I Won!

I Beat Cerebral Palsy

by

Danny Don Kitten

Copyright © Danny Kitten

All Rights Reserved

ISBN-13: 978-1514303191

ISBN-10: 1514303191

Introduction

Cerebral Palsy is a condition that affects the mind, body and spirit. I had to train my mind to control the muscles in my body. Persistence is the key to my success as well as my faith in God and family. I was born with this impairment. When I was young, I didn't understand why. I wanted to be like other kids and I went to many doctors who tried to 'fix it'. They could not.

I wasn't born the smartest one in the room. My sister read music and played the piano. She played with my dad while they entertained guests, but I had to stay out of the way in the kitchen. The music I made was only noise. The constitution says that all men are created equal. I question that, but I don't question that we have equal opportunity. One must ask in order to receive. One must seek in order to obtain. With all the hardships that came my way, I withstood them without destroying myself. I won. I beat Cerebral Palsy with the help and inspiration of those who have loved me.

≈1≈

I was born on October 16, 1944, at Mercy Hospital in Slaton, Texas. The nuns of St. Joseph Catholic Church in Slaton, also known as the Sisters of Mercy, were in charge of the hospital. Dr. James McSween was my mother's doctor. According to my mother, my birth was difficult and at the time was called a dry birth. I was extracted from her body during delivery with instruments, discovered to have blue baby syndrome and was not expected to live. Two weeks later I was still alive and diagnosed with cerebral palsy caused by damage to the spine, which was a birth defect. I became stiff as a board from head to toe and quickly taken to Scott & White Memorial Hospital in Temple, Texas. There were no hospitals in the immediate area of Slaton that could handle cases such as mine. While I was at

Scott & White, a team of doctors successfully released the pressure that had allowed fluid to collect on my spine. After that procedure, I was left with a twitching of the head, shaking of the hands and approximately 70% hearing loss.

Both my parents had to work the first several years of my life and since I required a lot of attention, my paternal grandparents, Clem and Lou Kitten, took care of me. I became very attached to them. They lived on a farm close to town and had all types of farm animals. What more could a young boy want!

I had a sister, Glenda Lou, five years older than me. According to her, I was delayed about two years in development, which included walking, standing and speaking. When I did begin to speak, my words were slurred and she was the only one who understood. My mother often asked Glenda what I was saying.

The year was 1950. It was the beginning of many things I remember - mostly about my sister. I was nearly six and I can still picture Glenda dragging me by the arm to a small house that had only four or five rooms with many windows along both sides. There were kids running and playing, and I realized some of them were my cousins. I wondered why everyone was there. I saw a lady, or at least I thought she was a lady, dressed in a black robe with only her hands and face showing. I had seen this before but didn't know the stranger. Sister Michael, as I came to know her, came out to the door every morning and every recess to ring a hand-held school bell. This was the beginning of what was to be my Parochial School Days, until the age of 14 years.

When Glenda was in the seventh grade and I was in the second, my Dad acquired a German Shepherd dog named Rex from an airman at Reese Air Force Base in Lubbock. The dog was already grown. It was Valentine's Day. Glenda and I had just gotten home from school and Rex was in the house and on a leash. Mom was on the phone talking to one of our uncles so I took the leash from her hand. My sister, Glenda, who noticed something on one of Rex's back legs, got a tissue to remove it. Suddenly, the dog turned, attacked my sister and began biting her. She screamed and tried to get away. I, too, was terrified and hid under the kitchen table. Mom heard the scream, dropped the phone and ran toward the dog and my sister. The dog again attacked, pushed Glenda on the couch and began to bite her arm. My mom straddled the dog and opened his mouth to make him let go. I can remember that I ran outside to get away. My sister went to the hospital, came home with stitches and has been afraid of big dogs ever since. Mom was also treated from the result of the bites she received. It is one of those memories a person tries to forget but seems to slip in occasionally as bad memories have a tendency to do.

School was a challenge. I can remember how difficult it was for me to read and write. I have memories of Sister Michael giving me a big, fat round pencil and a tablet with a picture of an Indian Chief on it. I had a terrible time learning to write because I could not hold a pencil the correct way and tore holes in the pages repeatedly. During those first years of school, I did not receive a report card because it had not been determined if I was capable of passing a grade level. I did spend two years in the 4th grade. I remember when I failed quite vividly because I received several spankings from my mother on arriving home, and many more after my father returned from a long day of working on the railroad. My parents were not abusive towards me, but they did believe in punishment.

$$\approx 2 \approx$$

The following spring of 1955, my whole world came tumbling down. Grandma Lou died of a massive heart attack as she was just beginning her day of normal activities. This was my first experience with death and very difficult to accept since I was so close to my grandmother. In those days, the body was prepared by the funeral directors and redelivered to the home for viewing for three days while neighbors and family dropped in out of respect. This was especially difficult for me as I had lived with my grandparents during every summer for many years and we were extremely close. Losing her was something I thought I would never forget, and I haven't. Seeing her profile in the living room, where we sat together for so many years, was hard. I slept nearby, close to my grandpa, while her body lay there. To this day, I can still see her profile every time I walk through that room. It is quite often as I still reside in that home all these many years later.

After losing my grandma, I spent all the time I could with my grandpa. We played and watched television together as much as possible. Every Saturday morning we watched *The Roy Rogers Show*.

Roy Rogers was my idol at the time, along with my Grandpa Clem. Since I was so captivated by this program, I invented my own western town. The old chicken house was the jail and the cream house was the saloon. Grandpa's barn was the main setting and the hayloft was my 'domain.' I threw forks full of hay down to the barn floor until I had a heap large enough to leap from the loft onto the hay, all along pretending that I was jumping from the roof of a building ahead of anyone pursuing me. Once I was done with my pretending, it was much harder to get that hay back up to the loft area! Tossing it down was always the fun, easy part.

Grandpa's old barn was enormous! It was at least twice the size of his six-room house. The wooden boards on the outside had turned a soft, velvety gray - weathered naturally by wind, rain, snow, and battered by time. The roof consisted of rusted sheets of corrugated steel, with a new sheet installed here and there as the need arose. Grandpa always cautioned me about playing on the roof because it could cave in so easily.

Big double doors on both the north and south sides of the building opened to form a breezeway though the center. Half the inside was used for farm animals; five stalls on one side for the milk cows, and stables for the horses on the opposite side. I still have several of these old weathered boards with the written names of cows and their calves. The remaining spaces were partitioned into a series of rooms. One of these rooms had a trailer full of cotton burrs; another stored corn, grain and cottonseed.

A small, closet-type enclosure contained some of my grandparent's personal items. This is where they hid my Christmas presents. On one occasion just before Christmas, I snuck out to the barn, got my new bike and rode it down the side of the field. After riding back, I cleaned the bike and put it away. When it came time for me to get the present, naturally I acted thrilled and surprised. I don't know if they ever knew I took out that bike.

There was another room inside the barn, hidden behind a camouflaged wall. A special wire was used to pull open a small, secret room which was off-limits to me, according to Grandpa. It had a secret door, but I wasn't allowed inside nor was I ever told about the contents. I never asked any questions about this *special* room, though I was always curious. Many years passed before I became aware that this was where Grandpa kept his moonshine still. Grandpa made moonshine, or as the German family members called it, hooch, throughout the prohibition era of the 1920's and was caught only one time. Due to a technicality, Grandpa only spent one night in jail. The liquor was supposedly made for medicinal purposes, which was the excuse of the time. He shared his makings with family and friends and of course for his own consumption. The still exists today, passed down though family members and remains a family tradition.

When I was playing in Grandpa's barn, I found an old hand-cranked corn shucker. The corn shucker stood three feet high and six inches wide. There was a round hole in the top and a square hole in the bottom. The large hand crank was on one side and the corncob dispenser was on the opposite side. The operator turned the crank to a fast speed and inserted a dry ear of corn through the round hole on top. The kernels fell through the bottom of the shucker into a bucket and the cob dropped through the square hole at the bottom.

While playing with the corn shucker one afternoon, I suddenly felt something crawl up my pants leg. I was startled and quickly grabbed the moving object and started running and screaming for my grandpa, all the while holding my pants where I had felt the object crawling. Grandpa ran outside, concerned by my screams. I told him I thought a mouse had run up my leg and he started laughing. He told me to let it go. I shook my head for fear the mouse would continue the rest of the way up my leg. Grandpa bent down to unbutton my jeans, still laughing. He attempted to pull my pants off and told me to let the mouse go. When I did, it fell to the ground, dead. I had been so scared and held so tight that I squished that mouse to death!

≈3≈

Like all typical boys, I liked sports and wanted to play them. I talked Mom into buying me a baseball glove so that I could practice and try-out for the local Pony League team. This glove was a little different than most of the gloves that all of the others had. If you have ever seen a picture of Babe Ruth with his glove, mine looked like that. I took the glove to school and practiced with my friends. Many times, I wasn't successful, but sometimes I was. Oh, what a good feeling that was! I got better as time passed.

One day my friend Eddie told me he was going to baseball tryouts. I thought since I had been practicing that I could do the same. The park wasn't too far from the house so I got on my bike and off I went.

I arrived at the park and climbed over the little picket

fence. After a moment, a coach walked towards me. I recognized him because he worked with my dad at the railroad and I knew that his wife owned the local flower shop on the town square. I remember my dad talked about him being such a loud and dislikable person. Right then, I discovered why. He started hollering at me even before he got close. He wanted to know *what the hell I was doing there and to get my Goddamn ass off the field*! I told him I wanted to play baseball.

He said, "Hell no. Get your ass out of here!"

I crawled back over the picket fence, climbed on my bike and rode crying all the way home. The people who knew me and the people at the church school had shielded me during my early years. I rarely dealt with others in the community and I was shocked by the way this person spoke to me. I could not understand what I had done wrong and why he was so mean.

I didn't tell Mom and Dad because I thought they would ask why I even went to tryouts in the first place. I never saw myself as other's saw me. I thought I had arms and legs just like everyone and could do what others did – run, jump and even play ball. After that experience, I never again tried to play baseball, but I still have my glove.

Dad and I had a good time when he wasn't drinking. He was fun. When he was home for several days, he took me on rides - usually down to the flats - the east side of town. Then we crossed the tracks and went to the Round House. At the Round House, men repaired wheels and brakes on railroad cars. The engineers also drove the engines inside so the rotating track could turn them around. Dad's brother, Ray, worked there. He let me climb into the caboose and go up into the lookout room. It was small, but I could sit in a chair and look out at all the other cars and engines. The caboose was designed for sleeping, cooking and had a small bathroom for long trips. In the corner was a coal-burning stove to heat the caboose. Dad said they could only use the toilet when the train was traveling down the tracks because there wasn't a holding tank. At the time, I didn't know what he meant and I didn't want to act dumb. Hold what?

≈4≈

As I grew into my teenage years, my sights started to wander into something a bit more exciting than playing in grandpa's barn. My first love was long and lean...her body was gorgeous! She had a 3-speed (gotcha!) standard transmission and a flathead six-cylinder engine. BOY! She was a beauty. 'My' very first car! I was sixteen years old and this 1950 Ford, 4-door sedan belonged to my grandfather. He always parked in the north side of the barn and sometimes when he took his afternoon nap, I went out and cranked her up. I then slipped into my world of imagination, dreaming that I was driving down the road towards my own ranch. Grandpa had a trailer hitch on the car so I pretended that I was pulling a horse trailer. My world of fascination was very vivid as I had developed it over many years. It was my only means of escaping from the body I loathed. Sometimes I backed the car out of the barn and drove to the pump house. There, I used several garden hoses to give the car a good wash job. She had wide white-wall tires and very small hubcaps, with the word FORD printed across them. The brake and clutch were small round pedals and the starter was operated by a push button, not a key. The paint on this first love of my mine was a faded yellow, the seat covers were worn and the doors squeaked, but to me she was beautiful. The highlight of my day was when Grandpa let me drive, even though I didn't have a license. We went on the country roads to visit my cousins and of course, it was fun to lead them to believe that the car was mine! Several of us often drove down the turn rows of the cotton fields to hunt rabbits. On one of these hunting excursions, I got stuck in a lakebed, in the middle of the cotton field after a long, hard rain. I was so afraid Grandpa would be angry with me so my cousins and I walked to our uncle's house, borrowed a tractor and pulled the car out. We then drove it to the well and washed it good! I suspect Grandpa knew about this, but he never mentioned it. His gentle and kind nature allowed him to look only at the things that were important and it taught me how to look beyond the negativity I faced - to always focus on the vision of what I wanted to accomplish in my life.

During my junior year in high school, Grandpa decided to buy another car for himself. He gave me the car I had fallen in love with. By this time, I had my driver's license and could drive it anytime and anywhere I wanted. I was ready to take on the world! Some of the first things I bought for my new car were flipper hubcaps, fender skirts and two rear speakers for the AM radio. I put miniature Hawaiian girls on top of the speakers so every time I hit a bump, the girls would do a cute hula dance in their grass skirts! Even today, when I see a car similar to my first love, my mind takes me back. I wish now that I had not sold the car. It would have been nice to have it today and be able to restore it after all these years. I look all the time, hoping to someday catch a glimpse of it. I am certain I would recognize it, even if it has been restored or lay rusting in a junk yard. I always glance when I pass a car lot because deep down I feel someday

I will find it.

≈5≈

I attended a Catholic institution all my young life and now, I faced a new and different school. Slaton High School was bigger, had more subjects and more students. One of these subjects that I was excited to take was vocational agriculture. I grew up on a farm with my grandparents and I loved to work with animals.

The teacher told us we had to choose a project for the year, either crop or animal related. I first wanted to raise a calf, but the cost of feed and time was too much for me. A pig was the next option and more in my price range. From experience, I knew that a pig would eat almost anything so I arranged to pick up the leftover food from the catholic school cafeteria. My only chore was to wash and scrub the container every day before I returned it. My agriculture teacher offered an extra pig he had bought - a Hampshire, which was black with a white stripe around its shoulders. That's the year I learned about all the different types of pigs.

My grandfather fed his pigs grain and table scraps, but I soon learned that wasn't the best for them. The food needed nutrition and to be processed with the right ingredients in order to gain proper weight and meat value. My agriculture teacher told the class that we would take our animals to a stock show in Plainview, about fifty miles north of Slaton. Our length of stay depended on how well the animals placed in the show.

Sometimes my father was in a good mood and sometime he wasn't. When I told him I needed money to eat on and that maybe ten dollars would get me by for a few days, he gave me five and said the school should furnish the rest of it.

We got to Plainview, did the paper work and unloaded the animals. Each animal was weighed and labeled according to its weight. My pig was heavy and I knew it was because of the food scraps from the school cafeteria. Then they were put into separate pens, each holding four animals. We began to wash and scrub them down with soap. Someone gave me a bottle of pleasant smelling dishwashing liquid and I got busy scrubbing. My pig couldn't have smelled any better when I finished. A friend gave me a jar of black shoe polish and a can of white talcum power. The black shoe polish was for the animals toenails and the talcum powder was for the white stripe across his shoulders. We repeated this process every time before going to the show ring.

This first showing was for separating the good, the bad and the ugly. Right before I entered the ring, a friend of mine put some Bengay ointment on his finger and shoved it up the pig's anus. This made the pig walk faster and tighten all of the muscles in his back so he wouldn't walk fat and lazy. I passed the first test and was in the group who needed to spend the night.

Because I didn't have much money, I figured to save it for food. I planned to sleep with the animals. I got the bedding for my pig and because there was an empty pen next to us, fixed a bed for myself. It had been a long day so I was ready to relax. The others left and after a few minutes, my teacher came looking for me, wondering what I was doing. I told him I was short of cash and needed it for food tomorrow, so would sleep with the pigs. He reached in his pocket, gave me a twenty-dollar bill and said I was going with the group.

The next day was show day. I repeated the same procedures that I did the day before and was ready for my number. I watched how the handlers who won, caught the judge's eye. I realized this was about showmanship as well as animal quality.

The Plainview show soon ended. I won fourth place and sold the pig for one hundred and forty dollars. Dad said that I should keep the money and do it again next year.

I learned a lot about representing myself. I learned about friendship. Most of all, I learned about being a teacher. Fifty years later that teacher had a son who was my superintendent at the school where I taught.

≈6≈

During my teenage years, I was the only child left at home. Glenda had married and lived several hundred miles east of Slaton. As a child, I always dreamed of being a cowboy and my dream became my sister's life. She married a rancher. To my surprise, life as a cowboy is much different than shown on television.

The first thing I learned is that real cowboys work hard and put in long hours. When we went to visit my sister and her husband, I rode with him to feed the cattle. I learned the difference between a steer, a bull, a cow and a heifer. Not long after that, I learned how to cut, brand and dehorn.

They had about seventy-five milk cows, which had to be milked twice a day. During the day, they cut, baled and ground feed for the cows. And if that wasn't enough, during the evening they rode and roped in local area rodeos.

I spent several weeks during the summer with them. This was the busy time of year for ranchers. They worked hard and played hard. The work didn't begin at sunrise; it began at four in the morning, rain or snow. The cows needed milking twice a day and every morning he woke me saying it's time to milk. I don't know if I helped or if I was in their way. I learned what it took to keep a farm running and to supply the family needs. The evenings were just as busy as the days for there was little time to sleep or rest. Depending on the time of year, the sport of rodeoing was always exciting. There was bull riding, wild cow milking, muttin' busting, calf roping and wild horse riding. My brother-in-law mostly roped calves because that's what he did on the ranch. We also did lots of hunting - not with guns, but with dogs - greyhound dogs. They were fast and strong. We hunted rabbits, coyotes, raccoons and possums. We rode in the back of a pickup using only a spotlight to see. If the driver didn't know the terrain of the field, we ended up in a ditch. We also hunted bullfrogs and rattlesnakes.

This part of the country is all about neighbor helping neighbor. Most everyone is related to each other, by either blood or marriage. During harvest time the feed that was planted months earlier, is ready to be cut, baled and ground up for the silos or stored in the hay barns. Everybody had their job to do, and helped wherever and whenever they were needed. Women worked as well, cooking big meals for all - chicken fried steak, corn on the cob, mashed potatoes, white gravy, cobbler and ice cream. After working in the dirty and hot fields or in the silos, the men removed their shirts and hosed each other down to remove the dirt, then washed their hands and faces before eating. Most grabbed a plate of food and found the nearest shade tree to eat fast and maybe get in a little snooze.

After the milking, baling, and feed grinding, it was time for the big cattle roundup. Every cowboy, young and old, had his own horse. My bother-in-law and his Dad had extra horses around the ranch and the one they picked for me was a Shetland. This horse was bred for inexperienced riders and children. It was not a working horse. I thought I was a good rider, but at the time, beggars can't be choosey. I had ridden this horse on previous visits, loading cattle and crossing creeks beds. During one of these crossings, the Shetland refused to move so my brother-in-law roped the Shetland to pull him across. I was still in the saddle. The next thing I knew, the horse and I were in the water. The water was deeper than I thought and the horse went under. I floated on top and as he was pulled from the water, I grabbed his tail and came out, too.

While looking for cattle, we rode through a mesquite bush area and surprised two deer. At that time of the year, the bucks were fighting each other for the rights of a doe. Two bucks had fought, locked horns and only one was alive, but trapped with his dead foe. He clearly had tried dragging the dead weight for a long distance and become exhausted. Coyotes must have smelled the meat and begun to consume it, trying to tackle the live deer as well.

My brother-in-law roped the dead deer, breaking the antlers to allow freedom. He explained that I should never rope a live deer. They are wild animals and someone could get hurt. Not only can the horns impale but front hoofs can be sharp and painful as well.

One day, my brother-in-law and his father were asked to help neighbors round up cattle. I could ride along but had to stay with the older group who knew how not to be in the way. A cattle round-up has many stages of work and each rider has his own job to do.

I looked for baby calves that wandered away from mothers. The fields were hilly and had many mesquite bushes on them. I found myself also looking for wild game and of course, rattlesnakes.

All of the cattle were brought into large holding pens where they were separated into size, age and sex. The bulls and older cows were moved back into the pasture for reproduction and the younger into another. This is where the castrating, vaccinating and branding occurred. If a man had good roping skills, this was the job for him.

The ranch where we worked didn't bring out the chuck wagon, but they did have a long mess hall that was used for feeding a large group of men. The meal was fantastic, with all the trimmings. After eating, we went back to work and I helped separate the young calves. My other job was to open and close the gate. What a busy and exciting time for a city slicker! I even wore boots, chaps and a cowboy hat. My dream had come true, just like the cowboys on a TV western show.

As we finished the job, loading horses and closing gates, the ranch boss came up and handed me a check for five dollars! Wow, I thought. I am being paid for having fun.

My sister and her husband had five wonderful children, three girls and two boys. We all sort of grew up together and I loved playing with them. Bob was the firstborn and grew up in the saddle. Everywhere he went, he had to have his hat.

Every year, Dad, Mom and I went to my sister's house for Christmas. It was a wonderful time and seems that it always snowed and was freezing cold. I went out to help rake the snow out of the feed troughs and chopped ice in the water tanks so the cattle could drink the water.

We went to midnight mass at the old tall and beautiful church that can be seen from the next town. The church was built on the highest point in that area. The church had wooden floors and the sound of all those boots echoed. I remember when Bob just started walking and talking that his Dad took him outside. When they returned he said, "Mom, I went potty on a rock." It was just as funny to all the others in the room as it was to me because the remark echoed off the walls.

I will always have a special bond with the family. I wish I could have had a tight knit family like they have. They always celebrate each other's accomplishments, helping one another when there's a need.

Every now and then one of them calls just to see how things are going and to update me on that side of the family. Almost all of our immediate family lives hundreds of miles away, but we do have good neighbors that drop in to check on us.

≈7≈

All through high school, I wanted to play football, basketball and run track. I knew that I would never be given a chance to try and was afraid that if I was, I might be injured. The teachers were always concerned about my getting hurt during activities as well. One of them told me if I wanted to run, to do it after school, when no one else was using the track.

Then I started noticing girls. I wanted to date but tended to be shy and was embarrassed easily. It was hard for me to ask a girl on a date. I later decided that the interest in my car was much more exciting than going out with girls.

I did manage to join the high school band. This was very exciting and allowed me to attend football and basketball games. I always had a love for music and still do to this day. After the football games, my cousin, Charlene, and I went to Tiger Town, the small dance hall where the school kids gathered and celebrated the football games after a big win. I wanted to dance and attempted to ask girls to dance but was turned down most of the time. But Charlene always danced with me. She was very pretty and popular. She and some other friends never hesitated to jump into my old faded yellow Ford and make the drag down Ninth Street. Sometimes we drove out to a local farm, stole watermelons and dropped then in the streets of town, just to see how far they splattered!

I always loved my parents and I did what I was told to do. Well, maybe not always. My parents smoked and drank a lot; sometimes the drinking went on for days and weeks at a time. I never knew what I would come home from school to see.

They even spent weeks in the Big Spring state hospital trying to 'dry out'. This happened repeatedly, and as always, they were never successful. I knew alcoholism was a disease and my parents had a difficult time controlling it. I often asked my mother why she argued with Dad when he was drinking. "If you can't fight them, join them," she said. And that's exactly what she did.

One evening as I entered the house, I heard Mom and Dad fighting and arguing with one another. That was normal, especially if Dad had been drinking all week. I usually tried to get to my room before either noticed but this time, his voice sounded different. As I entered the kitchen, I saw Mom lying nude on the floor in a fetal position. Dad had a rifle in his hand aimed at her. Without thinking, I stepped between them. I told Dad that if he shot Mom, he would have to shoot me, too. I could see the look in his eyes. He didn't want to do it. Something inside his head was driving him crazy.

Tears began to fall from his eyes. He put the rifle back in the corner and left the house. Mom then ran to the bathroom and I heard her sobs through the door. I was so scared that I shook from head to toe. I rushed out the back door, fell to my knees and began to pray. As I began the prayer with the Hail Mary, full of Grace..., I looked up into the sky. I saw the Virgin Mary just above the tree. She said that everything would be all right.

I never told anyone about this, not even my sister or my parents. I was so frightened at the time. I kept telling myself I imagined it and felt that I, too, was going crazy.

$$\approx 8 \approx$$

Like all car enthusiasts, I wish I had kept all of the vehicles that my father owned. I don't remember why, but Dad brought a 1959 four-door sedan home one day and told me to drive it until he found another. I wasn't much of a mechanic but I wanted to be. I needed someone to show me how, but all of the mechanics I knew were the old ones that Dad drank with and they were always busy drinking.

I did try a few things, like change a transmission, but I didn't know what I was doing. I had extra parts and bolts left. I had no tools and only a dirt floor in the garage but those were not the reasons I didn't pursue being a mechanic. I soon realized that my lack of coordination and physical strength would keep me from that career.

Being a teenager, I wanted to fix up the old '59 with

fender skirts and flipper hubcaps. I wanted dual exhaust and loud mufflers but I only accomplished the fender skirt and flipper hubcaps. One morning I got up and noticed my hubcaps were gone. I just happen to have an extra pair, so I took some baling wire and a short chain, bolted those hubs caps to the lug nuts of the wheel and wired the fender skirt latch. The next day I looked out the window and saw those hubcaps just dangling on the side of the wheel.

I needed more stuff. I found some caddy pointed tail lights so I took the backup lights out and put those caddy lights in their place. The instrument panel only had dials with lights but I wanted to know how the engine was performing so I needed gages. The gages had to fit in a hole two-inches in diameter in the dashboard. I found the perfect place for them but I had to cut the hole. All I had was an old hacksaw, so I went to cutting. While cutting, I noticed sparks coming out of the hole I made. I didn't realize I had cut a big roll of wires positioned under the dashboard. Yep, I screwed up again. I took the car to my cousin and after working several hours on it, he finally got the wires back together. Then I stepped on the brake pedal. The lights flashed on inside the car. When I flipped the left blinker, the windshield wipers erupted. But that gage I made a hole for worked just fine.

When I left my cousin's house, I decided to drive through town. As I was driving, I noticed a car in the bar ditch with a man slumped over inside. I pulled over and rolled down my window to see if he needed help. He said he ran out of gas and that he was cold. I saw something flicking on the other side of him and realized he had lit a fire in the seat. I asked him to put the fire out and he said no, he was cold. I drove back to my cousin's house, ran to the garage door and pushed it open shouting that a man down the road had a fire in his car. Of course, they thought I had lost it and told me I was crazy. By the time we got back to his car, the fire department was there along with the police. The man was sitting in the back seat of the police car. They said he was under the influence of something.

≈9≈

School was always hard for me. My grades were consistent: C's, D's and F's. I never thought I would ever have the opportunity to go to college, but more than anything, never thought I could make the grades to stay in and graduate if I did have the chance. My plans were always to stay on the farm and work the land. I knew I could do that.

Dad had a good friend who was a farmer. He was killed in a boating accident so his wife wanted to sell all the farming equipment and the house and move to town. The man had a John Deere Model G Popping tractor, with all the equipment to farm the land. I don't know how Dad got the money, but I'm sure he used Grandpa's farm as collateral.

I was fresh out of high school and had no job and no

experience in the business. A lot had changed since Grandpa farmed and sadly, Grandpa wasn't there to help me.

It took me a full day to change equipment from one set-up to another. On my Popper, the cultivator was on the front of the tractor. I had no power steering and no heater or air conditioner. It took all the strength I had to drive and to plow a straight row.

Dad decided we needed help. He called a cousin, whose father was in farming, had a fertilizer business, and was a good friend of the banker. Dad also agreed that the cousin should live on the farm so he could watch over it. I drove out to the farm to check on the buildings and animals and one day as I went down the drive, I saw a skunk headed for the barn. I drove my truck between it and the barn and had my window down so I could see the direction he was going. Suddenly he turned, raised his tail and sprayed the truck and me. The smell was so bad that I couldn't stop gagging. Then I had to go home standing on the running board of the truck with my face in the wind and the door wide open. When

I got home, I went to the back yard, took off all my clothes, used the water hose and scrubbed with all the soap I could find. I even scrubbed the truck, but it took days to get rid of that terrible smell.

We farmed together for a year, but my heart wasn't in it. I knew I couldn't support a family if I ever had one and there were many young men looking for land to farm.

≈10≈

I was in the house when my cousin Joe Bob, came by. Standing by the door and grinning from ear to ear, he said he just stopped in at the Dutchman to get a six-pack of beer. While he was there, he noticed some girls over at the house next door. The owner of the house also owned the Dutchman so Joe asked him about the girls. "Yep," he replied. "Those are my nieces from California and they are here for a few days. Would you like to meet them?" Joe met them and set up a double date for Saturday night. I was excited. Not often did I get a chance to go on a date.

Saturday I got dressed up with shirt, tie and a little Old Spice. I was ready to go. Joe picked me up and I met the three girls. The older two were both pretty women and the little girl, named Shirley, was cute. Joe liked

Beverly so that left me with Mary. We met and visited with the parents and then went to the movies and the Hi Di Ho for a coke. Joe and Beverly were getting on strong, but Mary wasn't too crazy about me. After the date, I thought that was the end for me.

I saw Joe two days later and he was still on cloud nine. He wanted to see Beverly again and was trying to make plans to do so. He wanted to know if I still had those free passes on the train and wondered if I would go to California with him. I wasn't working at the time and was a little low on cash, but he said he would help me out if I went along with him. I told him Mary didn't care for me and I didn't want to waste her time as well as mine. He said to just enjoy the trip and not worry about her. Since I was always looking for a way to get out of the house, I told Mom and Dad and packed for the coast.

California here we come. We got on the passenger train at Slaton and headed westbound to Los Angeles. The train was always exciting to ride. Even just standing at the station and watching that big engine with the sounds of the wheels on the track and the blowing whistle coming into the depot put a smile on my face. I always loved the sound and sight of a locomotive. When I could, I went to one of the local hobby shops and watched them play with the scale model trains.

It was hot outside, but inside the passenger car was cool and comfortable. The car had its train sound: clunk, clunk, and swayed from side to side. We could walk easily from car to car, but I enjoyed the club car the most. This car had food and drinks. Best of all, the roof was all glass. We sat for hours on end and watched the country, the towns and the people flash by the window. Sometimes we watched the cars traveling down the road trying to keep up with the train.

The train ride took two days and one night, and we were glad to get to our destination. The girl's parents picked us up and drove us to Long Beach, where our aunt and uncle lived. They had a small camper trailer behind their apartment where we stayed.

The next day we were scheduled to go to Seal Beach to swim in the ocean. The girls mostly sprawled in the sun and got burnt. I thought I was tan but my back and

legs began to look like red apples. The little girl name
Shirley wanted to play volleyball so I joined her. She was
always laughing and giggling, much more fun than Mary.
I think girls of that age wanted to be pretty and cute for
all those muscle beach bums and I was far from being
one of those.

Bev and Joe were together for most of the day and
evening. I enjoyed playing games with Shirley and
listening to music. The next day was Sunday so we
dressed in coat and tie and went to church with them. I
noticed that Joe was withdrawn and spoke very little. I
knew something had happened. He waited until we
were on the train headed back to Slaton before telling
me he asked Bev if she would consider marrying him and
moving to Texas. She said she had another friend she
was considering marrying. That just broke Joe's heart
and when we got back to Texas he stayed mostly to
himself.

Joe was a tall, good-looking man. He could have
gotten all the dates he wanted, but he was reserved.
Later, he and another cousin joined the marines and

went to boot camp in California. I don't know if he contacted Bev, but I suspect he did, just to make sure there wasn't a second chance. I know when he came home from the military he smoked and drank a lot.

Fifty years later, after attending a church service, my wife and I were talking to another one of our cousins. Two women came over to talk to us. When one of them confirmed that I was Danny Kitten, she started to cry. She told me she was Beverly from California and this was her sister Shirley. I then made the connection and returned the hugs. That's when my wife spoke up revealing her relationship. I laughed and told her the story that happened fifty years earlier but I am not sure she believed me.

I asked Bev were they were staying and she said next door to the Dutchman liquor store. I told her that I still had the pictures I took when Joe and I were in California. She related that while Joe and I were there, her mom told her not to marry Joe because she didn't want her to move to Texas.

≈11≈

I knew if I wanted to succeed and do something other
than farm, I had to figure out how to get into a
university or at least, a vocational school. All my friends
and cousins were going away to college. I remembered
when I was a senior in high school, I was called into the
office by the principal. He said there were some people
from Texas Rehabilitation who wanted me to continue
my education. They would help me find a school and
help finance it. I gave them a call. They told me there
was a junior college in Levelland, Texas with a two-year
agriculture program that might be just what I needed.
Levelland was 40 miles from Slaton so I went to check it
out. I was so thrilled to be able to do this! I just needed
to take and pass the entrance exam. A new chapter in
my life was about to begin.

South Plains College offered a two-year agriculture program that I began to work toward. Little did I know that some of these classes would be one of my key successes in later life. As I began to take these courses, I knew that I had to change my old study habits and work harder.

I met many good friends in college and found that most of them accepted me for who I was in spite of my disability. I also began to go out with girls and enjoyed attending the college dances and parties.

To help with the finances, I found local jobs on and off campus - from working in the cafeteria washing dishes to working at the local gins during the harvest seasons. The college also offered a band scholarship to pay for books, so I joined the college band. I had played the bass drum in high school so why not play the drums in college.

I never got homesick because many of my cousins also attended the same college and stayed in the same dormitory. I lived in Stroud Hall. Here I met lots of interesting people and had several roommates. Also in the dorms were some students who were from Slaton High School, so that made me feel good. I became close to the agriculture instructor and sought guidance. He encouraged me to aim for an Associate Degree in Applied Science.

Life in a dormitory at college can be the most exciting time of a young man's life, no moms and dads hovering. There was a dorm mother, but she never dared look down the hallways. There was only one bathroom and shower for each wing in the dorm, so there were a few rosy cheeks walking to and from the rooms.

The dorm faced the road and there were always cars driving by, the majority of them driven by girls. The windows on the dorm were large and open so we could hang out and watch the show. One of these cars was a Volkswagen and a few of us went out to the street to greet and meet the girls. We surrounded the car, grabbed the front and rear bumpers and picked it up. We carried the little bug into the lounge of the dormitory, set it down and walked off. Needless to say, the dean of men was called in and the entire dorm was under investigation. Everyone was questioned but I acted like an innocent bystander. Nothing came of the incident and the memory of it still makes me laugh.

In September, the fair always comes to town. I had some cousins who had rooms next to mine in the dorm and wanted to get out for some fun. The four of us piled into the car and away we went to the fair. We had college ID's so we got in free, walked around and saw the latest in tractors and farm implements. We were all farm boys and interested. Looking at all of the show animals was natural to us and we relived memories of our own experiences.

I don't think any of us had a lot of money - we did more looking than we did eating and riding the rides. We were there for a few hours and it was getting late, but decided to take one more ride before we left. This ride, like all of the others, went around and around. It was designed like a squirrel cage, with seatbelts for the occupants. The four of us got in and the machine started rolling, the cage tumbling over and over. About the second round, I felt my seatbelt come loose, and the next thing I remember, I was laying on the ground about ten feet from the ride with my head pounding. But no broken bones. The fair crew walked me to the first-aid station, but since I didn't have any broken bones and just a headache, I felt no reason to stay. Besides, I had to get back to the dorm because I had a test at eight o'clock the next morning.

I don't remember if I passed the test, but this was one of my hardest times in college. I spent many hours studying, just trying to keep my grades up to passing standards.

There was one guy in the dorm, just a few doors down, who was getting married. Being the good friends that we were, we decided he needed a bachelor party, a shave and a haircut before his wedding. It took ten of us to tackle him and get the job done. He wasn't happy with us but he didn't look all that bad for his wedding after he went to the barbershop.

Water guns were in use a lot, but there was always someone who had a better idea and soon the five-gallon pressure sprayer was the one to beat. All this play wasn't conducive to studying so in order to get any work done, I had to lock the door.

I did have a few dates while I was in college. I remember one girl I met at one of the church dances. We dated for a while and I took her to some of the spring proms sponsored by the college. Then all of a sudden, her mother met me at the door and told me never to come back - the relationship was over. I didn't know the reason but she never talked to me again.

I liked most of the classes. I had to stay within the degree that I had chosen so I took a lot of agriculture courses. My favorite was horticulture. In this class, we stayed in the greenhouse. I believe anything can grow in a greenhouse, where all elements are controlled. Little did I know this would be part of my twenty-year career. Like all courses, the instructor can make or break the class. I did spend extra time with him in his office. He knew I was struggling and was willing to tutor me and help me raise my grades.

About this time, I started dating a girl from Lubbock. She, too, was attending South Plains. We began seeing more and more of each other. She always smiled and seemed to enjoy being with me. Soon it was time for me to move on. I didn't graduate with a degree, though, because I still needed credit from a government class to receive my Associate's Degree in Applied Science.

≈12≈

I tried and tried to get a number of jobs in and around this area but most companies wanted individuals with a degree or some type of experience. Because of my condition, I knew education was the only way for me to make a decent living.

I spoke to the advisor at Texas Rehab who knew my background. That's where I learned about the school in Waco, Texas and that I qualified for financial help. It was a branch of Texas A&M, called James Connally Technical Institute, located on an old Air Force base. Because of conditions at home, I knew I had to leave and get out of Dodge.

I had just started dating this pretty little girl from college and was getting a bit serious about her. I thought if it continued, I would need a good job. Also, if this relationship was to develop into marriage, she might be willing to hang in there with me for two more years.

I called my cousin who went to South Plains College with me to see if he wanted to drive to Waco. Sure, no problem. The campus was large, very clean and orderly. There were airplanes and jets still flying in and out, but the air base was phasing out slowly. There were many programs available at this school; plumbing, mechanics (both auto and tractor), air conditioning repair, sewing machine repair, building construction, civil engineering, dentistry and others.

I chose civil engineering. On the air base and enrolled in civil engineering, I felt strong and important - almost as if I was in the armed forces that I so longed to be. If I was in the military, I would be normal – just like everyone else.

A month earlier, I had been drafted. I wanted to serve. I remember the day I rode the bus to Amarillo. While on the bus I saw a couple of my classmates from high school, but they didn't have much to do with me. We got to the armory base and marched into a large building. While we stood in line, they gave us a sack to put all valuables in and a piece of paper. We were to hold the sack in one hand and the paper, which had our medical history, in the other. We were to drop all of our clothes except underwear and stand on the long yellow line. When it was my turn, one doctor stood in front of me and the other doctor stood behind. One checked eyes, ears, mouth, teeth and so on. The other asked me to cough. When asked my situation, I told them it was on the paper. When asked if I could shoot a weapon, I said yes. Then he told me to go and urinate in a cup and follow the green line to the hearing test.

I saw the booth for the hearing test and I knew I would fail. I put on the headphones and listened for the beep. The headphones were too large. I tried to hold the paper, the sack, and keep the headphones tight to my ears, but I never heard the beep. The instructor opened the door and howled, "Can't you hear?" I said, "No sir." He told me to put my clothes back on and wait in a room until I was notified. They told me I was 1Y classification and that I would be on an emergency call list. Again, I lost this battle of being a normal person. In my mind, I am like everyone else and all my limbs work just fine. But, when I see myself in the mirror or on a video, I see what everyone else sees - a real dork. No wonder I couldn't get a job – who would want me? My condition hung over me like a shadow - it followed me day and night wherever I went. Not even the Army could help me escape from the monster.

After applying at James Connally Tech, I needed to make arrangements for school but first; I wanted to see where John Kennedy was assassinated. On the map, it looked easily accessible before heading back to Slaton.

Dallas, Texas is a big city and the map didn't show all the little streets we needed to follow to our goal. After driving around in a circle, we finally found Commerce Street. We saw the Texas School Book Depository where Kennedy was shot from and the underpass that the car went under. By this time, it was later than we thought and we only had enough money to buy a coke and gas to get home. So, we decided to find a vacant parking lot, get some rest and then drive home. We found one and parked, noting it was next to a burlesque club. Being twenty-one, we could have gone in, but we still didn't have any money. We thought about finding another parking lot that would be less busy, but we were lost. We stayed. My cousin was in the back seat and I was in the front. Neither one of us got any rest, for I found myself leery of anyone who came in sight and sat ready to start the car and drive away. I've had many long nights and this was one of them. The sun rose, we headed back home and finally got back to Slaton.

James Connally Tech was a great place. The location had lots of trees and lakes to explore. Lake Waco had good fishing and swimming spots and during the hot days of summer, a friend of mine and I went often. Baylor University was nearby and we could always find German food in the surrounding towns.

The classes were small and exciting. I was taking classes that weren't offered at South Plains, like slide rule and surveying. These were harder but I was willing to put in extra effort to learn. Not knowing anyone was a blessing as I studied more. I was in one of the barracks with no television and no roommate. At least, if I had one, he never showed. This was good quality study time for me. The teachers were supportive and willing to take extra time to show and explain how to solve the problems which was very helpful for me. I was more a hands-on learner.

I was taking eighteen hours of courses and attending a community college to get that last course I needed to get the Associate's degree from South Plains College. I maintained a B average at James Connally and a C in the night government class.

After six weeks, the instructor closed the class because I and another student were the only ones passing. I could come back next semester or choose another option. I took Building Construction because I wasn't about to leave without a degree in my hand.

I never had the chance to work with wood much. I remember when I was growing up and just big enough to handle a sander, Dad told me to sand off some rough spots on a piece of wood. He showed me how the grains of wood go in one direction and to sand in that same direction. While I was sanding with the grain, I noticed that if I sanded across the grain, the wood came off faster. So, that's what I did. Thinking I did a good job, I showed it to my dad. Wrong again. That good-looking piece of wood ended up on my hind side. My parents spanked me as a child. As a result, I now suffer from a psychological condition known as, Respect for Others.

James Connally had lots of construction going on and the class was truly involved in every stage. One of the classes I enjoyed was blueprint reading. I even learned how to draw my own house. I was amazed at how much detail went into a drawing. We cut wood down to scale and then built the house from the drawing we made.

The HemisFair was in San Antonio, Texas that year and we took our scale model houses. Vendors with new products for the building industry were endless and each one had something new to show us. While in San Antonio, we went to the River Walk, the big zoo and the tropical Chinese Gardens. Being an ol' country boy from the dry and hot flat lands of Texas, this was like the Seven Wonders of the World all in my own state.

Building Construction was a two-year course with no summer vacation. I met many people and from time to time, we shared rides going home for the weekends. My turn to drive came. There were four of us in the car and on the way back to school, about fifty miles south of Waco, my car stopped running. I had felt the motor missing for several miles, but hoped it would make it back to school. I was pulling a motorcycle on a trailer, so we weren't totally stranded. We pulled off the road and reviewed our options. It was two o'clock in the morning and the motorcycle owner said he'd go to a farmer's house to call his roommate. He was gone about an hour because he had a hard time waking his roommate and giving directions to get here. Another hour passed and the roommate finally showed. We got the chain out, attached it to both cars, put the bike on the trailer, and started toward Waco. It was pitch dark and my lights were dim but everything seemed to be going just fine. Suddenly the driver of the front car slammed on his brakes. I saw bright red lights, hit his bumper and the bike tumbled on top of my car. There were black cows everywhere. Someone had left the gate open and a whole herd of black Angus cattle surrounded us. One dead cow lay under the first car. Now what to do? We had two cars unable to move, so we all looked on top of my car at the motorcycle. Once again, the motorcycle and his rider headed off again, this time toward a ranch house, hoping to find the owners of the cows. Hallelujah! Luck was with us and the rancher told us he would help us get back to Waco and school. We helped him get the first car off the dead cow and drug the carcass in the ditch so no one else would hit it. We didn't need his help after all because the roommate's car wasn't damaged. We hooked ourselves to the first car and headed off again. I don't know how we managed to get back to James Connally, but we did - just in time for our first class.

I had been staying in the barracks and met the guys next door. We weren't in the same class but we did become good friends. They asked if I wanted to go to Galveston as one of them had a girlfriend who lived there and he knew a man who had a cabin on the shore where we could stay. It sounded like a great idea, so I went with them. When we arrived, we found where she lived, went inside and saw several college-aged kids breathing into paper sacks. I didn't know at the time what was happening, but later I realized that I was in the wrong place at the wrong time. We drove to find the beach house where I thought we had permission to stay. We found it. The screen porch was open but the house was locked. It was late so we decided to sleep on the porch and in the morning head on back.

I relaxed and drifted off to sleep. All of a sudden, there was a bright light shining in my face and someone asking who I was and what was I doing here. It took me a few minutes to realize what had happened. I looked around for the other guys, but they were gone. I was alone except for the police and the man who apparently owned the cabin. I told them I didn't know where the other boys went and I thought that we had permission to sleep here. I assured them that I wasn't there to rob the place. I told them I was sorry and I would wait on the beach for my friends to return. There were no charges made and the owner told me to stay in a motel. When I said I didn't have enough money for a room, he insisted on paying for it. He even took me to the motel but I had a sleepless night, wondering how I was going to get back to school. The guys returned but didn't say anything of what happened. It was a quite a drive back to the dorm.

Dad was still employed by the Santa Fe railroad so I had a free pass on the passenger train. It went from Clovis, New Mexico to Houston, Texas. I had to drive to Temple to catch it, which was about thirty miles from school. The train went back and forth every weekend so it was perfect for me. I caught the train on Friday at six in the afternoon, rode all night and arrived in Slaton at six in the morning on Saturday. I had a day and a half to visit my parents and, of course, my new girlfriend. Since I arrived so early in the morning I stopped in at the local bakery for the freshly made chocolate donuts - my favorites. Once, Mrs. Wilson, who was the wife of the owner of the bakery, made me a chocolate pie and wrote Happy Birthday in the meringue. Usually I walked home, but occasionally my parents met me.

For the ride back to James Connally, I caught the six o'clock evening train, rode all night and arrived in Temple at six the next morning. I drove to school just in time to catch breakfast and be ready for my first class. If I had any homework, I did it on the train.

As time passed, I visited my girlfriend more and more, beginning to feel like part of the family. My girlfriend's parents had good friends who lived in Arlington, Texas, which was about ninety miles from James Connally. The Waddell's often invited me to spend the weekend with them.

Mr. Waddell was a member of a Masonic group and he and his wife managed the home and farm for retired masons. This was a beautiful place with acres of green pastures, a little pond for fishing and a big garden in the back. The home was a long building painted white with white trim. I stayed in one of the many rooms when I visited. It had one large room filled with antiques from the people who lived there: old buggies, plows of all sorts, lots of old furniture and clothes. The home had a big dining room and a large kitchen that was always open and available. My new friends and their children lived within walking distance from the home. Their house was a large, brick, ranch-style abode. One evening while I was there, they invited me to have dinner with them.

We sat at a long table covered with white tablecloths, the silverware wrapped in linen napkins. People stood behind us waiting to serve. This was a full seven-course meal and as soon as I finished one, another course was put in its place. The waiters never let my plate become empty. Since I grew up learning to eat everything on my plate, I tried to do the same here. I was stuffed and I think my new friends realized it because there was a big grin on their faces when I refused the dessert – my favorite – chocolate pie.

Mr. Waddell wanted to know how far I lived from Lake Waco because he was big on hunting and fishing and wanted to take me fishing with him and his son, Gary. He had a good friend who lived in Waco and knew the lake like the back of his hand. I was overcome by this. Nobody ever asked me to go fishing. He kept his promise and made special arrangements for us to go fishing on Lake Waco.

Two years passed quickly. I was soon to receive my Associate Degree from Connally Tech and I had met many interesting people. I had passed that government class I needed and transferred it back to South Plains College where I walked across the stage to receive another Associate Degree. Now, I was about to begin another phase of my life. That girl I had been seeing back in Lubbock agreed to marry me and we would begin our life in Temple, Texas. I had a real job.

≈13≈

I married my college sweetheart, graduated from Connally Tech and started a new job all at the same time. Religion was a big factor for both of us. We visited several churches but since I felt strongly about mine, she agreed to take instruction and convert to Catholicism.

My first job was working for a construction company out of Temple, Texas. In the beginning, I was a go-for and machine operator. When we finished one job, we moved on to another, mostly staying in east Texas where there were trees and plenty of water. Driving to a big city wasn't a problem since there were several close.

At one town called Luling, the company built a large carpet processing plant. The job took about a year and while I was there, a steelworker named Rudy came up to me and asked if I was Danny Kitten from Slaton, Texas.

He once worked in the field across from me and knew I drove a Model G John Deere tractor. Rudy had lived in Luling for a while and invited me to go fishing with him. Boy, that sounded good. I always loved to go fishing even though I wasn't very good at it. There was a multitude of streams flowing in the area. We went down a dirt road to a waterfall where Rudy went under, stuck his hand down into the rocks and pulled out a large fish. I was reluctant to do so since I didn't know what was under those rocks. I felt much safer using a cane pole and a hook. I later learned Rudy's form of fishing was called noodling.

We often drove on the back roads to a bar to drink beer. There, he introduced me to a pickled egg. I was a newcomer to East Texas and several things were unfamiliar to me. The locals could tell right away. This pickled egg sat marinating in a big jar with a lot of others. I watched Rudy shell an egg and pop it whole into his mouth before I shelled mine. The egg got hotter and hotter and I felt my eyes widen as I reached for beer to wash down the heat. I suspect that's the idea - to buy more beer. Rudy and I spent good times together and he always had a good fishing story to tell.

The company was nearing completion of this job but the large boiler system still needed installing. When it arrived, I helped guide the boiler to its location on the cement slab. It was unloaded, hooked up to the pipes and connections, then secured and anchored. The men who installed it, lit the fire and turned on the gas. Everything was working to plan so the person I was helping showed me where to look to see if all was in order. The fire seemed fine to me, but I backed away so he could check. Boom! The big plate that had the little peep hole to see the flames, flew off and instantly killed the man standing beside me.

That's the day I decided I needed to be building highways. I found another job working with the Highway Department in Waco, building beams for bridges. The job was stationary so we didn't have to move often. We loved the location. It was outside the city, along the Brazos River that fed into Lake Waco. We still had our mobile home. The trailer park was across the highway from where I worked and there were young people in the park, so we felt welcome. When we left Luling, it took most of the money we had to move the trailer to Waco. It was around Christmas time so we decided to get only one gift for each other. At Target, we both had five dollars. My wife went to one side of the store and I went to the other to find a gift. Our choices were limited, but we got it done.

I worked at the plant for six months before getting raises and promotions. My boss talked a lot about fishing. He had an old boat and motor that he wanted to sell. I said I was interested so we agreed on a price and made a deal. My wife was pregnant at the time so she didn't go with me in the boat. It was a clear and calm day when I took the boat to Lake Waco, which was close to the house. I put it in the water and after starting the motor, went cruising with the wind in my hair just like the big boys on television. I had a good time enjoying my new toy but as I headed back to shore, the motor stopped. I cranked and cranked, then noticed water coming into my boat from the bottom. As long as the boat moved, no water came in, but now the floor was flooding. I cranked and cranked until my hand began to bleed. Luckily, the wind blew me close to the shore. The water was about five foot deep and the boat was sinking so I quickly removed the motor and drug it ashore. When I looked back, the boat was out of sight. I had to walk a ways to get my truck and trailer. I'm not sure the effort I used getting that waterlogged boat back onto the trailer was worth it since I never repaired the boat, but it didn't seem right just to leave it.

Soon our new baby was born. I asked the doctor if the baby was healthy, worried about complications since I didn't want to pass on cerebral palsy to any of my heirs. I had been very reluctant to have children. I knew all the problems I put on my parents. Thank God he gave us a strong, healthy and beautiful little girl.

One day in May of 1970, while driving to visit my wife's family in Lubbock, the radio station stated that a tornado hit Lubbock. Naturally we were worried, but all turned out fine. I didn't see much of my parents during this time because they were unbearable to watch or visit. I didn't want to witness their drinking or fighting. Actually, I didn't know how to deal with it so I just avoided them. My married life was fine; we were even looking for land to buy so we could move out of the trailer park.

One day I got a call from Mom. Dad had lost his mind and she committed him to the state mental hospital in Big Spring, Texas. She begged me to come home and help her. They were about to lose the farm and the house in town. She even promised to stop drinking.

I was torn. I didn't want to turn my back on my mother, but I had been married long enough to realize my mother-in-law would interfere in our marriage. Being half way across Texas worked but living just a few miles apart would not be healthy. I chose my mother and prayed I was wrong where the other was concerned.

I stayed with Mom while our trailer was transported. We got all the finances in order with the help from a lawyer and my wife and daughter stayed with her parents while I looked for a job. I did get small jobs, mostly construction projects consisting of painting and repair work.

I applied at a heavy equipment manufacturing plant in Lubbock and got a job driving a forklift. It was the big break I needed. We had our trailer on my mother's vacant lot in Slaton but that wasn't working as I seemed to always be in the middle of two women's opinions. My in-laws found a rent house in Lubbock, not far from where they lived, so we moved. Since we had only one car, I walked a mile to work and back, often riding with other workers.

Mom was doing much better, so she decided to go to nursing school. Eventually, the house on the farm became vacant and she wanted to know if I would live there rent-free and keep it repaired. My wife was very reluctant and only moved with me because she didn't have an income of her own. I soon got a promotion and a raise and bought another car so we both had transportation. I felt like I was back home. The farm was familiar.

≈14≈

My wife was incredulous that I would miss my daughter, Wendi's, birthday party. But Gary Waddell had asked me to go with him on his annual deer-hunting trip. I met Gary and his family, who lived in Arlington, before we were married.

Gary and his father were close and were great outdoor men. They leased a ranch in South Texas to hunt deer - the same place where Mr. Waddell had his heart attack and died. Gary continued the tradition even when he went off to college.

Gary, now in his last semester at Texas Tech, wanted me to go hunting with him. I had never been deer hunting and sure wanted to go. He knew I didn't have a deer rifle. It didn't matter because he had an extra so I just had to get a license. At that time, I had a four- wheel drive short bed truck with an overhead camper. We decided to take the camper and stay in it onsite where we were to hunt. I was excited about going on the trip. I didn't pay attention to the weather report and because we were going two hundred miles south, I wasn't worried.

We loaded our equipment and were on our way. The sun was shining but soon the clouds got heavier and heavier. I thought we'd drive out of the darkness because we were heading south but then the snow began. I still wasn't concerned because I had four-wheel drive. We were about thirty miles from our destination when the snow finally stopped falling, but the wind was blowing strong. Thank goodness I brought a heavy coat and an extra pair of long handles. We parked on the place we were to hunt. The electric heater in the camper was of no use. We did have a gas heater but since it used butane, we were concerned about carbon monoxide. We dang near froze.

Up at four in the morning, we walked to the blind and continued to be miserable since the wind and cold never stopped. There, we sat quietly for what seemed like hours.

We saw bucks in the distance and knew there would be more because the sound of clacking horns drifted in the wind. Suddenly a doe appeared and we hoped a buck would be right behind her. I slowly raised the rifle, wondering if one would get close enough for me to hit. Then it happened. A young buck. A five pointer was in my sight. I looked in the scope and put my hand on the trigger. I couldn't see the animal because my eyes started to twitch. I had a hard time controlling my breathing and then suddenly, he raised his head and ran away. I just couldn't shoot - it was such a beautiful animal. Gary saw a big buck, a twelve pointer, way in the distance up on a hill about three hundred yards. He shot. It disappeared and then he saw it again. He shot and the big buck dropped. We quickly left the blind and started toward the hill where he last saw the animal. As we crossed the hill, we could see him in the distance. On closer inspection, one shot was through both of the front legs and the second shot was through the neck.

We dressed and tagged the deer in the field according to regulation and Gary asked if I wanted to try again. I just shook my head. I wasn't the great white hunter that I thought I was. I never had the need to go hunting again. Even today, I have to force myself to shoot the rabbits that are eating up my hard labor in the gardens.

≈15≈

My wife began to change. She thought she was pregnant, but I reminded her I had a vasectomy. I took her to several doctors, even to the hospital. One day I came home from work and she was gone. My little girl was there by herself. We found my wife in the field, walking toward Lubbock and when I asked where she was going, she could only speak vaguely about a hospital.

She refused to attend church, be intimate or participate in life. She was only interested in eating chocolate candy. We went to several marriage counselors, different doctors and professors at Texas Tech. I couldn't afford all the bills so I worked on their yards or houses, reroofing one.

We joined a dance club, hoping that would give us a

joint interest and it did help. We met all types of people and the fun of dancing was rejuvenating as we traveled to different towns. Sometimes we went out-of-state. At one of the local dance clubs in Lubbock, I was dancing with another partner when an older man I didn't know told me to leave because I was an embarrassment to the club... that I should get my G—D--- shaky ass out of there. I went outside and wept. Then I got angry and headed back in the room to knock the lights out of the SOB. I had never felt such anger and hatred in my entire life. Just as I reached the door, another man I didn't know put his arm around my shoulder and said the old man was losing his mind. He had said that and plenty worse to others. Then I remembered my father, all the hurtful things he had said and done while under the influence of alcohol. The memories didn't make the hurt and shame disappear, but they did stop me from doing something foolish, like hit an old man.

When my daughter was school age, she went to Cooper public school. The priest at the church we attended asked why Wendi wasn't attending the church school. When I said I couldn't afford it, he insisted I enroll her and he would take care of the money. I did, knowing my daughter might not like it but I wanted her to have strong Christian values. My plans for a wonderful marriage and family were not reaching fruition and I felt I was losing control over the situation. I had been drinking beer only in moderation, but now I found myself drinking more and more, which only added additional problems to our relationship.

I was promoted from inspector to tool designer and worked with a great bunch of people, even making some good friends. After working ten years at the heavy equipment plant, it was shut down - moving to Mexico. I had to find another job. I worked at night at a nursing home changing bedpans, worked in a grain elevator, drove a road grader and worked in the garbage dump.

By now, my marriage was over and my daughter stayed mostly with my ex-wife. That was best, as I wasn't the greatest example of a dad. My lifestyle left a lot to be desired. I spoke to the priest and told him I didn't need to be part of the church, but he insisted we work together and after five years, I realized if I continued drinking, I would be a roommate with my father.

I had a job, and was very thankful of that. I liked the people I worked with, but something was missing. I checked on higher paying jobs, but they all required the one thing I didn't have, a bachelor's degree. I had to keep working to pay my bills, so the only alternative was night school. I chose Wayland Baptist University because of its size and personal attention. I wasn't a Baptist, but hoped they would accept my other college credits and help me finish. The administrator looked at my transcripts and told me I needed seventy-five more hours to receive a bachelor degree in occupational science and education.

≈16≈

I had been divorced two years, but was still active in the square dance club. I worked for the city of Slaton driving trucks, road graders and big heavy dirt hauling machinery.

While at one these dances I noticed this beautiful little Indian maiden that all of the men were fawning over. Her name was Petra. Not only was she pretty, she had beautiful dancing feet that were small and dainty. I knew, with my condition, I wouldn't have a chance of meeting her, so I didn't even try. She never noticed me. Sometimes she had a partner when she came to the dances, but mostly, she was alone. I knew she had been taking lessons from an instructor, and when I inquired, the instructor said her husband had died and she was living on a farm with her son. I thought we might have something in common. We both liked dancing and we both lived on a farm. Maybe she would talk to me. Nope, no communication. I kept wondering why I was so drawn to her. We did meet, even had several dates. I tried, like all men, to make a big impression and take her to a fancy restaurant but while standing in line, she saw a hole-in-the-wall place across the street. It had checkered tablecloths outside the restaurant. That's where she wanted to eat.

Another dance club was incorporated within the square dance. It was called round dance, which is ballroom dance with ques. She was taking lessons and seemed to enjoy this type more than the other. She said if I learned ballroom dance, she would dance with me. I was a bit distressed because ballroom dance requires body control, not my strong suit. This was hard for me, but I persevered. Not only did I get to dance with her, I learned that I could control my muscles and follow the music.

Dancing became the center point of our lives. We began travelling to other clubs and towns. After dancing all evening, we hung out with the group that enjoyed visiting over a cup of coffee or sodas.

While I was in college, I came across a poem that stuck with me. I don't remember the author or the title, but I was enchanted by the words. I memorized it and after twenty-five years, I wanted to share it with my new friend.

I do believe that God made you,
 for me to love.
He picked you out from all the rest
because he knew I'd love you best.
I had a heart I once called mine
but now you have two and I have none.
If I go to heaven and you're not there,
I'll paint your face on the golden stair
so everyone can see what you mean to me.
If you haven't come by Judgment Day,
I'll know you have gone the other way.
I'll give the angels back their wings,
their golden harps and everything.

And just to show you what I'd do,

I'll go to hell just for you.

I wrote the words as I remembered them, folded the paper and gave it to her while drinking coffee. I don't know if she read it then or later. She was gone for about a week because her daughter was having a baby but when she returned, I went to her house. I told her I would be moving on with my life and I would not bother her anymore. She cried and told me that she did care but needed two more years. I agreed to wait.

I had enrolled in night school and was working towards my bachelor degree. This would take about two years so I understood her need for time. We continued to see each other and danced.

I had some cattle and a horse on the farm. Petra came to visit and wanted to know if we could ride the horse so I saddled up the old mare and off we went, riding into the sunset. The mare didn't like the two of us on her back so she started to buck. I knew we would end up on the ground, and sure enough, we went flying through the air. I rolled Petra around me so that I would hit the ground first. This was our first and last ride.

I was doing okay in all but one of my college courses - English Literature. My mom saw that I needed help and called an old friend of hers that she met in AA group. She lived in Slaton just down the street and was a retired journalist who loved to read and stay up late.

I went over to her house. She seemed thrilled that I called on her and would be glad to help me. I told her that all my life I had trouble comprehending what I read and found no interest in literature at all. I did like to read but only about cars or cowboys.

I worked all day, went to class from six until nine, visited with my new girlfriend until nine thirty and only had the hours after ten to study. She said that was fine, as she didn't sleep much. I got off work at five and was at her house by ten. I gave her my assignments; she read them and then underlined the important parts she thought the teacher would ask. I also gave her a copy of some of my tests so she could understand what the teacher might ask. Sometimes I was so tired, she

97

punched me to keep awake while she read and reviewed. Most times, I got home at two in the morning. Thank goodness, I was able to comprehend the things she was telling me. My grades went from 50's to 80's and 90's. The instructor called me in and wondered if I had cheat notes. Why were my grades changing so drastically? I told him about my tutor and he was glad I was able to find help. She stayed with me all the way to the end, and then asked if I was going to get my master's degree. If so, I needed to hurry because she wasn't long for this world. I thought she was kidding. She came to my graduation, gave me a big, tight hug and kissed me on the cheek. She said I had helped her as much as she helped me. A week later, my tutor died. Thank you, God, for giving me this angel in life for without her I would not have passed English Literature or received my diploma.

Not only was I working on my degree, I was working on my annulment from my first marriage. I knew that I wanted to remain with the Catholic Church and this is one of the steps that I had to take. I was asked many questions. Did I try counseling? I told them that I did, reaching out to three that were sponsored by the Catholic Church.

By now, Petra had become my soon-to-be wife. She told me she was the mother of not one but five children, four boys and one girl. All were gone and on their own, living mostly in the Dallas area. Little by little, I met them all and they thought that I was okay. Then I had to meet Petra's mom and dad, brothers and sisters. I enjoyed them all, well most of them.

Mom got a call that my Dad was ill so I told her I could take off from work whenever she wanted to go. We decided to go the next day. Before we left, she got a call that said he died. The cause was emphysema. I wasn't surprised as he smoked constantly, even two or three cigarettes at a time. His mind had left him years earlier, though. The day he told me someone had stolen one of his testicles, I finally understood he would only return to Slaton in a pine box.

My Dad was an entertainer. He loved music. All his life he played some type of instrument, but his favorite was the organ and piano. He played for weddings, in bars and at festivals. He played both the organ and piano at the same time side-by-side and could listen to a song, then play it on the piano. I tried to play with him, but my hands shook too much. My sister played the piano and accordion and joined in with him but Mom said the only thing she could play was the radio.

I know that my Dad loved me very much but I didn't quite turn out to be the son he wished. He wanted me to be as quick-minded and coordinated as he was, but that would never happen with the muscles I had. My biggest disappointment is that he never got to see my daughter, to see my accomplishments and to see what we have done to the house where he grew up. The guilt, still in my heart, is that my mother and I didn't leave right away so we could be with him when he died. Before they closed the casket, I kissed him on the forehead, removed the ring from his finger and put it on mine.

≈17≈

The wedding day was getting closer. We wanted to remodel the house and add some extra space. There was lots of work to be done, inside as well as outside. We needed three bedrooms and two baths with a double car garage. The cost would have been less if we demolished and started new, but the house has character and lots of history.

Not only was our wedding day coming soon but my graduation as well. I still worked for the city driving dump trucks, but I knew with a degree in my pocket that I could open some doors and find the career suited to me.

While the house was being remodeled, I stayed with my mom and little by little, Petra moved her belongings to the farm and in the barn. The house was completed, she moved in, but because we weren't married yet, I stayed in town with Mom.

We were waiting on the annulment, but didn't know when it would be finalized. After consulting the parish priest, he suggested we marry by a Justice of the Peace and then later, marry in the church. On December 20, 1988, we got married by the JP in Mom's house. There were a few aunts and uncles in attendance and one bearded fellow who came with my cousin. Mom did a good job on the reception. She had a cake, finger foods and champagne. And of course, Petra was truly a beautiful bride.

We also had a square dance reception at the club where we belonged and there were many people who came to the dance, even some of Petra's family. I remember when we cut the cake that Petra bit my finger when we exchanged pieces. It was truly a wonderful wedding, enjoyed by all who helped us celebrate.

I arranged with one of the local inns to have a non-smoking room with a king size bed, some flowers and a bottle of champagne. It was a disaster. The room reeked with smoke, the flowers had a bad odor and the champagne was cheap. Sadly to say, she couldn't get out of there fast enough. We left the champagne behind unopened.

San Antonio was our honeymoon destination. The hotel room was great and the River Walk was beautiful. Christmas lights in that part of the country are always ablaze with lots of bling. A newlywed couple can't help but have a romantic stay.

≈18≈

I could hardly believe that I was about to graduate from college and receive my Bachelor of Science in Occupational Education degree. A few of our square dancing friends, my tutor, Mom, and my wife were at the event. To me it was my biggest accomplishment - now to find that open door to my new future. I told a few people, but had to work on my resume before applying for a position that I hoped would be a long career. I couldn't quit working for the City of Slaton because I needed a job, so I continued driving a truck while looking for another opportunity.

It wasn't long before I had a call from a friend I met at South Plains College. She was an administrator for a co-op in special education that had four local school districts. She heard that I just received my degree and might be looking for another career. There was an opening at Roosevelt ISD. I went the next day, thinking they might need someone to run the maintenance department. I met the principal and discovered he was a relative of my wife's deceased husband.

He said a special education teacher had quit and wanted to know if I could take her position. I reminded the principal, Mr. Wheeler, that I had no teaching experience, that I shook and stuttered at times. He said I would be perfect if I just went back to school to get my certification. I had two years to get it and could take the test as many times as necessary. When he informed me that school started in two weeks, I realized we had made plans to be out of town and that I would be a day late. Again, he said no problem and that he would fill me in on anything important. I went back to the house and told my wife to get in the car because I wanted her to meet one of her kinfolks. We got to Mr. Wheeler's office and he said, "Hi cousin." He was the gentlest person I ever met. He walked softly but carried a big stick.

Our six-day square dance vacation was in Missouri, at

Osage beach. Our dance instructors had arranged for us to attend. This is where one could eat, drink, be merry and dance all night. They had swimming, fishing, boating, skiing and parasailing. I tried them all and parasailing was my favorite. I got into a parachute on the back of a boat. It took off and I went up and up until I was flying with the eagles, so quiet and peaceful. For the first time in my life, my physical state didn't matter. As I hung from the harness, I didn't need the muscles in my legs to move. I didn't need my hands or fingers to grasp an object. I didn't have to speak or listen hard to understand. I only had to relax and absorb the pleasure of the sky. It was a beautiful place and a great vacation.

I had opened the door to a new beginning, spending hours studying, and hours telling myself I could do what a normal person does. Accomplishing my goal was not a single-person task. I had lots of help – teachers, tutors, well-wishers. Now that I stood at the door, I would have to succeed – not only for myself, but also for those who had faith in me.

≈19≈

Adopting, at the time, was the farthest thing from my mind. When Petra moved out to the farm, one of her sons, Max, came with her. He was bright, a very intelligent young man who loved the outdoors. When he was very young, Petra often couldn't find him at lunchtime when it was time to eat. Finally, she learned to look up in the trees. There he laid, arms and legs dangling over limbs like a lion cub.

Max kept the place looking neat and clean. He, like me, loved music, and he had speakers and a sound system throughout the farm. He wasn't a country music fan, but he did like Dean Martin's music. He also worked for Radio Shack, which gave him an abundance of resources.

I don't know why he took a liking to me, but he always

wanted to help me fix or do things that I usually had difficulty accomplishing. He even took me to different events when he had extra tickets, hockey and basketball games.

One day while he was helping me install some speakers, I said I wished I had a son like him. He responded, "Me, too." We both thought about the impromptu remarks. He was about to start a new life, along with a new wife. Did he want a new name as well? I didn't think the new wife wanted me around. She never said anything bad, but the vibes sounded like sour notes. But, as long a Max was happy, that was okay with me.

I did adopt Max before his wedding. We went through all the court procedures and I finally had a son. He married and we visited from time to time. Max's wife was attending college and before she graduated, they had two girls. They didn't come over a lot so we went to visit them. After the youngest one was born, his wife got a job and they relocated to San Antonio.

When I was young, I always wanted to be in my

grandfather's arms and to be with him. I was hoping, as a grandfather, to have my grandchildren feel the same. Max tries to visit and bring the girls, but it is a long way to travel. They still live in San Antonio where Max is a manager for a large chain store. He did call me often, but since he has gone through big changes in his life, the calls have gone by the wayside. Like all grandfathers, I was hoping for a grandson to carry on the Kitten name, but that was not to be. Thank heaven for little girls.

≈20≈

Grandpa built the barn and granary before he built his house. Since the family depended on the animals for its livelihood, they were the most important, needing not only shelter, but protection for their food as well. The granary had a loft to store smaller items and a breezeway. It was used for many things, but during the winter, the meat was hung there. While the house was being remodeled, Petra used it for storage. She had books, stamp collections, records, small furniture and many household items. In one of the rooms, I stored tools and building supplies, planning to make a woodworking shop to build toys and small furniture.

After we married, we brought some of Petra's belongings into the house, leaving the others until we found special places for them. Petra's youngest son was staying with us and one evening after returning from a trip to Dallas, Max said he heard something in the granary. He thought it was a cat or dog looking for mice. A bit later, he smelled smoke, looked out a window and saw flames from the outside building. He ran to our room and said we had a fire. Petra called the fire department and I went out to move my truck that was parked close to the heat. The flames were getting hotter and hotter. The tires were beginning to smoke. When the wind began to blow, it pushed the flames away from the house and away from the truck. Soon the fire department arrived but the building was too far gone to save. They did stay to keep the fire from spreading to the other buildings and the house and thought that probably the lightning storm which passed by earlier was the cause. Everything inside was lost: Petra's belongings, many of her family's possessions, but we were safe and the house was standing strong. It was a reminder of our many blessings remaining.

≈21≈

Mom stopped drinking and smoking some years back. She became stronger after Dad went to the hospital, making sure that all the bills were paid and everything was in order.

After retiring in her late seventies, she and a friend began traveling outside of the states, to Europe and Alaska. I was so glad she took the opportunity to do so as she brought back lots of pictures and memories.

Mom loved visiting Glenda, my sister, especially during Christmas time. She bought toys and gifts for the grand and great grandchildren all during the year, then put them together in a big box at Christmas time and drug it out. It is what her grandmother did when she was growing up, and it was such a great memory that she wanted to do it for her grandchildren. She also said her grandmother occasionally removed her teeth just to see the surprised look on their faces, so Mom did the same. My sister had five beautiful children. When her children had children, I got lost in all the names, but Mom remembered every one and enjoyed them all.

When she began losing weight, I knew something was wrong. I took her to the hospital and after what seemed like hours, we finally knew she had colon cancer. There was nothing to do but take her home. Our positions began to change and one day I realized I was taking care of her instead of the other way around. I paid her bills, checked on her daily and after speaking with her lawyer, discovered mom had taken care of all her burial arrangements.

I was always a handy man and could fix things with duct tape and bailing wire. However, this I couldn't change. I felt empty and lost. I was losing my mother. Within the next few days, Mom started doing weird things. She drove out to the farm and parked the car in the middle of the road, then walked to the house. Petra called me at work, so I came right home. Mom was lying down in the extra bedroom and when I checked on her, she seemed to be resting comfortably. Then we heard glass breaking and yelling. Mom had wrapped her arm and then busted out the glass in the window. She said someone was trying to get her.

I took her back home and called a sitter to stay with her until we made other arrangements. I called Hospice and they came right out and arranged for someone to stay with her. I called my sister and told her I thought she needed to stay with Mom one last time. She, her husband and the oldest daughter, who was a registered nurse, came to stay.

Early one morning Glenda called and said Mom slipped into a coma and for me to get there quick. I sat on the bed beside her, told her that I loved her and for her to go to the light and look for Jesus. It was as if she waited for me to come and tell her it was okay because she took one long gasp of air and was gone. We cried and prayed for her. Within a few minutes, there was a knock on the door. A priest was there to give her the last sacrament. The doctor, who lived across the street, came to check her vital signs and pronounced her dead.

Glenda told me that Mom got up during the night and packed her suitcase. She put in one shoe and one gown. Then she went to the refrigerator and got three bowls of ice cream and cake. She was going to a party out of town. That was my mom – she always enjoyed a party.

≈22≈

I am very lucky to have two daughters. One is biological, the other a stepdaughter.

My biological daughter, Wendi, was a shy little girl, but soon after entering high school, that shyness became a thing of the past. I remember at her birthday parties when she was little; I had to go find where she was hiding so she could blow out the candles on her cake.

She gave us a fright once and we feared we had lost her. I came in from work to find my wife crying - she couldn't find our little daughter. I looked in all the buildings around the farm, and called and called her name. We got the neighbor and began a search for her. His tractor was still in the field from where he left it to go in for dinner and when he drove past it, looking for

Wendi, he saw her in the shade of the big tires, playing in the dirt.

During my divorce, Wendi stayed mostly with her mother and grandmother. She did stay with us for a while, but there were too many chiefs and not enough Indians in the kitchen.

Wendi became a nurse, married and began her new life. She and her husband moved around often and sometimes I got confused as to where they were living. When the children began arriving, they settled into the Dallas area and now have a full beautiful family, three boys and one girl.

Papa, that is what Cathey calls me, is the only daughter that Petra has. She took a liking to me right away and always treated me with respect. She and her husband also live in the Dallas area and have two boys. Cathey is the one who keeps the family together, reminding me of a mother hen that always keeps an eye on and rounds up her chicks. She calls to check on us and makes sure we are okay.

Her boys have spent summers with us and enjoyed

the farm life. When they first arrived, they only wanted to sit in the house and play video games. I told them I had 160 acres of dirt and it lay waiting for boys to make some noise. They finally loosened up and we did play together and had lots of fun driving the tractor and playing ball.

Together we have six kids, fourteen grandkids and one great grandchild. I believe Cathey will be the only one to see if our needs are fulfilled. Because of the love and respect her family has given us when we visit, we enjoy travelling with them. Cathey's husband, Ed, is from the northeastern part of the country. He is also a history buff and a walking encyclopedia about the Civil War. On a trip across the southern states, he kept us informed about all the events during the conflict. Because of this, I became more interested in learning and reading about the heroes of the Civil War, sorry that I had waited until I was grown to understand the importance of their contribution to our nation's history.

≈23≈

I had been teaching for a few months when Mr. Wheeler told me to go to Midland, Texas. At the service center, they had a class called the Alternative Teacher Program. I was to take an entrance exam and be there on weekends for six months to be able to take the exam for special education certification. For every test that I have taken, I always had to take it twice. I even had to take the written test for my driver's license more than once. Written words are difficult for me to comprehend. This instance was no different. I took the test twice and passed. The class started on Friday, continued through Saturday evening and sometimes even on Sunday. I was back to school on Monday.

I got a room at a motel that was close to the class. It was clean and in a quite neighborhood, which I needed, in order to study and focus. I knew that I had better make the most of this opportunity because it might not come around again. The motel had a small restaurant where I could grab a bite to eat. But my favorite place was just down the street - the donut shop. The people who operated the store were Asian and they knew how to make those donuts melt in my mouth. At the end of that six-month course, I had gained ten pounds.

One day, while at home after the course was over, I told my wife about those melt-in-your-mouth donuts. She said, "Let's go get some." We drove a hundred miles to Midland to get a box of donuts.

The class had several instructors who taught, but one primary who was in charge. We talked about the laws involved, all the do's and don'ts, the types of handicapped conditions and how they affect the reason and learning capability of students.

We reviewed modifying different projects, purchasing aid devices, such as wheelchairs and walkers. We discussed working with support staff, such as physical therapists, speech therapists and occupational therapists. I didn't realize how many people were involved with a child's education. We needed to learn to work with nurses, doctor and caregivers, as well as all the other teachers.

I had been attending these classes for several months and the primary instructor came to me and said I had been chosen to be a participant in the 1,000 Points of Light initiative suggested by President George H.W. Bush. I was invited to be a guest speaker at the Alternative Teacher Convention on South Padre Island and received an all-expense paid trip. I was in awe, never before had anyone wanted to listen to me, or even to have me around. I, and two others, were chosen to go. This was my first public speech and I was nervous so I kept the talk brief and to the point. Afterwards, I received a letter from the White House congratulating me on my individual contribution to society. The letter was signed by President Bush.

The Alternative Program had other subjects and other classes but there were several requirements for completion. I had the Bachelor's degree but I would have to take the Special Education exit test. There were fifty people in the class and they were from all over Texas. The test was 4 hours long and intimidating to a man who always has to retake tests. I made a sixty-nine on the exam - one point away from passing. Instead of being proud that I was so close, I was frustrated and angry because I knew I could do it. There were ten who had to retake the test. I called a teacher and asked if we could get together on a weekend to compare notes and pass this test. She contacted others and we became a study group. The second time I took the test, I passed and received my certification in special education from Pre K to Grade 12.

With that certification in my pocket, my life was lifted to a higher level and I felt myself flying on that parasail again. Imagine me being a real teacher – no longer a little boy with cerebral palsy who ran away crying because a thoughtless old man told him to get his ass off the baseball field! But it took a while for me to realize that I was just as important as the teacher next door or down the hall. And they called me Mr. Kitten!

Sometimes while at the store, my wife and I would hear a voice say, "Hello, Mr. Kitten." Without even looking to see who it was, I knew it was a teacher or student from Roosevelt schools.

≈24≈

In 2002 I decided to restore my old 1950 Ford long-bed truck. I always had a passion for old cars and trucks and wanted to learn all that I could to build my own. I had to find someone who was willing to show me all the tricks of the trade.

While I was teaching at Roosevelt school, I talked often to one of the secretaries about my old truck. She said her husband worked on old cars and that I should meet him, so I did. Mike is an excellent welder and craftsman. He was a great and gentle person and was always there to help me out. We talked about my old '50's truck and what type of options we could change. I knew that I wanted a daily driver, easy to drive as well as quiet and comfortable - and eye appealing. With that in mind, most of the work could be done under the hood and on the frame; the body would remain the same.

The old '50 was originally designed to be a working farm truck and to haul heavy loads. The suspension was very hard and stiff. Mike suggested we change to a heavy-duty front end and that a Camaro engine would do the job. With this change, we would also have power steering for easier steering control. Mike had great ideas how we could reach my goals without the project being too costly. He knew a man who had a '78 Camaro clip and other parts that would add great comfort and control.

We soon had most of the parts to start this restoration and were anxious to get started. Mike told me to bring the truck to his shop and we were on our way to an improved classic ride. Mike worked almost every night and weekends. I tried to be there as much as I could to learn about every step. Although I could not do a lot of heavy lifting, I handed him wrenches or held things. I remember a time or two my wife said, "When are we going to move over to his house?" I took pictures of each change and add-on.

Once, I walked into his shop to see parts laying everywhere, a fender over here, a hood over there and the entire front-end lying outside. I just shook my head, hoping this man in front of me was as good as his wife said he was. To me, it looked like a big giant puzzle. Mike had done this type of renovation for some time. He had just about every type of motor, transmission and car part scattered around. The shop was larger than my house with all kinds of tools and a 1937 Chevy coupe, built with all the modifications of a modern day car.

Soon it was time to start putting this massive puzzle together; at least to me it was massive. To Mike, it was a piece of cake. He began putting the pieces together part by part and soon the truck was ready to roll off the assembly line. Then it was time to turn on the switch and listen to the massive machine as I drove down the road.

Mike talked about a trip he planned to take and wondered if I might be interested. We would travel seven days and stop at car shows in each town where vendors displayed their products. A concert and a meal were also included. Traveling from town to town with two thousand hot riders side-by-side sounded like quite an experience.

I told my wife I wanted to go and she encouraged me but also made it clear that on all other trips, she'd be along. She's a homebody, though. Her idea of a trip is one or two days.

Hot Rod Magazine and car vendors sponsored the tour. It started in Nashville, then on to Memphis, Jackson, New Orleans, Lake Charles, Shreveport and finished in Fort Worth, Texas.

Mike always led the way and I was hot on his tail. I knew if I lost sight of him, I would be in trouble because he had all the maps and locations of our motels. Whenever we got close to a major city, I was on his bumper so no cars could get between the two of us. I have been to several car shows, but nothing as big as this one. Cars, trucks and all types of motor machines were in the show.

While we were driving, I had to stop for gas so Mike said he would meet me down the road. I got my gas, started the motor and suddenly the passenger door flew open. A black man got in the seat and said, "Let's go." I told him I didn't allow any passengers and I wasn't leaving until he got out of my truck. He kept insisting that I drive but I continued to say no. I didn't know what I was going to do and kept looking ahead, hoping Mike would come back and check on me. Finally, the man got out and I quickly locked the door and breathed a sigh of relief.

Mike and I made it to New Orleans. We stayed a few blocks from Bourbon Street so we walked around to see the sights. I heard a little voice say, "Hi, Grandpa." It was my grandson, his father, his other grandpa and a neighbor I'd met. My son-in-law, Ed, had four of his classic cars in the show and was traveling on the tour as well.

The last stop was in Dallas. I visited with an old friend and saw my other grandson, who then rode home with me to stay a few days. Mike and I went on another trip to Austin, but then he retired from his job and moved to the Dallas area. We keep in touch and sometimes visit one another. Mike is a good friend and another angel in my life.

≈25≈

Not long after being hired at Roosevelt, I realized
teaching would be a different type of challenge for me.
Because I, too, had a handicap condition, I knew I had to
use a different type of teaching style. Each student had
his own way of learning and remembering. Some
learned by audio or visual, others by experiencing and
touching.

I had two different classrooms while at Roosevelt. My
first one was called 'The White House.' It was an old,
abandoned building, located between the elementary
and high school. This house had all the luxuries of a
home: a kitchen, a bathroom and two rooms that could
be used as classrooms. The rooms were small, though,
with small doorways – not conducive to wheelchairs and
my first class had two students in wheelchairs. One of

them was large, very large. I needed two big husky men to help me get this student to the bathroom because he had multiple sclerosis and could not stand on his feet.

The next year, our conditions improved and we had one large classroom. A lift was installed in the bathroom, so I didn't need those two husky men any longer.

My curriculum was based on daily living skills, concentrating on the students taking care of themselves in the bathroom and in the kitchen. That included cleaning and cooking. We worked on other skills - like dealing with money. It is a hard concept for a special education student to understand, but I only wanted my students to grasp that money is a means of exchange - this for that.

One of my students had his own way of recognizing money. I placed a one-dollar bill, a five-dollar, and twenty on a table. I then pointed to the one and he said Washington. Then to the five and he said Lincoln, then to the 20. Yes! You guessed it. Jefferson.

From time to time, several of the teachers asked me to give a Civil War lesson because they knew I had recently toured battlefields and was interested in the subject. I also had movies of Gettysburg and *God and Generals*, plus I took lots of pictures of the war sites. I blended the pictures and the movies to create a story about a twelve year old, involved in the war. I told the story about a father and son who fought on opposite sides from each other. The father was a doctor for the North and the son had studied music in the South before the war. There were many battles between the North and South and at one of these battles, the son was shot and lay dying from the wounds. The father, who was the field doctor, heard the crying boy and went to him, not knowing it was his son. The father couldn't save him and the boy died in his arms.

On many occasions, I took the students on field trips; to the store, to the mall, to the park – anywhere people gathered, just to get exposure. I wanted them to know they had a right to be in any public place.

On many occasions, people came up to my aids and remarked that the student in the red shirt who held the door open was so polite. That person with the red shirt was me. I was often mistaken for one of the special education students.

When we went to the South Plains Fair, all the handicapped students got free rides and were tagged at the entry way. I was tagged as well, and all the students and aids got a big laugh, but deep inside I felt marked and labeled. No matter how many degrees I earned, no matter how many years I spent in college, my handicap would keep me from being normal. All my life, I would be labeled.

There were times while walking down the hallways, especially in High School and Jr. High, I got a laugh or a smirk from students. But most of the non-handicapped students showed me respect as a teacher and addressed me as Mr. Kitten. I give this credit to all of the parents who properly taught their children at home.

My other classroom was in the elementary building. These were the Pre K to fifth graders, with young and innocent minds. They were the ones who asked me what happened or what was wrong with me. I always answered that God made me this way and that God had big plans for me and one of those plans was to teach children.

Because my students had so many different types of health and mental conditions, I had to be aware of where we went and who was around us. A lot of public buildings have double door entryways with automatic door openers. When a student with a high autism level walks up to one these - look out! He might run, scream or drop to the floor. My solution was to occupy his mind with something else and I always reminded the aid to have one hand on the student.

If my lesson was on baking a cake, we went to the store. I had a photo of all of the ingredients. As we walked down the aisle, we had a treasure hunt. Shopping wasn't fast, but neither is learning. When we got back to the classroom with all the items, it was their job to put all the food in the pantry or the refrigerator.

The High School teachers were very helpful to my students and me. Often, I asked the homemaking teacher to involve her students with mine, especially in cooking. Each of her students buddied with one of my students. We did this all year long, not only in cooking, sewing and crafts, but in other homemaking jobs as well. The students began to recognize each other and I noticed high fives in the hallway.

Every year I got the same students plus new ones that moved into the district. I even had one parent who drove thirty miles every day just to have her child in my class. I had one student for fifteen years and then there were some who died before they finished the program. I felt so badly for these students. I felt they could have experienced more in their lifetime. I also knew I had to draw a line with my personal feelings.

One year I had a handsome little boy I called Blue Eyes. He was timid and wanted to be left alone. It was difficult to get him interested in the classroom activities. Mostly, he hid in a closet or under a table. I needed a gimmick to bring him out of his shadow. The school district had just purchased a new refrigerator for my classroom. It came in a large box so I kept it to use as a class project. I told my class the box was put together in a specific way and we needed to study how it was done.

Blue Eyes became interested the minute I put it on the floor and opened one side like a door. He scooted inside and I knew he had claimed it as his. We began talking about making windows in the box. When I wanted little Blue Eyes to participate in the classroom activities, I just drug the box among us. The only problem I had was that the other students wanted a box, too.

Every year the public schools require teachers to take training in human management and self-defense courses, especially in special education. Each student comes from a different environment and has different reactions to stimulus. A teacher must learn not only to read minds, but also to study and read body language. Some students have difficulty in verbal expression, so it comes out in bodily outburst.

One day I had a student with severe autism who came to my class. The parents carried him; the mother held his feet and the father held his arms. The child squirmed and kicked all the way. My classroom was divided into several rooms, which could be closed off from others. As the student was brought in and placed on the floor, I told the aids to move the other students into another room and to close the door until the new student settled down. The parents stayed for a while, but I saw the boy was reacting to them, so I asked them to leave with reassurance that if I had any problems, I would call.

He was beginning to settle down until someone walked into the room. Abruptly, the boy began to throw things, becoming violent. I got the aids to keep everyone out because I knew I had to restrain him before he hurt himself. Following the training method, I stepped behind him, crossed his arms across his chest and we stood there several minutes. He was beginning to settle down when all of a sudden he raised both feet and kicked the wall. We both went flying across the room and hit the opposite wall. It was painful and I knew I had hurt something, but didn't know what. The student broke free and ran for the door. Luckily, he went out the back door into a cotton field and ran until he gave out. An aid brought him back to class. When the administrator heard this, the student was removed from my class and placed elsewhere.

I soon began having difficulties with my left arm and my neck. I went to the doctor and had an MRI. It showed damage to my fourth and fifth vertebrate. I began to lose strength in my dominant arm. When I wrote on the blackboard, the arm weakened as if all the air went out of a tire. I couldn't hold my arm up when my wife and I went to our dancing lessons.

Doctors in Dallas performed surgery and did a decompression on the fourth and fifth vertebrate of my neck. Afterwards, I felt no pain in my arms and neck, but I had no strength in my left arm. My right arm became the dominant arm. I could still grip with my left and use my fingers to hold on to things but I had difficulty writing and dancing.

The new student returned to my class. He had improved and was more in control of himself, however, noises disturbed him. One day another student, who had a birthday, walked into the classroom with a balloon in his hand. He rubbed it to make that crazy sound and the student with severe autism came unglued, screaming and shouting. Once we removed the balloon, everything was back to normal.

Most of my students were sensitive to sound and seemed to enjoy music. I set aside parts of the rooms to use as a relaxing and controlled area. I had soft music and soft lights. I also used water and bubbles to calm students.

One of the other special education teachers, whose husband was a recording artist, had a building that was sound controlled with built-in studio rooms. One day he opened this studio for my special students and they went wild. Some were rapping, some were keeping time to the music and some were singing. Hidden talents come out at the darndest times.

Jobs skills are important and can be taught. Modifying the training is a must. I had to keep it simple, not a lot of detail. There could be only one or two instructions. Because I was handy with tools and woodworking, I made jigs and holders to help with job preparation. I attended local job fairs and read listings to see what types of simple jobs were available in the community. I knew my students would never be rocket scientist, but it was my job to teach them and if I could teach them a skill, better for all.

We washed dishes and made beds, using a hospital bed in the classroom. We folded sheets and blankets. We did the laundry for one of the gym classes. I got a folding jig from one of the department stores and we folded shirts, t-shirts and sweaters.

Computer games were a delight for them and I used this as a reward. They could and did play games or parts of games over and over.

The administration supplied me with a greenhouse because they knew I had an associate's degree in agriculture. We planted seeds and grew fruits, vegetables, flowers, trees and bushes. We contributed to the Food Bank by planting vegetable seeds. When the seedlings matured, we took them to the Food Bank farm and helped plant the vegetables we started. Once a year the Food Bank had a banquet and invited my class – that's when they displayed the table manners we had practiced.

The green house was always full of plants and flowers

during Christmas time, especially poinsettias. During certain times of the year, elementary teachers brought their classes to visit my class and tour the greenhouse. They loved to see all the green plants and were amazed how warm the greenhouse was during the wintertime.

$\approx 26 \approx$

The City of Lubbock was very much involved with the Special Olympics and I asked the administrator if I could use the Roosevelt School name with my students. I also wanted to train them during the PE time in my class. The events were broken into two parts, track and field during the spring and bowling during the fall. Not all could do the track and field but most could bowl, even ones in wheel chairs. I went to a local blacksmith shop and had them build a special bowling ramp so we could practice.

I visited with the PE teachers and helped design a program for the students. The teachers were very thankful for that because they didn't have experience in the Special Olympics. I tried working with all of the teachers and most of them were receptive, but there was always one in the bunch that wouldn't give me the time of day.

The first year we participated in the track and field events, the students and I walked around the track to become accustomed to the surface. As we walked, the new head coach told me to get the wheelchairs off his track because the wheels would tear it up. He told me to go elsewhere. I did go elsewhere - straight to the principal's office and explained the need for physical fitness at all levels in a very loud voice. The next day I was back on the track. I can be pushed, but not into a corner when my students are concerned.

I tried to get all students involved in every aspect of the Olympics. We often had to go into homes to help the caretaker get students ready and then take them to the event. Every year became harder to get the students interested in the Special Olympics, each time fewer participated. Many of these special education kids were abandoned by their parent and left at a grandmother or great-grandmother's house. Grandmother didn't have the strength to get the student out of bed on a Saturday morning. Because we were participants of the school and school affiliated, a new regulation came out of Austin that ended our participation. If we drove a school vehicle, we could not leave it, which meant we couldn't go inside the house and help dress or get the student ready. Without aid, few of our students could participate.

While I was teaching, a college journalism student came to my classroom. Her name was Amy and she remembered me from her high school days. She worked part-time at the *Slatonite*, a newspaper in Slaton, and wanted to do a story about me working with handicapped students. Amy took several pictures and wrote an article for the newspaper. Afterwards, I received several letters and calls and realized the grown up little boy with cerebral palsy had made an impact on others.

We practiced lots of domestic skills in my class - one of them was cooking. It was fun. The food was good to eat, sometimes, and everyone was able to participate. I did most of my evaluations on this subject because I could involve the entire class.

Because we did lots of cooking, every year we had a Harvest Fest. I graded the students on domestic skills, as well as socialization skills - how they conducted themselves around other people and the type of hosts they could be.

We had lots of sweets, coffee, spice tea, chocolate fondue, small peanut butter sandwiches, vegetable plates, and small sausages with grape jelly. All the Roosevelt administrators, School Board Members and teachers who worked with the students were invited.

After retiring, when I met some of the teachers I worked with, they told me my shoes were never filled. They missed my presence, along with all the excitement that I brought to the classroom and to the school. My wife and I were in the grocery store one day and this woman came up to us and told me that she had taken my spot in teaching. She had come to realize that I was one awesome teacher. I thanked her and wished her lots of luck. Not long after that, I heard she had moved on to another position.

≈27≈

My mom told me I was born on the dance floor. She didn't mean it literally, but it was a compliment since my ornery muscles don't often do what I intend. Petra and I danced so often, my skills improved with age and the level of our dancing rose during our twenty years of participation. We were asked to dance with the professional instructors. This involved more travel to the larger cities, one of them being San Antonio. We enjoyed meeting new people, had the opportunity to dance and meet the professional people who wrote and choreographed the dances. The affairs lasted two days, one day for instruction and teaching, the next day for fun and entertainment.

Before we left San Antonio we stopped to eat at one of the breakfast restaurants and I got the Texas map and started looking at all the surrounding towns. I told my wife that somewhere close was a town named High Hill. My mother's father was from there. Just as I said it, someone tapped me on the shoulder and asked if I was Danny Kitten from Slaton, Texas? She told me her dad and my grandmother, were brother and sister. She was on her way home to High Hill and if we wanted to follow her home, we could stay for a visit.

We did have an extra day so I followed her car to High Hill. I had never visited, but heard Mom talk about the place with affection. We saw the beautiful old German Catholic church where my grandparents were married. Luckily that day, the church was having a Harvest Festival and like all little churches, trying to raise money for church repair. That evening they had fireworks, dancing and lots of beer. Afterwards, I got a good history lesson on the other side of the family and realized why my mother had such fond memories of High Hill.

≈28≈

As men baby boomers begin to retire, they are spending more time in the house with the commander in charge. As nature will have it, sometimes it gets a little warm in the kitchen. Lucky for me I can step outside and go to several locations that Grandpa left behind or some that I have built or purchased. Each one of these buildings has a name: garage, barn, cream house, and blue storage shed.

The garage is large enough for two cars with an extra concrete slab in front for working on other projects. It holds several important items: my 1950 Ford Classic Truck, my wife's Monte Carlo and most importantly, my tools to keep the Classic in top running condition. During the springtime, the local towns have car shows and swap meets. I get out the buffer machine and give the old

Fifty a good spit and shine. I also have my favorite music, classic country, playing in the background. I have three radios and one sound system hooked together, all on the same country classic music station.

The new barn started out to replace the old barn that was beaten by time, weather and nature. I wanted to rebuild the exact replica of the one Grandpa built, but the supply of money was limited. So I settled for a one-sided pole barn. The barn was built so I could add to it as money became available.

At one time, I had a few head of cattle in there along with some chickens and hay. That set-up went well for several years until I was injured and lost my arm strength. I settled on Plan B, sold the cattle and didn't mind when the coyotes enjoyed the chickens. I replaced the roof with new material and started installing a wood floor. The wall had metal panels and did not need replacing. Every year I added to the floor and purchased woodworking tools. I thought I could keep busy working with wood, having something to do after I retired.

I used the woodworking skills in my classroom,

teaching students how to use simple tools like screw drivers, pliers and hammers. I often went to tool stores where they had wood-making kits that can be assembled with small hand tools. I put pictures on the instructions to illustrate which parts went where. We made toys, benches, chairs, and the old favorite, bookshelves.

The barn filled up fast so I had to add more flooring and more space. It wasn't long before I had most of the tools to build anything small. I made projects for Petra: small tables, bookshelves and corner curio cabinets. We also built toys for the local children's homes. A friend of mine called one day and said he was going to South America to work with an orphanage and wondered if I would make wooden toys for them. I helped his group of church members make a hundred wooden racecars. The children were to paint them the color of their choice – that was a fun project.

It took twenty years to get the barn enclosed and the floor finished. I added thirty feet of five-foot glass windows so the natural light comes in during the summer time. I added two air conditions to cool down that hot tin roof.

My Dad was a railroad man and when I was young, he took me down to see the trains. A few times, he let me ride on the old steam engine. The engine was big, loud and hot. The wheels clanged on the track and the whistle had a magic sound. With all those memories returning, I built a train set in the barn, attached to the wall and designed to fold up when not in use.

I still had furniture that belonged to my grandparents. My grandpa was a tall, big man so the couch was extra-long. When he took his afternoon nap, he had enough room to stretch. I remember when my grandfather sat in his favorite rocking chair and listened to the weather and stock market report. I put the two rocking chairs and the extra-long couch in the barn and found a 1934 radio that fit nicely on one of the end tables my father made. Now talk about a man cave, this was a neat set up. My wife says that the add-on is large enough to have an old-fashion barn dance. Funny coming from her since she is a hard rock and blues fan.

I went down to the old basement and found the Hi-Fi record player I had when I was a teenager. Along with the record player were some old Elvis and Johnny Cash records. They fit in just fine in the barn. There are times when I go out to the barn, turn on the record player and plop down in that rocking chair to listen.

On the side, I have an overhead metal canopy, which contains my shiny, black Z71 truck and what my wife calls my sexy tractor. I am so blessed to have all this and I thank the good Lord for his blessing.

The oldest building on the homestead is the cream house. It was built for multi-purpose usage. Not only was the milk and cream separated by a hand-cranked machine but there was a fireplace in the building used to smoke sausage. Every year families and neighbors gathered and helped one another during the yearly butchering and meat processing. Afterwards the long links of sausage hung in the cream house to age.

This building was battered by time and weather, beginning to lean and look dangerous. My wife told me to fix it or push it down. I chose to fix it. I used my sexy tractor to straighten it and braced the walls and ceiling inside. I replaced the windows and now use the building for storage.

We have two other buildings, hers and his. The blue one is mine and the gray one is hers. The gray one is full of mom and Grandma things and the blue one has twenty years of teaching material and magazines. I plan to make this into my office when I get some time.

≈29≈

Twenty-five years ago, my uncle Clarence invited me into this group of men called the Knights of Columbus. I felt very proud and excited to be a part. For years, I had tried to join different associations and was always turned away. I worked hard to develop a place in this group, received the Knight of the Year Award and felt proud. During the turmoil of my divorce, I stopped attending the meetings but still kept my membership.

After my retirement from school, my wife suggested I become active again in the Knights. I started back and joined the fourth degree. I tried to help with some of the activities but I couldn't do much because I didn't have the physical strength. Something was missing. I felt like the fifth wheel in all of the activities. No one cared that I had a college degree. No one cared that I had taught school for twenty years. No one sat with me just to chat and I wondered if it was because I was handicapped or because I didn't have a beer in my hand.

One day I got a call from a friend of mine, Dave. He had always been friendly. Our families had gone to the same schools and church. Dave heard I had an old classic truck. He was looking at one to purchase and wanted my opinion. He brought it to the house and let me look at it. The truck was neat and clean. I told him whoever worked on it knew what he was doing and that it would be a good investment if the price was right, or worth having just to enjoy. He bought it and I invited him to a car show.

While at the car show, we had time to visit and I realized he had many of the same interests that I have. He likes old trucks, he likes working with cattle and likes restoring old barns. He is also a good talker.

While we sat under a shade tree at the show, I began to tell him about my childhood and the things I dealt with because of my physical condition. He said he knew I had a problem but didn't understand it. I also told him about the vision of Mary. He asked why I waited so long to tell it and I told him I didn't think anyone would believe me. Besides, why would it be of interest to anyone else?

Dave said a group of men gather at his place once a month. They flip burgers, drink beer, talk about God, and read scriptures from the Bible. He said all denominations attended. Then he asked if I would be a guest speaker, that I was inspirational and had a good message.

I did speak and was very nervous. Word got out that I had a vision from the Blessed Mother and people from Plainview drove down to listen. I have given four or five different speeches and each time there was a different message, but the concepts are the same - peace, love and prayer.

At these meetings, men come from all types of religions. They have different jobs and different problems and different types of families. Together, we talk about how we deal with our problems. Sometimes we talk about being angry with God and with our families. It's a gathering for support, reflection, well-being and prayer.

≈30≈

Years ago, the City of Lubbock purchased land off the Caprock to build a lake. This lake was to supply water for Lubbock. The crews had to dig a twenty-foot deep ditch, from the lake to Lubbock, and pump the water ninety miles uphill. They had to cross acres and acres of land, one of these acres being mine. A small corner of my land was used, lots of dirt was dug up and a twenty-inch pipe was placed in the resulting ditch.

Although West Texas is very flat, my land has a hill on it. When it rains, the runoff water makes deep trenches. Most farmers try to control the runoff and divert the water back into the field. I wanted to do the same and conserve the runoff. When the excavation crew crossed my land, they wondered if I wanted the extra dirt from the pipeline, since it was already my dirt. I had the perfect place. I drove my truck to the washout place and waited for the trucks to bring the dirt.

I planned for the drivers to come up the road, dump the dirt, turn right and move on to get another load - making a circle pattern. When they finished, a maintainer with a blade would smooth out the load. Simple, I thought. But the truck driver turned left instead of right and went in the wrong direction.

A cold, hard-blowing north wind blew across the field. I got out of my nice warm truck and stepped on the loose dirt, trying to direct the drivers in the right direction. Fighting the cold wind, I found myself face down in the dirt. I tried to push myself up but a sharp pain shot through my arm, my good arm. Two men saw me fall and came to help. One was the blade driver and the other was Lewis, who helped work the farm. Lewis looked at my arm, saw the break and said he would take me to the emergency room. I told him he had better take me to the house first to tell Petra. I knew I would get all those reasons why I shouldn't have gotten out of the truck in the first place, but she didn't say a word. That came later.

We got to the hospital and waited. The nurse gave me a shot for the pain and sent me for x-rays. The break was just above the wrist. There were two large men waiting for me in another room. They put my fingers into a finger lock, an instrument hanging from the ceiling. Then a heavy weight was attached to my elbow. I got another shot of pain medication because they were about to pull like crazy and push the bone in place. They told me to hold on. I hung as hard I could and was so thankful for the pain shots they gave me.

The nurses put on a half-cast and told me to check with the doctor after two weeks. Then I went home. My right arm was broken and my left arm didn't work well. I was weak and uncoordinated. Eating wasn't such a problem because Petra helped me, but I am a private person and attending to matters in the bathroom is definitely private. Putting aside my pride was hard to do.

The monthly man meeting was coming up, so I called Dave and told him I was laid up and wouldn't be at the meeting. He came right over to check on me, even offered to help with the bathroom situation. Now, that's what I call friendship.

I told him everything would be fine. I just needed a few days to recover. Sunday came around and he arranged for me to have Holy Communion from the church at my house. I was so overwhelmed by this I hardly remember if any of our children called to check on me. I know they did, but everyone lives so far away.

Two weeks slowly passed. After seeing another x-ray, the doctor said a tendon on the side of the bone was so strong it pulled the bone out of position. I needed surgery to have the bone reset and a plate installed so the tendon wouldn't do it again. He said it would make the healing of the break stronger but if I flew on an airplane, I'd have to tell the airline I had metal in my arm.

Surgery would be about two hours and I could go home the same day. I remember going to a room and a nurse putting a needle on top of my left hand. It burned and hurt and suddenly the lights went out. I heard someone call my name and said it was time to go home. Wow, that was fast. But then I realized several hours had passed. Petra was by my side the whole time but she said next time I was on my own.

≈31≈

When the wind is just right, there is one sound that makes me pause - the long blow of a whistle in the far away distance - a train going over a crossing.

My father was a railroad man. He rode up and down those tracks for many miles in rain, sleet or shine. Sometimes he was gone for one day, sometimes more. There were times I went with him to the station. While he checked to see when he worked next, I ran to the front of the station and listened for the sounds of that magnificent machine. If I was lucky, there would be one coming down track number one, lights flashing and bells clanging. Just the vibration of those giant wheels under my feet, the squealing sound of brakes and steam billowing from the engine sent chills down my back.

Sometime I saw the long, silver streak of the passenger train and I watched a conductor jump out of a small door. Groups of people mingled until he waved his arms and yelled, "All aboard". Those sounds and smells will remain with me forever.

During my early marriage with Petra, her son who was in his late teenage years, stayed with us. He brought lots of his toys and belongings. He soon went off to college and eventually got married. All his boxes stayed in my garage in my way. Little by little, I eased them out, box by box. Then I came across one box that had a train set in it.

I was still teaching special education and I needed something to hold the interests of my students. I thought we could build a track on a piece of plywood, cover it with green paper and run this train on it. I used basic math in my class with the project. We determined how many tracks we needed to cover a large sheet of plywood. We went on a special field trip to the local hobby and train shop. They saw a train already set up, in action with all the bells and whistles. Then they understood our goal. The hard part was explaining the difference between a toy and a hobby.

The train set I dug out of the box didn't have the bells and whistles so I went and bought some wooden train whistles they could blow and bells they could shake. To my surprise, some didn't know how to blow, so I started with a single candle and went from there.

The train set sparked an interest in the students. It sparked an interest in me as well. We got that train to run on the homemade track and I listened to bells and whistles for a long time.

Soon the train set went back to the original owner, but I stored that piece of plywood in the barn, knowing that one day I would return to that childhood experience.

Twenty years later, that piece of plywood got dusted off and mounted to the wall of my man cave. All I needed was a choo choo to put on it.

There is an antique store in Slaton where my wife loves to window shop. One day she saw a Santa Fe passenger train. The bells and whistles went off inside me. I knew that plywood track was about to see a new face lift.

The engine ran for a while but stopped. I needed a train to go around the Christmas tree and Christmas was fast approaching. I went to a family-owned store in Lubbock and learned that the train I bought had a bad motor. I purchased two sets before I was satisfied with the results and became good friends with the salesperson.

I now have two different sizes of trains, HO and O scale train sets. The scenery I am using for the O set is the farm like my grandfather built in 1912. I scaled it to one-quarter inch. The first building I made was the granary. It has five large rooms and a small room where Grandpa hid his moonshine. I built the loft as I remembered it along with a ladder and extraneous details.

The next building I made was the barn. I included the area for milking, stalls, hayloft and a protected space where the animals could get out of the weather. The cream house followed, the building where my grandparents separated milk from cream and smoked meat.

The last building was the house bought from Sears and Roebuck. I put in all the details I could remember from my childhood. Today, after nearly a century, my wife and I live in this same house, though with modifications.

I added one last element to the picture. The layout of the farm is complete inside the oval track, and as I fire up the old steam engine and travel back in time along the homestead, I see the little man looking out the top window of the engine and smile. That's how I remember my father.

≈ 32 ≈

My time with my grandparents was short, but they were an inspiration throughout my entire life. Yet, I knew so little about them. I began to research their history, dig into the soil and touch the buildings they left behind. The history has now become alive and every time I step out of the house that my grandfather built, the color and beauty of the land comes alive.

Clemens Henry Kitten and Louisa Anna Heilers were married on February 14, 1912 in Lawrence, Nuckolls County, Nebraska. They were to begin their new life and settle down in Slaton, Texas. They loaded everything they owned, including cows, horses, chickens and pigs onto a cattle-hauling train. Grandpa's brother and grandma's sister helped with the journey. They were about to be married and made the same journey to

Texas. The couples would end up living next to each other.

The land was flat, no trees or rivers. Everything they needed to live on or build had to be brought in or drilled. The trip to Texas normally took two or three days by train, but because of the time of year, they ran into a massive snowstorm in Canadian, Texas. The men rode in the cars with the livestock and nearly froze to death. They were stuck for three days, all the while having to find water and feed for the livestock during the freezing weather. After they arrived in Slaton, they had to find a place to stay and a barn for all the livestock while they built a house and barns. Those people had to be tough as nails. I can't imagine doing that in today's world. Back then, people had to and did depend on one another for help and guidance.

My grandparents didn't have any children because of health reasons. My grandmother had heart problems and later, cancer. There was a family in the area that was a step relation to my grandmother and in great need. Six children were left without parents, one of them being a newborn baby. Grandmother went to the aid of this family and found homes for the children. Some stayed with neighbors and some went to boarding homes. Since my father was the newborn, she kept him with her. She wanted to care for them all, but there was not enough food or money.

My grandparents adopted my father and changed his last name from Miller to Kitten, Clem Valentine Kitten. Born on February 14, 1916.

The original house was only one bedroom with no running water, so with the addition of a baby, they decided it was time to rebuild. Sears and Roebuck Company advertised a house that could be ordered and freighted in to a location. There was a loading and unloading port along the railroad at Posey, Texas so my Grandpa ordered the house. He took his team of horses and wagon to Posey and brought all the supplies to the farm and began building his new home with electricity, running water and a bathroom.

My grandparents had chickens, cows and pigs to live on and sold eggs, butter, milk and meat to help with the income. Grandfather worked the land, planted cotton and raised cattle to help. They had fruit trees and a big garden. I remember every year he walked in the field with his church key to check the corn for its ripeness. When he said it was corn-picking time, cousins and neighbors came to pick and can the corn and vegetables. The apple trees did well and produced an abundance of apples, more than everyone could eat. Grandfather knew what to do with the extra. It was a tradition handed down from generation to generation. It also helped with the farm income. Moonshine. Both he and his brother worked together, each one having their own skill. They used sugar water, yeast and apples. The mixture fermented for two weeks before they cooked off the liquid. Next, they poured the liquid into fruit jars and hid them in the fields. They fed the leftovers to the livestock causing sleeping hogs and staggering chickens.

The law got word of two brothers making moonshine. They stopped at Grandfather's brother's house to raid his farm, but the children had time to hide the jars in the field. Grandmother's sister, who lived across the road from them, had the old crank type phone. She called to warn them of the raid but it was too late. Grandfather had the last jar in his hand when the fed's arrived. They chopped up the still and confiscated all the moonshine they could find. They took him to jail and later, to trial. The judge asked him if he was making whiskey and Grandfather said no, so the judge dismissed the case. Grandfather didn't lie. Whiskey does not have the same ingredients as moonshine. Besides, the judge was one of his customers.

Grandfather was the man of the house, but like most marriages, the woman is in charge of the home. He was a giant of a man - stood six feet tall and weighed over two hundred pounds, but gentle and soft-spoken. His hands were so strong that he could bend a bottle cap with his bare fingers. I stood in awe every time I saw him do it. One of his favorite things to do was challenge another man to a grip contest with a broom handle. Both men faced each other, holding the handle, trying not to let it turn between their fingers.

Grandfather always teased and enjoyed laughing.

Although his hands were strong, they were always shaking. I remember Grandmother pouring only half a glass of milk or cup of coffee for him. He used both hands to hold the container to try to control the shaking. Mom said it was the Kitten shake, and most of the men had it.

I always played in the buildings and from time to time, stirred up a wasp nest. Usually I got stung five to ten times, swelled up and ran to the house in tears. Grandma always said, "He found another one." Grandpa waited until late in the evening to ask me where the nest was. I stood behind his giant figure and pointed to the direction of the nest. He then took out an old paper sack and with his shaking hands, very carefully opened the sack and placed the opening over the nest. Next, he squeezed the top of the sack until the nest fell to the bottom. While holding the sack with one hand, he took a match from the pocket of his overalls to strike on one of his buttons. After lighting the paper sack, he dropped it on the floor. I never saw him get bit. He said the trick is not to run.

Every summer Grandmother gave me a burr haircut and it lasted until the beginning of school. She made most of my shirts from the flour and cotton meal sacks and sometimes the buttons would be on the wrong side. As I got older, I was glad to get one of those store-bought shirts.

From the time I started school I always struggled to do well in my grades. I got by in addition and subtraction as long as I had enough fingers, but multiplication floored me. Grandmother stepped in to help. Every day during the summer, she took me to the back porch of the house where she had a small blackboard on the wall. I memorized the multiplication tables by the use of small flash cards. I was stubborn and wanted to play outside since it was summer but I realized she was stronger and more stubborn than I was. I finally learned them.

The morning of March 22, 1955, she was getting up to milk the cow and feed her chickens. She fell against the wall of the bedroom and died of a massive heart attack - a sad day for the Kitten family and especially, for Grandfather and me.

My grandfather was never the same after that, so lost and lonely. He sat in his old rocking chair and I crawled up into his lap and put my head on his shoulder. I stayed with him as much as I could and for a while, the whole family lived with him. That didn't last - too many people in a small house.

Grandfather started selling all the livestock and the farming equipment and rented the farm to one of the relatives, who was already in the farming business. He stayed in the house and drank his beer. I went with him to Big Spring, where he bought cases and cases of beer. He loaded that old fifty model Ford to the top. I was strong enough to help him carry all that beer down into the basement under the house. He could go down there without going outside and it was cool enough to keep his beer. As time went on, he became more tired and weaker. After a trip to the doctor and hospital, we learned he had liver disease.

We brought him to our house to live since we were close to the doctor and the hospital. I was in high school and involved in FFA. I had a project raising a hog for show and had it at his farm. I went out there every day and when grandfather was well enough I asked him to go with me. He never did. Once he left the farm, he never returned.

Both Mom and Dad worked and since the house was just a few blocks from school, I went home during lunchtime to check on him. Sometimes I made him a peanut butter and jelly sandwich. When Dad was gone, Mom asked me to help give Grandfather a shower. I had never given another man a shower before and was a little embarrassed, but we got it done. More and more he returned to the hospital and I knew the end was near. I didn't know how to talk to him or what to say to the person that I loved so dearly. He was so close to death. Oh, how I wish I had hugged him and told him how much I loved him; that I was sorry if I ever hurt him in any way and that I hoped to grow up to be half the man he was.

On November 18, 1960 he died. They brought him to the house and I cried for him. I looked at his rugged hands that worked the land, milked all those cows and squished all those bottle caps. They lay still. They were not shaking any longer.

≈*33*≈

In 2012, our homestead was one hundred years old. From the time my grandparents built the Sears and Roebuck house until I lived here, there have been over twenty couples who spent years under this roof. I saw some of these folks and asked them what they remember about the home place, hoping to get more information about it. Surprisingly, they remember little of the house, more about what happened behind the barn or up in the hayloft. There was never an answer, only a smile and a wink.

My grandparents worked hard to start it, but Petra and I put in lots of work, time and money, doing our part to keep the family farm an enchanted place. We planted over three hundred trees and shrubs. I have taken cuttings from one tree to start another tree. I even contacted the Texas Forest Service to get trees and shrubs that are adapted to this area. I began the plantings to bring in the birds, rabbits and other small animals. My plan worked, however, I had forgotten about the skunks, rats and snakes. I don't mind skunks from a distance but underneath my workshop is way too close to cohabitate with a family of them. I don't know how many constitute a family, but I witnessed enough of them waddling through a hole in the foundation that I was convinced it might be an army. I knew they liked cool, quiet places so I made it loud, really loud. I turned my radio to the loudest volume setting. I found a CD that had the song, *Who Let the Dogs Out*. I set the CD player on repeat and all night at full volume, the dogs were out. Then I sprayed powdered lime under the floor because it has real fine dust and makes breathing difficult. The skunks left.

I got pine trees that were drought tolerant. I always loved the smell and sounds of the whispering pines in the mountains, along with the trickling of flowing streams. Petra can't tolerate high altitudes, so I brought the trees to me. All I needed was the flowing streams.

From the road, you can't see the house because of the trees. When my grandparents built the place, Grandma planted elm trees and the ones that survived are over ninety years old. They cover the entire house and from time to time, I have to trim and prune them to keep them from damaging the roof.

The land was irrigated at one time. There were three wells but now only one is left in the field. I use this well to water the trees, grass and garden. Petra and I often sit outside in the shade enjoying the fruits of our labors, listening to the wind in the pine trees and listening to the water sprinkler in lieu of a trickling stream.

≈34≈

Every five years, the Kitten family has its reunion. Relatives come from almost every state and several countries. I am the fourth generation of descendants of Henry Joseph Kitten and the seventh generation of the original Kitten family who immigrated from Germany.

The Henry and Katherine Kitten family began in 1882 and had 1,429 members by July, 2010. Henry and Katherine's family with eleven children originated in Ferdinand, Indiana and ended up in Slaton, Texas. My grandfather, who was one of the eleven children, was the first to homestead here. Other siblings followed.

The Kitten reunion is a special event that brings generations together. I am always amazed at all the people who carry or have connections to the Kitten name. I am also in awe that when we travel out of town, if someone hears the Kitten name, they ask if we are from Slaton. I say, " Yep, I am part of the litter."

One year, the Martin Kitten family traveled all the way from Ibbenburen, Germany to attend the event. Martin still operates the original farm from the 1400's. Martin noticed my wife's name, Petra. There was a bit of a language problem, but he, too, had a girl friend name Petra. Now I think there are two Petra Kitten's

Because the Kitten's are of the catholic religion, there is always a big mass. Father Marvin, Clem Kitten, who is my grandfather's nephew, leads the celebration.

≈35≈

People who have changed my life.

Every time I see a rock star on television that takes a flying leap into the fans, I understand. All those hands support him in the air, and as one hand is removed, two more take its place to move him down the path and then gently place him on the floor. I often think about the footprints in the sand poem...while walking along I see two sets of prints and then only see one. When questioned, God said, "I was always there and carried you when the burden was too much for you to bear."

This is what I feel when I think of all those hands of angels that have guided me though life's changes and disappointments. Like the stars in the clear night sky, there are many hands, too many to count.

It starts with my parents, who gave me life and ends with the ones who will place me six feet under the ground. The ones who have stayed with me and supported me have influenced me the most: my wife, my children, friends and relatives.

I often hear successful people speak of their struggles, of obtaining their goals and doing it all by themselves. I find that hard to believe. So many have helped me, most importantly: my wife, my mom and my grandfather.

My wife has repeatedly told me that I am an intelligent person and my looks have nothing to do with the man I am. However, she can be and is, my worse critic. My mom suffered in pain to give me life and never gave me reason to think I wasn't normal. My grandfather was a father figure when my father was gone. He gave me roots.

There is a saying that you go around only once in life, but I have found this is not true. Both good and bad things have happened to me. I got a second chance to return to college and earn a long, awaited degree. Encouragement from the administration of Wayland

Baptist University and support from my family were key factors, plus the desire to better myself. "I can do all things through Christ."

I also have been given a second chance in marriage. Petra encouraged me to continue my education and helped me rebuild the old homestead and remodel the house.

I have been given another chance to regain my self-respect. Following my divorce, everything in life had just about fallen apart: I drank, I didn't care about my reputation; my family and I were growing apart; and life, in general, was going downhill. I even thought I might end up like my father, just like the saying, "That apple didn't fall far from the tree."

I am ever so grateful for all good things that are now a part of my life. Every day I am more and more thankful that I was a lucky one, that I did not just go around once, but was given a second chance.

≈36≈

When I was young, my sister, parents and grandparents protected me from the outside world. As I grew older, I wanted to see what was on the other side of that fence, yet society wanted me to sit and be quiet, labeling me different, unapproachable, odd, weird and handicapped.

I couldn't be still and quiet. Something inside pushed and urged me to do more, to be better – to be smarter than those labels I wore around my neck.

I wanted to fly with the eagles and be with people who were important, have decent conversations with interesting characters, experience what non-handicapped people experience. My body did not reflect that, but my mind screamed with normalcy. And there were many who encouraged me, many who helped me along my journey to become more than the man I saw in the mirror. I discount all those who say what I accomplished was given to me – their ignorance can be just as debilitating to them as my muscles are to me. Given and helped are two very different categories.

In 1951, a movie was produced, but it wasn't until 1989 when I studied it in English Literature that I recognized the concept. I realized that my life had been enriched far more by those who have helped me than by those who look the other way when I pass. The last sentence is still in my heart and because I have experienced it so many times, I know ..."I can always count on the kindness of strangers."

21962322R00112

Made in the USA
San Bernardino, CA
15 June 2015

10664372

RED STATE BLUES

OTHER TITLES FROM BELT PUBLISHING

The Akron Anthology

Car Bombs to Cookie Tables: The Youngstown Anthology

The Cincinnati Anthology

The Cleveland Anthology

A Detroit Anthology

Happy Anyway: A Flint Anthology

The Pittsburgh Anthology

Right Here, Right Now: The Buffalo Anthology

Rust Belt Chicago: An Anthology

The Cleveland Neighborhood Guidebook

The Detroit Neighborhood Guidebook

Folktales and Legends of the Middle West

How to Speak Midwestern

How to Live In Detroit Without Being a Jackass

In the Watershed: A Journey Down the Maumee River

The New Midwest: A Guide to Contemporary Fiction of the Great Lakes, Great Plains, and Rust Belt

What You Are Getting Wrong About Appalachia

The Whiskey Rebellion and the Rebirth of Rye: A Pittsburgh Story

RED STATE BLUES
STORIES FROM MIDWESTERN LIFE ON THE LEFT

EDITED BY MARTHA BAYNE

Copyright © 2018 Belt Publishing

All rights reserved. This book or any portion
hereof may not be reproduced or used in any
manner whatsoever without the express written
permission of the publisher except for the use of
brief quotations in a book review. Printed in the
United States of America.

First edition 2018
ISBN: 978-1948742061

Belt Publishing
2306 W. 17th St., Suite 4
Cleveland, Ohio 44113
www.beltpublishing.com

Cover and book design by David Wilson

TABLE OF CONTENTS

LOOKING TO THE FUTURE

CODA

INTRODUCTION
MARTHA BAYNE

A year and a half after the 2016 presidential election, Democratic voters across the country still carry visceral memories of the confusion, fear, and disbelief the election results engendered. Since November 8, 2016, pundits across the political spectrum have explored the electoral flip of traditionally Democratic states like Michigan, Wisconsin, Pennsylvania, and Ohio with expressions of grave concern. The national media, unused to getting the story so wrong, has visibly and often inadequately struggled to understand and explain this newfound exotic constituency of blue voters who swung red, and tipped Donald Trump into the presidency.

But what about those voters who remained true blue? With a broad swath of the Midwest now painted as "Trump Country," it's easy for outsiders to forget the election's razor-thin margins: 77,744 voters spread across Wisconsin, Michigan, and Pennsylvania turned those Democratic states Republican. That's less than the capacity of the University of Michigan's football stadium.

Red State Blues speaks to the lived experience of progressives, activists, and ordinary Democratic voters. It pushes back against simplistic "Trump Country" narratives of the Midwest—a narrative from which the region's rich history of grassroots, progressive politics has been erased. It gives the lie to lazy stereotypes about the white working class, who, by the way, aren't the only people living here by a long shot, thanks to waves of migration, from the Great one of the mid-twentieth century to more recent arrivals from the Middle East, Central America, and South Asia. The diversity, grit, and resilience of the Midwest has been an open secret all along, and as the essays in this collection demonstrate, it's a secret worth shouting from the rooftops.

By organizing the work here into a few loose categories, we've tried to bring a sense of, if not order, at least narrative chronology to a wide-ranging array of writing. Thus the first section, "Where We Live, Who We Are," interrogates Midwestern identity in the context of the current state of national politics. Here, reporter John Counts travels to Northern Michigan in search of answers; Annie Maroon muses on loving and leaving western Pennsylvania, the place, she says, "that taught me empathy."

Here at Belt, we initially (and lovingly) titled the next section "My $^@% Father Voted for Trump, Now What Do I Do?" ... but after some second thought decided to go with "Family is Forever" instead. Whatever you call it, this popular—and painful—genre examines the personal toll of this polarized election. Here, Trent Kay Maverick takes a long, wry look at his own father's penchant for "fake news," and Amanda Lewan tries to sort out the familial memories and conflicts kicked up by her move from stark-red Macomb County, Michigan, to a fixer-upper in Detroit, the city her parents worked long and hard to leave.

"Midwestern Bubbles" looks at those lighthouses of liberalism that have long anchored the Midwest, and which seem curiously invisible of late to the outside eye. Places as small as a Cedar Rapids gay bar where you can get an after-hours HIV test are counted here, as are sites like historic Yellow Springs, Ohio—home of Antioch College—and, of course, the bright blue city of Chicago, whose relation to neighboring Wisconsin is, as Bill Savage explains, forever fraught.

Finally, we turn to the hope on the horizon. "Looking to the Future" examines the ways activists and politicians alike are working to change things for the better. Journalists Sydney Boles and Rowan Lynam walk readers through the fight against an ICE detention center in Elkhart, Indiana. Kenyon College president Sean Decatur shares his personal narrative of moving, as an African-American man, to majority white Knox County, Ohio. And Pittsburgh city councilman Dan Gilman lays out his blueprint for building a progressive city.

We close the book with one of the best pieces of writing on Midwestern identity we've read in recent years: Phil Christman's "On Being Midwestern." While not explicitly political, we wanted to include it as a grace note. Originally published in the *Hedgehog Review* in 2017, this lyrical essay lopes from personal experience through Marilynne Robinson, Thomas More, and Slate political commentary to really explore the limits and possibilities of place-based identity—how much of it is real, how much is aspirational, how much rooted to nostalgia. We're happy he's letting us reprint it.

This collection is, of course, not in the least exhaustive. There's a lot more to read out there by, for, and about Midwesterners and their peculiar habits. If you're from some other place, we hope this taste will give you context and perspective for what you're seeing on the nightly news. And if you're one us, we hope you see a little bit of yourself reflected here.

—Martha Bayne

WHERE WE LIVE, WHO WE ARE

2004, EAST OF THE CROOKED CUYAHOGA
CHRIS DRABICK

Today, I picked the President.

I stood in line, in the rain. It wasn't so bad. It was morning, seven o'clock or so. The temperature was climbing, but it was still pretty chilly. I wore a hooded jacket. Even though the polls had been open an hour or less, already there were lines, which we were told to expect.

When I pulled my trusty Chevy Prizm into the parking lot at Forest Hill Church in Cleveland Heights, Ohio, the plethora of campaign signs made me wonder about the separation of church and state. Bush/Cheney. Kerry/Edwards. Yes on Issue One. No on Issue One. Eric Fingerhut for Senate. Re-Elect George Voinovich. Here I was, about to do my civic duty in a house of worship. There were people milling about, some in rain slickers, with clipboards holding paper that would soon be soaked by the precipitation.

There were three lines snaking outside of the church, with no signage or officials to explain the reason or reasons for the separation. I chose one, shoved my hands in my pockets against the wet chill and looked around. People were asking one another what line they were in. Was this the line for Precinct A or Precinct B? No one knew. The lines grew behind me, with many of the voters asking the same unanswerable questions. How long have you been here? When is this rain going to stop? Who are those people outside? Did you see the guy with the walkie-talkie? Who was he talking to? No one knew.

The line moved forward, still growing behind me. We shuffled inside, the hallway dark and wet from the shoes that had already trudged through. I pulled the hood off my head. The walls were those beige concrete bricks that comprise what seems like a majority of the interior walls of postwar churches. We moved forward, one at a time, slowly, surely. Confidently.

We were picking the president. I was picking the president.

As the hallway curved to the right, the reason for the three separate lines became clear. Forest Hill was housing three separate precincts that day. I was new to this area; I'd never voted in Cleveland Heights before. The rest of the crowd was confused. People, voters, looked to their registration cards, trying to match their precinct to the line they'd chosen. Some had guessed incorrectly. There was movement, shuffling.

People, voters, remained calm. Some bowed their heads and moved to the back of the line, out into the rain, ready to repeat the twenty-minute wait that brought them to this point. The line might have grown by that point, meaning a longer wait. A little old lady, her dark skin shriveled over her five-foot frame, looked at me with quizzical eyes.

"What precinct are you in?" she asked.

I told her. She asked if I would let her in line in front of me. Of course I would.

I was nervous. There was talk of problems at the front of the line. Registrations lost. People, voters, in the wrong building. Poll workers already getting short, annoyed, tired, stressed.

There had been talk for weeks about electronic voting machines, made by Deibold, an ultraconservative corporation from my semiconservative hometown of Canton, Ohio. People, voters, were worried that there could be monkey business associated with the electronic voting machines. Deibold was known to have made large donations to the Bush campaign. That made computer-vote tampering possible, maybe even likely, to the not-so-closeted conspiracy theorist in me. My mind wandered to that battered trade paperback I'd carted around since undergrad, *Conspiracies, Cover-Ups and Crimes* by Jonathan Vankin, written in 1992, in which brothers Ken and Jim Collier recount their experience with vote fraud in a local election in 1980 in Dade County, Florida, punctuated by something called a "hanging chad." In a book published in 1992. "Hanging chad." I was nervous.

To be fair, I was never in love with Senator John Kerry as a candidate. I'd preferred Howard Dean, who seemed ready to embrace progressivism, and would have made for some dynamite debates with Dubya had he just steered into the skid after that disastrous scream in Des Moines following his disappointing third-place finish in the Iowa caucuses. Kerry was a little milquetoast, too willing to run toward the middle in an attempt to sway those multifarious independent voters. Sure he had the pedigree, the "JFK" initials, the foreign policy experience that was needed that year. But I always liked the idea of promoting governors to the presidency—Clinton, Dukakis, my long-wished-for presidential campaign of former New York Governor Mario Cuomo—and "JFK" here was a senator. But what was I going to do? I would've voted for damn near anyone with a pulse who opposed Bush/Cheney.

I was there to pick the president.

The line shuffled forward. The fluorescent light from the large dining room that held the voting booths was visible in the short distance, but the hallway was so crowded with people, voters, that I couldn't see what sort of machines lay in wait. The earlier antsiness of the people, voters, was replaced by a calmer vibe, probably owing to the fact that we'd all settled in our proper lines.

It had been over a decade since I stood in a similar line. I didn't know what to expect. There were stories about invalid voter registration, precincts in Cuyahoga County that would be swarmed by Republican foot soldiers sent to challenge votes. I thought about the rain-slicker, clipboard people milling around outside. They may have been just those vote-challengers, ready to storm in and begin their day's work at any moment. The front of the line seemed calm, though, and there didn't appear to be any real trouble ahead. It was early, and things could change.

It was time. I signed the book. They waved me through. The machines were not electric, nor were they old-fashioned punch cards. Optical scan. Like filling in a multiple-choice exam in a large undergrad lecture course. Introduction to Voting. At least there would be a paper trail.

I took some time to look over the wording for Issue One, an amendment to the state constitution, the so-called "Gay Marriage Ban." I didn't pause in order to consider my vote, as I considered turning this down to be a no-brainer, personally. However, polling showed the measure to be a slam-dunk to pass, and I wondered if the other voters were taking the time to look at the actual language of what it was they were voting on. The amendment eliminated legal rights for all unmarried couples. There it was, in black and white. The homophobes probably didn't even realize that one was being slipped by them. It was a trick really; a ploy designed by state Republicans to make certain that fired-up evangelicals would turn out in droves and, while they're at it, cast a vote for their boy Dubya. It made me a little mad, but I didn't want to hold things up, so I filled out the rest of my ballot quickly and efficiently.

I picked the president.

The rain had slowed to a brief stop as I left Forest Hill Church. The rain-slicker crowd was still milling around the parking lot. Maybe they were exit pollsters, I don't know. I quickened my pace, not wanting to be interviewed or accosted or anything else, got into the Prizm and sped off to my job.

My duty was done. I'd made my voice heard for the first time in over a decade. I couldn't be silent any longer. I couldn't allow my abject fear of jury duty frighten me out of registering to vote. No matter how much I may have wanted to, I didn't feel apathetic anymore. It was fun while it lasted.

There was a lengthy period of time during which I was not registered to vote. By lengthy, I mean years. It might be true that I was not registered to vote for longer than I was registered to vote, but I can't be sure because I don't exactly know what causes a voter to become an ex-voter. Or when. But it was years.

In and of itself, this might not seem absurd. I am, after all, a pristine example of a Gen Xer; born in 1971, overeducated and underemployed, a latch-key kid with all of the inherent and inherited irony that gave rise to things like twenty-plus years of *The Simpsons*. In retrospect, it sure was nice to have the requisite comfort that allowed us Gen Xers to be so cynical for so long. The bulk of my 1990s was spent in the bliss of political apathy. I didn't vote in the 1996 general election, when Norm MacDonald's *Saturday Night Live* version of Senator Bob Dole neatly summarized his "Chinaman's chance" at winning the office. It was hard to vote against that guy.

Eventually, though, the Clinton presidency came to an end, the 2000 presidential election was decided in favor of George W. Bush by the Supreme Court, and it was a short ride from there to September 11, Afghanistan, the "Axis of Evil," Iraq, and "Mission Accomplished." The Clinton budget surplus came back to us in the form of $300 refund checks. Dubya had to go.

I remember little about my day at work that rainy November Tuesday. By the time my day was done, the polls were closed and I was ready to settle in and watch the results. I clicked around the networks and PBS for a bit, but it didn't take me long to realize that the internet was providing the quickest returns. After some trial and error, I locked into CNN. com, where I was able to watch continuously updating returns broken down by state and county. My internet connection was speedy, and I smoked Camel Light after Camel Light, filling the small black ashtray that sat next to my second bottle of Goose Island Honker's Ale. The polls were close, most of them showing a virtual statistical tie. In the final three Ohio polls before the election, Kerry carried a one-point lead in each, which in reality wasn't worth a good goddamn anyway.

As minutes turned into hours, I watched the states turn red or blue. New York predictably went to Kerry. So did Massachusetts. Virginia was hard-fought but captured by Bush. New Jersey, closer than predicted, went for Kerry. Bush took North Carolina. All eyes turned on Florida, but Bush pulled comfortably ahead. Arkansas, Alabama, Georgia went to the

Republican, too. Kerry held strong in Maryland, Maine and Michigan. But Ohio was too close to call.

The Central Time Zone states fell into place next. Kerry grabbed Illinois, but Bush routed him in Indiana. Iowa was close, but went red. Bush cleaned up in Kansas. Missouri wasn't as tight as some thought it might be, and Bush easily took the state.

But Ohio was still too close to call.

The polls then closed in the Mountain Time Zone. No surprises in Idaho or Montana or Nebraska, where Kerry voters needn't have bothered. New Mexico and Nevada were too close to call, and would stay that way for hours. But when the West closed up and California went to Kerry, as everyone knew it would, and Oregon and Washington turned blue, it was game on. New Mexico and Nevada were still up in the air, but with Pennsylvania's twenty-one votes firmly in Kerry's column, suddenly it was a numbers game.

It all came down to Ohio.

CNN.com posted county-by-county results, which updated with alarming frequency. I eschewed all other coverage, instead keeping my eyes focused on the monitor and my finger on the mouse. The smaller, rural counties tallied up some large pro-Bush numbers. Dubya took seventy percent or more of the votes in Auglaize, Clermont, Clinton, Hancock and Holmes. It was closer in the suburban counties, but Bush clung to leads in Lake, Medina, Butler and Delaware. The cities largely went for Kerry, with Franklin, Mahoning, Lucas, and Summit counties giving the challenger well over fifty percent of the vote, and because of the huge population differences between places like Columbus and Knox County, whose total population was less than 30,000, the margin stayed razor thin.

It all came down to Cuyahoga County.

I did the math in my head. If Kerry could pull seventy percent of the vote in my home county, he just might win this thing. This happened in 1964, with LBJ winning almost half a million votes. I thought about line that morning, in the rain. The line was confusing. People had to go to the back of the line and wait all over again. Did it get worse as the day went on? Did it get more confusing? What if enough voters had been turned away to keep Kerry from the seventy percent I was figuring he needed to win?

I thought about *Conspiracies, Crimes and Cover-Ups* again. I thought about the chapter in which it's outlined how shifting a few thousand votes in key areas could've swung the '88 election for Dukakis. I had the sinking feeling that "they" had picked their president.

Who are "they?" The millionaires and billionaires behind the "Swift Boat" attack ads on Kerry's service in Vietnam. Those behind the official-looking notices sent to people, voters, in the Columbus area, explaining that due to the expected high turnout, registered Democrats were to vote on Wednesday, November 3rd. "They" are the dirty motherfuckers who sent out letters on bogus Lake County Board of Elections letterhead telling newly registered voters that they had been "illegally registered" and would not be eligible to vote until the next election. "They" are the employees in the Secretary of State's office who decreased the number of voting machines available in Franklin County, so that machines were running at 90-100% over capacity, resulting in waits of three or four hours or even longer. The result was that Franklin County voter turnout was just over 60%, fully ten percentage points lower than the rest of the state. "They" are those responsible for successfully challenging individual voter registrations, resulting in over 155,000 so-called "provisional" ballots being issued, the vast majority of these occurrences being in urban centers. "They" are the those that purged 168,000 voters from Cuyahoga County between 2000 and 2004, resulting in mass confusion at the polls, with people, voters, showing up at the wrong precincts, waiting in the rain for hours, being told that they were no longer registered and subsequently adding to the many thousands of provisional ballots being cast, with fully one-third of that number being discarded (doubling the percentage from four years earlier). "They" are the 13,500 rural Southwest Ohio Republicans who voted for both Dubya and Democratic Chief Justice candidate C. Ellen Connally, a liberal Clevelander with little to no name recognition in a place like Sidney.

I picked the president, and "they" picked their president.

I watched the numbers swell for Kerry in Cuyahoga County. I wished I'd been able to go to the election-eve rally in downtown Cleveland with Bruce Springsteen, where tens of thousands of Kerry supporters overran Mall C, the Boss reminding the crowd to "believe in the promised land." But votes could be shifted, maybe not by hanging chad this time, but maybe just by Issue One and disenfranchisement and purposefully long lines. I started to sense my old cynicism welling up, feeling that my vote wouldn't matter. "They" had picked their president. The numbers continued to swell for Kerry in Cuyahoga County, but I'd seen the lines that morning at Forest Hill, and I knew without being told that there were lines elsewhere.

More than anyone else, the "they" of Ohio were represented by one man: Secretary of State J. Kenneth Blackwell.

It was J. Kenneth Blackwell who sent a letter threatening to fire the entire Cuyahoga County Board of Elections if they accepted provisional ballots in precincts other than where those voters were registered. It was J. Kenneth Blackwell who sent out voter registration forms, which he later refused to process because they were printed on incorrect paper stock. It was J. Kenneth Blackwell who was behind the Cuyahoga County voter purges, in which some neighborhoods saw as much as thirty percent of their numbers disenfranchised.

It can't have been a coincidence that those Collier brothers in Miami were witness to the "hanging chad" phenomenon a full twenty years before it occurred again in the same state. It can't have been a coincidence that thousands of inner city Ohio voters, reliably Democratic voters, were purged from the rolls just in time for the general election. It can't have been a coincidence that J. Kenneth Blackwell would fight so hard in court to preserve his "proper precinct only" rule about provisional ballots. It can't have been a coincidence that there were already twenty-minute lines so early in the morning at Forest Hill Church, where I was among what might have amounted to about a twenty-five percent white minority. It can't have been a coincidence that so many voters would swear out affidavits to the effect that their electronic voting machines would record either "no vote" or Bush votes each time they attempted to vote for Kerry. It can't have been a coincidence that tens of thousands of Bush voters didn't bother to vote either way on something as controversial as Issue One. It can't have been a coincidence that there were no bilingual translators at heavily Latino precincts. It can't have been a coincidence that the lines to vote in Gambier, near Kenyon College, lasted until well after midnight, while at nearby Mt. Vernon Nazarene College there were no lines at all from open to close.

Before I went to bed that night, I checked CNN.com one last time. Sixty-eight percent for Kerry in Cuyahoga County. On TV, reports were saying that, as the precinct results neared 100%, the election would remain too close to call for many hours. Others were already calling Ohio for Bush, some numbers showing Dubya ahead by over 200,000 votes. Only the provisional ballots remained. It was still possible, but increasingly unlikely, that Kerry had the numbers.

When I woke, whatever momentum was there as I watched Cuyahoga County vote overwhelmingly for Kerry was gone. Those 448,000 votes wouldn't do it. At around 11 that Wednesday morning, Kerry conceded the election to Bush.

Of course, it wasn't over. There were lawsuits to be filed, books to be written, blogs to be published, theories to be theorized, and tears to be shed. In the months that followed, the official story codified around Bush's superior campaign strategy and the push for Issue One, which passed with over sixty percent support. But underneath other stories emerged, themselves represented in the documentaries *No Umbrella* and *...So Goes the Nation*, as well as Michigan Congressman John Conyers's book *What Went Wrong in Ohio: The Conyers Report on the 2004 Election*. That one is a thoroughly sickening read, if you're so inclined. J. Kenneth Blackwell took a shot at the Governor's mansion in 2006, and thank goodness, Ted Strickland and the people of Ohio handed our friend an ass-whipping.

If *Conspiracies, Cover-Ups and Crimes* had taught me anything, it was that, no matter how hard the opposition tried, there would be times in which the people, the voters, would speak too loudly to be drowned out. We weren't heard in 2004, but a presidential candidate even less likely than Bill Clinton would ride a wave of "hope" and "change" to the White House in 2008. Of course, my cynicism could never completely abate. I knew Barack Obama had taken too much Wall Street money during his campaign to effect real change, and that Bill Clinton was literally from a place called Hope. In the 2008 primary, I voted for Hillary.

As 2012 rolled around, though, I got nervous again. Former Massachusetts Governor Mitt Romney was, to that point, the single worst presidential candidate of my lifetime, and possibly anyone else's. Need proof? Look at the parade of ne'er-do-wells that Republican voters attempted to award with their party's nomination in the "Anyone but Mitt" days. Minnesota Congresswoman Michelle Bachman, Texas Governor Rick Perry, pizza executive Herman Cain, former Speaker of the House Newt Gingrich, and former Pennsylvania Senator Rick Santorum. It says something that people, voters, took time out of their daily lives to go to the polls and choose any one of these nitwits over Romney. Anyone but Mitt.

When Romney finally sewed up the nomination, his campaign hinted that he'd be a sort of political Etch-a-Sketch, that they'd be unburdened by fact checkers. At first I thought the idea that voters would be fooled by a candidate so willing to brazenly lie his way into office was absurd. After the conventions, when Obama started to open up extremely wide leads in all sorts of polls, it looked like a done deal, the sort of election where I could sit back and sort of pretend that it was 1996.

But it wasn't 1996 or even 2004. It would have been easy to allow my cynicism to take over during the 2012 campaign, especially living in Northeast Ohio. The Supreme Court's *Citizens United* decision opened the floodgates for a ceaseless and increasingly absurd series of advertisements on television. Romney's promise was fulfilled, as he ran a shockingly dishonest campaign that somehow saw him closing the gap in the polls.

This made little sense to me, apart from the frustration caused by having to pull ourselves out of the worst economic crisis that the U.S. has seen in almost a century. I shuddered to think that people could blame the current president for this, or really any president for that matter. Wall Street was to blame, pure and simple, and while I was annoyed that Obama's administration was too willing to allow business to go on as usual, at least Dodd-Frank put some consumer protections in place. Romney's choice of Paul Ryan as his running mate was telling— this Ayn Rand–obsessed bro had authored the most brutal budget plan imaginable. If any single one of the grandmas and grandpas who were sporting Romney/Ryan bumper stickers and yard signs had bothered to look over that thing, its slashing of Medicare alone would be enough to make their blue hair stand on end.

But the ads on TV were constant and loud and jarring and disturbing, on both sides. I tried not to let it make me cynical. I tried not to allow myself to become convinced that money would determine the election. I tried to believe that the people's, the voter's, voices would again be loud enough to be heard. I knew the election would come down to Ohio once again, because the sheer volume (and volume) of the advertisements showed it to be true. The Republican-led state legislature did their best to fall in line, creating a sufficient enough fear of voter fraud to enact Voter ID laws that felt more like a poll tax than anything else. John Husted was the young secretary of state, and while he was no J. Kenneth Blackwell, some of his maneuvers, including trying to truncate early voting hours in inner cities while allowing suburban locations to remain open practically 24/7, turned him into a Blackwell-light. It was beginning to feel very familiar.

I worried I'd see long lines in my Akron precinct. I worried there'd be many stories about voter intimidation in my old stomping grounds of Cuyahoga County, where weeks prior there'd been anonymously purchased billboards erected promising jail time for vote fraud. I worried about the Romney family investment in InterCivic, a voting machine manufacturer that had apparently supplied a couple Ohio counties. I worried that John Husted's brazen attempt to increase historically Republican absentee voters by mailing out applications to every registered voter, whether they requested one or not, would have the desired effect. I worried that all of this added up to make 2012 feel strangely like 2004.

I needn't have been so scared. I didn't stand in line. There was no line. I walked right up. The sun shined brightly from morning until night. There was no dull, dreary, bone-chilling rain. I saw no voter intimidation, no scuffles over ID, no poll watchers bothering people, voters, outside of my precinct.

I again turned to CNN.com to follow the results. It was obvious to me within ninety minutes of the polls closing that the president would win re-election. There'd be no late night, nail-biting outcome. I could go to sleep early. I was no longer nervous, no longer worried. The people's, voter's voices, were heard.

We picked the president. I picked the president. On a sunny day, I walked from my beautiful home that I share with my lovely wife and our darling baby boy to a line-free polling place. I picked the president. "They" tried, again. "They" failed.

THE PENNSYLVANIA I CARRY WITH ME
ANNIE MAROON

Five years after I left, I got Pennsylvania inked into my skin. It was my second autumn post-college, and the notion that I might never live in my home state again was sinking in. So I decided to carry the state outline on my left shoulder, with the major rivers of the western third, where I grew up, drawn in blue.

I knew by junior high that I would leave Greensburg as soon as I was old enough. Both of my parents left the states where they grew up by their early twenties. My mom left Ohio for New Orleans, and my dad departed West Virginia for North Carolina. (Both eventually circled back to Pittsburgh; that part of the arc is only now beginning to seem relevant to me.)

At eighteen, I chose Boston. I almost never got homesick in college. That came later, once I became what you'd call a permanent resident of Massachusetts rather than a college kid. I spent a summer in western Massachusetts thinking about the mountains and creeks I grew up with, thinking about a cockeyed, hilly city where three rivers intersect, crossed by iconic bridges. I missed the geography, and I missed the people. My brother and I had left, but almost my entire extended family lives within a few hours of Pittsburgh.

And I thought a lot about the realization that hit me when I was seventeen and about to leave: that I would always be shaped by this place. I could roll my eyes and despair over the people around me in my rural-suburban county who never seemed to want to travel farther away than Pittsburgh. I could cast around for something fun to do with friends and wind up at the mall or the 24-hour Eat 'n' Park, because there was nothing else. But all that was part of me. I never wanted to get so far from home, mentally, that I forgot that.

Some states are iconic. Their names and shapes are evocative, synonymous with a way of life. Pennsylvania doesn't have that. It's a big state, but not big enough to have the outsized fantasies attached to it that California, Texas, or even Alaska have. It has major cities, but no New York or Chicago or Los Angeles. It's a perpetual swing state, voting Democratic in presidential elections all my life (until 2016), but never overwhelmingly enough to gain a reputation for it. People sometimes see the western part of my tattoo and ask if it's Massachusetts, mistaking the Allegheny River for the Connecticut. Others have squinted at it, running through the middle of the country in their minds: *Ohio? Colorado?*

In college, most of the real East Coast kids thought I lived somewhere in the suburbs of Philadelphia. Westmoreland County isn't fly-over country the way that, say, Nebraska is. From my parents' house, you can drive to D.C. in four hours, New York City in six. But I learned the term "Pennsyltucky" early to describe my homeland (long before *Orange Is the New Black* used it for a character who, in the show, isn't even from Pennsylvania, but Virginia). The term is a little too easy—dismissive of Kentucky as well as a huge swath of Pennsylvania—but while it irks me coming from New Englanders, I forgive it coming from others who grew up there.

The first election I really experienced was 2000. I was nine years old, in fourth grade, and it was the first time I realized just how different my family was from the families of my classmates. Kids talked, in the way kids do, about how they would vote for George W. Bush, because their parents were. In my fourth-grade class of about 25 kids, only two of us—my friend Marissa and I—were in Al Gore's camp. (One other boy implied that he might have been with us, but he didn't exactly want to stick his neck out. He and I are Facebook friends now, which means I see his pro-Trump posts.)

That was it: Marissa and I, taking whatever insults a bunch of vaguely conservative fourth-graders could hurl at us. We snapped back at our classmates pretty well, as I remember it, and the election went on for a month. At the end of it, George Bush was president, and I felt somehow separate from the kid who had entered the school year, terrified of having anyone pay attention to her. I was different, and now everybody knew it.

In eighth grade, my mother took me to a rally in downtown Greensburg before the 2004 election, where I hollered across the street at a friend's father, who was waving an inflatable dolphin to mock John Kerry's "flip-flopping." I absorbed my parents' lukewarm acceptance of the Democratic nominee and wore a Kerry button to school on Election Day. It was still pretty much just Marissa and me, but I was settling into my identity as one of Latrobe Junior High's token lefties.

The summer before senior year, I spent two weeks at journalism camp in Washington, D.C., with kids from all over the country. I made friends from New Jersey and Los Angeles and Queens, all of whom were astounded when we watched the documentary *Outfoxed*. OK, but nobody really *believes* what's on Fox News, they said. Nobody actually *watches* that stuff and thinks it's true.

I remember exchanging looks with a girl from Tennessee. We tried to explain that, well, yeah, some people—including people we love—*do* watch Fox News, and they do think it's the best place to get their information. We disagree with them, but we love them and want them to be safe and healthy and happy. Sometimes we're alarmed by the things that come out of their mouths, though, and the violence with which those things come out.

I don't know if it is better or worse to grow up in a place that does not share most of your values. I do know that it forces you to see people who are different from you as human, rather than as some faceless concept (like the mythic, monolithic "white working class," or the occupants of something called "Trump Country"). They are your day-to-day life, the people you joke with on the afternoon bus and the people who sit by you in class. Sometimes you settle for rolling your eyes when they talk politics, because arguing with them is too exhausting. In rare triumphant moments, you stand up to a smarmy Republican teacher who takes for granted that everyone agrees with him, or at least that everyone will shut up and pretend they agree with him.

Since November 2016, "empathy" has become a loaded word. Empathy is something western Pennsylvania taught me. As a writer, empathy is something I can't help, and can't afford to lose; I want to understand other people. Flat characters are for formulaic superhero movies with Good Guys and Bad Guys, not the stories I want to tell.

But empathy does not mean a free pass. My empathy for your real pain and hardship doesn't get you off the hook for deciding that a candidate's racism, xenophobia, and misogyny weren't that big of a deal, because you didn't think they'd affect you directly, or just didn't think they mattered that much. And nothing rings more hollow than a think piece pleading with the people in the line of fire—black folks, Latin folks, immigrants, queer and trans people, Muslims, women, Jewish people, people who need Medicaid for life-saving services—to empathize with those who put them there. Why should they be obligated to peer into the souls of people who couldn't be bothered to do the same for them?

In the summer of 2016, I drove from Massachusetts to Greensburg. The last leg of the journey took me from featureless, gray Route 22 onto Route 119, through little towns like Crabtree and the rolling green fields that signal home to me. I used to get lost on purpose in these hills coming back from college, soaking in the scenery. This time, every pocket of civilization I passed was scattered with Trump signs, like clusters of fungus on fallen trees. This wasn't surprising; after voting twice for Bill Clinton, my county had gone Republican since 2000. I have always known who my neighbors are. But I felt sick in a way I hadn't felt about the John McCain signs that sprouted all over my hometown in 2008. I might have rolled my eyes, or sighed, at McCain and Mitt Romney, but I did not feel afraid at the sight of them.

On election night, I watched the results with my colleagues at our office in Springfield, Massachusetts. I didn't leave until Pennsylvania had been called, around 1:40 a.m. The next morning, I began sorting through my emotions. I considered the facts. In total, just about six million people, half the population of Pennsylvania, had voted at all. The winning candidate's margin of victory was narrow, not even a majority—just less than 49 percent of the vote to just less than 48. I knew all this, but still I felt, that morning, betrayed by my own skin.

But I am proud of what western Pennsylvania made me. I am proud of my mother, who took me to ragtag protests throughout my youth, who is so vocally opposed to this administration that acquaintances and friends often send her private messages on Facebook, thanking her for saying things they aren't bold enough to say themselves. I am proud of my father, who provides medical care to kids in the poor, rural areas that voted hard for Trump, the areas in desperate need of help from someone who cares about them outside of an election cycle. I am proud of my friends and relatives who still live there, and of all the members of the community who do the crucial, unglamorous work of making people's lives better.

What was killing me November 9, 2016, was the small, irrational hope I'd held that the people who sat next to me at my brother's hockey games, drove me to and from practices, and came to my graduation party would be decent enough to look at Donald Trump and say, enough is enough. Yes, we are conservative, we are Republicans, but some things matter more than party lines, and this is not a normal Republican presidential candidate.

Some of them were decent enough, of course. But a lot of them were not. And the people of whom I'm thinking are not all members of that much-scrutinized White Working Class with all of their Economic Anxiety. They are all white, yes, but many live quite comfortably. Their cars are large, with trunks big enough to carry multiple hockey bags, and their spacious homes sit in immaculate housing developments. Some are old classmates who, in the culture vacuum of the suburbs, embraced a certain "redneck" identity that celebrated their realness, their true American-ness, which they demonstrate largely through drinking at country concerts.

I don't know whether their feelings are changing now that white supremacists feel comfortable enough to openly display their colors all around the country, some of them saying outright that this administration has emboldened them to do so. I have stayed Facebook friends with some acquaintances from the area; there are times to unfriend and un-follow, but I am afraid of what happens if we all cut ourselves off completely from people with whom we disagree. One woman, who posted in November that she voted for the president based on his position on abortion, voiced disappointment and a sense of betrayal in August, in the days after Charlottesville. I haven't heard much from anyone else.

Three years ago, when I got my tattoo, I figured the odds were better than not that I would never live in Pennsylvania again. Kids like me flee towns like mine all over the country, for all sorts of good reasons, and a lot of them don't come back. My county lost more population between 2010 and 2016 than any other county in Pennsylvania. Some people leave seeking jobs. Others leave seeking safer places that will fit them better, or threaten them less; my queer friends from home left for bigger cities. I left in part because I wanted to explore a new place, to start over in a city where nobody knew me. Somewhere along the line, I put down tentative roots; the hills and old mountains in the northwest part of my adopted state have been a good enough facsimile of home. The fall of 2018 will mark my tenth in Massachusetts.

But now I can see myself in Pittsburgh. Maybe in a year, maybe further off, but I can imagine it. Maybe if I want to keep talking up my unromantic swing state, I need to put my money where my mouth is. There are people in western Pennsylvania, and in Ohio and West Virginia, who deserve better than a president who will play to their fears and anxieties in election season and strive to leave them without health care months later. They deserve someone who will speak honestly about how we got this way and provide real solutions, rather than taking the cowardly cop-out of casting immigrants and people of color as convenient enemies.

But maybe it is too easy for me to give a rousing speech from western Massachusetts, where Bernie Sanders dominated the bumper-sticker race from the start and won my town's primary vote with ease. The week before Christmas in 2016, my brother and I were driving home through the center of the state—the white-hot core of Pennsyltucky, if you must—under an astonishing pink sunset that stayed with us as we wound west, past barns in picturesque fields covered with snow.

I tried not to think about politics. I wanted to fight for the land and sky themselves, to protect them somehow from harm. It is easy to romanticize from the highway, and easy to dismiss, or speak grandly, from hundreds of miles away. That day it was hard, maybe impossible, to hold everything I felt about Pennsylvania in my heart at the same time.

AMERICAN CARNAGE IN PENN'S WOODS: A HISTORICAL PARABLE

ED SIMON

"Were they not suspected of hostile designs? Had they not already committed some mischief? Some passenger, perhaps, had been attacked, or fire had been set to some house? On which side of the river had their steps been observed or any devastation been committed? Above the ford or below it? At what distance from the river?"
—Charles Brockden Brown, *Edgar Huntly,*
or, Memoirs of a Sleepwalker (1799)

"He sees where blows with Rifle-Butts miss'd their marks, and chipp'd the Walls. He sees blood in Corners never cleans'd. Thankful he is no longer a Child, else might he curse and weep, scattering his Anger to no Effect... What in the Holy Names are these people about? ... Is it something in this Wilderness, something ancient, that waited for them, and infected their Souls when they came?"
—Thomas Pynchon, *Mason & Dixon* (1997)

Pennsylvania's frontier in the decade after both the Seven Years War and Pontiac's fearsome Indian rebellion was a paranoid place. In the 1760s, Pennsylvania was not yet even a century old, but the settlers had feared the howling wilderness since they laid the first red brick of Philadelphia. As it was in New England and Virginia, here in the middle colonies fear of not just nature but the Indian Other would be the birthright of these new Americans. King Charles II—that drunken, womanizing, dandyish monarch—granted a proprietary charter for the colony to that stolid, sober Quaker William Penn, in recognition of naval service that the latter's father had performed in the 1650s, which resulted in Great Britain acquiring Jamaica.

Penn was on fire with that Inner Light of the Society of Friends, and he believed in Christ's prophecy that swords would be beat into ploughshares, and though Penn took the injunction that "Though Shalt Not Murder" as absolute decree of the Lord, his new experiment in utopianism on the shores of the Schuylkill and Susquehanna is intimately tied to the blood-soaked success of his father on those warm Caribbean sands. After all, "Pennsylvania" was named by the King after the father, not the son, as many have assumed.

Though the colony was generously defined by an incredible diversity in religion, ethnicity, and language, there were also deep fissures that developed in the decades after Penn's death. Tensions between white and Indian, English and Scots-Irish, Quaker and Presbyterian, east and west, and as always (and still) between urban and rural. For in what would be the largest private land owning in human history, this combustible combination would alight in terrifying, unprovoked violence one winter day in 1763, when innocent blood stained new snow red.

Right as dawn broke on December 14, a crisp, clear winter morning when winters were still cold, a masked group of vigilantes snuck into a Conestoga Indian village not far from where Millersville is today and killed six Susquehannock men, women, and children as they lay sleeping. The militia—prefiguring the posses that would later define America's violent history—was composed mostly of settlers with Scots-Irish background from the borderlands on the western frontier of Pennsylvania. The Conestoga Indians they attacked hadn't just laid down their arms; they had never picked them up to begin with. For if the shivering settlers at Fort Pitt had feared Chief Pontiac arriving from the west to cut their throats while they slept (and in turn decided to ameliorate their fears by inventing biological warfare, as the forks of the Ohio was the first place where smallpox blankets would be distributed amongst the natives), these murdered Conestoga at Millersville were good Christians who posed no threat to the men who killed them.

The theoretician of this murderous crew—who heard Iroquois war cries in their nightmares even when the Iroquoian spoken in Millersville was more often than not offered up in Christian prayer—was a minister named John Elder. Charmingly referred to as the "Fighting Pastor," as if he were the mascot of some sleepy Christian liberal arts college's football team, Elder was in reality by every definition of the word a genocidal war criminal guilty of ethnic cleansing. Elder preached his sermons in a town called Paxtang, and from a bastardized, Anglicized pronunciation of that place-name his gang would come to be called the Paxton Boys. In those frosty years after the French and Indian War, the Paxton Boys marauded through the backcountry, massacring innocent Indians and murdering those they viewed as white race traitors. Settlers on the western frontier had suffered mightily during that war, and they sometimes did not receive the resources or assistance that they could have from the colonial government. But the Paxton Boys departed from mere martial logic and embraced the totalizing reasoning that justifies genocide.

As historian Fred Andersen writes, "The message of all these losses, for the colonists, could be reduced to the syllogism that lay behind the Paxton Boys' plan... if good Indians did not harm white people, then the best Indians must be those who could do no harm, for all eternity." Something occult had indeed developed in the backcountry. Surprise in Philadelphia can only be accounted to their not paying attention, and their not understanding their own relationship to men like the Paxton Boys, who would soon turn and threaten the city as well. As the violence spread, Rev. Elder refused to identify which of his congregants had blood on their hands from cut Indian throats or who had scalps affixed to their belts as if they were animal pelts. For that the minister was relieved of his manse by the Presbyterian Church, who didn't countenance the mutilation of praying Indians.

In the wake of the Conestoga massacre, Governor John Penn offered a reward for the capture of the Paxton Boys and ordered that the surviving Susquehannock be placed in protective custody at a prison in Lancaster. On December 24, Elder's clan broke into the prison, and there they murdered and then mutilated the remaining Indians who had seen their friends and families killed by these same men only ten days before. Six adults and eight children were killed on Christmas Eve. Jesus may have loved the little children, but his minister broached no such affection, for an Indian infant was still first and foremost an Indian.

Participants in the lynching were never identified, but as one witness to their attack, William Henry, recorded, the posse of some two dozen were "well mounted on horses, and with rifles, tomahawks, and scalping knives, equipped for murder." After the Paxton Boys had departed from their crime, Henry was able to take stock of the hideous scene. He came upon the corpse of Will Sock, beloved among whites and natives alike, "on account of his placid and friendly conduct." Next to the old Indian and his wife were two children "of about the age of three years, whose heads were split with the tomahawk, and their scalps all taken off." He saw the corpse of a man, "shot in the breast," whose legs and hands were chopped off, and who was finally shot in the mouth with a rifle, "so that his head was blown to atoms, and his brains were splashed against, and yet hanging to the wall, for three or four feet around." There had been peace with the Indians for a decade, and these

Susquehannock, who lived among the men and women of Lancaster in a spirit of mutual affection, had endured their illusory protection in that prison cell by singing psalms and reading their Bibles. And yet the Paxton Boys—and the demagogue who had inspired them—indulged in this orgy of supposedly preemptive violence to protect the safety of the white settlers on the western horizon.

Elder responded to the latest atrocity by washing his hands of it. The minister saw the tomahawking of a friendly old man, the scalping of toddlers, and the decapitation of an innocent Indian not as his fault, even if he'd been preaching a scripture of cleansing atrocity for months now. Rather, it was the fault of those elite city-dwellers off in distant Philadelphia, those rootless cosmopolitans who didn't understand the reality of life in the backcountry. He wrote to the governor that "Had Government removed the Indians, which had been frequently, but without effect, urged, this painful catastrophe might have been avoided."

Elder implored, "What could I do with men heated to madness? All that I could do was done." Furthermore, the Philadelphians didn't understand that the Paxton Boys aren't violent men, for "in private life they are virtuous and respectable; not cruel, but mild and merciful." Though the massacre was "the blackest of crimes," Elder justified the tomahawking of children as simply one of those "ebullitions of wrath, caused by momentary excitement." Really, Elder informed Penn, you had to kind of be there to get it.

The Paxton Boys took aim not just at the Indians but at their fellow white colonists as well. Literary scholar Scott Paul Gordon explains that they reserved just as much opprobrium for who we might think of as "liberal" whites, writing that the "Paxton Boys targeted whites, English Quakers and German Moravians, when they believed that these groups, too, jeopardized the security of the backcountry." Elder had triggered a culture war. Educated, worldly, sophisticated inhabitants of a city like Philadelphia, used to hearing not just English but German, and Swedish, and Dutch, and indeed the Algonquin and Lenape languages of the Indians, were horrified by the atrocities to the west. Shortly after the New Year, a popular pamphlet titled *A Narrative of the Late Massacres, in Lancaster County* was read from Walnut Street to Rittenhouse Square, in taverns and coffee shops and churchyards. The writer, a revered printer named Benjamin Franklin, feared not the Indians, who had lived in peaceful coexistence with settlers since Penn's original commission, but rather the "white savages from Peckstang and

Donegal." Placing their trust for protection with the "good" whites, the Indians found themselves slaughtered by the savage ones. The author's lament is that the natives "would have been safer, if they had submitted to the Turks; for ever since Mahomet's Reproof to Khaled, even the *cruel Turks*, never kill Prisoners in cold Blood." Pennsylvania may be where the lamb was to lay down with the lion, a peaceable kingdom, but in Lancaster those "poor defenceless Creatures were immediately fired upon, stabbed and hatcheted to Death!"

These Paxton Boys fetishized their weapons and their masculinity and most of all their whiteness. They saw no compunction in putting innocent men, women, and children to the blade so as to preserve whatever they imagined and defined their sacred honor to be worth. They were "barbarous Men who committed the atrocious Fact.... Then mounted their Horses, huzza'd in Triumph, as if they had gained a Victory, and rode off—*unmolested!" A Narrative of the Late Massacres* was a furious document, which reminded its readers that "Wickedness cannot be covered, the Guilt will lie on the whole Land, till Justice is done on the Murderers. THE BLOOD OF THE INNOCENT WILL CRY TO HEAVEN FOR VENGEANCE." If the Paxton Boys and their defenders were wrong about their fear of supposed, imminent Indian attack, then they were correct that the genteel inhabitants of Philadelphia were unaware that in the backcountry a malignancy was growing, not among the Indians but among the settlers, who increasingly festered in resentment against enemies imagined. And where there are enemies imagined, soon there will be enemies discovered (or invented). And then blood will be shed. The Paxton Boys had practiced on Indians, but Franklin feared that their rage would soon be turned against those whom the Paxtons believed protected the Indians. He turned out to be right. The Paxton Boys would soon march on Philadelphia.

Andersen explains that as "word spread that the vigilantes intended to kill all the Indians in Pennsylvania, their popularity and their numbers mounted fast." By early February fully 500 had assembled to march upon the largest city in colonial America, threatening to massacre every Indian who had taken up sanctuary in Philadelphia. One of the Paxton Boys wrote "When we go there, we'll be sure to bring back Quaker scalps." Another claimed that after that, the Paxton Boys planned to range some seventy or so miles to the north, where "not one stone should remain upon another in Bethlehem," as there were designs to murder both Indians and the Moravians whom the rebels saw as the former's protectors.

Gordon writes that the Paxton Boys targeted a "multiracial set of victims," where the nativist fury of the mob could focus on not just Indians, but also "Quakers, and Moravians," all of whom would collectively come to "define the frontiersmen's category of 'enemy.'" When the Paxton Boys came to Penn's city, the potential list of victims in this planned pogrom was long.

The mob was met at Germantown by an assortment of government leaders, including Franklin, and armed guards. Franklin negotiated with the rebels for the safety of both the city and the Indians hiding within. An understanding was reached—the men would spare the second largest city in the British Empire, the largest metropolis in English-speaking America, in return for assurances that the Paxton Boys would never be charged, convicted, or punished for what they did to the innocent Indians of Lancaster.

America—one huge Indian burial ground. Pennsylvania is the story of America writ small. Historian Peter Silver explicates what he calls "the anti-Indian sublime," the dominant mode of American culture, where what an "American" is must always be violently defined against some exoticized Other. From the Indian to the slave to the papist to the Muslim and the Mexican. We're in part so fearful of the Other because we know precisely what it is that we did to the Indian—not just in Lancaster, but in the Pequod War of seventeenth-century New England, or the plains wars of the nineteenth century—and we know our guilt. The very landscape heaves under the accumulated weight of so many ghostly corpses, where branches once dripped with human blood, and might yet again. Peter Silver recounts how a few years before the Paxton Boys crimes, a "raider named James Kenny passed up the Cumberland Valley from Maryland into Pennsylvania... he found that many people thought the snow-covered landscape around them charged with the presence of the dead." Silver also recounts how the *New American Magazine* of Woodbrige, New Jersey printed a poem in 1758 entitled "On the Late Defeat at Ticonderoga," memorializing felled settlers from the French and Indian War. The poet, travels through fields of "empurpl'd bodies," the fetid, stinking, decomposing mass of corpses, white and Indian alike, which fill the fields of western Pennsylvania. Finally the poet comes to the banks of the Monongahela River, to encounter "gore-moisten'd banks, the num'rous slain,/Spring up in vegetative life again:/While their wan ghosts, as night's dark gloom prevails,/Murmur to whistling winds the mournful tale."

A gothic story, no? But then the story of America's settling has always been a gothic tale. That anonymous poet of 1758 might as well have written in prophecy; his visions are that of Ezekiel in the desert. And like Ezekiel's dry bones, those waterlogged corpses in the Monongahela would surely rise and walk again, haunting and compelling us in that cycle we dare not escape from. The poet's narrative of defeated pioneers hacked to death by some unseen barbaric force served only to instigate men like the Paxton Boys as the American frontier continued to stretch ever westward.

Our stories haunt us, even if we don't specifically know or even quite remember the shape of their narrative. And yet, those corpses—Indian and white—can't help but "Spring up in vegetative life," just as surely as Ezekiel's field of dry bones would stand "upon their feet, an exceeding great army." The Paxton Boys remain an exceedingly great army. They march on Lancaster and Philadelphia still. Whatever their new names be, wherever the new Lancasters and Philadelphias are. Nor are we innocent, ensconced as we are, surrounded by the comforts of our diversity and our education. Just as the Quakers let those low church pioneers fortify that boundary between civilization and its discontents, so too have we turned a blind eye to the distasteful and uncouth Paxton Boys of our own era, who brutalize whomever they deem the Other of today.

Herman Melville wrote of a "metaphysics of Indian hating" which defined the American experiment: a rancorous, poisonous worldview that now and again infects the body politic. In America, the Indians were only the first of many to be hated, and there are always and forever new Indians. Perhaps an argument could be made that large gatherings of diverse people affect a certain herd immunity to the worst of that disease, but that's a secondary observation, for the Paxton Boys can live in any city, any neighborhood. They can live next door to you, drink coffee at Starbucks, shop fair-trade at Whole Foods, and hate you while they do it. The Paxton Boys wear khakis and drive nice cars. They part their hair. The Paxton Boys aren't out there; there is no frontier, and there never has been. Only the vagaries and contradictions of the human heart. If you pay attention, you can meet the Paxton Boys even today, forever marching on the city, forever drawing closer. Too often we look the other way and let them scale the fortifications, where those whom we've promised to protect dwell. A promise of security for only so long. If the time comes, will you be willing to name every one of the Paxton Boys, or will you let them slink away, their victims not remembered, their crimes unnamed?

I never heard about the Paxton Boys until I went to get my PhD, but I still somehow knew the story. Not just because I'm a Pennsylvanian through and through, and am thus as privy to those ghosts as any other, but more importantly because I am an American, and that haunted gothic tale is all of our sinful inheritance whether we choose to collect or not. One could reduce an analysis of the contradictions of a place like Pennsylvania to that old joke about it being two big cities with Alabama in the middle, which I suppose is sociologically true, though equally accurate about all states and the country as a whole. Yet this parable should not be read as a reductionist allegory about urban versus rural, or town versus country, or liberal versus conservative. That some of that is in there, no doubt, would be accurate. But it's not the whole story. Nor should it be read as being in the mode of the ever-popular white working class ethnography, where some coastal liberal makes condescending apologies on behalf of people with hateful beliefs by recourse to some misguided, sentimentalized class politics which is actually anything but. No, if anything this parable should make clear what's incomplete about that particular genre, for those threatened and killed by the Paxton Boys were often working class, just as the good Rev. Elder was a distinguished, wealthy graduate of the University of Edinburgh. And as Gordon makes clear, the supreme irony is that many of the frontier Quakers and Moravians threatened by the Paxton Boys had previously been threatened by Indian attack during the Seven Years War.

What is most important to take from this parable is that there have been many Conestoga massacres. Being blind to those ensures that there will be many more in the future. While there are no Conestoga left to remember the names of those who died in December 1763, we remember those murdered in the hope that someday, somebody will remember us. And we pray that we can somehow exorcise the land of these ghosts, the hateful vigilantes and the tortured innocents alike.

SEEING RED IN MICHIGAN
JOHN COUNTS

The Iraq War veteran wore a bent-brimmed baseball cap that shaded his grease-covered face. I was interviewing the young vet-turned-mechanic, a defeated Bernie Sanders supporter, at his small town auto garage when a dark pickup pulled up into his driveway. The mechanic saw the truck and laughed.

"That's Jim," he said excitedly. "You've got to interview Jim. Ask him if he's voting for Hillary. Just ask him."

Jim peered down at me from the high cab. He was a big, older guy in his 70s, bald except for some gray stubble that spread from his dome down to his face, clad in sweatpants and a sweatshirt. His wife sat in the passenger seat, her reddish hair stiff with hairspray. I did what the mechanic said and asked Jim about Clinton. Jim gave me a look of pure disgust.

"I'd vote for the devil himself before I'd vote for that lying, stealing bitch," he said.

I looked to Jim's wife for any reaction to the sexist slur her husband used to refer to the first female major party presidential candidate, but she stared straight ahead. I'm guessing she'd heard her husband use that word about Clinton a thousand times while living out their days in some cozy ranch on a couple wooded acres up there in the hinterlands of Northern Michigan. There are thousands of couples like that in the state. You see them eating gravy-covered meals at small town diners wearing boots and insulated flannels. They are retired from well-paying auto jobs and have either moved north to vacationland or are sticking it out in the blue-collar suburbs of Detroit. They play bingo and fish for walleye. They are the "regular Americans" the network media only pays attention to come election time, when television cameras whisk from the coasts into middle America, when those of us in Michigan and the rest of the nation's interior become "folksy" instead of "flyovers."

"Did you vote Trump in the primary?" I asked Jim.

"Hell no. I voted Bernie. But I'm voting Trump now."

I should have known then, in July 2016, that some metamorphosis was taking place. That a toxic anger was fermenting in white guys like Jim and their silent, forward-staring wives.

But I didn't have any idea it would lead to a Trump victory. Like the rest of the media, I assumed Clinton would clean up on Election Day, but not just because of the disastrously wrong polls. This was Donald Trump we were talking about, whose expressions of incredulous, indecorous incivility could seemingly fill as many pages as *Infinite Jest*. I had faith not just as a reporter but as a human being and an American that my fellow Michiganders ultimately knew better. That they would see through the charade. That the white, working class families in my beloved home state—who have long been put on a pedestal for their sense of community, humility, and decency—would surely be able to see through a man so narcissistic, prideful, and indecent.

I was wrong.

I failed to see that the election wasn't just about Trump. It was about anger and hopelessness. It was about Jim and other white voters who felt forgotten, alienated, and ultimately pushed off that pedestal of respect.

In 2016, Jim's rage trumped everything in Michigan.

I've known guys like Jim my whole life.

I was born in Bay City, Michigan in 1977, the year after our state's previous red dip. In the 1976 presidential election, homeboy Republican hero Gerald Ford cleaned up with 52 percent of the vote while losing to Democrat Jimmy Carter.

It was an era of transformation in Michigan. When I was a kid in the 1980s, an 18-year-old with a high school diploma could still expect to walk into any auto factory and get a job on the spot that would guarantee financial safety for life—a satisfying payoff for the monotony of the work and years of sometimes violent labor struggles.

There was no need to study hard or go to college.

"I'll just go to the Chevy," said the older kids who skipped school to smoke pot.

My house was different. Mom and Dad were both from Detroit. Dad had a college degree and worked as a reporter at *The Bay City Times* for what was then Booth Newspapers, which owned papers in several mid-sized cities across the state, including Grand Rapids and Ann Arbor. It was expected that my brother and I would do more than just graduate high school and get a job at the Chevy. In fact, it was journalism that brought me to Jim's pickup truck to ask him about his political views this past summer. I now work for the same newspaper chain that once employed my old man.

For most of the year, I'd been hacking away with other reporters at a large investigative project on the Flint water crisis—probably the most chilling story of government failure in our lifetime. We were still working on it during the presidential primaries.

But there was no way Michigan could go for Trump. Not in a million years.

Trump had been around most of my life, of course, flashing his self-satisfied grin in pictures and onscreen, another tanned face in the trash heap of late twentieth-century television culture. I never thought much of him. I never watched his reality show. I never read his books. He was just that rich guy with the atrocious combover who talked a lot. Like much of the world, I was shocked at his rise to power.

Once we wrapped up the Flint project, I thought I'd look into which Michigan county had the highest percentage of Trump voters during the primaries. I crunched the results versus county populations and determined that rural Atlanta, Michigan—an unincorporated county seat located in Briley Township—was our state's Trump Town. I wanted to touch base with someone up there so, from my home near Ann Arbor—a few hundred miles away—I emailed the township supervisor and the county sheriff. I'm still waiting for the sheriff's response. The township supervisor, however, emailed me back that same night.

"Yes, I can meet with you," he said. "Just let me know a time. Don't bother with a motel. You can just stay the night."

Michigan has its share of business class Republicans—auto executives, engineers, pizza magnates—who live in the tony Detroit suburbs of West Bloomfield, Birmingham, and the Grosse Pointes. But for the most part, Detroit suburbs aren't the suburbs of, say, John Cheever. There aren't many swimming pools. Mom and Dad probably don't have a college degree. They drink Bud Lite tallboys, not gin and tonics. They live in brick ranch houses where you can vacuum the entire downstairs without changing electrical outlets, not stately colonials. There's probably a muscle car out in the garage being restored. There's probably more television sets inside than books.

The last time Michigan turned red—1988 for George H. W. Bush—my family had just moved from Bay City to the Detroit area between the same east-west cross streets of Plymouth and Joy where they'd grown up in the city a few miles to the east. They grew up in the 1950s and 1960s, in the illusory America Trump promises to bring back—a time of strong manufacturing jobs that supported a household with Dad's one income, clean city streets, and the tacit but unspoken preference of white lives over brown lives in our society.

I joined the renegade crowd growing up. The skaters. The dopers. The punks. The burnouts. We liked drugs, art, and rock and roll. We worked menial service jobs at pizza joints and donut shops—the only kind of jobs around in the 1990s—to support our passions. We snottily stereotyped the working class "Michigan guy." He worked a trade job— the assembly line, construction, a factory. He played football in high school. He was too macho. He didn't dance. He drove a pickup truck. He had a fishing boat. He religiously went deer hunting. He listened to country music. Most of all, he had a moustache.

There's a Nirvana song called "Mr. Moustache." This is what we called that stereotypical Michigan guy. Mr. Moustache.

I brought along a tent to Trump Country, just in case I ended up camping, a determination I'd make when I saw what kind of hospitality Atlanta, Michigan had to offer. A night on the ground in a state campsite is sometimes better than a cockroach motel. The township supervisor—the de facto mayor—had offered an extra bedroom, but I wasn't banking on that, either, though I did hope to catch up with him that night because I wasn't sure if he would evaporate in the morning. Plus, I don't generally agree to sleepovers until I've met someone in person.

I hit the road, I-75 north through Flint, Saginaw, Bay City—towns that peaked twice: first in the lumber era, then the manufacturing era. They aren't bound to peak again in the near future, though the Mr. Moustaches of the world would like to believe otherwise.

North of Bay City, the terrain changes, as do the attitudes of the locals. This is the area known as Northern Michigan (not to be confused with the Upper Peninsula, which has a different, though related, cultural identity). People who live in Northern Michigan refer to the urbanized south where I live as "downstate."

The urban working class isn't the same as the rural working class, though Trump got both votes. While the Detroit area suffers from stark segregation, the urban working class is made up of many different races and ethnicities. The pay is good thanks to decades of collective bargaining.

The rural working class of Northern Michigan, on the other hand, is almost uniformly white, and lucky to even have a job. Vast stands of white pine used to cover the tip of the mitten until they were clear-cut by the lumber barons of the nineteenth century. It was never very good soil for farming, though hearty folks tried. Now, "Up North" is mostly a tourism economy. The old lumber towns host fishermen, hunters, hikers, bicyclists, bikers, ATVers, campers, off-roaders, boaters, and cottage owners. Many downstaters own a family cottage somewhere "Up North." The townies work in the hotels, motels, restaurants, bars, gas stations, and golf courses, serving the more well-heeled Michiganders.

Atlanta was no different. On my way up, the township supervisor, Mike Wurtsmith, emailed to say he had to work the late shift at a nearby golf course. We'd tentatively planned to meet up that evening as soon as I arrived for an interview. But he'd been called in to the golf course, where he managed the bar.

"I'll meet you at my house," he wrote. He wouldn't be home until late.

As a reporter I'm always anxious about subjects bowing out of interviews. The more people put you off, the harder you try to nail them down to a time. I wasn't going to miss this one, but had about four hours to kill before meeting up with Wurtsmith, so I went to the only logical place to while away the time in small town America: the bar.

The older I got, the more I understood and embraced the blue-collar identity of my home state. I grew up hunting, fishing, and wearing flannel, after all. I'd also survived two Detroit stick-ups as a kid and partied in the city's abandoned buildings as a teenager. Our white guy rock stars— Bob Seger, Kid Rock, Jack White—are always described in magazine profiles as "gritty." Our white guy writers—Jim Harrison, Elmore Leonard, Philip Levine—get similar treatment.

Middle American white guys are taught to take pride in our slightly ruffian, uncivilized nature. In a way, Michigan—along with the rest of the nation's vast middle—is the Huck Finn of America, with the Aunt Sallys of the coasts perennially telling us to smooth down our cowlick, sit still at the dinner table, and speak in complete sentences with proper diction.

No one is going to tell us what to do. No one is going to decide who our president is.

In this way, a Trump vote was nothing more than a simple exercise in rugged American individualism.

I bellied up to the bar and ordered a beer and cheeseburger. I'd come up to Atlanta without too much of a plan beyond connecting with the mayor. I'm of the "let it happen" school of journalism. I've always ascribed to the notion that a journalist needs to be a mash-up of historian, sociologist, poet, and barroom hustler.

So, I drank a beer. Then another. Then started hustling.

I struck up a conversation with a fellow who had wandered in not long after me and sat a few stools down the bar. He looked close to retirement age and was wearing a sleeveless shirt. I learned his name was Gary Michalak and he was a former postal employee who had just returned from the larger town of Gaylord west of Atlanta where he'd bought several firearms, including a handgun that shoots shotgun shells.

He was an amiable guy who was all in on Trump. But despite being an outspoken critic of the "liberal media" that I represented, he gleefully agreed to take me out into the parking lot to show me his new guns.

Like a scene in a Tarantino movie he opened the trunk of his black Cadillac and proceeded to show off his new firearms, including the small, large-barreled hand cannon that shoots shotgun shells. The pictures I snapped of him with the guns and the Caddy made him look like a criminal or the dictator of a small country.

But he was just a retired postal worker. An American.

The township supervisor's house turned out to be a cabin on the lake amid other vacation cottages. After more communication, he talked me into coming over before he got home.

"The door's unlocked. Just make yourself at home," he texted as the summer sun was sinking in the sky.

When I got the message, I was at a campground on a nearby inland lake, ready to pitch a tent and call it a night. The back and forth texts, emails, and calls had gotten confusing. He was going to have to work until eight, then nine, then ten.

"Just go to the house and I'll meet you there when I can," was the summation of his texts.

So I did.

There is nothing more unnerving than walking into a stranger's private space when they aren't there. I made sure I was at the right cabin, confirmed by a wooden nameplate next to the door, and hesitantly went in. It was a homey affair. The first thing I noticed was a picture of my host shaking hands with Joe Biden.

I'd assumed he was going to be one of these "Don't Tread On Me" type of Tea Party Conservatives who got so hot under the collar when Obama was elected. But when Wurtsmith got home, I quickly realized he wasn't. His passion was community health, something he'd worked at for decades, making sure the people in his rural part of Michigan had access to doctors. That passion is what brought him to Washington, D.C. He later tells me he was locking hands with the Democratic Vice President at a health care conference.

We talked politics deep into the night on his back patio overlooking a small lake rimmed with pontoon boats. Wurtsmith, a tall man with piercing blue eyes and a crisp voice and haircut, still considers himself a conservative. When I came out and asked him if he was planning on voting Trump in the election, he hesitated.

"I just don't know if I can," he said.

The total population of Montmorency County is 9,259. Of that, 1,046 people voted Trump in the primary—11.28 percent—giving it the highest percentage in the state. Most of those folks are older, middle class white people who never went to college, according to the U.S. Census data. Thirty percent of the population is over the age of 65. The county is 97 percent white and only 10 percent of the population older than 25 have a college degree. The median household income in 2014 was $36,448.

The general election results were no surprise: 70 percent for Trump, 26 percent for Clinton. The actual number of voters may seem like peanuts, but taken in aggregate all across America, these are the places that gave the election to Trump.

The town of Atlanta is at the crossroads of two state highways. Certain Northern Michigan vacation towns appeal to different classes of people. The wealthy flock to the west side of the state, in mansions and condos along Lake Michigan near the Leelanau Peninsula, where the novelist and screenwriter Jim Harrison lived for many years and where the chef Mario Batali has a house. Those towns feature bakeries with scones, wine bars, and high-end clothing shops.

Then there are towns like Atlanta, which have a more working class vibe. The big thing to do in the winter is to get in jacked-up trucks and go driving on the icy back roads. There are plenty of deer hunting camps out in the woods. The strip of storefronts in town include a gas station—called the Freedom Market—a hardware store and a gun shop. There are also three different taverns.

Wurtsmith gave me a tour the next morning, taking me into a diner, gun shop, the local newspaper office, and the Iraq War vets' new auto garage, which had just opened up. The common theme of the interviews was that the good people of Atlanta watched a lot of Fox News, were very worried about gun rights and, like Jim in the pick-up, had a palatable disgust of Hillary Clinton.

Here's a sampling of the quotes:

"He doesn't stop and think for a minute," said Susan Reed, the manager of a diner in town. "He's honest."

"We lost jobs something terrible when the Democrats took over," said John Renshaw, a retiree from Flint's Buick City. "I think [Trump] can bring business back and put people back to work."

"I think Trump has a wonderful family, he has wonderful children," said Brenda Birchmeier, a school bus driver. "I can't see him being against women where he has helped women all his life."

"I feel like Hillary wants to take our guns away," said Sarah Reed, a college student. "It's weird to me that people don't care about gun rights."

We heard quotes and sound-bites like this all throughout the election at Trump rallies. The media wrote them down and filmed it, but we weren't listening close enough. The fear and rage of white people all over Michigan is what turned the state red for the first time in decades—and what tipped the election.

All anger does is beget more anger and now, in the Trump era, we are in a national frenzy of rage.

THE BURGERS AT MILLER'S (OR, DEARBORN'S CHANGED)
TARA ROSE

It was the winter of 2004, at a bar and grill in Dexter, Michigan. I was quietly chewing my salad, purposely avoiding conversation with my boyfriend so I could continue eavesdropping on the discussion at the table behind me. The group included a man, his wife, and their woman friend, all middle-aged. They were chatting about my hometown thirty miles away.

"We used to love going to Miller's," said the wife as her husband and friend groaned with great longing. "Their burgers are amazing."

"Oh, the best!" the friend agreed.

They paused. I knew what was coming next, just as soon as they were thinking it.

"But you know," the husband said, "Dearborn's changed."

His wife sighed in agreement. "It used to be a real nice area."

"Those people are awful," I said to my boyfriend. I could tell from his wide-eyed glance that, even if he'd been eavesdropping along with me, he wouldn't have deciphered a code that had been obvious to me for decades.

When white ex-residents of my hometown sigh and say, "Dearborn's changed," what they're really saying is that it was a lovely place before the Arabs "took over." White Dearborn's pride is embodied by the towering figures of the past—world famous entrepreneur Henry Ford and longtime mayor Orville Hubbard. During his 36-year tenure as mayor, Hubbard delivered an impressive array of city services, but that wasn't the only reason he was beloved by some. Hubbard died in late 1982, a few months after I began kindergarten at a public school built with Ford money. From that point forward, I got used to hearing elderly white neighbors lament the lost days of Orville's administration, "when things were different." It was always understood, without anyone needing to say so explicitly, that the olden days were better because people of color weren't tolerated.

Orville Hubbard did his best to ensure black people stayed out of Dearborn. During his decades in office, he successfully fought against public housing, warning residents that the town would become "a black slum" if it welcomed a subsidized population. He spoke openly and often about his segregationist views, even bragging about the ways in which he'd mobilize police and firefighter sirens to harass African-American residents who had the gall to break the color barrier. His legacy of anti-black racism lived on throughout my childhood, adolescence, and all the way until I finally left town at age 20. During the 1980s and '90s, few black families moved into my east Dearborn neighborhood, and those that did usually didn't stay long. But during those years, I watched the Arab community grow and prosper in the east end. And the whole time that was happening—many years before 9/11 and the widespread anti-Muslim hysteria that followed—I saw a lot of white people lose their minds over the weirdest things.

"Those Arabs smell bad."

"Look at how many of them live in a house together. Aunts, uncles, cousins, and grandparents all under one roof. Every one of those kids has a million cousins, and they'll get all of 'em to gang up on you if you cross them."

"Watch out for the boys. Don't let your daughter date one. They treat women like property. No woman in her right mind would dress like that in the summer. They're brainwashed."

"They know English. They're just being sneaky. Like how they sneak around the tax codes, and sell their gas stations from one family member to the next. It's so they never pay taxes."

Throughout my elementary and junior high school years, I got so used to hearing white people bitterly regurgitate these claims that I didn't even consider whether or not they were true. Back then, before I was aware that these stereotypes didn't hold water, I could never figure why most of these things would even make a person mad. I mean, the "treating females like garbage" part was upsetting, but I knew too many white girls from abusive families to see that as something specific to the Arab community. As for the other claims, who cares about big families living in little houses, speaking a different language, and possibly gaming the tax system?

But in junior high—when academics mean nothing and school becomes a nonstop, social-climbing death match—I noticed that even the dorkiest white kids could always cash in on whiteness. Toward the end of eighth grade, I remember walking home from school with a few of my fellow nerdy white girl classmates. We were talking about our mutual friend Jackie, who was the only black girl in our grade. Jackie got picked on a lot, and we all agreed that some of the kids in our class were just being racist. And then one of these white girls, said, "I'm not racist. I like black people. I just hate Ay-rabs."

By this point, I'd heard so many different people, kids and adults alike, make this statement so many times it had become hackneyed.

In 1991, this was what passed for a progressive mindset among white Dearbornites. You could shun the obvious racism of your parents and grandparents, yet still see yourself as superior to the "Ay-rabs." But we all knew the "A-word" was derogatory, so I called them out on it. My observation had little impact and was shrugged off quickly. Seeing themselves as superior to Arabs wasn't the point of the discussion. It was just an afterthought.

In high school, I met and began dating Sam, who was the only Arab in my hipster friend group. At our largely Arab-American high school, hipsters—a.k.a. "alternative" kids—were not considered cool. But he was quite the tastemaker among us weirdos with his blue hair, flannel shirts, Doc Martens and anti-establishment column in the school newspaper. The thing our alternative pals didn't always understand was that Sam came from a long line of hardcore leftist, anti-racist activists, and he wasn't interested in being deemed worthy by our white standards.

I can still see the withering expression on his face when one of the guys in our after-school theater group said, "I hate Ay-rabs, except Sam. He's not one of them. He's one of us."

"Hey, don't say that," said Sam.

"Say what?"

"Ay-rab."

"Oh. Sorry, man."

Sam later told me in private how much that guy pissed him off, how he could somehow see Sam as "not one of them." Indeed, when it came to the alternative crowd bagging on the rest of the student body, it wasn't always easy to tell where a healthy hatred of the popular kids ended and anti-Arab racism began. Because at my high school, Arab-American culture had become the standard for what was considered cool. While those in my social group (and at the whiter high schools across town) were embracing grunge rock, most of the student body enjoyed Middle Eastern pop and freestyle dance music. Secular girls wore their hair big, while religious girls wore hijabs. Boys favored slicked back manes, black leather jackets, and heavy cologne. Many of the white kids mimicked the secular Arab trends because that's what was fashionable. For my mostly white alternative crowd, resenting the dominant culture meant resenting the things Arabs celebrated.

But I was used to being an outsider with weird taste and didn't mind being different. By junior year, I figured out that most classmates who teased me were just messing around, and some of their jokes were pretty hysterical. If I could maintain a sense of humor about myself, I'd be fine. So I learned to relax. High school still felt endless and boring as hell, but at least I no longer suspected the more "normal" kids were out to get me. It also helped that I was spared the usual conventions of high school misery. I was one of the weird weed-smoking, sex-having kids in a school where there was very little social pressure to do these things. If I'd been trying to fit in with a more conservative crowd, I might have been less happy.

Even if most of the other students thought I was weird, I always knew I benefited from the unfair advantage of the teachers' favor. In the early 1990s, the white portion of the student body at my high school was dipping below 50%, but every single one of my teachers was Caucasian. Many of them liked me because I was studious. Some clearly preferred white students to Arabs. I knew that to them I was more "normal"—from the way I dressed, to the Catholic church I attended, to the simple fact that I spoke only that one language they knew.

Right when I was making my peace with life, I began working at the Henry Ford Centennial Library, a midcentury marble fortress located on a long strip of Ford-developed land dividing Dearborn's east and west ends. The full-time library staff consisted mainly of middle class white ladies from the west side of town, most of whom fit a certain type: stuffy, staid, fearful, racist, and very big fans of Miller's.

I'd never heard of Miller's until I heard the librarians rave about their famous burgers. The way they fetishized it always irked me. "You've never been to Miller's?" they'd gasp, as if it were odd that I didn't hang out at a bar five miles from my house in a neighborhood I rarely visited. It's like they thought I'd missed this key rite of passage as a Dearborn person who hadn't been initiated in the cult. I automatically associated Miller's burgers with racist whites because the same people who couldn't believe I'd never eaten there also couldn't believe I actually lived in east Dearborn.

"Aren't you scared? It's so close to Detroit. I don't let my kids go there. This is as far east as I'll go. It wasn't always this way, but it's really changed. The people have changed. The men are very rude. You see these women and girls come in here, wearing scarves on their heads. I feel so sorry for them. I can't believe there are men who still treat women that way."

On one occasion when I heard a librarian named Connie make that last claim about young Muslim women, I thought of Maha, a girl I'd known since kindergarten who came to school wearing a hijab one day in fifth grade. I remembered Maha calmly explained to us other girls that she had a dream in which Allah told her she was ready.

"Um, I think a lot of these girls decide to wear the scarf on their own. It isn't always like someone told them what to do," I said.

"Oh, no! That's not true. They just get tricked into thinking it's their choice," Connie said with the same gentle yet self-assured firmness one uses to explain "stranger danger" to a child. I can still see Sarah, our tattooed teen girl coworker nodding in solemn agreement. What struck me most in that situation was how these two women who usually hated each other's guts were suddenly united in their shared assumption that all Muslim girls are victims. That's what I think of whenever I hear the term "white feminism."

That job was my first lesson in the way white outsiders perceived the post-white neighborhood where I was raised. And more often than not, the outsider perspective was (and still is) quite racist. But dealing with those awful white librarians had to be way worse for Sam, who worked there at the same time I did. He and I remain good friends today and I chuckle remembering one of his observations about the 2016 presidential primary election. He compared every Republican candidate to the worst faculty members at our high school. Jeb was the bumbling guidance counselor, Rubio was the slick young science teacher, Trump was the sleazy, out-of-shape gym teacher.

"And Hillary," he said, "is every awful white woman who worked at the library."

Just days after he said that, I saw footage of Clinton in a coffee shop, sneering at a Somali-American woman who questioned her support of black communities. "Why don't you go run for something then?" she responded to the young lady with a dismissive chuckle. The expression on her face immediately reminded me of the way some librarians would talk down to Sam. And it also reminded me of Connie and Sarah lamenting the poor, misguided hijabis. One of the perks of white feminism is that when women of color disagree with your actions or your worldview, you think you can treat them like idiot children.

A week after that Hillary video went viral, Dearborn's Arab-Americans and Muslims voted overwhelmingly for Bernie Sanders, helping him achieve his unexpected win in Michigan's primary election. Many pundits were stunned to see this community throw their support behind a Jewish candidate, but assuming the opposite result only makes sense if you also assume this community is necessarily anti-Semitic. Hillary Clinton's primary loss in Dearborn makes more sense if you consider her history of policy affecting the Middle East—from voting for war in Iraq to embracing the use of drone warfare during her tenure as secretary of state.

I've been living in the South for the past seven years, and anyone down here who's heard of Dearborn knows it mainly as a Muslim enclave. A few years ago I met a Michigan guy at a bar in Chattanooga, Tennessee, and when I told him I was from Dearborn, I swear his immediate response was, "Dearborn's changed, huh?" Groan. I'm always quick to explain, perhaps a bit defensively, that growing up there and attending diverse schools was good for me.

But the simple fact is that I love my hometown because it's where I'm from. I spend a lot of time in Dearborn whenever I go back to visit family and friends. The familiarity of it comforts me, even the gridlike streets and cookie-cutter tract housing that I found so dull and stifling when I was young. But mostly I enjoy the people, the blunt and funny yet easygoing manners that remind me of the best parts of high school. Southeastern Michigan will always feel like home to me. Even from hundreds of miles away, I still care what happens to metro Detroit as it reimagines itself in this post-industrial economy.

So I follow news from that region, which is how I happened to notice a Twitter post from a *Detroit Free Press* journalist just days before the 2016 presidential election. "Hillary Clinton came to Dearborn today, but like her husband in March, goes to west side place, avoids mosques, Arab centers, Muslim clergy." And in the tweet quoted beneath his post were the words, "Clinton swung by Miller's bar in Dearborn, Michigan this evening."

I literally screamed. It was too perfect. I messaged Sam with a screen cap of the tweets and the words, "FUCKING MILLER'S" He replied with an "LOL." We traded jokes about the stupid, infamous burgers and the librarians who loved them. We prayed that Hillary would beat Trump anyway, but I remained bitter.

"I swear it's a dog whistle," I told my husband. And instinctively, I still believe that. Clinton took the Arab and Muslim votes for granted. She laid all her money on those white swing voters and she met them at a place that remains, to this day, a landmark for west Dearborn's shrinking white population.

I'll fully admit that I've never been to Miller's, but as far as my subconscious mind is concerned, it's a "safe space" for every white person who's ever sighed and uttered the words, "Dearborn's changed."

SEVEN YEARS IN INDIANAPOLIS
ALLISON LYNN

When I moved to Indianapolis in 2010, I imagined myself as an anthropologist—which, in retrospect, is a pretty rude way to move anywhere. But I was a native Northeasterner: I spent my childhood in Massachusetts, went to college in New Hampshire, and then lived for nearly two decades in New York City before my husband and I relocated to Indianapolis for university teaching jobs. With those jobs came the promise of no longer having to panic every time the rent was due, but at the cost of leaving my liberal bubble.

Sure, there had been Republicans in my circle in New York, but even at the time I understood that they were fake Republicans: socially liberal or financially greedy voters looking out for their own interests. One hedge funder I knew openly talked about how he intended to switch his party registration from Republican to Democrat as soon as he'd socked away his millions. He wasn't a real Republican, just an idiot.

Another woman-in-media friend attempted to vote in the Republican primary, only to find that her Greenwich Village polling place had no machines set up for GOP voters. "We didn't expect any," the poll workers apologized, giggling amongst themselves. On her walk home that day, my friend asked herself why, in fact, she was still registered Republican if she was pro-choice, pro-woman, and pro- so many other equal opportunities. She switched parties before the next election. She wasn't a real Republican, just lazy.

But now, four decades into my life, I'd be moving to a place with actual Republicans as my neighbors. I steeled myself for debate and argument and a reckoning with why, exactly, so much of the country voted in ways that seemed a mystery to me.

Bring it on, I thought as I packed the car and headed west.

In his 2006 profile of Axl Rose in *GQ* magazine, John Jeremiah Sullivan writes: "Given the relevant maps and a pointer, I think I could convince even the most exacting minds that when the vast and blood-soaked jigsaw puzzle that is this country's regional scheme coalesced into more or less its present configuration after the Civil War, somebody dropped a piece, which left a void, and they called the void Central Indiana. I'm not trying to say there's no there there. I'm trying to say there's no there."

My first year in Indianapolis, I thought I understood what Sullivan was talking about. I had come to Indianapolis with my liberal talking points in hand, ready to argue and yell and maybe, after a few of the excellent Indiana microbrews I'd been reading about, to even listen to a different point of view. Quickly, though, I discovered that there were no raging arguments or debates at my local pub, and my new neighbors, if they *were* the ultra-conservative radicals I had expected, weren't talking about it. Instead, the populace was quiet.

And frankly, so was the downtown scene. In fact, there was no sense of an active downtown at all. The city as a whole felt numb. When I asked where to eat, more than one local told me to head three hours up to Chicago for good food. As for shopping, a West Coast transplant explained to me that "Indianapolis is a good place to live, value-wise, but we do our consumption elsewhere, when we're in California or New York."

By my second year, though, Indianapolis began to undergo a dramatic cultural change, so much so that central Indiana was no longer a place you'd feel entirely comfortable describing as a void. Things peaked when chef Jonathan Brooks opened the restaurant Milktooth —serving modbar espressos and brulée grapefruit and miso soup with pickled kombu—and landed on *Bon Appetit's* list of "10 Best New Restaurants in America." Down the street from me, Benjamin and Janneane Blevins opened a bookstore called Printtext in a whitewashed single-room storefront whose tables were piled with stacked issues of *Dissent* and *n+1* and *Cherry Bombe* and vintage literary magazines and journals where the essays appeared in both Lithuanian and English.

The *there* that began to fill in around me resembled more and more the there familiar to those of us from elsewhere. The city suddenly seemed full of hipster Latin-fusion restaurants and artisanal donut shops and experimental food trucks and legitimate tacos. As I type this, a restaurant serving $85 omakase meals is getting set to open.

My fourth year in the city, I was invited to an Easter egg hunt (chocolate eggs and coolers of microbrew) in my neighborhood, where the other guests were longtime Hoosiers, all of whom vote blue. This blew apart my theory that the blue streak running through Indy was entirely powered by transplants (the same transplants who were eating the legit tacos and Latin-fusion but couldn't quite keep all of the artisanal donut shops in business). And it reminded me of all the judgmental shit I'd cast on Indianapolis before I arrived. So maybe it's not that Indianapolis was undergoing so much change, at its core. Maybe it's that I'd finally lived long enough in the place to begin to understand it—a process that doesn't take months, or years, but years-and-years-and-years. Especially in a city where so much of what's going on is under the surface.

I've been assured by people who've been here for decades that the food scene really is getting better. The food scene as a culinary development, they mean, not as an indicator of some sort of swing toward blue politically. The microbrew-swigging egg hunters assure me that city's blue streak has a long history. Because while the city voted red in nearly every presidential election prior to 2004 (and has voted blue since), the democratic slice of those pre-2004 elections consistently hovered at around forty percent—sometimes nearing fifty. That's not nothing. Especially in a state known as a conservative stronghold.

What is new, I'd argue, is the *volume* of that blue-streak's voice. Thanks to Mike Pence's attempts as Governor to wrest the state even further to the right, the political numb silence that greeted me in 2010 was replaced by serious Midwestern can-do in 2013. My neighbors rallied and wrote letters in support of same-sex marriage. Lawns on my block sprouted signs that read "Pence Must Go" and "Fire Pence: Your Rights Could Be Next." My son, age 6, begged for an "Expel Pence" sign for his birthday. *Everyone else already has one, Mom!*

I started to understand that if Indianapolis is a blue bullseye in the middle of this doggedly red state, the bullseye grows bluer and bluer as you move toward its center, until you come to its very, very middle: the streets where my house sits. When I first moved in, a new friend described a woman on my street as "a good Democrat"—her way of explaining that the woman was someone I'd be glad to know.

It's easy, as I write this from that street, to think the new blue voice has grown deafening. It's only when I venture into the outer rings of the bullseye and beyond, that I'm reminded how truly atypical my neighborhood is. This grand change, this opening up, this loud blueness, this application of Midwestern can-do to defeating the far right—it isn't happening all over. Drive an hour west of Indianapolis and, in reaction to the South Carolina statehouse debate, you'll see trucks flying Confederate flags. In Greencastle, students of color tell me they've been pelted with sodas thrown from the windows of those same pickup

The Indiana I've experienced these last seven years is not the same that others know.

I was out of the country during Trump's election. I had been in Paris for the year, where my husband and I were working on books. In the months after the vote, I commiserated with French friends, who themselves were nervous about Brexit and the specter of Le Pen. I traded worst-case-scenarios with the expats I knew—mostly other parents of kids at my son's French (with a bilingual-English bent) school. We protest-marched together and followed Twitter and talked theories about the election during school potlucks. At one afternoon pickup in December, I was cornered by two dads, both American.

"You must know lots of people who voted for Trump," they said, "in Indiana, and all."

But here's the thing: I couldn't think of a single one. I explained this to them using the bullseye metaphor, a metaphor that quickly expanded into some sort of theory about the widening divisions in our country as a whole.

When I moved back to Indianapolis in the summer of 2017, I still couldn't think of a single person I knew who would have voted for Trump. With this in mind, I attended a fundraiser for Rep. Andre Carson, the Democrat who represents the streets just south and west of mine—though my house falls one block into the district of Republican Susan Brooks. I arrived to the fundraiser feeling good. Our city's got a Democrat in the House, and all of us who were gathered want to prop him up. There are a lot of us on the left, my friends and I told ourselves. We just need to ensure we're heard. But then a young campaign donor asked Carson how he should talk to his own family members in the south of Indiana. He said that outside of Indianapolis, everywhere he goes all he meets are Trump voters who, nearly a year into this disastrous presidency, still see Trump as some sort of hero. "What should I say to them?" the young Democrat asked Carson.

Carson didn't have an answer.

How do we talk to them? is really what the guy wanted to know.

It seems increasingly the answer is that we don't.

In Indianapolis—in all of the Indianapolises in America's Midwest—we're getting better food and leftist bookstores and expanding contemporary art scenes and choosing, so often, to read this as a new political reality. But these bookstores and art scenes and pour-over coffee bars aren't replacing what was here before. They're co-existing just out of eyesight. We're two sides at a standoff with a wall between us—to use the right's terminology—preventing us from even seeing each other.

What it boils down to, it seems, is that there are two Indianas just as there are two Americas. And there are two Indianapolises, as well. The city is home to Democrats who are museum fundraisers and poets and sound artists and fiction writers and lawyers and bankers and CFOs. We are transplants and natives and teenagers and retirees. And we are surrounded by churches full of Republicans, by art classes packed with GOP-leaning novice painters, by right-wing financial managers, college students, and orthodontists. Conservative marketing professionals drive past my house to go to work downtown every day. Even if our voice as Democrats is amplified in this city, it remains barely a whisper in the greater fact of our state.

So if I'm still pretending to be an anthropologist, what have I found? Seven years in Indianapolis, and what I've come up with aren't answers, but questions: What happens when one Indianapolis stops talking to the other? What happens when there are evangelicals next door but you no longer hear them? When you no longer even see each other? Where does this leave us? Where does it lead?

DOWNSTATE HATE

EDWARD McCLELLAND | PREVIOUSLY PUBLISHED IN THE CHICAGO READER, NOV. 15, 2017

On an Amtrak platform in Springfield, I met that rarest of an Illinoisans: a woman who divides her time and her loyalties between downstate and Chicago. Pat Staab lives in the state capital most of the time, but she was on her way to Chicago, where she keeps a condo in River North.

"I'm from New York," she told me. "I need a big city."

As a result of her peregrinations between upstate and down-, Staab is well versed in how the state's rival regions view each other. Downstaters think Chicago is "crime—you're gonna get mugged," she said. Chicagoans think downstate is "rural, all farms. I tell them we've got museums here. We've got a symphony."

"There are people from Springfield who've never even been to Chicago," Staab said.

"I'm sure there are people from Chicago who've never been to Springfield," I replied.

"Except maybe on a field trip."

The animosity between Illinois's largest city and its smaller towns is almost as old as the state itself. I say "almost," of course, because Chicago, incorporated in 1837, is 19 years younger than Illinois, which is set to begin a yearlong celebration of its bicentennial on December 3. Downstaters have always thought of Chicago as a black hole of street violence and political corruption, sucking up tax dollars generated by honest, hard-working farmers. Chicagoans have always thought of downstate—when they've thought of it at all—as an irrelevant agricultural appendage full of Baptists and gun owners who'd just love to turn Illinois into North Kentucky.

For most of Illinois's history, the two spheres have been evenly matched in influence, with downstate contributing some of Illinois's most important political figures, from Abraham Lincoln to Adlai Stevenson. Downstate was also the forcing ground of internationally known industries: Moline gave us John Deere, Peoria gave us Caterpillar, and Decatur gave us Staley, which in 1920 hired George Halas to coach a company football team he would move to Chicago the following year and rename the Bears.

More recently, though, the misunderstandings and alienation between Chicago and downstate have been ramped up by two particularly 21st-century phenomena: globalization and political polarization. As the big global city in the northeastern corner of the state sucks jobs and college graduates out of the rest of Illinois, downstate is becoming older, less educated, less prosperous, more reactionary, and more Republican. Politically, downstate is in complete opposition to the Chicago area, especially on such culturally charged matters as gun rights, LGBT rights, and abortion. But it lacks the votes to bend the state to its will on any of those issues. This was never more evident than in 2010, when Governor Pat Quinn defeated state senator Bill Brady, a social conservative from Bloomington, despite carrying only four of the state's 102 counties—and could've won by carrying only Cook County.

"Illinois needs an electoral college," a Republican friend from Decatur groused after that election.

On a statewide level, that would violate the constitutional principle of "one person, one vote." So the next year, state rep Bill Mitchell, a Republican from the Decatur area, came up with another solution for ending Chicago's political dominance over Illinois. He introduced a bill to divide Illinois into two states: one comprising Cook County, the other the remaining 101 counties.

"It's very simple folks: we just do this and we'll resemble Indiana more than the present, debt-ridden state of Illinois," Mitchell said at a press conference to promote his bill. "We can resemble Indiana, which has a lower debt, a lower unemployment rate, and a lower deficit."

The split between Cook County and the rest of Illinois would be "just like a divorce; there's irreconcilable differences between the state of Illinois and Cook County," he said. "Cook County, you go your way. Let the state of Illinois go its way and try to live like a family lives on their own budget. I think it might be in the best interest of both parties to go their own way."

This was far from the first Illinois secession proposal. In 1925, the Chicago City Council passed a resolution in favor of forming the state of Chicago because rural legislators were refusing to reapportion the General Assembly to reflect the city's growing population. In the 1970s, western Illinoisans upset over a lack of transportation funding declared their corner of the state "the Republic of Forgottonia." In 1981, state senator Howard Carroll of Chicago actually passed a Cook County secession bill through both houses of the General Assembly, just to scold downstaters who were complaining about funding Chicago's mass transit. (It was pulled back by then house speaker George Ryan.) Even if a bill were to pass, dividing Illinois would require the consent of Congress. (In our internet era, this view is represented by the Southern Illinois Secession Movement, whose Facebook page has 106 followers.)

Since downstaters complain so often about sharing a state with Chicago, it's important to remember that they wanted it this way. Nathaniel Pope of Springfield was the territorial delegate to Congress in 1817, as Illinois was preparing to enter the union. Pope wanted Chicago for the very same reason Mitchell wanted to get rid of it: because it adds a metropolitan, northern character to Illinois.

Originally, the Northwest Ordinance, passed by the Second Continental Conference in 1787, declared that Illinois's northern border would run along a line defined by the southern tip of Lake Michigan. Had that plan been followed, it would've stretched from Calumet City to Moline. What we now know as Chicago would've been part of Wisconsin.

Pope proposed pushing the boundary line north. There were both commercial and political advantages to possessing a Lake Michigan port. The new state could build a canal connecting the Mississippi Valley to the Great Lakes. Most of the Illinois Territory's early settlers were southerners. Pro-slavery sentiment was strong. But since Mississippi had just been admitted to the union, and would soon be followed by Alabama and Missouri, it was essential that Illinois be a free state to preserve the balance in the Senate. Pope wanted to attract Yankees migrating westward across the Great Lakes.

At the time, of course, no one knew that the trading post at the mouth of the Chicago River would burgeon into one of the world's great cities. But Pope realized it would be essential to shaping the state's character.

Even so, throughout the 20th century, Illinois political power was closely balanced between upstate and downstate. The Republican Party dominated the Chicago suburbs and the farm counties, while the Democratic Party held sway in Chicago and Little Egypt (as southern Illinois is nicknamed, possibly because the meeting of the Ohio and Mississippi Rivers is said to resemble the Nile Delta). As a result, "downstate was the swing area," says Kent Redfield, a former legislative staffer and professor of political science at the University of Illinois at Springfield. "Having downstate candidates was important for balancing the ticket."

That need for geographic diversity helped build the political careers of such influential downstaters as Democratic senators Alan Dixon and Paul Simon and Republican governors Jim Edgar and George Ryan. But at the beginning of this century, as the rest of the nation divided itself into urban blue and rural red political enclaves, Illinois did the same.

The Chicago suburbs became more ethnically diverse, and college-educated professionals repelled by the Republican Party's virulent Bible Belt conservatism began voting Democratic. Meanwhile, downstate became more Republican, as college graduates left the region and the loss of coal and factory jobs decimated labor unions that had formed the bulwark of the Democratic Party. When Bill Clinton won Illinois in 1992, he carried Chicago and downstate Illinois while losing most of Chicago's collar counties. In 2016, Hillary Clinton carried all of northeastern Illinois but won only a handful of downstate counties—those containing cities and/or college campuses. (Clinton began her political career in 1964 as a "Goldwater Girl" from once staunchly Republican Maine Township—which voted for her by 20 points.)

"Downstate is solidly Republican, but it's much less important," Redfield says. "Look at the legislative leaders." House speaker Michael Madigan and senate president John Cullerton hail from Cook County. So do the last three governors: Rod Blagojevich, Pat Quinn, and Bruce Rauner. The only downstaters currently holding statewide office are state treasurer Michael Freirichs of Champaign and Senator Dick Durbin of Springfield.

No place exemplifies downstate's changing political and economic fortunes better than Decatur, the hometown of secessionist Bill Mitchell. I lived in Decatur in the mid-1990s when I was a reporter for the local newspaper, the *Herald & Review*. At the time, it was a heavily unionized town loyal to the Democratic Party. But it was undergoing a series of labor disputes that made it a "flash point of globalization," according to its then congressman, Glenn Poshard. Tate & Lyle, a British company that had bought Staley, provoked a strike that lasted two and a half years—one of three labor disputes that resulted in a drastic reduction of union jobs in Decatur. Workers at Decatur's Caterpillar plant went on strike. So did workers at the city's Firestone plant, which eventually shut down after a scandal over faulty tires. Decatur is now Illinois's fastest-shrinking city. Macon County delivered majorities for Bill Clinton and Barack Obama, but it voted 55 percent to 38 percent for Donald Trump, who promised to renegotiate the North American Free Trade Agreement and other Clinton-era trade deals that he claims have hollowed out midwestern factory towns. (NAFTA, which was unpopular with unions from the start, has been blamed for allowing Maytag to move refrigerator production from Galesburg to Mexico, and for Roadmaster moving bicycle production from Olney to Mexico.)

"I backed Bernie Sanders," says Jay Dunn, the Democratic chairman of the Macon County Board. "I had to hold my nose to vote for Hillary; a lot of people didn't hold their nose and voted for Trump."

Beyond its loss of blue-collar union jobs, Decatur also lost a significant element of its professional class when its most important food-processing companies, Tate & Lyle and Archer Daniels Midland, moved their headquarters to Cook County, which is more appealing to the executives it wants to attract. (Caterpillar recently moved its headquarters from Peoria to Deerfield.)

"That didn't help the feelings of the Decatur people, losing the status of that," Dunn says. "The economic part of it is we've lost a lot of air traffic, people flying in to visit the president and the higher executives. Our airport's kind of struggling. Houses are sitting empty, because most of the executives lived in expensive houses. It's stupid to blame Chicago, though. The company's just making business decisions. ADM and Tate & Lyle are international businesses. People flying in, there's not a lot to do in Decatur, Illinois, compared to Chicago."

Dunn also disagrees with downstaters who think they'd be better off if they didn't have to share a state with Chicago.

"We got some people who just hate Chicago, ignorant of the fact that without Chicago, we'd all be broke," he says.

In 2016, Governor Rauner tried to inflame the Chicago-downstate divide. Speaking at a prison in Vienna, he attacked a $900 school bailout plan that would have devoted more than half its funds to the Chicago Public Schools. "The Senate and House are competing with each other [to see] who could spend more to bail out Chicago with your tax dollars from southern Illinois and central Illinois and Moline and Rockford and Danville—the communities of this state who are hard-working families who pay their taxes," Rauner said.

"Rauner's rabble-rousing against Madigan and the mythical Chicago machine, which is informed by polling and focus group data that I don't have, suggests that the ill-feeling remains general enough to be exploitable," James Krohe Jr., author of *Corn Kings and One-Horse Thieves: A Plain-Spoken History of Mid-Illinois,* published by Southern Illinois University Press. "Chicago and downstate are like conjoined twins, one of whom has a weak heart and is being kept alive at the expense of his stronger sibling. Great swaths of downstate are dying, demographically and economically; parts of the region remain viable only because assorted transfers of wealth from greater Chicago and Washington sustain it in the form of social security and disability checks, crop supports, and university and prison funding. (Deep southern Illinois, for example, has only two industries worthy of the name: SIU and road building.)"

If legislators actually did divide Illinois into two states, one comprising the six counties of the Chicago area, the other comprising the rest of the state, here's what each would contain, and contribute. Downstate can keep the name, since the Illinois (aka Illiniwek) Indians didn't live up here. Chicagoland would call the new state Potawatomi.

Population
Potawatomi: 8.3 million
Illinois: 4.5 million

Fortune 500 companies
Potawatomi: 30
Illinois: 2 (State Farm, John Deere)

State universities
Potawatomi: 4
Illinois: 8

Prisons
Potawatomi: 1
Illinois: 40

State parks
Potawatomi: 6
Illinois: 35

Per capita income
Potawatomi: ranges from $23,227 in Cook County to $35,546
in DuPage County
Illinois: ranges from $13,325 in Pulaski County to $23,173
in Sangamon County

Tax revenue
Potawatomi: $10,207,787,779
Illinois: $4,485,087,020

Gross state product
Potawatomi: $532 billion
Illinois: $120 billion

"Once upon a time, Chicago and downstate belonged to the same economy," says Richard C. Longworth, author of *Caught in the Middle: America's Heartland in the Age of Globalism* and a fellow at the Chicago Council on Global Affairs. "Factories downstate made things Chicago needed. That's gone away. What's replaced it in Chicago is the global economy. What economic vitality there is in Illinois is in Chicago. The economic fortunes of Chicago and downstate are diverging."

Obviously, a lot of downstaters are mad as hell about losing political and economic influence to Chicago. But do Chicagoans even notice? And if they notice, do they even care? No, and probably not. Culturally, Chicagoans don't identify with—or even think much about—the state they inhabit. As a friend puts it, "I'm not an Illinoisan. I'm a Chicagoan." I once mentioned to another Chicago friend that I'd just visited a small town in southern Illinois, "down by the border with Kentucky." She looked at me quizzically. "Illinois doesn't have a border with Kentucky," she said. (This is someone with a master's degree—but not in geography.)

If someone tells you, "I'm from Illinois," it means that (a) he's not from Chicago, and (b) he'll be annoyed if you ask. (Matt Weidman is from Berwick. As he puts it in the bio of his Twitter feed, @forgottonia, "Is that near Chicago? NO, it is not.") Kevin Cronin, the lead singer of Champaign's REO Speedwagon, once introduced "Ridin' the Storm Out" in concert with a story about how it was inspired by a Rocky Mountain thunderstorm, an astonishing sight for "an Illinois band." (Another musician who tried to promote pan-Illinoisism: Musician Sufjan Stevens (who was born in Detroit) offers a pan-Illinoisan view in his album *Illinois*, which includes songs about Decatur, the Rock River Valley, and Metropolis as well as Chicago.) But Chicago's lack of identification with the rest of the state has prevented Illinois from developing a distinct identity like that possessed by so many of its neighbors. Wisconsinites drink beer, fish for muskie, and drive snowmobiles across frozen lakes. Minnesotans are passive-aggressive, play hockey, and eat hotdish. Iowans grown corn and sculpt butter cows. What does it mean to be an Illinoisan?

"When I'm in other states, and I say I'm from Illinois, the first question I get is 'How far is that from Chicago?'" says East Saint Louis native Ray Coleman, who helped sell Barack Obama's 2004 Senate candidacy to downstate voters. "Chicago always comes up in the conversation. In Metro East"—the trans-Mississippi suburbs of Saint Louis— "everybody feels forgotten. It's Chicago, the collar counties, and that's all that matters."

This ignorance is partly a result of the fact that Chicagoans don't consider the downstate Illinois a vacation spot—it's flat, it's hot, it doesn't have any big lakes. Chicago is a Great Lakes city, so it's more convenient, and more congenial, to spend a weekend on the water in New Buffalo, Michigan, or Door County, Wisconsin, than on the Mississippi River—even though Illinois has more miles of Mississippi riverbank than any state. Dan Krankeola, president and CEO of Illinois South Tourism, which serves 22 counties south of Interstate 70, says he barely bothers marketing to Chicago.

"We find the majority of our tourists are coming from Saint Louis, Indianapolis, and farther south of us," Krankeola says. "If you live in a big city, you love that environment. Our character is very different from Chicago." (If you're thinking of heading downstate, Krankeola says, "We've got a World Heritage center at Cahokia Mounds; we've got Gateway Motor Sports Park, Shawnee Hills Wine Trail, Carlyle Lake Wine Trail. A lot of opportunities for a staycation.")

It literally took an act of God to lure Chicagoans to downstate Illinois. That act was this year's so-called Great American Eclipse, whose path crossed far southern Illinois on August 21. Chicagoan Eric Bremer and his wife, Helen, went to see the rare spectacle. A Decatur native whose grandparents lived in Metropolis, Bremer was familiar with Little Egypt, which lies in the northern salient of the Ozark Mountains, but it was a revelation to Helen.

"I think it was one of Helen's first trips," Bremer says. "We went down, and I sort of forgot—you get down into the Shawnee, and it's very different, and it's not the Illinois that you think about. We went to Bald Knob Cross, which was fantastic for eclipse watching. It's beautiful, looking around there and seeing the valleys. It's a different world, even culturally, because it's entwined with the Ohio River and the Mississippi Valley. She had no idea that sort of place existed in Illinois."

Bremer is already planning a return trip, to the New Columbia Bluffs, in Massac County, which mark the northernmost range of southern flora and fauna, such as bald cypress, magnolia—and poisonous snakes. (One of the last remaining tourist attractions in Cairo is Magnolia Manor, a 19th-century mansion with the namesake tree growing in the front yard.)

When Chicago alderman Ameya Pawar was growing up in the north suburbs, his family vacationed on Michigan's Mackinac Island and at Niagara Falls, but rarely ventured downstate. So when he launched his shortlived 2017 campaign for governor, Pawar made it a point to venture into "Forgottonia." He even chose as his running mate the mayor of Cairo, a town as close to Jackson, Mississippi, as it is to Chicago. They bused Cairo public housing residents to the Department of Housing and Urban Development's office in Chicago to protest plans to close down their buildings and scatter the residents. Many were making their first trip to Chicago. On his downstate campaign stops, Pawar inevitably had to overcome local suspicions of the "corrupt Chicago politician," but once he did, he found commonalities between the two spheres of Illinois. Galesburg, which lost its Maytag factory, and Newton, which lost a Roadmaster plant, are undergoing the same economic dislocation as the south side of Chicago when the steel mills shut down in the 1980s.

"Cairo, East Saint Louis, the south and west sides of Chicago, Freeport, Galesburg—they're all dealing with the same problems of disinvestment," Pawar says. "The assumption is that people there are weak. But these communities often have the most resilient people, because they have to stitch things together after government has left them behind. What happened 40 years ago in black and brown communities is happening now in small towns, with the opiate crisis. Now it's considered a public health problem."

One of Pawar's campaign themes was "One Illinois." After ending his campaign, he announced the formation of a political action committee with that name. And in February 2018 he announced the launch of a media platform as well.

"I want to bring people together from small towns and big cities to tell stories about what it means to be an Illinoisan," Pawar says. "Bring people together, and you can say, 'Look, let's see the commonality. The economy changed. Why are we fighting each other? Why are we allowing our leaders to tell poor whites that black and brown people are a threat to them? We end up fighting around race, class, and geography when really it's the system that's the problem."

In 2012, Pawar was part of the inaugural class in the Edgar Fellows Program, which brings young leaders from around the state to the University of Illinois Urbana-Champaign for a series of seminars hosted by former governor Jim Edgar.

"On our second day of the fellowship, Governor Edgar put all of us on a bus and he's like, 'Look, I want to take all of you to a working farm,'" Pawar says. "So he goes to a farm outside Champaign. He looks at the Chicagoans and said, 'I'm glad you got to see a working farm. What's grown on this farm gets traded on LaSalle Street.' Then he turns to the rest of the fellows. 'You've got to stop complaining about the CTA getting funding. The structure that supports LaSalle Street doesn't exist without the CTA. If there's no LaSalle Street, you have no place to trade your grain.'"

From its very origins, when Nathaniel Pope shifted the state's border to balance southerners with northerners, Illinois was never designed to be a monolithic state. We're not Nebraska or Delaware. In its nearly 500-mile run from Galena to Metropolis, Illinois cuts across multiple linguistic, cultural, and topographic regions. Illinois is Yankee and southerner, Catholic and Baptist, immigrant and native, town and country, Great Lakes, prairie, and foothills. Illinois's demographics are closer to the national average than any state's. We're the middle of Middle America. That's why "Will it play in Peoria?" means "Will it appeal to the average American?" It's also the source of Illinois's unique role in American history, as the proving ground for racial progress. Abraham Lincoln won the Republican nomination for president because he was seen as a candidate who could reconcile the conflicting views of slavery held by the north, the midlands, and the upper south of the country, all represented in Illinois. Barack Obama prepared to sell himself as the nation's first black president by selling himself to the diverse voters of Illinois—who have elected more black members of Congress than those of any state. Illinois is riven by the same urban-rural animosities that have divided the rest of America, but it's also the perfect laboratory for figuring out how to overcome them. Chicago and downstate need to stick together, because the rest of the country needs us together too.

FAMILY IS FOREVER

BLOOD IS THICKER

DANA ARITONOVICH

Uncle George was lying on the floor in his hallway when a friend saw him through the window as she approached the front door. He was carrying a roll of paper towels from one room to another when his legs suddenly weakened. Once his body was down, he couldn't get himself back up. It was the day before Hillary Clinton won the popular vote and Donald Trump was elected the next president of the United States of America.

A few weeks later, we learned that Uncle George had cancer. By February, he was gone.

I never found out if he voted early.

As a first-generation American who grew up in a politically conservative outer ring Cleveland suburb, surrounded by chain restaurants, strip malls, and plain white people as far as the eye could see, I sensed that conformity was the key to getting along. But I was never one to keep my mouth shut when I had an opinion.

My grandparents were Democrats from the time they became American citizens. My grandfather thought that choosing your own government was the most incredible thing in the world, and he knew that was what made America great. He was around twenty years old when conscripted into Tito's Communist Yugoslav Army in World War II. He despised Communism and eventually went AWOL to join the rebel Četniks and fight alongside the Allies. The rest of our family seemed to perceive Democrats as being too close to commies on the political spectrum, and since they could never return to the old country for fear of retribution from Tito's dictatorship, they wanted to stay away from anything remotely left-wing. But for my grandparents, there was something about the Democratic Party that appealed to them. They thought Republicans were full of shit.

Serbs are loud and opinionated and eager to start arguments about all the things you're not supposed to discuss in polite company. During family gatherings, the men are usually yelling about politics over beers and shots while the women are in the kitchen yelling about everything else. When I was in eighth grade one of my mother's cousins, a staunch conservative and a Teamster, asked me at a holiday dinner whether I supported the Contras or the Sandinistas. Ollie North was in the news every day and Johnny Carson made jokes about Fawn Hall, so I had a general idea that the U.S. government was involved with some sort of shady weapons deal. But I didn't know how to answer the question. Thank God my mom, well-versed in current events and packing decades of experience defending her views, stepped in to show me how it was done. It was at this moment that I realized I had to study much harder before visiting the relatives so I could talk politics with the grown folks.

When Michael Dukakis ran in 1988, I was all in right away. He was Greek, so my Serb senses were excited. He was also, to me, super liberal, and that sealed the deal. My parents and grandparents were ready to pull the lever for him that November, and I got into a lot of arguments at school for supporting such a lefty. I excitedly stayed up all night watching the election results, confident that we'd be seeing an Orthodox Easter in the White House for at least the next four years, and I was devastated when he lost. Four years later, I cast my first vote ever for Jerry Brown. I wasn't too sure about that Clinton guy, but after his acceptance speech at the convention that summer I was excited about him. I worked for his campaign that fall, and saw him—from very far away—speak at my campus a week before the election.

The Clintons have never been popular with Serbs. Yugoslavia broke up and war began the year before Bill was elected, and it was quite fashionable for American politicians to be anti-Serb. I just couldn't bring myself to vote for him a second time because of his administration's ignorant actions regarding the former Yugoslavia. Serbs are not inclined to forgive and forget, and are understandably still resentful. Many have long harbored a hatred for Hillary in part due to her alleged role in influencing her husband's anti-Serb stances. But it wasn't until Barack Obama ran for president that I noticed a shift in the tone of relatives who were always flapping their right wings. I don't remember Uncle George ever saying much about politics except for union stuff (and he didn't have much good to say), so his political transformation was pretty startling.

I didn't really look at anyone differently because of their political views until Obama was elected. (Thanks, Obama!) Prior to that, I would jokingly recoil in disgust when somebody told me they voted for one of the Bushes or McCain-Palin. Not that I never judged anyone by their politics, because I sure as hell did; some opinions deserve judgment. But there was such an ugliness, such an overt hostility toward President

Obama. It's no secret why that was, but not everyone wanted to admit it. But I just *knew* that all the haters were racist assholes who failed government class and probably beat their wives. Decent people couldn't possibly hold these views.

Uncle George loved The Beatles and The Who, played in a band called The Deadbeet's (unnecessary apostrophe and all) when he was a teenager, and bought me the first Led Zeppelin boxed set when I was in high school. He shopped at Marc's all the time and went to Indians games with us for 25 years, never leaving early because he didn't want my mom and my sisters and me to walk back to the garage without him. When I was fortysomething and having car trouble, he told me to let him know if I needed a ride and he'd get up well before his normal 3:00 p.m. wakeup call to drive the thirty minutes to my place and take me to work. For my parents' fortieth anniversary dinner, he grabbed the check and paid for all ten of us without blinking an eye. He randomly brought me cases of bottled water when he found them on sale really cheap. A few years ago, I began writing for a friend's new LGBT magazine, and when I posted my first article my uncle shared it on his Facebook page. One day, he slipped me some cash when I needed it most and told me my dearly departed grandmother wanted me to have it.

But Uncle George was also waiting for Obummer to take away his guns and enact sharia law across the country. For eight years, he forwarded thousands of emails with patriotic quotes falsely attributed to Paul Harvey, questionable conspiracy theories about President Obama's secret Muslim wedding ring, and dire warnings about scary illegal immigrants living on welfare and voting for the dastardly Democrats who encouraged them to flood across the border to birth criminal anchor babies. At a three-year-old cousin's birthday party, he claimed that the Saudi government was paying families $250K a year to move to America and have children so that by 2020 we would be a majority-Muslim nation. When I asked him for the source of this ridiculous claim he hesitated to respond, but eventually sneered that he saw it on "the internet."

His Facebook posts were mostly absurd articles from right-wing websites, with the occasional family picture thrown in for good measure. When I challenged the fake news he shared online, a friend of his would mansplain and call me uneducated, Uncle George never replied. I'd post evidence that proved everything in his various posts was wrong, but still, he never wrote a word in response.

It was upsetting to see somebody I loved willfully suffocating themselves in such filth, consciously choosing to believe these outrageous lies and obviously Photoshopped pictures. So I decided, for my own sanity, to stop following him on Facebook as the 2016 election drew nearer and his posts grew increasingly deplorable. I would never have deleted him altogether, of course, but I did delete—and block—another older male family member who made a rape joke when the "grab 'em by the pussy" tape was released. Several other relatives of the Republican persuasion deleted me from their friends list during Obama's second term, but nothing was ever said about it and nothing seemed different between us when we saw each other in the real world. There were still hugs and kisses and laughter over succulent roasted pig and warm krofne.

I wasn't surprised that so many of my relatives were excited about Donald Trump. But I was still disgusted by their support—and amazed at our shared DNA. It hurt my heart to try to reconcile how people I had always known as honorable, hardworking, and family-oriented could cling to these abhorrent opinions. How could such an excellent father and husband praise a man who bragged about assaulting women? Why would an educated, well-placed young lady give her vote to a womanizer who wanted to take away her right to decide what to do with her own body? When did an immigrant from a small village without toilets, a man who, after more than fifty years in the U.S., still sounds like a Serbian Ricky Ricardo, whose citizenship was sponsored by his own brother who came to America as a refugee, decide that his candidate would be the one yelling the most ferociously about refusing entry to refugees and only allowing people who already spoke English or had a college education into the country? What did I not understand about them after knowing them my whole life?

Uncle George and I never talked politics again once we knew he had that bastard cancer in his body. It felt like a decision we somehow made, silently, together. It was impressive that he didn't gloat about Trump's victory, but if there happened to be a Trump story on the news when we visited him in the nursing home, none of us said a word. He was usually watching *American Pickers* and other nonpartisan fare anyway, instead of the Fox News he had streamed 24 hours a day at home. I wondered if he wanted to argue so we could pretend everything was normal. Could

I make a snotty comment to provoke him into battling it out with me? How I wished he had the energy to fight.

After he died, we realized that he had been sick for a lot longer than we knew. He had grown into a grumpy old man even though he was only 66 when he took his last breath, but he was also very private and independent and didn't want us to worry about him. He wanted everything to be as it always was.

Now, I get even more anxious before family events. I pray that nobody brings up whatever political story is dominating the news, but I still study so I can shut down anyone who starts some shit. I'd rather hear about babies and food and everyone's health problems. *How are the new meds are working out? What's going on with your asshole neighbor? I'd love to hear listen to another story about you beating up a kid in seventh grade!* Please, anything but current events. We're not really who we vote for. Right? Besides, blood is thicker than politics.

AN ODE TO CHRISTOPHER COLUMBUS, THE SECRET JEW WHO DIED OF SYPHILIS

TRENT KAY MAVERICK

A few weeks after the election, I'm at my father's nice house in the suburbs, talking politics over sushi and wine. Fox News blares from the other room, while his wife reads dubious articles out loud from her Facebook feed about Muslim hordes attacking nursery schools with machetes and drinking the blood of Israeli babies. His in-laws jabber in a mix of English and Russian, gloating less over their recent political victory than my apparent loss. And my father, bless his heart, calls me a "liberal cupcake," having misheard the slur somewhere.

I live in Beachwood, a clean, safe, well-off suburb on the east side of Cleveland that's probably, and no stretch here, 90 percent Jewish. Seventh grade was an endless parade of catered Bar and Bat Mitzvah parties complete with custom-printed yarmulkes, disco versions of "Hava Nagila," and kosher buffets. My father is a doctor, one brother each a lawyer and a CPA, just as God intended. I can still recite a three-hour Shabbat Shacharit service from memory, and whatever it is, I'm not buying it until it goes on sale.

My father has been a Republican for as long as I can remember. As a kid, I considered him a curiosity, a political aberration in the overwhelmingly blue county that encompasses downtown Cleveland and its suburbs. When my parents were still together, they would go to the polls every election to cancel out each other's votes. Growing up I trotted out the line that my pro-choice, professional, educated, Jewish father "voted his wallet"—it wasn't that my father hated the gays, exactly, it's that he liked his money more. At least, that's what I believed.

My father remarried when I was in my twenties, to a Russian Jew who started out a dirt poor and illiterate immigrant, and now makes six figures as an anesthesiologist. Her parents remind me of my grandparents, with the same thick accents and grooved facial features, the same taste for fermented fish and weak tea. They are traditional and judgmental and gently sexist, nurturing yet patronizing at the same time ... and, to my initial surprise, hard-core right-wingers.

Before the election, I saw my father, smart and Jewish and somehow tempted by the right, as an anomaly. I imagined his fellow Republicans were mostly poor, angry, gun-toting, Bible-thumping, rural and disenfranchised, and definitely, definitely not Jewish. I couldn't believe there were more conservatives out there like my nerdy, nebbishy father and like his wife and in-laws, too.

My father was born in Israel in the 1950s, to young Holocaust survivors who met and fell in love in the new Jewish state, then set their sights on America. He is emblematic of the American dream: He arrived in this country at age two, the son of a devout carpenter and a mother who never learned to drive, both of whom spoke Yiddish exclusively in the home. He excelled in school, and though he maintains to this day that he was denied admission to a certain Ivy League university because he was Jewish, he went to medical school and now makes more money than I ever will.

And yet here he is a few decades later, parroting blatantly ridiculous (and thoroughly debunked) statistics to me about how 25 percent of all Muslims are radicalized or how 80 percent of white homicide victims are murdered by black people, or how outdated voter registration information allowed three million people to vote illegally.

My father's wife came to America to escape communist Russia. Now she's first in line with the Muslim panic. When I go to London to visit a close friend, she warns about Muslims bearing bombs in airports and how it's not safe for Americans to travel abroad, though I'm statistically more likely to be killed by some white guy right here at home. When she reads that a presidential executive order has enacted the Muslim ban, her mother, who barely speaks English, simply announces, "Goot!"

The cherry on top is when her father, speaking in his heavy accent, proclaims that "the Mexicans" entering this country should be forced to learn the language or be deported, and his wife responds affirmatively, enthusiastically, in Russian.

It's at around this time that, emboldened, he further informs us that Christopher Columbus, zealous expansionist and torturer and mass-murderer of Native Americans, was actually a secret Jew.

"Hmm, sounds like bullshit," we all say, and out comes the iPad.

Now my father's wife is on the Internet, searching for evidence of this claim. It amounts to a few suspicious symbols in private letters and weird requests in Columbus's will. It's a tinfoil theory that a Jewish Columbus pretended to convert during the Inquisition but secretly remained loyal to his faith, and even planned to resettle the Jewish community in the New World. It's flimsy and fantastical at best. In fact, the more we read, the more it seems Columbus was very, very Christian. He promoted the conversion of native people, quoted Bible verses in his writings, and even considered his explorations a fulfillment of Catholic prophecy.

But, "No, no," the old man insists, despite all evidence to the contrary. He read it on the Internet, so it must be true.

"What ever happened to Columbus?" I ask, hoping to change the subject.

In chimes my father, "Everyone knows Columbus died of syphilis." And we're back on the iPad. His wife finds numerous articles blaming Columbus for the precipitous spread of syphilis in the New World, but alas, the man himself died of gout. Still my father holds firm. Gout, he says, is clearly a cover-up. I mean, no one wants to say the man who discovered America died of syphilis. Besides, he says, "Everyone in those days died of syphilis." To my father, the gout thing is the ultimate fake news.

In the era of alternative facts, here are two intelligent, cosmopolitan Jews refusing to back down from some insignificant nonsense they read on the Internet, holding fast to false claims that seem unlikely in the face of mounting evidence. How are they supposed to now critically analyze and dismiss propaganda about Muslims and blacks and immigrants and those pesky liberals and whatever else is pissing them off this week?

The inability to think critically and course correct when faced with facts seems part of a larger cognitive dissonance. Here are Jews with a painful history of genocide and persecution falling prey to the same hate-fueled rhetoric and scapegoating used against their own people a generation ago. As if they themselves are not immigrants, refugees born in foreign countries who came here seeking a better future. As if they are not intimately acquainted with religious intolerance that rounded up and killed off their families. As if they have ascended to some higher plane of Americanism, and the past doesn't matter. Dayenu.

My father's Republicanism, I could handle. Our disagreements about health care, taxation, school waivers, environmental protections—these were normal, logical debates that occasionally flared my passions but largely came down to academic differences of opinion. The current climate, with its rising tide of hate, anger, and intolerance, now goes beyond politics as usual.

In supporting this administration, my father's family has become complicit in its hate speech, misinformation, and persistent othering of Muslims, immigrants, and other minorities. I have to assume support for Trump is support for the wall, for deportations, for the Muslim registry and travel ban, for the narrowing and sullying of what it means to be an American. My father and his wife, whose families both fled persecution, now can't help but participate in the casual persecution of others.

I can almost understand how rural white America could feel this way, alienated and angry and afraid—it makes sense for folks so insulated to fear outsiders. What I can't wrap my head around is the same ignorance and intolerance espoused by children of Holocaust survivors and Russian Jewish refugees. The Jewish people are intimately involved in the story of persecution. It is deeply woven into our histories and identities as Jews. To ignore where we came from, what we went through, and to actively wish it upon others, goes against the very fabric of what it means to be Jewish—and American.

I view our modern political climate through a uniquely Jewish lens. The house I live in was owned by Holocaust survivors who sealed up the milk chute and installed five separate deadbolts on the back door. Now, the threat of a Muslim registry brings up images of sewed-on stars. The president of the United States claims that Islam hates us and calls for a religious test to enter the country ... to a roar of claps and cheers. As a Jew, I'm chilled by all-too-familiar horror. If I were Muslim, I'd be hiding under my bed. I fear my father, in standing by his party and his vote, by refusing to speak out and by readily absorbing Trump's rhetoric, is enabling the exact brand of hate that murdered our own people not so long ago.

I don't believe my father is a hateful person. But the fact remains that he voted for racism, for xenophobia and Islamophobia and the arrogance of "America First." Perhaps he was duped by alternative facts, by misleading statistics, by fear-mongering and propaganda. Or perhaps he felt a fever pitch of fear and hatred toward minorities was an acceptable byproduct of a conservative agenda. Perhaps, because it's a different group at the wrong end of Trump's wrath, a group that doesn't include him and his own, it doesn't seem like a problem. History has shown what happens when hateful rhetoric becomes commonplace, when it is not challenged, and no one is blameless. It is our responsibility as Jews to honor the legacy of the Holocaust and our history of persecution, to stand up, to not be silent, to never forget.

Sitting at the dinner table, I realize that I sort of hope Christopher Columbus was a secret Jew (I'm less bothered by the syphilis). In a time when Spain turned its back on its Jewish populace, our hero Christopher

Columbus, the theory goes, was looking for a haven in the New World, a place where his people would be safe to practice their religion. He imagined a country built for immigrants, for refugees, for the persecuted, for people in search of religious freedom—a diverse and welcoming nation.

Though, if it's true that Columbus was a secret Jew, I suppose it follows that somewhere along the line, he lost the thread, and forgot what he'd originally set out to do. He sailed to the New World in search of refuge for his people, but was swayed instead by riches and a bloody campaign to keep the godless natives in line. Just like my Jewish family, who fled Eastern Europe only to be consumed with fear and mistrust of immigrants, refugees, and religious minorities, it seems Columbus found in America a new group of people to despise.

APPALACHIAN YANKEES IN MICHIGAN

WENDY WELCH

Call us Appalachian Yankees. My family has spent three generations driving up and down I-75 looking for work someplace between Michigan and Tennessee.

That's not the only road some of us have tried to leave. Working class folk descended from mountain Christianity with a capital C: that's my people. When you look up fundamentalist in the dictionary, you find a picture of Grandma Mattie. In 1937, she and Grandpa Alex abandoned a crossroads general store in Tazewell, Tennessee for a slum-burb in Detroit, where he became a bricklayer and she raised five children.

The Tazewell church they never left behind didn't hold with adornment: no curling of the hair, no wedding rings, not even reading glasses. If God hadn't equipped you with it when you came out of the womb, you didn't need it. No good ever came of reading too much anyway. The purpose of life was to glorify God and take good care of your family. This is our creed.

Three out of four aunts agreed, but Aunt Lelah struck out sideways, settling in rural Ohio with a Navy man. No one can explain why this loosened her up a bit, but theirs was the first daughter to show up at the annual Christmas gathering in blue jeans. Scandalized glances fell aplenty, but family is family. In later years two sisters and a brother used Lelah's house as a stopover en route to destinies of their own as teacher, nurse, and preacher back in the region Mattie and Alex had left the generation before.

We cousins retraced Grandma and Grandpa's route back and forth, spreading out into Chicago and a few other offshoots of the 75 corridor, aiming at ever-moving targets of jobs and theology. Sometimes steel mills and college classes proved infertile soil for Tazewell's brand of Christianity. Some cousins raced through life well above the speed limit aided by an excess of substances; others navigated with caution, compliant to their raising. More or less. Blue jeans gave way to pierced ears, which caused Grandma Mattie to pray until the Christmas ham got cold that first year. But we were still family.

Grandma's funeral was well before the 2016 election, and—unbeknownst to us—the last Golden Day. We cried and laughed and sat at the wake eating Aunt Pat's Orange Delight Bundt Cream Cake and watching the children run. Wedding rings had created a whole new generation with different names but the same faces we remembered from childhood. We knew they would inherit our family creed and Aunt Pat's cake recipe along with those faces: glorify God; do right by your flesh and blood; avoid curling irons; cream the eggs and butter together before adding them to the dry ingredients.

By the time we gathered again to say goodbye to the first of the uncles, years had passed and we needed more than eggs to bind us. At the wake, the now-adult children of cousins, working their way through graduate school or a steel mill, offered jokes wrapped around baited hooks.

"That March of Women abomination in D.C. got more people walking than Michelle Obama ever did! Ha! Seriously though, he's gonna drain the swamp."

"You mean drain the Federal Reserves, don't you? Do you know how much golf he's played since becoming president? And his scores are worse than mine! Haha!"

The fundamentals felt the same—take care of your own, do what God says—but carefully manicured nails and upswept curly hair dominated the room. The Aunts passed each others' great-grandchildren back and forth and kept silence against their granddaughters in business suits. The granddaughters responded by twisting their wedding rings and sharing about the churches they had settled into back home— home being everything from Hugeopolis to Nowhereville along I-75. Churches where "family" meant ALL God's children, red and blue, black and white. They spoke of living wages at $15 per hour, single payer healthcare systems, and staying out of Walmart.

Their cousins who worked in what Tazewell had become, who had fled Flint and given up homesteading in Detroit after a bullet lodged in their Valu-Village stove, grimaced and said they'd have been glad to have a Walmart near them, all that time they were trying to rebuild a country ruined by entitlement. They narrated first-person experiences that proved God hated freeloaders. A family took care of its own. A real family, at least.

The Orange Delight cake stayed on its plate because half the room were on a plant-based diet after hearing a TED talk about the links between global warming and personal health, and the other half were diabetic from eating out in Hazard, Kentucky.

The aunts could see what was happening, so they did what Appalachian Yankees do in times of crisis.

"Y'all quit that politics talk and get over here and finish up this ham. We're fambly," said Aunt Evelyn.

"It can be difficult to understand God's word in the context of today's challenges." Aunt Edna shoved paper plates of Orange Delight into our hands as she spoke. "But you can't argue with your mouths full. Eat."

Aunt Lelah looked sideways at Aunt Edna. "God's word never changes."

Aunt Edna blinked, fork halfway to her mouth. Her granddaughter Sally answered instead. "No, but life's circumstances do, and God gave us brains for a reason."

Uncle Ernie jabbed his plastic fork at Sally. "We must not question God's word. It tells us that Earthly governments are ordained by God."

Cousin Alannis rolled her eyes and opened her mouth. Within ten minutes, people were leaving. I think it will be the last time I'll ever see some of them. We will tell ourselves that this is the way family works, breaking down into smaller units after the loss of Grandma Mattie. That time's inevitable march dictates the aunts become matriarchs of their own tribes. We will not allow ourselves to believe that anything else happened here, this day we didn't know would not be golden with family and Bundt cake.

God love Cousin Alannis with her MBA and spiked heels. In her life, in the lives of her brothers and sisters, respect never became a word that shielded others from consequences. God bless Cousin Sally in her long denim skirt and sneakers, yards of poker-straight hair piled atop a head full of brains; she taught her nine children to question everything, just like she'd been doing since age three.

Did the women at wakes and weddings those hot summer days in 1860s Tazewell think similar things, gluing their layer to the Apple Stack Cake built family by family, each adding a piece to the whole? Did they watch the heat storms roll toward them from the edge of the valley, listen to trapped thunder beat itself to death against the mountain walls, and hear warnings of what was coming? When they prayed for rain, perhaps it was to cool the land and grow peace in their families, while brothers argued states rights over picnic tables laden with food and cousins spit watermelon seeds at each other across the creek. Maybe they prayed for the safety of cousins gone north, whom they would never see again.

When did they know seeds would turn to bullets? When did they rec-ognize that even families come apart at the seams so carefully sewn for generations by advice at the breakfast table, through careful introductions of cherished daughters to boys with no plans to move away, with recipes in scrawling script on scraps of paper stuck between pages of college textbooks for grandchildren headed toward The City?

The aunts looked defeated as they gathered up plates of uneaten Orange Delight from around the room. It is not an expression I am used to seeing on these faces my family have been sharing for so long.

Politics is one thing, family another. How much power does a president have, to reach into the very hearts of people and turn watermelon seeds into bullets?

FROM MACOMB COUNTY TO DETROIT CITY
AMANDA LEWAN

We moved into our first house together. The house is a big colonial with a brick face and navy blue shutters. White columns stand in front of a red door. Two large flower pots sit empty and peeling. The porch is a pedestal waiting for our arrival, and arriving at first feels grand.

"A red door stands for prosperity," a friend says when I show her a photo.

"Good. We're going to need it," I say.

Three stories is far too large for the two of us and three dogs, but it's the smallest house we could find in the neighborhood we chose, Detroit's historic Boston Edison area. I have never been one to want to own things. I don't dream of houses and linens and other homely things. But if I *did* dream, then this house would be it. I love everything from the glass door-knobs and original keyholes to the cornice edges around each window, etched white and sealed in light grey walls. It feels like a place of lightness.

Moving in, however, does not feel so light. I carry a bag of emotions with me, one not well-packed and wrapped in too much silver lining.

I grew up in Macomb County, north of Detroit. That is where, as a child, I enjoyed a good school system and dance classes and band practice. It's also the county that went red in 2016 for the first time in over a decade, tipping the state in a heated election year and becoming a national symbol of white working class frustration. It's the county with "Trump" plastered on nearly every car and billboard. This is the county that shot down our region's public transit proposal, the county that seems to want to stay set apart. A majority white county, outside a majority black city. This is the county I come from but do not call home.

Members of my family spent their entire lives trying to get out of the city in which we had just purchased our new house. They leave for logical reasons: better schools, better jobs, safety, cities with more op-portunity. It was once a symbol of success if a family member got out of Detroit, knowing something better was supposed to be around the cor-ner. My uncle moved to the country beyond the suburbs; an aunt moved to Macomb. One cousin couldn't find a job working in the city during the recession and moved to Atlanta instead. Jobs in the city of Detroit are so few and far between that 64% of Detroit residents commute to work outside the city, and residents have little access to public transportation that is reliable and speedy. Perhaps you saw the story about the man who walked 20 miles to finish his morning work commute? My grandma is the only one who still stays in her home of 50 years on Detroit's east side. She has retired but not moved out. She was the only one left until I moved in.

I ask my dad what he thinks of the house.

"It's a nice house," he says.

There are no fatherly warnings. No stories from his twenty years of boarding up abandoned homes in the city. No reminders of the times guns were pulled out on him, and drugs were found in the way of his work while he was doing his job. No comments of our block of beauty surrounded by what most see as blight, streets of emptiness that he used to try and fight. He closed down his construction business many years ago. He works as a janitor. He voted twice for Obama and surprised me when he voted for Trump, believing in the dream that things were better in the past. He points to things he likes about the house, buys the moving crew of brothers their lunch, and leaves without leaving approval.

Right next door to us the house is empty, but not really. Cars sit in the driveway and backyard. Plants remain scattered around as if someone lives there. Our house was similar to that one too, owned by a family holding on. No one was living in it, but the owners kept it until it until a neighbor made an offer, took its shell, and infused it with necessities, made it a home again.

I wonder how many drive by our neighborhood and see blight? How many see opportunity? How many dream of the past?

Next to us a piece of plywood stays wedged in a window; two white circles and a small half-moon are painted on it. It is smiling at us over a hole that is empty inside. I am sitting across from it from my brand new kitchen island drinking my fresh coffee. It is smiling at me from across the way. I want to smile back. History can't be shut up with plywood.

I ask my aunt: Why leave Detroit?
I ask my uncle: Why leave Detroit?
I ask my mom: Why leave Detroit?
I ask my grandma: Why stay?
I do not ask my father anything.

Two old friends come to visit. They are moving into their first home together soon, too. We walk through every room of our new house, talking and catching up. The men are insisting on family donated furniture while the women want to add their own touch. Then, at the end there is a subtle ask. They are settling down in a neighborhood outside the city where this question would not come up. But there's much unsettled here, empty, abandoned, and it's past dark. They ask: What's the best way to get out of here?

How do we get out of here? That is not the question I want to ask myself but: *How did we get here? And how do we get back together?*

Like my grandma, I am set apart in my ways. We have found our home and we will stay here for what I hope will be another fifty years. I think of all my relatives spread out across our divided region. I want to bring them back, one by one, to be a closer family and a closer region. I sit in my second story office writing this where I am surrounded by the trees. In it is the silence of a sky opened up around me. In this space I hope for possibility. In this city I hope we can all return to as home someday.

KICK ASS: MY DAD, THE AMERICAN DREAM, AND DONALD TRUMP

ANGELA ANAGOST REPKE

"Kick ass."

This was my dad's sign-off and direct order at the end of his letters to my three brothers and me while we were in college and into young adulthood. His letters were usually scribed on his yellow legal pads. They would include some Greek philosophical quote like "everything in moderation," or a gritty, yet quirky anecdote of his own, like this one:

> *My Dear Children,*
> *I guess it's time for more stuff on my life.*
> *I do not recall much about the seventh grade except that I was still working at the restaurant on the weekends—the late shift from 10:30-3:00 in the morning.*
> *One of those nights this motorcycle guy came in drunk and he was abusing this woman that he was sitting with. My dad went over to interrupt the abuse in his Greek accent. The guy grabbed a ketchup bottle in his hand and hit my dad right on the side of the head with it. Ketchup and blood came out all over the place and knocked my dad down to the floor. That scared the shit out of me. Fortunately, he only had a couple stitches. I was so upset I wanted to go around to all the bars and get some of my little friends to catch this guy and kick the shit of out him somehow. I wanted to kill that evil sonofabitch.*
> *Presently, Mom and I are doing quite well although she is on my ass about something every day. I almost never argue since I am generally out in the world, still exposed to its main festivities of good and evil.*
> *Kick ass,*
> *Dad*

He'd stick a twenty-dollar bill in sometimes, too—beer money. I don't know why, but as we became adults and he grew into an old man, he stopped including "kick ass." Maybe it's because at eighty-one, he himself has stopped kicking ass—or at least stopped trying as hard.

My dad's name is Christ—pronounced Chris. He stands tall at a portly 5'7." He is the only child of two Greek immigrants who had an arranged marriage. His father pushed an ice cream truck in Downtown Detroit so their family could survive in a filthy one-room apartment before moving north to Saginaw—where they still struggled. He's done nothing but work his ass off, beginning as a ten-year-old boy in a restaurant as a dishwasher and busboy. Clawing to the top, he fumbled through five different colleges until he finally graduated from Wayne State Law School. His father died when he was thirty, so he busted his ass to support his mother, Angeline. He built his own life with his own damn fortitude.

He is the American Dream.

As kids, he instilled in us character and integrity. School was important, but not as important as doing the right thing—choosing good over evil.

So, as the presidential election came around, I expected that he himself would do the right thing.

Saginaw is known for its high homicide rate, segregated schools, and that house that sold for one dollar. But, it wasn't always this way. Greeks began coming to Saginaw as early as 1910. My grandfather landed at Ellis Island (for the third time) with his young bride in 1929 and found his way to Saginaw by 1931. By the time my dad was a kid, the city was pretty integrated. "I don't remember any race issues. Everyone was too busy working their asses off," is how my dad put it. Most Greeks worked in business, especially hotels and restaurants.

My dad always used to tell me that when an out-of-town immigrant would come to a restaurant, "they would never charge another Greek. That's just how it was." Without a church in Saginaw, the young immigrants worked hard to preserve their heritage by holding American Hellenic Educational Progressive Association meetings above the Vlassis Brother's Restaurant at 411 Court Street. This is where the development of their church finally evolved. Without these men, I never would have learned how to crack my red, not pastel, Easter eggs. They protected our traditions so that I can now teach them to my kids.

Garrison Keillor came to visit Saginaw a couple of years ago to celebrate the great poet and hometown son Theodore Roethke. Said Keillor, "It will be a reminder to Saginaw that out of suffering come gifts of great beauty." All Greek immigrants are this beauty.

Many of these people, people like my dad, are still alive. With the election around the corner, I wondered what the people of Saginaw would do, too. Saginaw County hadn't gone red since Reagan in 1984. And in 2016, although nervous, I hoped the streak continued.

A fall in Michigan is better than in any other state. Period. All of nature is at its absolute best, a bright myriad of colors before it all becomes naked, gray, and dies. It was no different on a cool mid-October morning when I drove from my parent's home in Saginaw across the state to Grand Haven for a baby shower. The foliage was at its peak. Trees were set ablaze all along M-46. Flames flew across my Ford Edge windshield.

As I drove through the first rural city of Hemlock, I saw my first pumpkin patch. My dad took my brothers and me here a couple of times as kids. A small family-owned one ran right out of their home, the kind where you walk up to the owner himself and pay for the pumpkin you choose. But there, smack in the middle of all of that orange on the lawn, I saw it: TRUMP. MAKE AMERICA GREAT AGAIN!

Must be a fluke.

Living in the township of Grand Blanc, a suburb of Flint, I hadn't seen many Trump signs—yet. Or maybe as a new stay-at-home-mom, I just didn't get out enough.

The sun had started to melt the dew on the green grass, but it still sparkled. I drove through rural town after rural town with the sun chasing me. Merrill. St. Louis. Breckenridge. Lakeview. More TRUMP signs. I approached Edmore. There was a farm with an average red barn upon a little hill. The vast lawn had what seemed to be one hundred tiny TRUMP signs and right in the middle—the biggest TRUMP sign of them all. It looked just like the others, blue with a little red trim, only blown up to the size of a billboard.

I'm not sure if it was the signs or the black coffee sitting in my guts, but I had to pull over at a gas station to empty my nerves into a hadn't-been-cleaned-in-months toilet. I bought a bottle of water so I didn't just deliver my insides to their establishment.

I continued to pass through rural towns until I got to US-131 to Lake Michigan. More and more signs for Trump. I seldom saw one for Clinton.

He could win.

This was the first time I admitted this.

This was no longer just a *Saturday Night Live* skit that my husband and I laughed at.

After the baby shower, I wanted to take a different way home, but it would cost me more time. I wanted to get back to my parents and my two small children.

That night, after tucking the kids into bed, I sat down with my parents. I drank a glass of wine; my dad had Scotch. He was half-watching CNN and reading *Hamilton*. I told him about all of the TRUMP signs I had seen that morning.

"So what?" he said.

"So what?" I asked.

Smoke began swirling in my chest. Two sticks rubbing together—at any moment a full-blown fire could have erupted.

My mom interrupted. "Why don't you tell her, Christ."

"Tell me what?"

"He might vote Trump," my mom said.

I forced out a laugh to prevent the fire from igniting.

"But Dad," I said, "that's not how you raised us. To be for a person like that."

He rebutted. "I just don't trust Hillary. I don't believe a damn thing she says. She's just like the rest of them."

While flailing my hands as Greeks often do as they argue, I asked, "Dad, how would you like it if a man talked to Mom, your granddaughter, or me like he talks to women?"

"Well, I'd beat his ass," he admitted.

We bantered back and forth about Hillary's dishonesty and Trump's disgusting, vile, behavior—until finally, the two sticks made a spark.

"Dad. Donald. Trump. Is. A. Motherfucker."

He looked at me unrattled, took a drink of his Scotch, scoffed and said, "you're right."

Good, I thought.

Since my dad was 81 and my mom was 68, they could vote early by absentee ballot in Michigan.

On November 1st, before the rest of the country could vote, my mom called me around 9:30 as she does every single day. As I folded laundry, my two-year-old daughter threw it in the air and snickered at herself.

"Well, you're not going to be happy with your dad," my mom said. "I can't even look at him."

Thinking he pissed on the floor or forgot to pick up her meds again, I asked, "What now, Mom?"

My graceful, full-of-class mother said, "Trump. He fucking voted for Trump."

"No," was all that would spill out of my mouth.

This was the first time in my life that I was disappointed in my dad.

The big day came for the rest of us. November 8th.

It was raining hard that election-day morning. But I didn't care, I wanted to get my vote in early. So, I put the kids in the car and headed to the elementary school around the corner. I carried my daughter while my son and I tried to dodge the bullets of rain, but it was useless.

When we got inside, I asked a volunteer how long the wait was. Two hours. Hell no—not with a four and two-year-old. I'd come back later.

The rain stopped before dinner. Standing in the parking lot, we remained small below the all-gray sky. This time the wait was about an hour, but I came prepared—with Dum Dums. I carried my daughter as the line curled around the gymnasium. My son got antsy in ten minutes. I couldn't blame him. He started snaking around on the floor. Some of the voters made small talk about my cute kids, but the gym was tense.

When we were finally done voting we took the obligatory selfie with our "I voted" stickers. No tantrums in the one-hour long line—a truly victorious mother. So I thought.

That night, as I tucked in the kids, he polls started to close. As they were shutting their eyes, my husband poured the wine. Here we go, another *Saturday Night Live* show.

I kept my thoughts to myself. I couldn't say it out loud.

As the wine went down, more and more states turned red. Indiana went first, only to be later followed by two pillars —Ohio and Florida. Wolf Blitzer became visibly agitated.

My mom and I called each other every thirty minutes or so. But I never talked to my dad. I pictured him oblivious, reading another historical nonfiction with CNN on in the background—barely paying attention.

Flipping back-and-forth between the very pregnant Savannah Guthrie and Wolf Blitzer, I couldn't decide who was pissing me off more, them or my dad. It didn't matter. There was a bomb sitting in my stomach, ticking louder and louder as each state fell.

Finally, after midnight, I gave up. Hillary hadn't conceded, but my gut knew it was heading that way.

This was no longer a bad joke but an American tragedy.

Executive Order 13769. On January 27, Trump shouted to the world what kind of country he wanted to run and who he wanted in it. The travel ban was not only devastating, but scary as hell.

Upon learning about the ban and getting the tears out once again, I went to my basement and rummaged through a drawer where I keep my old journals and letters from my dad. I found it—the one where he tells the story of his parents immigrating to the United States from Greece.

October 8, 2006

To my beloved children: Tom, Nick, Angela, and Deno,

We are all products of our accumulative history, heritage, family, and lifestyle inherited from our parents and grandparents. Too often, we are worried about the problems at-hand and other necessities that we don't have time to contemplate where we have been or where we are going. I'd like to give you a little more history, specifically of your grandmother...

The young bride, Angeline, came to the United States, lost two children, struggled financially and left Greece never to hear the voice of her mother or father again. She had no contact except by mail and it took two or three months to get a letter across. There were no telephones in Greece yet.

The worst was yet to come in Greece, even after WWII. There was a great Civil War where her brothers and over one million Greeks perished. There was extreme, poverty, famine, and chaos. But, your grandmother was dedicated to her relatives and her new husband's brothers and sisters. Every two or three weeks, she would tie a box up with cords, and taped addresses all over it, telling me to haul it down to the post office. The box was full of clothing, medicine, and articles. It was a ritual for many years. This became a religious experience for me—a dedication to the family.

Your grandmother was a tough cookie. She was in a strange country without the benefit of language or education. She handled things for herself and by herself.

Your grandmother had terrific pride and I believe her fear of failure is what pushed me through to become an attorney. Back then, there were very few professionals of Greek descent.

So, in conclusion, I would say I'd like you to be very proud of your heritage, where you came, survived, and occasionally even prospered under difficult conditions. Our predecessors should never be forgotten. If I'm ever in the mood, I'll write another one of these notes.

Kick ass,

Dad

At one in the morning on Memorial Day, I heard a high-pitched "bing" from my phone. It was my mom. "In the ER. Dad's rectal bleeding won't stop. I'll keep you posted. DON'T COME."

I went. My mom sat shaken and my dad was asleep when I got there. This was not a new scene for me. I hate seeing my parents in hospital beds. Every time, it's haunting.

"Your dad will pull through," my mom said.

"I know," I responded.

I believed my mom—for the most part. My dad beat cancer's ugly ass and survived a sepsis attack that led him into a medically-induced coma for twenty-one days. He fights. He "kicks ass."

But this time was different, By the time my father got out of surgery my mom was exhausted but he was still full of wit. As the nurse came into his room, I discovered that she was one of my old students from when I taught in Saginaw. A skinny, feisty little troublemaker. I loved her. My dad asked her, "Was my daughter a good teacher? Did she kick your ass?" My old student immediately fell in love with my dad. His charisma got her. Just like it does everyone else.

Once my dad got out of the hospital, all of my brothers flew in. We were sitting in that family room of his American Dream home. The home that he worked for since he was a ten-year-old boy. The news was on as we talked over it. Trump was on Twitter again, this time with the proposed ban against transgender people in the military. My oldest brother, Tom, said, "I haven't turned on the news since the election. I just can't."

We all shared in the Trump-bashing a bit. The presidency does not belong to Trump, but to the people, we said. Things may only get uglier for our country, but we will recreate ourselves. We'll be the place where people come to dream. This may just have to be the crooked route we have to take to get there.

I wasn't sure if my dad was even listening. He sat in his faded corner of his brown leather sectional—rubbing the wooden floor lamp with his thumb as he always does. He was silent, his glasses nudged down his nose, taking a break from reading *A Life of Ulysses S. Grant*, which was folded open, hugging his belly.

Finally, I mustered up the balls to ask.

"Dad, do you regret voting for Trump?" He turned his stubborn, chubby face turned to me and, curling one side of his lip upward, he nodded.

DEMOLITION DERBY AND THE CHAUTAUQUA COUNTY POLITICAL MACHINE

JUSTIN KERN

Everyone honked as they drove by our house. This meant nearly everyone who drove through this part of Dunkirk, New York, was either "horny," "gay," or in agreement with epithets oddly singling out pilgrims.

At nine years old, I had only this information to go on, this statistically curious range of public sexual expression in my new hometown, based on the spray painted requests of passersby on the bodies of two demolition derby cars parked in our side yard. The cars were owned, eviscerated, and soon-to-be driven by my Uncle Paul and (unrelated) Uncle Buck, two laboring men who, like my dad, I admired much in my youth for the charisma of their rugged economics and coarse tongues.

It was 1989 and my first summer living in Dunkirk. My parents moved me and my two sisters there from suburban Dallas. Carrollton, Texas was certainly not like Dunkirk, an empathetic and tree-lined dichotomy, that probably saved my soul. But Dunkirk also didn't seem like New York, the place that was a planet in three letters—NYC—and from whence TV shows beamed; the place everyone expected when you say "New York". Dunkirk was a place where you lived across the street from your dad's childhood home, where his mom still lived, in the shadow of a hulking specialty metals manufacturer, and where your uncle and your fake uncle parked a demo derby car next to your house that, in no-missing-it red block letters, invited the rest of the city to "BLOW ME, PILGRIM."

Chautauqua County is one of two consistently Republican blocks in the Empire State, the rest of New York a call-it-by-9:00 p.m. shade of blue. (Cattaraugus County next door is its consistently red first cousin.) Gubernatorial candidates in the '80s and '00s were geographically correct in calling Chautauqua County part of Appalachia, though they meant it as a diss to titillate the tony people downstate.

Dunkirk, at around 10,000 people, is the second-largest municipality in Chautauqua County and named for another shorefront city in

France, the one of movies and World War II miracles. In Dunkirk, N.Y., industrial train tracks make for the fastest walking routes across the city's four wards. Marx and Engels name-dropped its factories once, I heard at a college party, and longtime Buffalo Bills play-by-play announcer Van Miller edges out Civil War veteran Thomas Horan and filmmaker H.B. Halicki as its most famous citizen. As far as those in or running for office on the nightly news, our household took the political stance of deriding them all while sometimes voting for who knows who.

The single annual event that brings people to Dunkirk each year is the Chautauqua County Fair and the biggest attraction at the fair is the demolition derby. It is a multiple night affair with preliminary heats leading up to a thunderous finale, plus special blocks for jalopy football, women drivers, or cars that are overly welded (my dad's specialty, being a welder and all).

Dunkirk has its own spin on the stinking and blinking of the American fairgrounds. Wafts of tangy Chiavetta's BBQ and savory smoke from a *pinchos* truck; carny dares in front of rickety games and total cow butthole in barns where farmers worked in ease. Polka bands and a bingo knockoff called "I Got It" for the *bushas*; a 4-H stand where I once stared at Gov. George Pataki unceremoniously inhaling a pale hot dog for a photo op before leaving town.

Into the grandstands, you'll find up to 2,000 demo derby fans, people rearing for smashed metal, fires, and burnt fuel, all that kicked up dust and mud. Hours of heats amplified by the dangerous rev of motors not meant to sustain certain levels of stupidity, punctuated with multiple fire truck horns at the flicker of flame. Rows of barking joy from the peanut gallery, with not-infrequent fights and spilled cups of Genny.

Those first years we went, I cheered simply at any smashing by my family and friends-called-family. Dad could never hold my interest in fixing up the 25-year-old cars that we inevitably drove around town, but with the demo he had me. It's easy to succumb to the freedom of being as loud as possible while you soaked up swears and clumsy *entendre* that had made it onto the demo cars.

A few years on, summer car preparation became a tactical matter. Junkers were hidden for months in cornfields and behind garages to avoid city zoning infractions. Spring meant shop bays reserved for cars pounded into place for repeat thrill rides. The paint jobs also got serious. Out were sleazy gags and lame shout-outs. Mom tapped the bliss of art school she couldn't finish on account of dropping out to have me.

She gave serious treatment to logos for Ford and Strike's Bar. Proudly, she covered one hood with a fiery orange-and-white rendition of Ghost Rider from a Mark Texeira cover she borrowed from my comic book stacks. Cars and driving in Texas felt all about intimidation and machismo. Everything blunt and no interest in other people. At the Dunkirk demo, there was group acceptance in destruction. We would gather to root on your neighbor's decision to gut his grandma's Pontiac, paint it purple, and drive it a lopsided 30 m.p.h. for a collision with a station wagon that just … won't … restart.

Could be we were all gormless hicks, an easy answer, if that's all we're after nowadays. Through the 1990s and early 2000s, the demo grandstands had plenty of rednecks from various body shops but also not a small number of adjunct professors from the state college up the street. Drunk cops off-duty, rowdy unionized teachers and boilermakers, cheering black families, hustling photographers from the right-wing hometown newspaper … a loose, yelling and joyous conglomeration of people, in a split-in-half political city surrounded by an island of Republican counties in a Democratic machine state.

A sliver of Donald Trump's potential to actually fucking win was in plain view in summer 2016 at the fair.

In my first trip back to the fair in about a decade, the typical political party booths and Pataki hot dog consumption had given way to a more splintered climate.

First was, a mixed bag of Libertarian ideologies sold at a fair stand as a party platform that was one part anti-Federal Reserve, another part pro-prepper, with random nods to the First Amendment, aliens, and pot. Really, this wasn't too surprising, at least judging proclivities of a few of my friends who had stuck around Dunkirk. In a city swatted back from the supposed gains of the rest of the country, it may have seemed downright foolish to stick with mainstream Albany and Washington, D.C. hucksters.

Next up was a longstanding suspicion of the Democratic frontrunner. In western New York, Hillary Clinton had already been the subject of special dismay from the empty promises of a Senate election. Incumbents were lousy enough. But a presumed incumbent so clearly using your placement on Lake Erie as their stepping stone? On demo cars, then, there was space reserved on rear bumpers—that best spot to beat and be beaten—for rival cars to "hit Hill." For sale in the expo hall were stickers with cartoon character Calvin pissing on the word "Clinton" (your preference which one, I suppose) next to more traditional cartoon urine targets like logos for Chevy or the Miami Dolphins.

And then there was Donald Trump. He might as well have sponsored the fair. His mirage bid for the Buffalo Bills and outsized television personality had cast a spell on enough locals to make an impact. For sale in the expo hall and midway were any number of memes-turned-shirts: a silhouette of Trump firing terrorists or illegal immigrants or Hillary Clinton. Next to POW-MIA and Confederate and Seneca Nation flags were red "Make America Great Again" designs. Heat after heat rolled out demo drivers who had carefully professed their allegiance to Trump on the untouchable tops of rickety Dodges and Toyotas.

My wife and I took this as an outlier. Dunkirk and Chautauqua County had been left to their own devices for too long, right? Sure, we had seen a bit of the same months prior in Texas, on a visit to those who have since retreated down South, including my mother and little sister's family. But the lawns of the Lone Star state lacked the enthusiasm they displayed during the Bush years. More, it seemed just a seething resentment that this would all drag into high school and Cowboys football season.

Back in Wisconsin, where I live, political problems are easily split along that common Midwest line between a blue city or two (Milwaukee and Madison, in our case) and the rest of the state. And so, in our sneaky cool lakefront Milwaukee neighborhood of Bay View, in a Democratic city that was once downright socialist decades ago, it was easy to insulate ourselves. Outside, far away, are the frothing right-wing rants of surrounding Waukesha and Ozaukee counties, two of the most stalwart GOP bastions in the U.S. With Joe McCarthy's witch hunt conservatism since shaken off, this part of Wisconsin conjures a particular electoral party champion, from Scott Walker to Paul Ryan to Reince Priebus to F. James Sensenbrenner. All cut from the same overtly political mold, echoing Ronald Reagan. As a result, election night in Milwaukee simply exacerbated the ultimately unsurprising chasm between those who heard what they wanted and those who hadn't heard all that had been happening.

By mid-2017 in Dunkirk, handfuls of locals were disappointed, already, in President Trump, whose rudimentary electoral map of course included

Chautauqua County but also bled across the center of the state. Pissy retired white guys at one of the two Polish Falcons clubs muttered about Trump both not getting a chance and not deserving one. Some people, like my mellowing father who followed the union line and voted for Clinton, have lost that freaked out election night edge. Even the treason or impeachment talk has softened. Outside decisions across the board. Mostly, a familiar feeling that has settled in—one where you're left to fend for yourself.

In the last few years, the pier has gotten prettier while the coal-burning power plant smack on the Lake Erie waterfront went dormant. Social club members stay buzzed on sign-in weekdays while no one still quite knows how to treat the ailing populace easily connected to painkillers. Delays plagued a promised pharmaceutical manufacturer, the first big potential project in 50 years outside of the Nestle factory's steady growth and a Saturn plant that never materialized. The mayor, Willy Rosas, became the first Hispanic mayor elected in the state, a nod to the city's long-present Puerto Rican population. One of the recent mayors, Richard Frey, died not too long after he was sentenced to six months of home confinement for federal wiretapping related to his use of campaign money.

When you've had working parents and family sent to prison for dealing drugs across the first Bush Administration and into Bill Clinton's, you learn different. If you've lived in Dunkirk, stuck around, left and came back, you're inevitably, confusingly suspicious. And if the result is a hodgepodge of political decisions out of step with the state or nation or big city one county away, so be it.

At the 2017 Chautauqua County Fair, the demolition derby may have hinted at a nadir more inevitable and deeper than politics. The nights of demo heats and side action were reduced to about four rounds. Patches of the stands were empty, according to my sister Barb, a creative lightning bolt who works in manufacturing logistics and had my wonderful nephew with her longtime electrician boyfriend whose presidential pick I never asked.

Turns out the heavy metal Imperials and Cutlasses are gone, and the primarily plastic Neons and Camrys hardly make for smash 'em up fun. With fewer icons of America's chrome automotive hubris left, there's a smaller bang for the drivers and the crowd. The chance to smash into your neighbor, and secretly tell off the ghosts of a too-big-to-fail car industry, fade from the rearview mirror you already ripped out as per demo heat regulations. Call power whatever you want when you hardly have any, for high-up decisions. Rather, go crashing through political norms and social expectations. Bash out the windshield of a Ford Country Squire, if you can find one without a lot of rust, and cover it with crass rhymes about the president or Plymouth Rock settlers or Ghost Rider before you speed it rear-end first into cheering public ruination.

MIDWESTERN BUBBLES

THE OTHER "FORGOTTEN PEOPLE": FEELING BLUE IN MISSOURI

SARAH KENDZIOR

In January 2016, shortly before the inauguration of Donald Trump, I was invited to a conference for people in the media and tech industries to discuss the future of news. Like every conference of this nature to which I've been invited, it was held in a city I could never afford to visit on my own, much less live—Palo Alto, California, where the average home sells for three million dollars. That would be two million, eight hundred and seventy thousand more than what the average home sells for where I live, in St. Louis, Missouri: a struggling, blue city in a once purple, suddenly bright red state.

I arrived at the conference anxious to share my concerns about the future of media under Trump: the role Russian propaganda had played in the election, the mainstreaming of white supremacists by the national press, the gutting of local papers that had steered so many to conspiracy sites as an alternative.

These concerns, while shared by some attendees, were mostly dismissed, since the prevailing belief in blue, wealthy, tech-savvy California was that somehow democracy would work itself out. Once in office, Trump would surely be checked and balanced, they told me; freedom of the press could not seriously be challenged, as it was a constitutional right. What they were really struggling with, they said, was how to better understand "the red state people"—those poor, exploited Midwesterners who had bought into Trump's fantasy and shocked the nation by propelling his win. Those poor, exploited Midwesterners who had somehow—according to the coastal publishers and tech gurus in attendance—all suddenly become white, male, conservative manual laborers.

It is a terrible thing to be in pain and ignored—as a place, as an individual. It is perhaps worse to finally be recognized, but only as a symbol—to be given a mask and told that it's your face.

This is what it has been like to be both a member of the national media and a citizen of the Midwest since Trump's win, as the coastal media views our long-ignored region through a narrow journalistic kaleidoscope, twisting and turning on the same images again and again until the view is utterly distorted. It is true that the national media—so disproportionately represented by the coasts that one out of every five journalists now lives in New York, Los Angeles or Washington DC—had long ignored the white, male, conservative manual laborers of the Midwest. But now, apparently, their plan was to ignore everyone else who lived there too: black, brown, Muslim and Jewish citizens; workers who toiled not in a field or plant but in a Walmart or a university; intellectuals and immigrants; and anyone else who was appalled at the election of Donald Trump. We lived in Trumpland now, we were told, and our blue city was an inconvenient island.

In some sense, this dynamic is not new. For decades, as national media consolidated on the coasts and regional papers died out, the Midwest got used to being ignored. The national media would show interest when there was a disaster—a tornado, a murder, an act of negligence so spectacular it would merit the occasional check-in (Flint still doesn't have water, by the way) or, in the case of 2016, a grotesque election. Now, due to surprising Republican wins in Michigan, Wisconsin, and Pennsylvania alongside more predictable wins in every state but Illinois and Minnesota, the Midwest was suddenly standing in as Trump's mandate.

This, of course, was a lie: the Midwest boasts an incredibly diverse array of citizens held together, perversely, by little other than a shared sense of neglect. We are not red or blue but mixed, purple like a bruise. But that wasn't the kind of pain or complexity the national press typically examines—not an individual level, where the ambiguity of lackluster choices propelled votes certainly as much as fanaticism; and not on a structural level, where the irregularities of our voting system have left the legitimacy of the election somewhat in doubt.

With a few exceptions, the national press was not interested in the gerrymandering that had plagued our states for decades, or the new voter ID laws that disenfranchised over 200,000 people in states like Wisconsin, where Trump won by a miniscule margin of roughly 20,000 votes. They were not particularly interested in *how* Trump won—that is, in structural barriers that challenge the narrative of ideological conformity within the Midwest—but in who Trump claimed as the "new winners" of his America, the "forgotten people" whom he claimed to have uniquely remembered. In order for the self-conscious coastal press to lay claim to Trump's narrative—to prove that they were not, as he claimed, the "media elite"—another group needed to be forgotten for Trump's "forgotten people" to shine.

And that group of "forgotten people" was the group who remain an inconvenience to everyone: the mostly liberal, often non-white residents of the Midwest's sprawling cities, where people are far more likely to work in the service industry than in the manufacturing fields Trump presented as the heart of the "real America". That heart was torn out decades ago, and while Trump was correct in identifying the pain of that economic loss and the social upheaval in its wake, he showed no understanding or even interest in our current plight.

And why would he? Blue city Midwesterners were, by and large, not his people. Blue city Midwesterners were, to his horror, his *protesters*—the people most likely to see through Trump's bullshit due to a lifetime spent navigating an abundance of bullshit in their midst; the people most likely to see Trump's autocratic policies not as horrifying fantasies, but as a federally instituted implementation of what they had witnessed on a local level for a very long time.

When Trump arrived in St. Louis for his first rally in March 2016, he was greeted by a large, ethnically diverse array of protesters, including members of long-standing citizen movements fighting for higher wages, LGBT rights, and, especially after Ferguson, an end to racist police brutality. Having suffered under local and state repressive policies, this was not a group of people who would take Donald Trump in stride, or dismiss him as a joke or a longshot. St. Louis was the first city to shut a Trump rally down, though Chicago got the credit after his appearance there was canceled hours later.

As the campaign wore on, and Trump's team began proposing a series of measures so autocratic that many pundits dismissed them as unfathomable, urban Missourians countered that this was indeed possible: Trump was merely a variant on what we had known. (You may recall we spent the bulk of November 2014 under martial law.) And life has only gotten worse for us since. The 2016 election turned the Missouri legislature overwhelmingly Republican, and they have passed policies so sadistic that outsiders often mistake them for a sick joke: *lowering* the hourly minimum wage from $10.00 to $7.70; being so racist the NAACP gave Missouri a travel warning and told black people not to visit; passing a law making it possible for your boss to fire you if he discovers you are taking birth control; being one of very few states to give private citizen voting data to the Trump administration under the pretense of countering "fraud", and so on.

Often thought of as an irrelevant backwater, Missouri is arguably a harbinger of America's brutal future under Trump. We are indeed the "Show-Me State", as in Trump says "Show Me" and our legislature of lackeys—in violation of basic democratic norms and laws—complies.

As I write this, the Trump administration is considering an array of policies that mirror those Missouri has managed to pass on a local level. These policies will disproportionately affect the red state voters about which he pretends to care. His tax plan will raise taxes most on households making $75,000 or under, meaning the bulk of states affected are in the Midwest or the South instead of the wealthier blue states on the coast. The possible repeal of Obamacare similarly hurts red state voters, who are poorer and more poorly served by their state governments in terms of receiving basic medical care than blue states. If net neutrality is eliminated, the vast rural stretches of the Midwest that are already denied affordable broadband access will find their prices raised even more, while Midwestern media—already gutted—may die out completely if fewer residents can afford to access it.

We are in an incredible amount of trouble out here in the red state of Missouri, and over the past year there have been an incredible number of protests in our blue cities—and even in our redder cities in the Ozarks, like Springfield—that reflect this anxiety. Missourians have protested against low wages, for women's rights, for immigrants' rights, for LGBT rights, for black rights, for a full investigation of the Russian interference scandal, for science, for healthcare, for tax transparency, and more. Indivisible and other new activist groups have joined an already robust protest and organizational infrastructure. This is a painful fight, as we watch our friends and neighbors lose their civil and economic rights, but it is one to which we are sadly accustomed.

But it is a fight that is scarcely covered by the national press. It was only after the neo-Nazi Charlottesville that the media began to consider that it wasn't "economic anxiety" that guided the Trump case after all. This is not to say that people in red states don't have economic anxiety—pretty much everyone does, given that the recession never really ended here. But that does not seem to be what attracts Trump's hardcore base—and furthermore, that hardcore base is not particularly representative of the electorate even in red states like Missouri. Trump's numbers sit as a record low, while protests against a sitting president occur, arguably, at a record high. That story remains largely untold in my state, along with the fear and determination that propels those attempting to hold the administration accountable.

In January 2016, in Palo Alto, an executive at a major media company asked me how to capture what's really going on in the red states. My answer was simple: "Hire locals," I said. "Don't send parachute journalists. Hire people who live there year-round, who know the system, who have a stake in what happens, who strangers will trust because they won't really be strangers."

He laughed. "But we can't do that," he said. "I mean, we need to hire intelligent people. We need people who know how to write."

I told him I lived in St Louis and smiled, and he blanched, perhaps because I had proven Missouri journalists are real, perhaps because he was startled I still had all my teeth. He then asked if I'd be interested in writing about "rural life" and I explained I lived in a metropolitan area of nearly three million people and he should find someone who actually lives in a rural area. He stared at me blankly, and I felt that familiar sense of rage—the rage, horribly, that Trump had tapped into, the rage of being condescended to and ignored.

That rage is still burning in Missouri, where, as usual, we in the blue cities have learned that we have to fight our own battles—because many of the people in the coastal blue states think we do not deserve support, and because our own state government holds us in contempt. We are fighting as much for conservative residents as we are for fellow progressives, as many structural injustices—economic inequality, healthcare, the right to free speech and media—affect everyone. We are fighting against what's coming, because for us—the blue voters in the red states, the other forgotten people of Trump's America—the grim future has already arrived.

"WE HAVE A GAY BAR HERE": YOU DON'T NEED A COAST TO BE COSMOPOLITAN

GREGGOR MATTSON and TORY SPARKS

"We have a gay bar here," the waitress informed me after I told her how impressed I was with the offerings in downtown Lima, Ohio. I hadn't even told her that I already knew. I was in town for the book project that had taken my research assistant Tory and me through twenty-seven states, interviewing gay bar professionals. I'd driven to this small city of under 40,000 souls for the express purpose of interviewing the manager of Somewhere, Lima's LGBT bar and club since 1982. At some point the bar stopped using its original name, "Somewhere in Time When Even the Moon is Not Enuff," before it was fictionalized in the Fox sitcom *Glee*, which introduced the world to a shinier, more musical Lima.

Gay bars are a marker of cosmopolitanism for small cities. They are the only physical places where LGBTQ people gather in public, and they serve multi-county regions of multiple states. Patrons of Fort Wayne, Indiana's, Babylon Nightclub, for example, told the drag queen who brought them on stage one evening that they'd driven from hometowns more than an hour away: Muncie, Indiana; Coldwater, Michigan; and Fort Shawnee, Ohio. Small-city gay bars like those in Lima or Ft. Wayne offer more than a night's entertainment or a place for patrons to be themselves. They are institutional histories of a region, a safer place to meet strangers, escape families, or bump into old friends or new lovers. And as the fictional depiction of a small-city bar in *Glee* should remind us, there are 147 small cities with a lone gay bar which, when added together, constitute as many gay bars as in New York, Los Angeles, and Chicago combined.

The Zone Dance Club is the hub of Northwest Pennsylvania's LGBT community and the last bar standing in Erie, which had three as recently as twenty years ago. The "world's smallest gay pride parade" that musters in the club's parking lot was featured in a popular 2011 podcast and a 2017 magazine article, leading the city's tourist office to launch a regional campaign advertising Erie as "your off-the-beaten-path gay-cation destination." A television spot, featuring The Zone, aired on Buffalo, New York-area televisions, promoting Erie's beaches, art galleries, and nightlife.

Though big-city journalists think gay bars are closing because of an influx of straight people, integrated nightlife is nothing new for Erie, explains DJ Joe Totleben. "We've always had lots of straight people here." This surprises some of the tourists who visit PA:

> Last year we had some boys up here from the South, where was it now? Georgia or someplace like that?—and they were just amazed! They said, 'down South the gay bars are gay bars and there's no straight people.' [Here] we've never had a problem. You could just say we've always been integrated.

Acceptance may have just brought integration to the big cities, but small Midwestern cities have been living an integrated life for 25 years. A straight woman showed her comfort in The Zone when she turned to my gay friend at the bar, told him he was a beautiful transgender woman, and stuck out her hand: "I'm your goodwill ambassador!"

Sure, LGBT-acceptance has meant that gays and lesbians have more choices in going out, as Joe explained: "These days our biggest competition are the straight bars in town. One of them has an outdoor bar in the alley between the buildings and they have block parties in it, and there's more gays there than here." Alex Sphon, President of the NW PA Pride Alliance disagreed: "LGBT culture is dying because of integration." Joe countered that the reason Erie's gay bars are failing isn't due to more choices, but fewer patrons: "Everyone isn't going out as much as they used to." This he attributes not to social attitudes, but economic realities: "The city's economy is in the toilet and has been, and when manufacturing left they never made any plans to do something different." Without money, people can't afford the $5 cover charge that helps keep the lights on.

The cost of doing business was also highlighted by Mary Green, owner of Sneakers in Jamestown, New York, in the far west of the state near Lake Chautauqua. "When we first opened, we were selling 12-ounce drafts three for a dollar, now a keg has gone from $30 to $80, and that's a lot of money. All the decent booze is $40, so you have to charge $4.50 and they can't really afford it, or they can only afford one." One of her patrons leaned forward to add, "The economy went to shit 10 years ago."

In post-industrial middle America, going out is an expensive option, and not an easily accessible one, either. While big cities boast extensive public transport systems, smaller cities face an obstacle completely unrelated to social attitudes: the drive. Club Icon is in Kenosha, Wisconsin, a bedroom community midway between Chicago and Milwaukee. An employee who declined to give his name attributed the bar's struggles to a changing car culture: "The kids today don't want to drive, whereas we couldn't wait to drive! We're in the middle of nowhere—we only wanted to drive! If you don't wanna drive you can't get here. Maybe they just don't want to drink. Things change. They could just be afraid of drunken driving." DUIs were cited as obstacles to patronage by other bar professionals, including the Lady LaTweet Weldon of The Velvet Room in Columbus, Georgia, and Derrick Nelson of Omaha Nebraska's The Max, the bar that describes itself as "America's Best Gay Nightclub." Take that, San Francisco!

BJ Hunt, the new owner of Kings & Queens Bar in Waterloo, Iowa, cited a combination of LGBT acceptance and car culture for the declining patronage in his bar:

> UNI (University of Northern Iowa) is in Cedar Falls. I think it's the drive here, basically. They have different areas—Downtown, College Hill and Main Street—where they can go out only a few blocks away. It's all on campus, walking distance, so they don't want to [drive] down here to drink. We have Uber now, that happened like a month ago, so we have a few more people coming in here. I guess it's not cool [for LGBT college students] to go to the gay bar anymore because all the other bars are more accepting.

One of the country's newest gay bars is using rideshare apps to address the decline of driving culture in the Fargo-Moorhead area. The Sanctuary Bar and Bistro of Kragnes Township, Minnesota, population 322, provides one free drink to patrons who show an Uber or Lyft receipt. Another owner, who spoke off the record, has no faith with the sharing economy, however: "there's been a couple of incidences where the Uber driver was a friend of the other bar that was open. 'I was just there, it's dead, why don't you go to this other place?' If Yellow Cab did that, no way! Uber's not regulated like that, so we don't Uber, we just call a cab."

Acceptance has opened new possibilities for some bars. Aut Bar of Ann Arbor Michigan runs print ads that promote their famous brunches, as co-owner Keith Orr explained: "Discover what gay Ann Arbor already knows—We put that in the straight press. We make it clear we're not a gay-friendly place, we're a *straight*-friendly place!" That a university town has a gay bar isn't surprising, although there are plenty of gown-towns that don't have any. What's surprising is that Aut Bar is the economic engine for one of the most innovative LGBT business models in the country, funding an adjacent community center and LGBT bookstore, one of the last dozen in the country. What started life as a Mexican restaurant for co-owner Martin Contreras' mother now anchors the "homoplex," a name coined by lesbian arts icon Michelle Tea. The buildings share a cozy paved courtyard under the canopy of a huge tree, its branches festooned with rainbow fairy lights spreading over cafe seating, a fire pit, and a sometime-outdoor stage.

Martin and Keith transformed the restaurant into Aut Bar because the existing gay bar was straight-owned, run-down, and wouldn't respond to the AIDS crisis. As Keith explained, "having seen so many friends and lovers succumb to AIDS, it became depressing that that was our only community space. That became one of the motivations for us to open a place. It wasn't just about being a bar, it was about being part of the community." As he continued, "I have said this for the 21 years we've been open, our mission statement is about serving the men and women of the gay community, their family and friends. Since day one." To people who claimed that Ann Arbor was so accepting that gay bars weren't needed anymore, Keith demurred: "the mission statement is about a safe space. People would look at me these last couple years, 'oh, isn't that quaint! Gays in the military and marriage equality—'safe space,' really? But since the November [2016] elections there's been a resurgence, 'Oh, we do need safe spaces, don't we!'" Both nodded somberly.

When asked if it was a business necessity to be straight friendly, Keith disagreed, explaining that what he and Martin wanted, and what a small city gay bar can be, were one and the same: "It was part of what we envisioned as sort of a modern day gay bar. Not just a men's bar, or a lesbian bar, or a suit bar, or a leather bar. Big cities have those, they have a huge community and can subdivide like that. We're just a little town and this is the gathering place for everybody." Being a bar for lesbian, bisexual, gay *and* transgender patrons meant welcoming their families and friends—the integrated acceptance for everybody that small-city gay bars have long embraced.

Being open for everybody is especially fraught for lesbian bars, however. Milwaukee, Wisconsin is home to Walker's Pint, owned by Bet-z Boenning for the last 16 years. It houses a world-class collection of funny bumper stickers and the wooden bar is adorned with brass plaques that remember each of the departed bartenders. Walker's Pint sits amid four other gay bars in the gay neighborhood of Walker's Point, facing a "boy bar" across the street with a "gentlemen's club" in the back.

For Bet-z, the secret to surviving the decimation of lesbian bars over the last 20 years is to welcome everybody, but only if they respect who the space is really for: "this will always be primarily a women's bar. This is a safe place for lesbians first, women second, and then everybody after that, but you can't kick out people that are going to support you." Her philosophy was innovative when she started the bar: "when I first started coming out, boys stuck to boy bars and girls with the girls." Upon opening, she walked across the street to the "boy bar," Fluid, and informed them: "'Just so you know my staff and I are going to come support your bar.' And we started doing a lot more together. Showing that we can work together for things, for charities, support each other's staff even though we are furthest away from each other on the spectrum as far as boy-boy vs. girl-girl. We should take care of each other." This philosophy informed how she treated her patrons, and insisted they treat others: "if women were being rude to men, I would say, 'You need to go, I'm just not dealing with it.' Basically, as long as everyone can respect one another and understand the mission is here women first, everyone's welcome as long as you're not douchey. So I think that really helps us to still stay here."

If Walker's Pint operates as a small bubble of "lesbians first, women second" in a national sea of gay boy bars, small city gay bars are often small blue bubbles in a sea of red. Jason Zeman, the owner of Iowa City's Studio 13, feels his bar excels because of this blue-bubble advantage:

> Iowa City has always been extremely liberal. I think the college is a big part of it. We have the second oldest gay pride in the country, it started a year after Stonewall, because a group of lesbians marched that next year with the university... Iowa City is very unique for the Midwest in this area, at least.

Small-city gay bar owners know each other across the miles, and they all acknowledge there is no one-size-fits-all business model. As Jason explained the difficulty of owning a gay bar in redder areas:

> I can see that being a challenge especially in a blue collar city like Cedar Rapids, it's completely different, it really is. I appreciate that. I feel bad for Pretty Belle [owner of Cedar Rapids' Belle's Basix] sometimes because it is such a different animal.

In some cities, like Cedar Rapids, the gay bar is the blue bubble, while in others, like Iowa City, the gay bar sits comfortably within a larger blue city.

Cedar Rapids didn't always have only one gay bar, but Belle's Basix is the last one standing. The bar has a down-home, homemade feel: nothing flashy, but a roomy drag performance area, a small shrine to the Chicago

Cubs, and a politically themed drink special called Moscow's Fool: "Stolichnaya Orange Vodka, Pussy Energy Drink, Mexican lime juice, ginger beer, and very simple syrup." As owner Pretty Belle, AKA Andy Harrison, explained, "We used to have like four or five gay bars back in the day. One catered to lesbians, one would cater to the leather crowd, one would cater to the twinks, [another for] the drag queens and all that stuff, and I miss that." Belle's Basix exemplifies the complex relationship between a small city's vision of itself and its gay bar. As the bartender who gave his name only as Damien explained:

> To a certain degree, we're the right-sized city to continue to support it. We're a small enough community where the gay community is exactly that: it's a community. For the most part if you're gay in Cedar Rapids, you know most of the people in the community—that's not the case in New York or Chicago— [but] not so small that it's closed-minded.

Belle's is the only place in town where you can get an after-hours HIV test, one of the many social service offerings found in gay bars that operate as much as community centers as businesses. As Pretty Belle says, "We're open every day. If there's a blizzard, we're open." Belle cut back on her drag performances because of the daily stresses of being the owner. "It's hard to perform and have a patron complaining 'oh, my girlfriend's here and she's gonna kick my ass!' Like, okay well, I'm performing right now! Just calm down! Or the bartender comes up, 'we're out of ones!' because people are tipping me ones."

As Damien continued, he could have been describing any number of small overlooked cities, little blue islands in the sea of the red Midwest:

> You'd never vacation here—nobody comes to Iowa for vacation. But it's a great city. You won't tear it down! But Iowa is wonderful: it's cheap, it's safe, it's quiet. For the asshole of America, it's kind of progressive.

If you find yourself in a small city with a gay bar, drop in. You'll be welcome, whoever you are. You might see a RuPaul's Drag Race celebrity: Alaska Thunderfuck 5000 got her start in The Zone of Erie, Sasha Belle at Studio 13 in Cedar Rapids. Tip your bartender, don't be shy about getting extra ones to tip the queens, and ask anyone you meet about their stories. You'll feel more worldly by the end of the night.

RACE AND KINDNESS IN YELLOW SPRINGS, OH
MARK REYNOLDS

Take Interstate 70 into Ohio to U.S. 68 South, and roll past the rural houses, the cheap gas, and Young's Jersey Dairy (which will be crowded), until you see a yellow banner stretched across what has just become Xenia Avenue. The banner says KIND NESS. No one quite knows how it got there; its twin stretches across Xenia Avenue on the other end of town. It seems to be part mantra, part code of conduct. This is how you know you've arrived in the Village of Yellow Springs.

The banner is above the crosswalk for the Little Miami Scenic Trail, a seventy-three-mile paved path that runs from Springfield through Yellow Springs, past the 1,000-acre Glen Helen Nature Preserve, all the way to just north of Cincinnati; locals ("Villagers") merely call it the bike path. Just past the crosswalk on the right is Ha Ha Pizza, where pizza has been available on wheat crust since the '70s. Across the street from Ha Ha's is a Subway, the only national retail place in downtown Yellow Springs (unless you count the Speedway and the US Bank); there's a sign in front of one of the numerous downtown gift shops that says "Friends don't let friends shop chain stores."

Ha Ha's shares a building with a store that sells t-shirts, incense and various other stuff you'd expect to find in a Summer of Love time capsule. Around the corner is a mini-arts district of galleries and craft boutiques. Across the street is the town dive bar, next to the dive bar is a comic book shop, next to that is an antique shop, and down the street in the other direction is a bike shop. There are almost as many coffeehouses (three) as traffic lights (five) in town.

Every Saturday at noon, a group of people stands at Xenia and Limestone Avenues, across from the Mills Park Hotel (a recent addition, verandah and all) waving a purple flag of the earth and asking people to honk for peace. Back when the Standing Rock protests were at their peak, they had #NODAPL signs. Sometimes their signs say Black Lives Matter; none of the people are black.

And on this or any other picture-perfect summer Saturday, motorcycles from wherever are rolling down the street and the sidewalks are busy with people from wherever hanging out, people who don't live here but come on the weekend to walk around and check the place out, and maybe buy something and catch a taste of culture and lifestyle that they won't see anywhere else in southwestern Ohio between Columbus and Cincinnati, except maybe in the hipper parts of Dayton. (Some residents prefer to steer clear of downtown when the tourists invade.)

Truly, Yellow Springs is a different kind of place. It's garnered accolades galore: Coolest Small Town; Best of the Road Most Fun Town; Most Amazing Place in the Midwest to Retire; and more. It is entirely possible to spend a week or an hour there and fall in love with the coolness, the quiet, the vibe. You could take in all the offerings from shop to shop, or the Prince mural in the alley behind the Xenia Avenue businesses, or the eclectic housing stock of improvised add-ons, works of art and McMansions (those are on the south end of town, an area some call "the suburbs"), and come to feel that you're in a bubble. A precious, cozy little bubble, where not only time but attitudes remain rooted in a post-hippie aesthetic, both cultural and political. A bubble where the mean old outside world, with its relative lack of progressive trappings-per-capita and abundance of fast-food joints, does not exist. A bubble where the name Donald Trump is hardly ever uttered unless accompanied by hand-wringing, or obscenities, or both. Yes, you could get lost inside that bubble, and not mind it one single bit.

But bubbles can be deceptively seductive places. Beyond the bubble, life is markedly different. The area surrounding Yellow Springs— nondescript towns like Fairborn, Clifton and Xenia—is considerably further downscale. The opioid crisis looms over those landscapes, partly a result of the utter lack of economic opportunity. Nearby is Wright-Patterson Air Force Base, whose only real connection to Yellow Springs is through the town's exemplary school system, which attracts numerous families with young children (which, in its way, has driven up housing prices far beyond most neighboring towns and 'burbs). It all adds up: while Yellow Springs (population 3,500) voted 89 percent for Hillary Clinton, the rest of Greene County voted 64 percent for Trump.

As you might expect with numbers like that, villagers walked around in a collective fog after the election. But Yellow Springs soon recovered its post-hippie swagger, and redoubled the will to maintain its quirky progressivism. Most helpful to that effort was a swiftly arranged live broadcast at the movie theater of the post-election *Saturday Night Live* hosted by Dave Chappelle, the town's most famous resident.

But not long after the election, that deceptively seductive blue bubble was pierced—from within.

Like in Times Square, Yellow Springs drops a ball at midnight to ring in the New Year. But seeing as how there are no skyscrapers there, the ball descends from atop the hardware store in the middle of downtown. It's a pleasant event that draws folks from around the area; no other nearby town does anything special for New Year's Eve.

Most years, the event is pretty laid-back, like Yellow Springs itself, and the street is clear by about 12:30 or so. But not at the dawn of 2017. For some reason, police cruisers began blaring sirens and pinching off Xenia Avenue from opposite directions at 12:08, causing mass confusion in a two-block area. The noise was deafening, children were scared. No one could understand why this was happening, since the crowd would have dispersed peaceably on their own with limited nudging, just as they'd always done. They also couldn't understand why police cruisers were showing up from surrounding jurisdictions.

At one point, a black man ran up to one of the cruisers, banging on the door to get the (white) police officer's attention. For his efforts at trying to extract some sense from the madness, he ended up in a wrestling match with the officer and almost got tased. And then he was arrested, charged with felony obstruction and an additional misdemeanor (a Village Council representative, a seventy-two-year-old white woman, was later charged with two misdemeanors).

The taser got lost amidst the ruckus, which went on for almost an hour. But the damage had been done. Idyllic, quirky Yellow Springs had its very own police misconduct crisis, taking its place among the Chicagos, Clevelands, and Baltimores of the nation.

Three nights later, villagers and TV stations packed the community center for a quickly-called Village Council meeting. The meeting began with the announcement of the police chief falling on his sword (he was not on duty during the incident) and tendering his resignation. That did not appease the dozens of people who gave impassioned statements decrying the behavior of the police. Some even went so far, this being Yellow Springs and all that, as to call for the total disarming of the police and reorientation of them as "peace officers."

But there was another current running through the comments. Residents gave accounts of previous aggressive policing in recent years. Some became emotional in recounting what had happened to a loved one. Villagers had been troubled by an increasingly non-Yellow Spring-sian tenor to the police, and the town's Human Relations Commission had attempted to mediate concerns throughout 2016, but not until the New Year's Eve incident did the concerns become a front-and-center issue for the village.

And that's not all that blew up. Many of those on the business end of hard policing were young people of color, who felt themselves sin-gled out and targeted. Their concerns, as it turned out, went insidiously deeper than just bad encounters with the law.

Two weeks later, at the village's annual Martin Luther King, Jr. Day commemoration (a silent march through town, culminating in a choir concert), a black middle school student read her prize-winning essay, or at least did her best to make her way through it. She recounted the way some of her classmates treated her, calling her "monkey" and making other references to how they thought people who looked like her resembled animals. She was too overcome by the hurtfulness of the scene to finish the essay; someone else finished reading it for her. The audience, appalled by the events she described and moved by her courage to describe them, gave her a standing ovation.

But even that would not be the end of it. Later that afternoon, sev-eral young people met with a *New York Times* reporter to talk about their experiences. The reporter had ties to Yellow Springs, and found out about the New Year's Eve incident via a Facebook friend. The stu-dents told him about their treatment across the town, by shopkeepers as well as police and classmates. They described a sense of being in-visible, which would seem to be hard to happen in a place this small. They were accompanied by members of The 365 Project, a local group working to address racial relations and understandings in the village.

That such a group would be necessary seems at odds with Yellow Springs' bonafides. The town was founded in a spirit of early 19th Cen-tury progressivism (and also tourism even then, as the town's name-sake water supply drew folks from miles around in search of its healing qualities). To this day, there is a remarkable diversity of faith commu-nities, from traditional religions to Baha'i, Buddhist. and Quaker; the only place of worship missing is a mosque. Horace Mann chose Yellow Springs as the home of the pioneering college he envisioned, settling Antioch College there in 1852. Ever since then, Antioch's progressive bent (first to allow women to present their academic work, first to hire women as faculty, and many other achievements) went hand-in-hand with Yellow Springs' essential self-definition as a place where all were welcome.

Except when they weren't. After World War II, blacks working at the Air Force base and other neighboring companies found it hard to find places to live in Yellow Springs. Eventually a new housing development, a cul-de-sac of ranch houses known as Omar Circle, became the village's first black neighborhood. In the '60s, a major conflagration ensued after a white barber refused to cut a black man's hair, claiming he didn't know how; eventually the barber closed his shop.

Despite these incidents, Yellow Springs maintained its reputation as a tolerant community, with a healthy population of black professionals, educators and business owners. Two churches, First Baptist and Central Chapel A.M.E, served them. The police chief in the '70s and '80s was a still-beloved black man; a street bears his name as an honorific.

But as housing prices started rising in the '90s and '00s, many blacks found themselves priced out of the market and moved out, and other blacks did not move in to replace them. From a peak of about 30 percent, today Yellow Springs' population is around 12 percent black (and affordable housing remains a challenge).

And in those intervening years, many blacks came to see the kindness and tolerance Yellow Springs espouses as, if not a lie, then at least a platitude that masked the complicated realities of living inside a deceptively seductive blue bubble that, even if it's nowhere near the mainstream, is hardly immune from any of the issues bedeviling America. Thus, they were not surprised by the February 5, 2017 *Times* headline: "A Small Ohio Town Tries to Curb Aggressive Policing." They were not surprised by the accounts of young black people in the article. And, presumably, they were not surprised by the responses of white residents, which can easily be summarized as "We know we have to do better."

For white villagers, the moment became something of an existential crisis. Attendees at a Village Council meeting in March sat raptly as a report on the New Year's Eve incident, damning the conduct of the police, was read into the public record (Chappelle was there; his comments towards the end went viral). Around that time, the town newspaper ran a series of articles about the nature of local policing—and was called to task by one letter-writer for not having any blacks on its reporting team.

But in time, the tension dissipated, at least visibly. A new police chief was hired, by all accounts inclined to a community policing approach more in line with civic values. The charges against the black man and the white council member were eventually dropped. Life didn't get perfect for aggrieved young people of color, but at least the truth was out in the open. Later in the year, a book club was announced; its text was Shelly Tochluk's *Witnessing Whiteness: The Need to Talk about Race and How to Do It*.

Thus was Yellow Springs able to breathe easier, the resilience of its values having carried the day once again. But the cozy blue bubble would soon be pierced again, this time by strangers in its midst.

Antioch College has a legacy of incubating activists, change agents, and assorted rabble-rousers; Coretta Scott King and Congresswoman Eleanor Holmes Norton are among its alumna (Coretta's husband gave the commencement address in 1965). Students have historically lent their time and energy to fighting the powers that be; those ranks include Michael Schwerner and Andrew Goodman, two of the three civil rights workers infamously killed in Philadelphia, Mississippi in 1964 for trying to register black people to vote.

So it was not particularly surprising that three Antioch students went to Charlottesville, VA in the summer of 2017 to counter-protest the "Unite the Right" march. Word got out that they had been there, and they were interviewed by the local news.

Perhaps it was that flash of notoriety, or Antioch's historic reputation, or both, or something else entirely, that prompted someone to paste racist leaflets on stop signs around town.

The only previous defacement of signs was by someone who scribbled "Trump" under the printed "Stop" on several signs across town; the public works department was none too pleased by the graffiti, but months later the signs were still there, and some folks considered them cute. This incident was different, and not cute at all.

Sometime on a late August 2017 day, several stop signs had been adorned with flyers touting Identity Europa and the National Vanguard, two of the groups who descended upon Charlottesville. They bore messages like "Serve Your People" and "Protect the Family: Reject Degeneracy," and images of Greek statues. *The Mockingbird* blog reported that later that day, other fliers were posted on downtown buildings, coincidentally on buildings where folks were meeting to discuss the acts.

On the same day, someone saw a pick-up truck bearing stickers for the West Ohio Minutemen parked in the grocery store lot.

This had people wondering: was the alt-right about to start it up here? Could Yellow Springs be the next Charlottesville?

For their part, a Minuteman leader denied his group's responsibility for the fliers. No one came forward with an explanation. There was no further sighting of any such propaganda, and the whole thing had receded back outside the bubble by the end of the week. If the intent was to recruit people from Antioch or Yellow Springs to the alt-right cause, the perpetuators clearly did not do their homework.

But the incident served as a reminder that Yellow Springs is not surrounded by a moat or a concrete wall. The environs beyond the village boundaries can be treacherous; ask the students at predominantly black Central State University, just down the road in the isolated hamlet of Wilberforce, about the last time they saw Klan activity near campus. The sense for people of color has always been: Yellow Springs may be cool, but be careful after dark on the back roads.

Indeed, venturing into Xenia or Fairborn is like going into another world. Xenia's the county seat, yet there's no downtown to speak of beyond the county buildings, a new eatery or two, and various pawn shops and cheap retail. Fairborn isn't much better, except for the Kroger superstore near I-675. The people in those and the other nearby towns may be as decent as any, but the tenor of those locales is anything but idyllic and quirky.

The nearest sign of economic life outside of Yellow Springs is the sprawling bastion of Mallified America along both sides of Fairfield Road in Beavercreek, an exurb between Yellow Springs and Dayton—and the site of the Walmart where John Crawford, a black shopper, was killed by police in 2014 for holding an air rifle on sale in the store (villagers and Antioch folks joined Crawford's family in a vigil at the store in 2017 to note the third anniversary of the murder).

Given all that, it's no wonder Yellow Springs becomes a tourist town on the weekends (and especially during its Street Fairs in the spring and fall). If you want to people-watch the folks with their eccentric hairstyles and fashions, or admire the shops with their original artworks for sale, or have anything approaching a beyond-the-Southwestern-Ohio-norm cultural experience, this is where you venture. The harsh extremes of the broader world will not intrude upon your pleasant day trip into post-hippie kumbaya and commerce.

And if you have any leftish or countercultural leanings at all, this is the only place for miles in any direction where you feel like you can breathe.

The end of that picture-perfect summer Saturday took me back down Xenia Avenue, to pick up a few things at the store. One of the local jewelers spotted me across the street, and we shouted a quick chat at each other before the traffic picked back up. The street was still busy, with diners filling up the restaurant patios. That night, I sat on the front stoop of my domicile, and enjoyed the calmness and quiet. The deer weren't walking about, just the neighborhood black cat across the street. No existential angst about the fate of society, at least not outwardly. Just another serene and charming day, just like so many others there.

Yes, Yellow Springs, for all its faults and vulnerabilities, is a deceptively seductive blue bubble, and many villagers are proud about it. And yes, the world outside it is scary, and sometimes the world inside it can be scary too. But when the leaves change color in the fall it's glorious, and no one much thinks about the mean old outside world lurking just beyond the mysterious KIND NESS banners.

FIBS AND CHEESEHEADS, FROM CHICAGO TO CHETEK.
BILL SAVAGE

I first heard the term "FIB" while tending bar on the north side of Chicago in the late 1980s. A few regulars had returned from a fishing trip to some obscure lake town in northwest Wisconsin, and were regaling each other, and everyone else in the place, with epic bullshit tales of huge fish caught during the day and vast quantities of beer downed by night.

The fish stories I doubted; the beer tales I believed. I'd seen it often enough.

One complained that he didn't like the attitude those Cheesehead bartenders had about FIBs.

"FIBs?" I asked.

"Fucking Illinois Bastards," another responded.

A third chimed in, "Yeah, they don't like us much, but they need our money. We don't go up there and spend it, their towns die. They know it and they resent it."

A few years later, I became one of those FIBs, in that very same obscure town.

In 1992, my mother and my stepfather, Jerry, bought a cabin on the narrows of Pokegama Lake, in Chetek, Wisconsin. It's common for Chicagoans to have such getaways. North-siders tend to go to Wisconsin, south-siders to Michigan, which makes sense: when you're trying to get out of the city, you don't want to drive all the way across it first.

My stepfather's Aunt Hattie and Uncle George had owned a place on a small island in Chetek since the 1950s, and Jerry had been visiting since then, to snowmobile in the winter and fish in the summer. My mom loved the area, but not so much the need to boat on and off the island, so they bought on the mainland.

The Cabin, as it was inevitably called, had been built by a carpenter who lived in the northwest suburbs. Tucked between two small resorts and a handful of other seasonal buildings, it had two bedrooms, a kitchen/common room, and a screened-in sleeping porch. Out back, a fish house to clean the day's catch, and a small pond. In front, a wood pile and a fire ring with a grill.

A three-season place, the cabin had to be shut down for the winter and reopened each spring, and for fifteen years I was part of that opening and closing crew, along with Jerry's nephew Marty and sometimes his son, Marty Joe. For fifteen years, I travelled north in late spring and again in autumn. The interstate to Eau Claire, then about an hour north on US-53 to Exit 126, County SS into Chetek's main business strip, 2nd Street. Drive through town, over the New Bridge, into farmland for a half mile or so, then right down a side road over a slough, then left to a driveway paved in pine needles. The pond's frogs provided a welcoming chorus when I pulled in around dusk.

My mother and Jerry, and other family, used it all season, but I only ever came for opening and closing. (I'm not a fan of the mosquitos and jet skis that dominate much of the summer.) After the first year, we honed our work systems, and closing and opening took just a few hours of the three-day weekend we insisted we needed to properly do the job. The rest of the time, Jerry and the guys fished, I sat around reading, or went for bike rides. At night we ate what they caught—or Jerry's world-class chili or gumbo—and sat around the fire pit with drinks: Manhattans prepared by ancient family recipe for them, beers for me. We'd watch the wildlife, muskrat and deer, owls and bats, occasionally a bald eagle. On clear nights, the Milky Way, and once, the brilliant green Aurora Borealis. We'd critique each other's fire-building skills and talk about the Cubs or Bears or family stuff.

Over the years, I came to love Chetek and look forward to the seasonal trips as markers of the year's progress, seeing familiar faces and places. The people at the bait shop, the bakery, the diner, and the bar were all friendly. It's not like we became real locals, though Jerry and Marty did subscribe for years to the *Chetek Alert*, the weekly newspaper, to keep up on events in the off-season. When I was there, I sometimes drove as far as Rice Lake or back to Eau Claire to get the *New York Times*. I had to have my crossword puzzle fix, and liberal op-eds.

Which might have made me stand out had I gotten to know any Chetekers better.

Chetek is in Barron County. In the 2016 election, 169 people there voted for Jill Stein, and 726 for Gary Johnson. Hillary Clinton got 7,881 votes. Trump won big, with 13,595 votes, 60.4 percent of the total ballots cast. In Chetek itself, Stein got 6 votes, Johnson 22, Clinton 375, and Trump 650.

Jerry and my mother sold the cabin in 2006, as her health was deteriorating, and the lung condition that would eventually take her life could not tolerate the campfire smoke and pollen count. After she passed in 2008, Jerry and Marty and I did our best to get up there at least once a year anyway, staying at the resorts we used to drive past. Our last visit was mid-May in 2016.

As I pedaled my bike through town and out to Dallas—a small hamlet ten miles away with a fine microbrewery, Valkyrie Brewing Company—I noticed lots of Trump yard signs, a few for Cruz, and zip for Clinton. I pondered the relationship between this rural and Republican place and my urban and liberal point of view.

I knew about the economic stuff. Whenever I visited, I made it a point to spend money in Chetek, to keep the local economy going. I gassed up for the drive back at the Lakeland Co-op rather than the BP station. I always bought presents at the consignment store, which consistently offered great jewelry, sports paraphernalia, and Wisconsin kitsch. When the local historical society opened a small museum, I happily paid my entry, left a donation, and bought a t-shirt memorializing the wooden "Chetek Boats" that were manufactured in town for a few decades. I'd bring the seedless rye and the M&M cookies from Chetek Bakery back to friends, and I always loaded up on postcards at the one bait shop that sold them.

These postcards were like a time capsule from the past. Except for some depicting the New Bridge, they could be anywhere in the state, featuring generic Wisconsin scenes or gags—deer in a meadow, astonished fishermen landing a bass bigger than their boat. CHETEK WISCONSIN was embossed on the front image, and I pictured salesmen selling the same cards in other small towns, other names stamped on the same images.

I sent these postcards back to friends and family all over the world, but mostly in Chicago. Like FIBs, big cities subsidize rural parts of their states with the tax dollars generated by their larger and more dynamic economies. Despite the fact that rural white folks in the Midwest seem to vote against government and taxes, they get more back than they pay. A recent study in Illinois showed that the urban counties around Chicago got 80 cents back from Springfield for every dollar sent there, while some rural counties got more than two dollars back. I suspect the same dynamic takes place in Wisconsin.

That's structural, but the personal matters too. While I'd been coming to Chetek for decades, it'd be a lie to say I'd really gotten to know anyone there beyond the shallowest acquaintance. The servers at Bob's Grill, where we usually came into town for breakfast, changed year by year. I did frequent Mary's Pub, where I liked to sit and write my postcards in the mid-afternoon. Mary was usually there, and over the years she remembered me, and would comment on what she called my "notes" as she served me a $1.25 Leinenkugel or, more recently, a $2 New Glarus Spotted Cow.

Jerry had a different experience. He spent much more time there, and got to know lots of people just going about the business of having a cabin with a boat. Every spring, the dock had to be re-set after the ice cleared. Every fall, the boat had to be put in storage for the winter. Buildings and vehicles had to be maintained or repaired, and so the hardware store was a frequent stop. And you have to eat, so he was well known at Chetek Bakery and various grocery stores.

These relationships start out as economic, part of the cash nexus that lets FIB money flow into Cheesehead bank accounts. But people are people, and friendships inevitably happen. The owner of the resort to our north kept an eye on the cabin when it was empty, and when Jerry's sister was there alone, as a break during chemo treatments, he watched extra close, and alerted the local paramedics that she was there, just in case she needed emergency assistance. Guys at marinas would put a repair Jerry needed to the front of the line, knowing he might only be in town for the weekend—but also because they'd gotten to know each other over decades. Once, Jerry needed a small part to repair a water ski, and it would take a week or more for it to arrive. The mechanics took the part off their display model, knowing that the grandkids were only visiting for the weekend and it'd be a shame if they couldn't get some skiing in.

These were some of the stories told around that fire, but there were no Chetekers sitting there with us. We might have been in Chetek, but we were not of Chetek.

When it was time to sell the cabin, Jerry never formally put it on the market. As he brought the boat to its winter storage spot, he mentioned to the guy renting him the space that they were probably going to sell soon. Word travelled through the grapevine to the grandson of the carpenter who built the cabin and sold it to Jerry. The young man hadn't been able to afford it then, but he could now, and so the cabin returned to its family of origin. A very small-town transaction with folks from the big city, a bit of a karmic subsidy.

Current political debates about red state/blue city identity politics often revolve around the question of bubbles. Are liberal "elites" in big cities somehow unable to see or imagine the concerns of "real" Americans in small rural towns? Or are those red state Americans disconnected from political and economic realities, not to mention urban diversity and progressive ideas that would actually help them?

Everyone lives in some bubble or another, but the ongoing re-lationships people develop in resort towns like Chetek can perhaps pierce them a bit.

Contemplating my experiences in Chetek, I recall how damn hard people worked. Everyone seemed to have multiple jobs. At shift change, the bartenders were all either coming from their other job, or leaving to go to it. Folks I met at Mary's had day jobs with the county or some of the remaining light industry in Rice Lake or Eau Claire, but also rented cabins to FIBs like me, or stored boats over the winter, or worked as fishing or hunting guides, or repaired cars out of their homes, or did house-cleaning for resorts they didn't own or stay at. This seems not unlike the growing "gig economy" that post-industrial urban Ameri-cans are being trapped in. But that's a political reality still very much working itself out, some yet-to-be articulated experience blue city and red state people might share.

Chetek also is connected to the American political divide in two other ways, one historical and kind of comical, the other contemporary and deadly serious.

At Bob's Grill, there's a funny connection to the Cold War and the origins of the space race, back when most Americans agreed that Russia was not on our side. While the United States was inspired by the Soviet launch of Sputnik to increase spending on science and education, one citizen of Chetek had another response, the "Spudnik." As their menu recounts: "In October 1957, the Soviet Union stunned the world and set opened [sic] the 'Space Race' when they put Sputnik I into orbit. [Own-er] Gert Pabich decided to boost America's spirits in the fall of 1957 by launching the Spudnik. The potato based donut-hole was born and has been a part of Bob's fare for near 70 years." The English prof in me loves the perhaps-unconscious poetry of "boosted," as in rocket boosters and raised spirits both. I cannot speak for all of America, but Spudniks have certainly boosted my spirits more than once, along with Bob's pancakes and sausage links. This, I sometimes thought, was hilarious: a small-town diner responds to an event of vast geopolitical significance with . . . a high-calorie food item. Hatred of the Soviets, and love of sweets, united Americans, at least in 1957. Nowadays, maybe not so much.

More recent visits have involved other manifestations of red/blue political divisions over energy policy and environmentalism. The post-glacial geology of Barron County includes significant deposits of the silica sands required for fracking in oil fields from the Great Plains to Canada. Some local farmers sold their land to multinational corporate mining interests, which moved in to extract this resource. Disused rail lines were put back in service, and new sidings built. What had been a bucolic countryside now hosts vast industrial sites, and the road between Chetek and New Auburn, County SS, handles massive truck traffic. Whether locals in Chetek support fracking in the abstract—Drill, baby, drill!—plenty of people I overheard in the bar were not happy with this transformation in their landscape. So much of the local economy is based on people coming there to hunt or fish, and giant mountains of freshly mined sand, along with trains and trucks, all visible from the highway into town, wouldn't appeal to nature lovers, FIBs or otherwise.

Of course, the counter-argument is classic contemporary conservative "philosophy": the farmers who sold to the silica miners could do any damn thing they wanted with the land they owned. Private property rights matter more than any common good or shared ill. I wouldn't claim to know anyone's particular opinion about climate change, but it seems that climate change denialism and love of private property rights correlate closely, and always on the red side of the argument. But, as many have said and written, Republicans can ignore the facts, but the facts won't ignore them. On May 16, 2017, an EF-3 tornado struck Chetek, killing one, injuring 27, and leaving dozens of families homeless. The tornado's path was the longest single tornado track in Wisconsin history. Not Harvey or Irma, but perhaps another extreme weather event with some global warming behind it. But when Chetekers talk climate, I just write my postcards.

In the twenty-five years I've travelled from Chicago to Chetek, I've seen many changes, one of which speaks to the distance between locals and out-of-towners. The old bypass off I-90 onto US 53 in Eau Claire got so built up with malls, super stores, and stoplights that the state built a bypass around the bypass. So much of America's infrastructure (literal highways and informational ones) is designed to allow swift passage through the landscape (natural or political) without any direct contact between traveler and local. Whether my Chicago family's long-term connection to Chetek will ever add up to anything is an open question. But one thing is for sure: as much as I depend on, and love, Chetek for recreation and connection to nature, Chetek depends on the likes of me, and my tax dollars, to survive at all. Like it or not, we are all connected.

LOOKING TO THE FUTURE

WHEN ICE COMES TO TOWN: LESSONS IN RESISTANCE FROM ELKHART, INDIANA

SYDNEY BOLES and ROWAN LYNAM

In Pembroke, Illinois, it started in Hopkins Park; in Gary, it started right across the street from their small airport; in Crete, it was Balmoral Park. In Elkhart, Indiana, it started at the intersection of county roads 7 and 26. It was a stretch of weeds and snow next to the county's correctional facility and its huge, methane-leaking landfill, catty-corner from the well-worked farmland of German immigrants.

This unremarkable piece of nowhere, Indiana would have held over a thousand immigrants in ICE civil detention. They would have been held in a private, maximum-security facility with the capability to hold 60 in solitary confinement, encased in a total visual barrier.

Would have—because Elkhart, like so many Chicagoland towns before it, said no.

CoreCivic Comes to Town

Civil immigration detention in the U.S. is growing. Since President Donald Trump's directive to Immigration and Customs Enforcement to round up and deport undocumented immigrants regardless of priority status, federal agencies and private prison companies alike have been preparing for a capacity expansion of nearly 10,000.

The Midwest is a primary target for that expansion.

The region lacks any private detention facilities, instead splitting its immigration detention capacity between several county jails that have contracts with ICE. The country's two major for-profit detention players, CoreCivic (formerly Corrections Corporation of America) and The GEO Group, have been struggling to change that since 2012, when CoreCivic set its sights on Crete, Illinois.

CoreCivic has withdrawn its proposals for immigration detention centers time and time again over the past six years, but it has continued to search for a home in the greater Chicago region. In Gary, Indiana, there was a riotous anti-deportation campaign, and the proposal never came to fruition.

But this time, in Elkhart, CoreCivic was seeking to open a detention center securely in "Trump Country." A full two hours' drive from Chicago, this county voted 68 percent for the President and seemed far away from the coalescing immigrant and labor forces to the west.

Evidently, it wasn't far enough.

An unlikely pair lead the Coalition Against the Elkhart County Immigrant Detention Center, which formed immediately following CoreCivic's proposal. Richard Aguirre, a fiftysomething professor at the local Mennonite university and longtime progressive activist, is a mustachioed Mr. Rogers type, soft-spoken and thoughtful. Marbella Chavez, 22, came back to her hometown specifically for this fight, having grown into activism at college in Bloomington. The two organized a consciousness-raising event at the Concord Junior High School cafeteria on December 14, 2017, where about 300 people, bundled in coats and scarves, made their way over a parking lot slick with black ice to attend.

The cafetorium, as it would be affectionately introduced by the superintendent, was packed with rows of green plastic chairs crowded with coats slung over the backs. Residents reached across rows to shake the hands of people they recognized from neighboring counties or church congregations. Nervous energy buzzed in the room. A single person brought a poster-board sign: "Immigrants make America great."

Aguirre waited with a soft smile in front of the projector, an image of the Statue of Liberty behind bars casting bright yellow and blue light on his face. The light caught his round glasses so you couldn't quite see his eyes. It was time to start.

The City With a Heart

Elkhart is a city of 60,000 with a bustling main street and picturesque river views. It's called both the "RV capital of the world" and the "City with a heart." Bordering the snowy downtown streets, standing almost as a symbol of midwestern determination in the face of economic struggle, is a 25-foot-tall traveling statue of Grant Wood's *American Gothic*. The resolute couple stands, pitchfork and suitcase at the ready, staring out over Elkhart as snow once again begins to fall. They will remain with Elkhart as silent, colossal watchers until February 2018, when they will continue on their midwestern journey.

This is a city on the mend, bouncing back from the 2008 economic crash that left the RV industry in tatters and Elkhart with the highest unemployment rate in the state, at nearly 20 percent. Now unemployment hovers around 2 percent, a number economists deem well above full employment. In other words, most people who want a job can find one.

County Commissioner Mike Yoder, a centrist Republican torn between his Trump-voting constituency and his own track record of supporting immigration reform, is one of three commissioners who would have voted for or against the detention center. Once the CoreCivic proposal got approval from a zoning board, Yoder and his two fellow commissioners, Suzanne Weirick and Frank Lucchese, would have voted the final yes or no. It was towards these three local politicians that the coalition directed their substantial activism.

He was the only commissioner who showed up.

The point of the event, Chavez would say later, was to make opposition to the facility easy to spread from neighbor to neighbor. "You can't really mobilize people to do something if they're not informed about it," she said.

It was a tactic Chavez learned from Black Lives Matter events at the University of Indiana. After the 2016 death of her uncle at the hands of the Oklahoma City Police, Chavez learned how affirming it could be to stand up in front of a crowd and tell her story.

Just over five feet tall with bright eyes, Chavez spoke with a practiced calm. The eldest of four children born to Mexican immigrants, she grew up translating for her parents at doctors appointments, school meetings and immigration proceedings. When her family moved from Chicago to Elkhart 12 years ago, neighbors spray-painted racist slurs on the family car within weeks, she said.

But the racism she experienced didn't keep Chavez from believing in Elkhart. "The number of people who are supportive of Latinos and immigrants coming to the community far outweighs the number of people who are resentful of us," she said.

"I think they [CoreCivic] hope that our momentum dies down," Chavez told the audience, laughing. "But I am here to tell you that this will not happen." The crowd laughed with her. She directed attendees to the back of the room, where she had laid out postcards and letter-writing materials on folding tables.

Chavez intends to continue pursuing a career in medicine, but she put her education on hold—and her family at risk—to defend the town. "If this gets passed the commissioners," she said, "If they try building this, you bet I'm gonna sit in front of a bulldozer. I'm going to put myself on the line to do whatever I can to help stop this."

In the coming weeks, Chavez and Aguirre would hold prayer vigils, conference calls with activists who had beaten CoreCivic in other towns and reach out to the local business community. Chavez even mobilized her three younger siblings to contact their friends via Snapchat. The only worry was that the white Republican business leaders who relied on immigrant labor wouldn't dare come out against the center.

Elkhart's Hispanic population has topped 20 percent in recent years, and Aguirre has spoken with business leaders who, despite being Trump supporters, fear they could lose their minority workers if a detention center came to Elkhart.

"[One manager] said, 'I love the Latino workers because they work hard,'" Aguirre recounts. "'They showed that they are just the greatest employees and I don't want this facility here because they'll leave.'"

But when Aguirre asked if the businessman would speak out against the center, "It's the same story," Aguirre said, sighing. "Of course not."

But they did—weeks later, as a group. And it mattered.

Playing in Grey

On January 18, 2018, Jeremy Stutsman, the Democratic mayor of the Elkhart County town of Goshen, posted an open letter to the community on his Facebook page. It read, in part: "CoreCivic... would create jobs we don't need at wages we don't want. Any tax dollars generated by the project wouldn't be enough to offset the long-lasting damage such a facility would do to our county—both in terms of perception and in terms of creating an unwanted unwelcoming reputation." Below the mayor's signature were the names of prominent community members, business leaders and two towns' chambers of commerce.

The following day, CoreCivic formally withdrew their proposal.

But for a long while, the future of Elkhart was in the hands of three county commissioners who had a hard choice to make.

Back in December, before CoreCivic withdrew, Yoder considered the political consequences of his vote over a ham and cheese omelette at Angel's House of Pancakes, an all-day breakfast diner tucked into the corner of a strip mall.

"If we said yes to this, it would be politically potentially really bad," he said, shrugging. "People's memories are short, but I would be up for re-election the year that this opens." It's not just about welcoming all people, he explained: It's about welcoming all industries, too, even if they might not be the most palatable.

(The night before, at the school, he had joked about the high barrier that would encase the CoreCivic facility. "The only thing you'll see is a welcome sign. Huh. Oh sorry. A bad joke.")

In five-minute intervals, Yoder would gently decline a refill on coffee from Angel's attentive waitstaff. It was already close to 11 in the morning, and the breakfast crowd had begun to empty out of the spacious diner. Something about the interior felt too big—like it had had another life as a department store before transitioning to pancakes.

The decision would have defined the small-town official's political identity. He'd either be the fear-mongering racist who was comfortable alienating Elkhart's large Hispanic minority, or the bleeding-heart liberal who kept good jobs out of Elkhart. But there was something aspirational in Yoder's eyes when he talked about the vote.

He knew about CoreCivic's well-documented history of civil rights abuses. For him, that history wasn't a deterrent. It was an opportunity to exert oversight, something private prisons have always resisted. He wanted to make a real difference in a problematic industry.

"Regular oversight," he stressed, looking over the top of his glasses. "Not just once a year or whenever there's complaints. Regular."

Now he won't get the chance.

"There was absolutely no community interest in [oversight]," Yoder admitted over the phone in late January, just days after CoreCivic withdrew. The organized opposition to the facility didn't want to play in shades of grey; they wanted Yoder to say no. "It was my attempt to make a little bit of lemonade, but it was essentially DOA."

The Battle and The War

Based firmly in the local faith community, the Coalition in Elkhart attacked the CoreCivic proposal from multiple fronts—with land use, economic, humanitarian, and moral arguments against immigration detention. It brought Catholics together with Mennonites, union workers together with immigration activists, and the white community together with the very people who would be affected by an increased ICE presence.

Sreekala Rajagopalan was a small middle-aged Indian woman who held her hands close to her chest when she talked. She'd lived in Goshen for 45 years, and it was her timorous voice that resonated the loudest among the arguments against the center.

"I feel that the attack will be on all brown people, whether they are documented or undocumented," she said, her voice beginning to wobble. "Am I supposed to carry my—I'm sorry, I'm vibrating with emotions." Rajagopalan paused and breathed, closing her eyes for a moment. When she spoke again her voice was hard. "But am I supposed to carry my documents showing that I'm a citizen in my pocket all the time?"

Commissioner Suzanne Weirick, another of the three who would have decided the fate of the detention center, said she received more than 300 letters and postcards from the vocal coalition opposing the facility, and just a handful supporting it. Throughout the process, Weirick solicited evidence and opinions from all sides to make the best decision for the county. But she couldn't let emotional pleas distract her from practical concerns, she said. She figured that most of the immigrants in detention would have been convicted of crimes. "I'm sorry, if you're a felon, your rights are kind of suspended while you're serving your conviction. Whether you're in detention in Indiana or in Arizona, you're probably not going to be getting Ben and Jerry's."

In fact ICE detainees are going through a civil process, not a criminal one. De jure detention has never been intended as a punishment; it's meant to hold people until they're processed through immigration court.

Misinformation swirled around the proposal—would the facility hold felons or just undocumented people rounded up by ICE? Would they be held in minimum or maximum security? No one seemed to have the exact answer, making the commissioners' decision all the more harrowing.

Ultimately Weirick felt it was a clear decision for the commissioners. "Overwhelmingly, the community said that this was not a vibrant community initiative."

Frank Lucchese, the third county commissioner, did not return requests for an interview.

Yoder said there was "obviously a sense of relief" about CoreCivic choosing to leave Elkhart. He chose his words carefully, pausing for long moments. The community would have to evaluate what almost happened to them, and Yoder wasn't sure what the next steps would be. He laughed over the phone. "I've not really given you anything there, have I?"

But Marbella Chavez knew exactly how to proceed: A party. "Stay tuned," she said in a text, followed by a smiling emoji.

OTTAWA COUNTY: MAKE VACATIONLAND GREAT AGAIN
VINCE GUERRIERI

For most of its 227 miles, Ohio Route 2 runs not far from the shore of Lake Erie.

A stretch of the highway in Erie County is named for 1965 Miss America Jackie Mayer, who grew up in Sandusky. And on the west side of Cleveland, Route 2 is the Shoreway—where a key scene in *Captain America: The Winter Soldier* was filmed (although you might not recognize it now that the highway has been transformed into a scenic boulevard).

But in Ottawa County, it's the main thoroughfare through the northern end of the county. As a highway, it goes through the Marblehead Peninsula, home to beach and summer homes, and into Port Clinton, the county seat. Then it turns into a rural road, going through acres of farmland and past Camp Perry, a National Guard training and marksmanship facility, and the Davis-Besse Nuclear Power Plant before heading into Lucas County, where it becomes a main drag into and through Toledo.

In 2012, Barack Obama took Route 2 to get from Toledo to an appearance in Sandusky, stopping at a local fruit stand and a local coffee shop. Every election year, it's always been dotted with campaign signs—and in 2016, it was filled with signs for Donald Trump, who ended up winning the county with 57 percent of the vote on his way to taking Ohio.

If Ohio's a bellwether state in presidential politics, then Ottawa County is its distillation. In 1944, it picked Thomas Dewey over Franklin Roosevelt—which might have been due to the presence of John W. Bricker on the ticket. (Bricker, a former governor, remains the last Ohioan to appear on a major party presidential ticket.)

In every presidential election but one since then, it's gone with the winner. The lone exception? In 1960, when it voted for Richard Nixon, despite John Kennedy's last minute push in the state. The early pages of Theodore White's seminal *The Making of the President 1960* chronicle Kennedy's disappointment, noting that on Election Night, he took off his jacket and rolled up his right sleeve to show a hand and forearm scratched, swollen and callused from meeting what he thought were adoring crowds, and said "Ohio did this to me."

About two months before the 2016 election, I talked to former Ohio Democratic Party Chairman Chris Redfern, who lives in Ottawa County, for a news story that never saw the light of day. He said then that Trump was able to tap into a lot of disenchantment and voter frustration, noting, "If yard signs could vote, Trump would win Ottawa County in a walk." But still, Redfern seemed sure that Hillary Clinton would triumph.

My introduction to Donald Trump was my grandmother's *People* magazines in the 1980s. He seemed like a buffoon who was far enough away from me as not to be toxic. I covered his performance in the first Republican presidential debate in 2015 for *Belt Magazine* and assumed it was just a matter of time before he would be seen as the snake-oil salesman he was. I too figured Hillary Clinton would win.

When Ottawa County voted for Dewey and Bricker in 1944, it, like a lot of Northern Ohio, was filled with heavy industry. Port Clinton was home to the Erie Ordnance Depot and factories like Matthews Boats, Celotex and Standard Products, while the Marblehead peninsula was laden with limestone quarries. The atomic age led to a need for beryllium, and Brush built a processing plant in 1953 in Elmore, in the western end of the county.

Ottawa County was a perfect representation of the Democratic New Deal coalition at the time, with agriculture in the western end of the county and factory workers, many immigrants or first-generation Americans and almost entirely unionized, in small towns like Port Clinton and Oak Harbor.

In the 1970s and 1980s, the western end of the county started to vote more with the Republican Party, and deindustrialization took its toll. Matthews declared bankruptcy in 1975. Standard Products closed in 1993 and Celotex followed in 2001, just leaving behind sites that needed millions in industrial cleanup before redevelopment took place. There's only one quarry left on the Marblehead Peninsula. Manufacturing dropped from 55 percent of total employment in the county in 1965 to 25 percent three decades later.

Sociologist Robert Putnam grew up in Port Clinton, and used the city in his latest book, *Our Kids*, as shorthand for the disintegration of the American Dream. (As he was writing it, he actually called me to verify my account in the local paper of a Port Clinton High School graduation as being a packed house.) The Port Clinton he grew up in provided enough economic opportunity for him to attend Swarthmore after a relatively middle-class upbringing. Today, Ottawa County's poverty rate approaches 11 percent—still below the state and national average, but a vast increase in just fifteen years.

The county regularly has one of the highest unemployment rates in the state—but only in the winter. It's become a seasonal area, taking advantage of its lakefront location and really embracing tourism, one of the remaining growth industries in Ohio.

The region was known as Vacationland in the 1960s, with small rental cottages and tourist attractions like Prehistoric Forest, a ten-acre site populated with statues of dinosaurs (as seen in *Tommy Boy*, which takes place in and around Sandusky, and was filmed all over Northwest Ohio). The soil around Lake Erie and its islands made it ideal for growing grapes and winemaking. And of course, Port Clinton still bills itself as the Walleye Capital of the World, and has an annual Walleye Festival in May and a Walleye Drop on New Year's Eve.

Now, tourism is big business, generating $371 million in revenue in Ottawa County in 2015, according to Lake Erie Shores & Islands, leading more than $42 million in tax revenue. It's estimated that half of the houses in Catawba, Portage or Danbury townships—all communities on the Marblehead peninsula—are second homes for vacationers or retirees who want to spend time on the lake.

Nostalgia remains a driving force—as it is in every tourism-driven area, with business dependent on good feelings and warm memories. And it's not always a force for good. The Port Clinton Robert Putnam grew up in is gone, and a lot of people want it back.

"Economic anxiety" has become an excuse to provide cover to Trump voters who might not be racists themselves, but certainly weren't turned off by his bigoted displays. And I'm certain there are people like that in Ottawa County, if for no other reason than the county is 97 percent white and 99 percent native-born citizens (although I take a little pride in the fact that the only Confederate flags I have ever seen were for Civil War re-enactments or at Johnson's Island, the former Confederate prisoner of war camp that still contains a Civil War cemetery).

But in Ottawa County, economic fears are legitimate. It's difficult to make a living in agriculture anywhere. Good-paying non-seasonal jobs were hard to come by. One of the county's largest (and best-paying) employers is the nuclear power plant. The plant has had problems with cracks and repairs for years, and owner First Energy announced plans in 2017 to sell it or close it down. Absent a state bailout, options appear more likely for the latter than the former.

Even seasonal jobs remain in jeopardy. The biggest thing Ottawa County has going for it is Lake Erie. Fish available at the restaurants and diners along the lakefront come from there. The charters and recreational boaters use it. Some municipalities even get their drinking water from it—including Carroll Township.

One of the last things I covered as a journalist in Ottawa County was a brief crisis in Carroll Township when algae made the water undrinkable for a few days. The largest threat to Lake Erie—indeed, all the Great Lakes—is algae blooms that could choke off sea life and make the water undrinkable for humans. The blooms are fed by excessive phosphorus in the water, which comes from waste, either from runoff from improperly spread fertilizer or improperly treated (or entirely untreated) sewage from larger cities.

The water crisis in Carroll Township was the metaphorical canary in the coal mine. The following year, the same thing happened in the city of Toledo—which also draws water from Lake Erie's western basin—this time affecting hundreds of thousands of people. The situation was remedied in a couple weeks, which doesn't seem like a long time until you can only drink bottled water. It hasn't been as bad since, mostly because of dryer conditions and not any real steps taken to remediate the problem.

And with Donald Trump in the White House, that might not change for the better. Cuts to the Environmental Protection Agency certainly won't help Lake Erie, and Ohio's representatives, in a rare moment of bipartisanship, joined together to fight for Great Lakes Restoration Initiative, which was to be drastically slashed in the Trump administration's first proposed budget.

Since he took office in 2011, Gov. John Kasich has promised a more pro-business Ohio Department of Natural Resources, and although he came down firmly against Trump in 2016, his potential successors on the Republican side are trying desperately to out-Trump each other.

"Make America Great Again" has turned into a siren song.

LIFE AND BELONGING IN KNOX COUNTY, OHIO
SEAN DECATUR

Once you start to see them, you see them everywhere. You may think that at some point they will fade into the background, become just a part of the landscape, but each sighting is as jarring as the first. Each raises questions about whether I belong.

I drive by one of the local fire stations in Monroe Township, just a bit outside of my town of Gambier, in Knox County, Ohio, and what catches my eye is not the Stars and Stripes flying in front of the station, but a Confederate flag, atop on an even higher pole, on neighboring property, just close enough to make the distinction hard to see. Is this a statement?

An aggressive driver honks in the grocery store parking lot, and when I look over into the cab of the pickup, I notice a Confederate flag draped over the seat. Was this normal angry driving, or something more sinister?

I go to pick up my son and his friends from a movie on a Saturday night. In the parking lot I see another truck with a Confederate flag in the back. Almost instinctively I think, is my son OK? He soon comes out of the theater, laughing with his friends, and they pile into the car. Does he see the flag? Or has this been such a common sight during his formative years that he fails to notice?

This is one of the many paradoxes of life in Knox County. Ohio was, of course, with the Union during the Civil War. Kenyon College, where I am president, takes pride in having educated not only Civil War generals but also Lincoln's secretary of war, Edwin Stanton. The town square of Mount Vernon, near Kenyon, features a monument to veterans from the area who fought to preserve the Union. That rich history would suggest that a public display of loyalty to the Confederacy would not be justifiable on the oft-expressed grounds of "history and heritage." And yet, less than half a mile away from that monument, several homes regularly fly Confederate flags on its front porches.

I grew up in Cleveland, and I consider myself a loyal son of Ohio and the Midwest. Throughout the thirteen years I spent living in New England (while I was a chemistry professor at Mount Holyoke College), I missed the friendliness of the community and the sense of connection found in a place where neighbors greet and welcome new arrivals. And of course I missed the deep local connection to the sometimes frustrating professional sports teams. My wife is from the Cleveland area as well, and we were incredibly excited when job opportunities at Oberlin College brought us back to Northeast Ohio from New England in 2008.

When I was offered the opportunity to come to Kenyon, my family had much to consider. Kenyon is an excellent institution, with a renowned reputation and international student body. Most of my life has been spent at small residential liberal arts colleges, and I felt instantly at home on its campus. And, it was in Ohio, still close to family and part of the culture I loved. But, central Ohio—in particular, a largely rural and white section of central Ohio—was very different than our familiar terrain of greater Cleveland, and as an African-American in a multiracial family I wasn't sure whether the transition would work for us. But we decided to take the leap, and we became blue-state Ohioans living deep within red-state Ohio.

Five years later, I am happy that we made the move. In many ways, we felt at home from the start. That famed Midwestern friendliness does reign supreme here, just as it did closer to Cleveland. We've made friends, and our son had a remarkably smooth transition into a new school. Like many of our neighbors, we spend a lot of weekend time on the sidelines of youth athletic events; we commiserate with our fellow parents when it is cold and rainy, and we celebrate victories or just good, solid play of all members of the team. There are many opportunities to share in the pain of being a Browns fan with our friends and neighbors, and the eruption of joy over the 2016 Cavs championship was felt in Knox County as well.

Yet there are still difficulties, like the flags. I cannot separate the Confederate flag from its function as a symbol of racial intimidation and white supremacy, so living in its midst is discomforting, to say the least. There is the annual music festival named for Dan Emmet, a Mount Vernon native and "pioneer" in blackface minstrelsy who is credited for writing the song "Dixie" (though scholarship suggests that authorship rightly belongs to a local family of black music performers from the same era; so the festival manages to celebrate cultural appropriation as well). I know that an overwhelming majority of the people I have had the chance to know well would never brandish the Confederate flag with pride, nor would they espouse an ideology of white supremacy. But, their silence on these issues, which reifies the invisibility of the concerns and feelings of people of color here and across the country, is disturbing.

And yet race is only part of the complexity at work here. With a college president married to a tenured professor, our family is marked by financial privilege—especially in a region shaken by poverty and its effects. This is a county hit hard by the rise in opioid addiction; where new jobs require a level of technical skill that many are not equipped to meet; where parents in many households are holding down multiple jobs, working long hours, and still feel like they are not getting ahead. Despite the constant stress and burden of race that my family feels, we have an economic security and confidence in our long-term socioeconomic position that many of our neighbors do not share.

And Kenyon's role within the region is complex. Kenyon has been home in Knox County for over 190 years, and the histories of the college and the county are deeply intertwined. However, over 85 percent of Kenyon students are from outside the state of Ohio, many from large urban areas and/or one of the coasts (there are nearly as many Californians as Ohioans at Kenyon). Not surprisingly, at times this produces a cultural divide between folks from Kenyon and longtime residents of the local community, to whom Kenyon can seem elite, aloof, and unwelcoming.

All of this was made more visible in the election of 2016 and its aftermath. Knox County was "Trump Country" in 2016: visitors to campus from liberal enclaves in New York and California would often comment with surprise on the number of prominent Trump/Pence yard signs, and in the end Donald Trump carried Knox County with over 70 percent of the vote. If you discount the almost 1,000 votes from Kenyon students—which went almost completely to Hillary Clinton or one of the third-party options—the percentage of the vote to Trump is even greater.

The election reminds me of thestrals from the Harry Potter series, the magical creatures who can only be seen by those who have seen someone die; invisible to most, they are made visible by the trauma of witnessing and accepting death. Similarly, race, class, and culture divisions in Knox County and elsewhere existed before the election of 2016; these divides were not created on Election Day, but rather like the thestrals became visible, and the appearance was shocking and disorienting.

Confederate flags were always here (though they seemed to proliferate during the 2016 election), and the occasional racist shout from a passing pickup truck driving through Gambier occurred before November 2016, but in the time since these incidents seem to have taken on new meaning and weight. Politics always felt like a tricky subject for small talk on the sidelines of a sporting event, but now everyone works hard to avoid it at all costs.

Yet the thestral-like appearance of these community divides also gives me a hope that a path forward is also becoming visible. The actions of the new administration have provoked serious conversations on race, religion, and immigration in our community, and several efforts have arisen in the past year to have community conversations on race, some led by local clergy (this is a deeply religious community, so clergy-led efforts have particular power and resonance). Nearby Mount Vernon is in the midst of unprecedented investment in its downtown community, not only improving the quality of life for residents but also generating serious discussions about what is needed to make the town a center for entrepreneurial development, and I know that, historically, economic growth is key to bringing about social and cultural change.

And at Kenyon, we have launched a strong effort to reach out from behind our gates and into the community. Instead of isolating the campus from the town in the wake of a cultural divide, we are leaning in, doing our part as an institutional citizen to invest in the community and to help move important conversations forward. We approach this work not as outsiders attempting to remake a community in our own image, but rather as partners in a shared commitment to ensure that all in our community thrive, now and in the future.

Do I belong here, on the sharp edge between red and blue? It is not always comfortable, nor should it be—but the work of bridging divisions, taking the risk of building community where it is hard to do so is meaningful. There will always be moments when I feel like I don't belong (and fortunately, Cleveland is not too far away, so neither is familiar barbecue, haircuts, and other features of urban life). But I feel confident—perhaps naively so—that the Midwestern values of community building will be embraced by us all, and help to move us all towards a more inclusive future.

GUIDING A PROGRESSIVE PITTSBURGH THROUGH THE TRUMP ERA

DAN GILMAN

After the election in 2016, the roles of Pittsburgh and cities across the country have shifted. State legislatures, the United States Congress, and the White House have become more conservative than ever, focused on reducing access to health care, maintaining stagnant wages, creating little opportunity for people of color, attacking the LGBTQIA+ community, and criticizing immigrants and refugees as a threat to our democracy. Cities across the country are taking a leading role in creating jobs that pay, more sustainable and safer communities for families, and a more welcoming city for people of color, the LGBTQIA+ community, and immigrants and refugees. With a City Hall that is more progressive than ever, Pittsburgh has seized the moment and stood up for its inclusive values, using both ordinances and the bully pulpit to do so.

Shortly after the election, cities across the country reflected on their core values and the threat posed by the newly elected administration and its allies in Congress and state legislatures. How will mayors, city councils, and county commissions govern and advance progressive values in the Trump era? How do "islands of blue in large seas of red" resist state legislatures moving determinedly to the right?

In increasingly conservative Pennsylvania, cities face the seemingly insurmountable challenge known as state preemption, which prohibits municipalities from superseding state law with legislation. The charter prevents cities like Pittsburgh from advancing progressive ideals through legislation. In addition, Pennsylvania is one of the most gerrymandered states in the nation. Despite a sizable edge in Democratic voter registration statewide, our congressional delegation is comprised of 13 Republicans and 5 Democrats and our state house and senate have a near veto-proof majority. Our state's conservatism has forced Pittsburgh's leaders to legislate creatively and effectively use our voice to defend and advocate for the progressive ideals on which our city was built.

As city councilman for the 8th district, for instance, I introduced legislation to ban forced conversion "therapy" for LGBTQIA+ minors, a psychologically and physically harmful process that was championed by the Vice President during his time as Governor of Indiana. The legislation, which was introduced as a measure to protect the well-being of minors rather than a new regulation on business, passed unanimously and earned Pittsburgh national recognition for our efforts to resist the President's agenda.

A few months later, the nascent presidential administration began publicly speaking out against immigrants. Considering its history as the nation's onetime leader in steel production and other industries, Pittsburgh was built by the hands of hardworking immigrants who first came to the city in search of better lives for themselves and their families. As a new generation of immigrants and refugees come from across the globe to live, work, and learn in Pittsburgh, our corporate, university, nonprofit, philanthropic, and government leaders across all sectors understand that our city must extend the same welcoming hand it did for previous generations. The threat posed by the new administration compelled our Mayor William Peduto, myself, and my council colleagues to act rapidly, to legislate where we can, and to use our influence to affirm our core values as a city.

In the weeks following the inauguration, as headline after headline declared the Trump administration's intention to divide our country, break up families, and ramp up deportation, I convened a meeting with people from all sectors to identify the most pressing needs of our immigrant neighbors. A roundtable of immigrants, refugees, union leaders, educators, advocates, faith leaders, and organizations serving immigrants and refugees shaped the narrative surrounding the treatment of the newest Pittsburghers and those from around the world who have called Pittsburgh their home for decades. Through an all-encompassing package of legislation, we created an Office of Multicultural Affairs within the City's Department of Public Safety to affirm that all are valued here. We also reaffirmed that city services are available to all individuals regardless of citizenship status, improved language access for all Pittsburghers, and we restated that in Pittsburgh, we refuse to act as an arm of the Immigration and Customs Enforcement agency.

Later in the tenure of the new administration in Washington, at a news conference declaring his opposition to the Paris Climate Accord, the President uttered the now-famous words: "I was elected by voters of Pittsburgh, not Paris." Mayor Peduto responded swiftly, noting that Secretary Hillary Clinton won the city of Pittsburgh with over 80 percent of the vote and reaffirming Pittsburgh's commitment to a sustainable future. The quip earned Pittsburgh the international spotlight, with many global news outlets highlighting Pittsburgh's remarkable transformation from an industrial powerhouse to a city that has shaken off its rust and diversified its economy, which is now based in education, medicine, technology, and green energy. The mayor also issued an executive order to power our city's government on 100 percent renewable energy by 2035. This exemplifies the ability to not simply legislate, but also, to advocate for progressive policies.

Pittsburgh will continue to legislate where we can and use our bully pulpit to stand up for progressive values despite threats from conservatives in Washington, D.C. As scandals continue to rock the White House and as our state and federal governments become increasingly conservative, our city is looking ahead to the future as a gleaming example of the power of inclusivity and sustainability.

A DEMOCRATIC HOPEFUL FROM RANCH COUNTRY
CHRISTOPHER VONDRACEK

"You're on the fastest route," Siri told me about a mile outside Bonesteel (pop. 216). I buzzed down an empty country road, passing by a brown calf staring curiously from behind a mesh fence. Between the Christian radio stations, I heard a scrambled NPR news report announcing that President Trump had yanked the U.S. out of the Paris Climate Accord. Beside me, yellow ditch flowers sprouted along the green fields and rolling hills ended in summits over the Missouri River. Pro-life billboards crawled up wooden posts standing in grass, and the mud on inert ATVs—seemingly paused mid-torque of the steering column—crusted over in the sun.

Entering a place is not the same as knowing a place, but the drive from Sioux Falls, South Dakota's largest city at under 150,000 people, had been a journey of years, not hours. And I'd come for a purpose. After eight miles, my dented Volvo scaled a winding gravel road, passing picks-ups, Subarus, and black SUVs. Some folks were walking. I'd foolishly worn sandals, so I hiked up my jeans so they wouldn't drag on the rocks. Later, woman in line for the beef brisket asked me—a total stranger—"where's the flood?" I smiled like she hadn't insulted me, but I had thought we were allies. We had all come for the main event: 33-year-old Billie Sutton, a former rodeo star and four-term state senator from Burke (pop. 600), was about to announce he'd thrown his hat in the ring for South Dakota's highest office. As a Democrat.

"We rise to the occasion together," Billie said that day on the stump. "No matter what the obstacles ahead, no matter what the challenges, we can work together to make South Dakota everything it can be."

South Dakota is a small state, and earlier that night Billie gave the same speech to the faithful gathered in a dingy American Legion off Minnesota Avenue in Sioux Falls. Billie had used his notes during that event, but now he had memorized it. But, to me, the night belonged to Rep. Troy Heinert, who strolled up to the pulpit in his black coat and cowboy hat.

"I'm a rancher, a Lakota ... and a Democrat," he said, repeating a surprising line that had gotten him big applause weeks earlier at the McGovern Day dinner. Democrats—especially *West River* (what folks in South Dakota call those people west of the Missouri, a rougher, rowdier, rangier kind of living)—are more endangered than the black-footed ferret in the Badlands.

When I talked to Billie, I offered to help him with his speeches if he wanted. What I wanted to say was, *I can help you talk more about being a Democrat or even mention it at all,* but Billie is obviously the savvier politician. And it wasn't an oversight that the "D" word didn't get mentioned this day on his family's ranch north of Burke.

A few weeks earlier, at a coffee shop in Sioux Falls, I bumped into the former chief of staff for former Republican governor and congressman, Bill Janklow, who lamented the gridlock in the state house. South Dakota is ground zero for the much ballyhooed colony collapse of rural Democrats in the twenty-first century.

He told me there are three parties in Pierre. He saw far-right conservatives and mainstream Republicans as the power structure. Democrats are barely in the calculation. There are only 6 Democrats out of 35 seats in the Senate. One of them is Sutton.

The state's Republican governor, Dennis Daugaard, is a moderate by western-state standards. He vetoed a transphobic bathroom bill and mostly stayed away from the state party's invitation to anti-Muslim extremist groups touring local churches and hotel ballrooms.

It didn't always used to be this way. My mom grew up in South Dakota and talked of the prairie populists—George McGovern, Tom Daschle—who were giants on the state and national stage. During the Great Depression, Tom Berry from Belvidere, South Dakota—now a dried-up town hugging a steakhouse and gas station adjacent to Interstate 90 that belts across the state—was mighty popular and earned the "cowboy governor" moniker. But there hasn't been a Democratic governor in my lifetime. Or Billie's.

Billie is a local banker. His wife is an attorney. They have a child. And as he does at every stump, Billie rolls on stage buoyantly in a wheelchair and gives his speech.

"We need to change the same-old, same-old!"

A political reporter in the state recently called Sutton "is the real deal." But it's hard to know if this will stick.

A cowboy string band plays "In Heaven on a Horse." Near the vats of tinfoiled-over food stand the Rosebud Rancherettes. On a flatbed stretching over a grassy bluff along the Missouri, adjacent wagon wheels and hay bales covered in stars-and-stripes bunting, Sutton wears a white Stetson hat. A lot of people with belt buckles have gathered—horses swish tails on hill stretching behind him. Sutton's voice is small and airy, like a rancher clicking his horse, as he runs off his platform.

"In college, I was a nationally ranked bronc-rider, and up in Minot, North Dakota my horse flipped over on me in the chute. I was paralyzed instantly."

Baby blue placards with Billie's name in yellow wave around the yard and hang from the hay bales on stage, adjacent the American flag, but "Democrat" doesn't appear anywhere. Days earlier a few hours to the west, Montanans elected a Republican who body-slammed a journalist over a banjo-picking Democrat. The week before, at a bar in Ft. Pierre, a progressive man considering a run for the state legislature told me over beers that he wanted to run as a Republican in his deeply conservative district of central Sioux Falls.

"Democrats get crushed," he said. "I want to move the conversation from here to here."

His hands wavered over the bar, like two needles on an old pick-up truck. I've heard this before around here.

"You get accustomed to losing," a Democrat from Yankton County, the old territorial capital, told me. He's considering running for the state legislature, too. "Democrats want to be martyrs. They get used to losing, and they forget how to win. You don't win by being a purist."

The previous fall, a computer programmer—Jay Williams—lost to incumbent senator John Thune, a Republican, by double-digits. I had listened to a debate on the radio, agreed with everything Williams said, and knew he'd be slaughtered.

In August, I found myself in the backyard of a retiring theatre and English teacher—a known, rabble-rousing liberal—in a verdant patio with other Democrats. One, a magazine publisher who ran and lost for governor in 1998, told me about living in D.C. during Nixon's presidency.

"We were on the Potomac one afternoon during the summer recess, and it was just days before Nixon would resign, and suddenly this big yacht came driving down the channel, and there he was, Nixon, and he looked over and waved."

The tempo and direction for the state's Democrats wavers. A progressive who lives and works out in Rapid City for cattle ranchers told me it doesn't happen from liberals.

"It's not going to be because we're fighting for trans-rights," she said. "We need kitchen table issues."

A few weeks later, this same woman stuck up for the party's current chair, who during the annual McGovern Day Dinner faced a coup attempt from supporters of Paula Hawks, who ran last fall against the state's immensely popular congressional representative, Kristi Noem.

After Sutton's event in Bonesteel, South Dakota's Republican party director called Sutton a "hyper partisan liberal Democrat." But he's not. Maybe the best thing a political party can do is get out of its own way.

At lunch, after Billie's announcement, I sat with a former state legislator from Wessington Springs—where the black-cowboy-hatted string band opening up the announcement descended from—shared a picnic bench with me, as we sipped lemonade and ate our fruit kabobs and pork sandwiches.

"I've seen it before," he said, "As Democrats, we just got to wait until the other party screws up." He took a moment, skewering a piece of pork stuck between his teeth with a toothpick, perhaps pondering the same thought I was.

A cloud of dust swirled up as a stagecoach—carrying the Sutton family name—pulled up, and some children got out, their hair glowing in the sun dazzling in that blue western sky.

"And I think we're getting there. We just have to have one of our own ready."

NEIGHBORS
BRIDGET CALLAHAN

After the August rally, the atmosphere in Wilmington was weird. September felt violent. There was tension in the air, bumping between people like streams of fleas, or viruses. Everybody's aura was poisoned. No one felt good about talking to anyone they didn't know. Strangers were might be your enemy. The polarization of ideas was a tangible, electrical thing, a strange force of psychology as powerful as gravity and physical magnetism.

There are a lot of transplants in Wilmington. It's a North Carolina beach town, full of international tourists, and New Yorkers who move south to "get away." There is a Cleveland Browns tailgating club.

When I first moved here, I would get pissed when people asked me where I was from.

"Cleveland."

"Oh, my boyfriend is from Cincinnati!"

Cool. That might as well be an entirely different state. Weird spaghetti-eaters. But a ton of people from Cincy. Lots from New Jersey. A sizable delegation from Illinois.

For the last two decades, the city has also been chock-full of the film industry, and all those resulting characters. Actresses who taught yoga. Dorky townie gaffer guys. Stunt doubles who taught at surf camps in between jobs, and always the ubiquitous super rich: producers, directors, "artists" who talked gaily at parties about "how, of course, it's hard being in the South culturally, there's practically no liberals here, they're all rednecks, however the tax rates are great."

It would be a mistake to think this was a liberal place, some sort of Yankee bastion. The highway was only built forty years ago. Twenty minutes of driving and you are in rural North Carolina, where people sell boiled peanuts by the side of the road and take out second mortgages to buy farm trucks. Maybe the liberals were the people we met at the cocktail bars, but the people not at the bars were the thousands of nice, church-going evangelicals who populated every place outside of downtown. We forgot about them, because we never saw them, except sometimes shopping at Whole Foods if their kid had a gluten allergy, or on the local news when there was a horrible accident and their church was trying to raise money. They weren't on our Twitter feeds. And they forgot about us, because they didn't go out to bars, we didn't come to their church events, and we weren't on their Twitter feeds either.

But after Donald Trump came to town we were all, loudly and relentlessly, reminded that we were neighbors.

I stopped playing with Tinder. I was scared of confrontation, resentful of photos of people in camo, or holding guns, sporting military haircuts, or riding in big trucks with tow-headed children who were making more dignified smiles for the camera than their father, who stuck his tongue out arena-rock style in the background, proud of his possessions. Princes of the South standing atop their car dealership boats, holding giant ocean fish like scalps they had won in war. No, Tinder was out.

It was hard to find anyone to sleep with actually. My sexual organs were shriveling up, crumbling like burnt kale as the electricity of the culture war heated up. The guy I had been sleeping with kept saying stupid stuff about politics not mattering: "You know, the World Bank is just orchestrating all of this." And every guy I knew hated Hillary because she was so "unlikeable," like they were auditioning to be part of a Pew Research poll. The lack of physical affection was making me sensitive. I flinched like an animal who has found itself in a cage with snakes. I longed for the comforting blue of Cleveland.

Despite the looming election, it was still summer in a beach town, and we were all busy working three jobs, trying to harvest as much money from tourists as we could before they left us again. They were at least a welcome distraction from the news. They showed up with their kids and cousins, got blisters from walking around in flip-flops, complained about the drivers, and spent their savings accounts. The early summer tourists were all richies from up north who rented beach houses at the height of season. But as the summer dragged on, it shifted, to relative locals from Greensboro or Raleigh. The people who knew to wait till the hotel prices went down a little, and then they could afford a weekend at the beach before the kids headed back to school.

One Saturday night I was giving a ghost tour downtown, a thing I did for extra cash. Summer nights in Wilmington are full of college kids, marines, and tourists. Dusk is sweet in the South. Everyone is a bit happier once the sun goes down because it's no longer one hundred degrees. They like to have some patio beers and find touristy things to go on: carriage rides, boat tours, ghost tours.

There was a large group for this tour even though it was the end of the summer: families, older folks, grandmothers visiting, couples from

Jacksonville. It was the end of the night, I had walked them past most of the cool houses, and we were all having fun.

On the corner of Dock and Front Street, right in the middle of the rowdiest stretch of college bars, I stood in front of a joint called the Husk, and told a story about a river captain and his brave dog—a good one for families and people who cried at ASPCA commercials. The dog dies, see. Everyone loves a ghost dog.

As we stood there, me in black witchy garb gesturing towards the bar, this crowd of white people in polo shirts, flip-flops, and pastel shorts circled around me, a towering guy approached. He looked like the kind of Marine you see in movies or GI Joe commercials—huge arms, bald head, the tendons sticking out around his neck. There are a lot of Marines in Wilmington, they come down on the weekends, to go on dates or drive for Uber. In general, I like them. We don't have a lot of Marines in Cleveland, and so my first exposure to them was here, drinking usually, and they are always polite and respectful in ways that the townie college boys are not.

You can tell the Marines apart because there's his particular smoothness to the way they move, always keeping their spines straight, in control of their muscles. Like ballerinas. This guy was very tan, with a tight pink shirt, and Jersey Shore jeans, and his ballerina was wasted. He walked drunkenly right into the middle of our group, then stopped abruptly, as though suddenly aware he was surrounded by people.

"What is this?" he said, swaying.

"It's a ghost tour, "I said brightly.

He stopped moving and looked more intensely, at the people, and then at me. Just staring us down. I smiled again, half laughing at his swaying, waiting for him to move on. Then, as if a lightbulb had gone off, he got it.

"No you're not. I know what you are, don't try and lie to me. No, you're a f--king feminazi Hillary supporter. You're all f--king feminists. You can suck my f--king cock, bitch," and he started vehemently miming the action of me sucking a cock, which was in fact just him pretending to suck a cock. But I wasn't going to point that out.

A middle-aged guy, his sunglasses perched on his slightly balding, burnt hairline, stepped forward. "Dude, this is a ghost tour. There are children and women here. You are ruining it for everyone."

The crowd murmured its support.

"Shut the f--k up you weak libtard. This is my country."

"Leave my dad alone." A prepubescent girl in Walmart punk clothes stepped forward and screamed. Her voice was shot into the air like a cannonball. We all waited for the splash. It didn't come. Even the drunk guy looked startled.

"If you don't leave, I'm going to call the cops," I said.

He leaned in, yelled in my face. "Go ahead and f--king call the cops. I know what this is. I know what y'all are doing. I've got rights!"

"Look, dude, I don't know what you think this is." Another older man moved up next to me. He was wearing a shirt that read "Jesus Saves", and his wife was gathering their children in her arms and backing them away. The whole family was a cause-and-react swing: he stepped forward, they moved back. "This ain't nothing political. She's just telling stories."

"I'm not letting bitches like you destroy this country," the drunk guy said, pointing at me, and I could feel people tense up, like he was going to hit me and they knew they were gonna have to do something.

"OK guys, listen," I said to the crowd, "we're just going to leave. Ignore him." I started walking the group across the street. He hollered expletives after us, but as soon as we were a block away, he stopped yelling and continued his wandering.

We stopped to gather ourselves. A couple of the tourists came over and asked if I was OK. They surrounded me protectively like a group of clucking hens.

I wasn't really fine. I was shaken. I was furious. But I smiled professionally, said I was fine, agreed with them the guy must have been out of his mind. It reminded me of the time my boyfriend and I were mugged, how the real shock had taken time to wear off and then the fear had come days later, when it made no sense to be talking about it still. I could feel that shock coming and fought it off. No weakness in front of strangers.

"Did you know that guy?"

"How dare he talk to you that way, with kids around!"

"What do you think he was on?" an elderly white lady asked. She had a little gold cross at her throat. I saw it, and remembered to not swear. Don't crack some joke about cocaine.

"I don't know, but definitely something. What a jerk!" one of the other men said. " As if anything about us screams "political rally!" We're just trying to have fun with our families, and assholes like that..."

A supertan woman, her perm frizzing in the humidity, put her perfectly manicured hand on my shoulder. "You handled that very well, dear. If that was me, I would have lost it," she said in a thick Jersey accent. "And I don't think you look like a feminazi at all."

They all came back to the shop with me and wrote feedback forms for my boss about how wonderful I had been. "Handled it like a pro" someone wrote.

Back home, I opened a bottle of wine and chain-smoked on my porch. It was 80 degrees and the trees were humming in the thick North Carolina darkness. The worst part was that he had been right. I was a Hillary-loving succubus feminazi. I did want to change his country. I hated men like him. Like a well-trained predator, he had smelled it on me or seen it in my face. Maybe he had just seen a pale fat girl, dressed in black, without a ring on her finger, and guessed. Nobody else had seen my difference though, or more likely they hadn't cared, and I clung to that thought for comfort. That at least, in person, they had my back.

INTRODUCTORY COMMUNICATION: TEACHING ACROSS MICHIGAN'S URBAN-RURAL DIVIDE

LORI TUCKER-SULLIVAN

Introductory Communication

In the fall of 2016, I put a few thousand miles on my car working as an adjunct professor of public speaking. As an adjunct, I accept positions wherever I find them, and that semester was no different. I had three classes—one in a rural Michigan community college, and two in an urban four-year institution. My students varied in age, socio-economic status, and intent with regard to their educations. Though most kept quiet about their political leanings, they were usually easy to discern, whether from comments they made or the speech topics they chose. From week-to-week during that fall, I taught, counseled, and heard the stories of immigrants, refugees, unemployed housewives, a cancer patient, and others. (All names have been changed to protect students' privacy.)

September

If I'm lucky and miss the grain haulers and school buses, I make it from home to class in just over an hour. The drive is always lovely this time of year with leaves turning and wheat casting a gold glow across the suburban acreage. I begin by pairing students up to introduce one another to fellow classmates. I hear repeatedly about their majors, former high schools, and how much they hate public speaking.

Debra is older, perhaps thirty-five. I often have two or three students returning to school after being laid off, or after being told by their employer they must have a degree. Debra is a slight, perky redhead. A stay-at-home mom, she's returning to school to major in environmental science. "I decided to do something with my life now that my kids don't need me so much. If I'm going back to school, it should be for something important," she says to the class. She remains after class to tell me she's nervous.

"My husband is pretty ambivalent about this," she confides. "He owns a business and doesn't think I should worry about a career or money. But it's not about that, you know?" I do know. I tell her she'll do fine. I'll be flexible with her work if she gets overloaded; she can email if she needs to miss class with a sick child. We'll make it work.

Later, I meet Sean, a suntanned high school senior taking classes that will allow him to graduate with an Associate's degree. These students are always motivated and eager and I enjoy them. Sean fits that description, though he is quieter than most of the high schoolers I've taught. When he asks if we can talk, his face is serious.

"My parents are divorcing and my mom just moved out," he says. "She bought a house closer to work, so I may be late on days when I stay with her. I'll try not to be. I just thought you should know; if I'm down, that's why."

There are a few others who stand out that first week. Some I'll come to know pretty well. Others will float just below the radar and skate out with slightly improved skills and understanding.

The following week, I'm in a very different setting. Looking out at my urban class, I see young women in headscarves, young men with sagging pants, and a few students wearing expensive sneakers. They are kids figuring out schedules, navigating campus, and reuniting with friends. The classroom is filled with technology—whiteboards and giant screens from which I can project lecture slides.

The students' introductions are also different. Their majors are bigger—biochemistry, engineering, pre-med—this is career prep, not simply job planning. They are more confident. They talk about communities where they grew up, but also about international travel and community service. It's clear their worlds are bigger than their peers' at community college. But they are not without challenges.

Carla is a quiet African-American woman with short-cropped hair. Adorned with tattoos bearing the names of those she's lost to illness or violence, she projects a shy vulnerability. She refers to me as Miss Lori. I sign papers allowing her to join though the section is already full. I count seven times that she thanks me for the opportunity.

The students are uncertain as they approach the front to speak, except for Billy. He stands at the whiteboard in full animation, waving his arms, rubbing his hand over his blond crew-cut, and shouting his introduction as though auditioning for a stand-up comedy act. I can't tell if this is bravado masking fear, or if he is truly this outgoing. He tells of being teased about his clothing choices in high school. Pointing to the blue hoodie he's wearing, he says he's worn it every day for the past four years, the hood mostly up around his face.

"I read like a book a week," Billy says. "And I'm a pretty serious gamer. But it won't interfere with my studies," he promises. The animated bravado appears to be a new approach for Billy. I picture him in front of a mirror, pep-talking himself that college is a place of reinvention.

Fatima is waiting outside my next class. I sign papers stating I understand that she is to have extra time for test-taking and speech preparation if necessary. She is a Syrian refugee who, despite having lived in the States for four years, still suffers PTSD and anxiety attacks. I ask if she's certain she should be taking a speech class. She says yes, she wants to study medicine and needs to overcome issues with talking in front of groups, among other things. She is sweet and soft-spoken in a bright yellow head scarf, long-sleeve t-shirt, and blue jeans.

Urban or rural, all the students are eager for the semester to start. It's a new beginning for them: new classmates and experiences, broadened horizons, finding themselves for the first time in a long time, or the first time ever. I spend the weekend setting up gradebooks, preparing lectures, and finalizing rubrics.

With a few productive hours remaining on Sunday, I volunteer at Hillary headquarters. Today I'm phone-banking—rustling up volunteers for three upcoming rallies. I'm not worried about the election. I've volunteered and canvassed before, for Mondale, Bill Clinton, and Obama. The convention was exciting and historic, the opponent is stumbling and deplorable, but campaigns go on regardless and I feel better doing my part.

October

As autumn arrives, I get into a routine of classwork and commuting. The students are getting to know one another and feeling comfortable. We discuss the differences between informing and persuading, what it means to be extemporaneous, and what topics are appropriate for speeches. At the community college, the students struggle with schedules—children are at home with the flu, jobs have hours that increase near the holidays; two students are dealing with unemployment benefits.

Tanner is a strapping young man broad-shouldered from farm work. I've seen him a few times being dropped off by his even younger wife, a toddler in a car seat squealing with delight as daddy kisses him through the window. Tanner is cheerful and focused. He left the farm at nineteen to work in a local canning business. While there, he was given an opportunity to do IT work and found that he had a knack for such things. "Go to college," the company told him, "and we'll give you a better job when you graduate." So Tanner is here, completing an associate's in cyber security. His soft spoken demeanor belies the bulk of his chest and shoulders. For his first speech, in which students bring a physical object and tell the class what it represents about them, Tanner brings in antlers that he's found while hunting. It's a clear representation of the person—though he participates peripherally in the sport, he prefers collecting artifacts left by nature, not taken by force.

Recently, Tanner missed a few classes, including the first chapter test. He asks if he can speak with me.

"So I had a few doctor's appointments last week, that's why I missed class. They found a mass on my thyroid and they're not sure what it is," he says. "They say it's nothing to worry about, though. They'll go in and remove it and either way I'll just not have my thyroid any more. They did a biopsy and I'm just waiting to hear.

"My wife works part-time and since I left my job we didn't have insurance until last year when we got Obamacare. Before that, we were going to clinics and the ER. So I didn't really have a family doctor to see when I started having stomach pain. I guess I put it off longer than I should."

"You have a doctor now?" I ask.

"Yeah, I like this guy I'm seeing, but it's still three weeks to get an appointment. There aren't a lot of docs out here anymore so I'm going to one in Ohio. But he's good, I like him."

I tell Tanner to let me know how things work out, to not worry about classwork as we'll work things around his schedule. He is driving a hundred miles round-trip to see a doctor, is only twenty-two and has a two-year-old son. Having lost my husband to cancer, and a close friend to thyroid cancer, I can't stop thinking about Tanner and his young family as I drive home.

Through their speeches, I get to know my students. Sean brings in tennis trophies and speaks of dedication and teamwork. Jose brings in a voltage tester and talks of becoming an electrician; Erica shows a tattoo. Debra is the first to be political. She brings in her Bernie 2016 t-shirt and talks about what it means to be politically engaged. She's careful not to campaign, but rather to talk about her political activism during her earlier years of college when she volunteered for Al Gore. She tells the class it's important to believe in something bigger than oneself.

Colleen balances out Debra with a talk about hard work. She brings in a perfect attendance certificate from her nursing home employer and tells the class that she had second thoughts about bringing it because, really, she only did what is expected. "I loathe freeloaders," she says. "I am always on time, and I show up when I'm expected to. Nothing in this world is free, you only get anywhere from hard work."

Ahmed is one of very few Middle Eastern students in the community college. A US military veteran, he has lived here for twenty years, though his English is still quite broken. For his speech, he brings his Iraq War license plate and tells the class that his next-door neighbor, Jim, wouldn't speak to him when he moved in. "He tell me not to talk to him or his wife. Once I try to mow his lawn to be friendly and he make me stop, half-way done. But then I go to the Secretary of State and they tell me I can get this special license plate for my car. I park in my driveway with the new plate and Jim ask me, why do I have this. I tell him I was in the army in Iraq. I was a soldier and translator. Next day, Jim leave flower on my porch. His wife leave cookies. We are now friends."

After class, I ask Ahmed about other experiences in this rural community. He says most everyone is nice, but he knows the current election has driven people apart. "I'm Republican," he says. "I love George W. Bush. Someday history books will look good on Mr. Bush. He freed many people from despots. You don't know what life was like. Whole Arab Spring happened because of America."

"You really think the Iraq war was a good thing?" I ask.

"Yes, definitely. But this new guy? He will start a war with his thumbs. He say things to make others mad and make him look good. He will have us in war very soon. I worry. I am signed up to go back to serve as a translator and that could happen any time. I will let you know if I get called up."

In the city, students perform speeches using objects that mirrored their wide variety of religious and cultural beliefs. Lily showed the headscarf she no longer wears because she discovered feminism. She still believes she made the right choice despite being shunned by her family. Fatima brought in the Colorado Rockies t-shirt from the Red Cross she was wearing when her family left Syria. Once in the U.S., the sponsor organization asked her father where they wanted to go and he pointed to her shirt. "Colorado," he said. And that's where they spent the next four years before moving to Michigan to be with family. Students consider how these connections that could determine someone's future could come to be.

Their bravery in sharing these speeches leaves me humbled. One young woman shows the tattoo she got after coming out to her parents. Mira shows the scrubs she wore while delivering a baby in Guatemala. There are student athletes and debaters with awards, cheerleaders with hair ribbons, and metal screws removed from someone's healed leg.

Billy is still animated as he talks about gaming. Holding an X-Box controller, he talks about the lesser-known benefits of video games. But when I assign Billy to a small group of female students to complete a citation exercise, a verbal altercation erupts. I separate the group and take them outside.

"I'm tired of every other week, somebody telling me they want power from me," Billy says. He was uncomfortable with the leadership roles taken by two young women in the group. "I'm the target of everyone's hate because I'm a white male. I can't help that. I work two jobs to be here. I don't have 'privilege.' It's like they're ganging up on me."

I referee as best I can, asking the women if they understand that no one, male or female, wants to be assumed to have certain attributes because of their gender. Then I ask Billy if he understands that people aren't trying to take power, only to join him in a place they feel they've never been allowed.

"As a woman, it's important for me to have a place at the table. You've been at that table all your life. I understand that you don't have the same place at that table as some of your classmates who don't have to work, but you are there. Many of your fellow students are barely allowed in the room, much less at the table. And all they want is to join you. They're not asking you to leave, nor should they. They're only asking for you to scoot over. The more people and voices around that table, the better we'll all be. That's just my way of thinking about it," I say.

"I never thought about it that way," Billy responds. "It feels like I'm being blamed for being who I am. And being asked to give up what little I've got." Billy is the white working class male whose votes may swing the election. I don't believe Billy is inherently racist or misogynist, but he is impressionable and has verbalized what many in his economic situation believe is true.

As they leave, I notice Billy walking with one of the female students, continuing the discussion. They sit together during the next class.

The last speech is Carla who steps up with no prop. She's listened to students—white, black, Arabic, Hispanic—tell of accomplishments, and hold up mementos of family trips, obstacles overcome, and dreams realized. She holds out empty hands and says, "I have nothing."

With that she tells us that she is lucky to be alive, having seen family members shot, assaulted, and riddled with cancer. She's never vacationed, gone to camp, or learned to play an instrument. What is the value of our lives, she asks her classmates. Can it be summed up in clothing, athletic equipment, or hair ribbons? She is the first in three generations to not be pregnant by age sixteen. She has courage, a heart, a brain, and a strong, straight spine that allows her to stand up to anything. Some lines rhyme, perhaps from practice or perhaps from serendipity, it's impossible to tell. By the time she finishes, the class is left silent and staring; many, including me, are in tears. She receives a standing ovation.

If this class learns nothing else, I think, over the past three weeks they've learned empathy and some level of understanding of the differences and commonalities between them. Everyone is trying to overcome challenges. Sometimes we can see it in the looks on their faces, the clothing they wear, or the way their shoulders hunch. But sometimes we have to listen and bear witness.

November

On election night, I canvass in a Bangladeshi neighborhood with a friend. We knock on doors asking if residents voted and offering directions to the elementary school if not. Most proudly show their "I Voted" stickers. I have a full heart as I walk to a neighbor's place to watch the election returns. Of course, that feeling dissipates as the night unfolds, until the beer is gone and we watch, disbelieving and sad. I answer text messages from my daughter, away at school and confused by what is happening. I sense her tears and wish to be with her, but can only tell her that it isn't as bad as it seems, despite not feeling that myself.

As I drive through the farmland, the previously ignored Trump-Pence signs make me angry. The two-lane road is mostly empty but I notice a pickup truck ahead, parked on the shoulder, Confederate flags waving from the truck's bed. As I pass, slowing slightly, the driver whoops and hollers from the truck, waving his arms in celebration. I am enraged, disgusted, and fearful for the first time in this place.

I try to keep class focused on the task at hand. Debra, the Bernie supporter, is distraught. After class, she says she almost didn't attend, having stayed up until the bitter end at 3:00 a.m.

"I don't understand this. I'll never understand how people could vote for him," she says. I give her a quick hug before we part. Tanner missed another day of class and I'm worried. I make a mental note to send an email.

The tone is far more somber in the city, with two female students nearly in tears. Mira has been a vocal Hillary supporter during class, wearing t-shirts and pins. The previous Friday, I attended a Hillary rally and there was Mira, in the bleachers waving a placard. She could be seen on the CNN event coverage. Now she sat in my class, shaking her head, reading aloud the terrible online comments made to a Jewish reporter who questioned the outcome.

"These people are frighteningly anti-Semitic," she says.

Billy is shocked as well, and tells me that his family is full of union plumbers and auto workers, none of whom would vote Republican. "They may be on the conservative side, but they all thought he was a doofus. No way they voted for him."

We spend time in class debriefing. I don't voice any disappointment or frustration as I feel that it's not my place, but the students need to talk, to try to understand and make sense of it. I spend a few minutes during the next class talking about fake news. "My generation has created lots of problems for you to fix, but this one is all yours. You must learn to listen and discern reputable sources," I warn.

December

One of the most troubling aspects of this new breed of conservatism is the disdain for post-secondary education and the branding of such as the playground of the liberal elite who no longer care about the working class. I see it as a ploy to keep the undereducated ill-informed and easily manipulated, but I see it play out routinely in community college. Numerous very bright students—like Andy who spoke six languages and was learning Mandarin by tutoring Chinese students online at night—ignore my questions about four-year degrees because their parents don't want them in college. Some transfer to the small private college nearby, but many others select two-year programs when they could do much more. It took weeks of prodding and introductions to university professors to convince the smartest student I ever taught to apply to Michigan. He was accepted with a full scholarship to study philosophy. No one had ever suggested that a four-year degree was an option.

In class, we're discussing the power of words and language. I show a clip of a debate about use of the "n-word" and we have a respectful discussion about who is permitted to use this word and why. We discuss labeling and words that stereotype. This is always one of my favorite sessions. Sean speaks up.

"I love my dad, but when I started playing tennis and had matches around the state, I made African-American friends and he wouldn't let me post pictures of us on Facebook. He called them the n-word. I know he'd do anything for me, but it's not right that he feels that way. These are friends who go through the same things I do, cutting weight and stuff. I also realize that my mom's a feminist and that's not a bad thing. She's an engineer in a plant and gets harassed all the time. People use the word feminist like it's bad, but it's just women wanting equality. I'm proud of her."

I'm proud of Sean for articulating all this. I've said nothing all semester about how I lean or vote and I didn't need to. I'm not brainwashing Sean. He is seeing the world in new ways because of new experiences. The more he is educated, the more likely he is to be progressive in his thinking. It's about understanding nuance and gray areas.

Tanner emails that he'll begin treatment in a week. I arrange for him to take the final before class ends so that he doesn't have to worry. Once he's taken the final, he'll be finished with class. I am tempted to buy his family Christmas gifts, but I don't know them well enough to know if that would be appreciated or if it would feel too much like charity. He is worried about health care and may return to full-time work just to make sure that he has insurance.

Ahmed makes it to the last class, but tells me he will ship out the following weekend. He cannot tell me where he'll be or what he'll be doing. I shake his hand and thank him for his service, though he barely passes the final.

I trudge through the gray-black slush across campus to hear the last university speeches. We wrap up the semester and I wish everyone well. They are tired and excited and want the semester to be over. Billy tells me this was the best class of his first semester of college. I take that as a win. Carla gives her last speech on the need for more job counseling in college and I'm proud that she's taking a stand on something that impacts her directly.

After class, as I'm packing up to leave for the last time, Mira asks if she will see me at the Women's March in D.C. in January.

"Absolutely," I say.

CODA

ON BEING MIDWESTERN: THE BURDEN OF NORMALITY

PHIL CHRISTMAN | This essay originally appeared in The Hedgehog Review, Fall 2017, hedgehogreview.com. Reprinted with permission.

After my Texas-born wife and I moved to Michigan—an eleven-hour drive in the snow during which time itself seemed to widen and flatten with the terrain—I found myself pressed into service as a regional expert. What is the Midwest like?, she wanted to know. Midwestern history, Midwestern customs, Midwestern cuisine? I struggled to answer these reasonable questions, about a region where I was born and where I have spent most of my life, with anything more than clichés: bad weather, hard work, humble people. I knew these were inadequate. Connecticut winters and Arizona summers are also "bad"; the vast majority of humans have worked hard, or been worked hard, for all of recorded history; and *humility* is one of those words, like *authenticity* or (lately) *resistance*, that serves mainly to advertise the absence of the thing named.

I soon learned that I was hardly the only Midwesterner left tongue-tied by the Midwest. Articulate neighbors, friends, colleagues, and students, asked to describe their hometowns, replied with truisms that, put together, were also paradoxes: "Oh, it's in the middle of nowhere." "It's just like anywhere, you know." "We do the same things people do everywhere." No-places are as old as Thomas More's *Utopia*, but a no-place that is also everyplace and anyplace doesn't really add up. Nor, at least in my experience, does one hear such language from people in other regions—from Southerners, Californians, Arubans, Yorkshiremen. Canadians live in a country that has been jokingly described as America's Midwest writ larger—Canada and our Midwest share, among other things, manners, weather, topography, and a tendency among their inhabitants to downplay their own racism—yet they are hyperspecific in their language, assuming a knowledge of local landmarks that it never occurs to them non-Canadians may not possess. They assume that whatever their setting is, it is a setting, not, as Midwesterner-turned-expatriate Glenway Wescott once wrote of Wisconsin, "an abstract nowhere."[1]

When pressed, a person might explain these tropes of featurelessness by pointing out the similarities imposed across the Midwestern landscape by capitalism. Boosters sometimes still call the region "America's breadbasket," and for much of the late nineteenth and twentieth centuries it was also, to a large degree, America's foundry, and, during World War II, its armory.[2] (Such is the extractive quality of Midwestern economic history that some historians have proposed that we take seriously the painter Grant Wood's irritated description of the region, in his 1935 pamphlet *Revolt against the City*, as a colony of the East.[3]) What all of this means in practice, of course, is vast visual repetition: mile upon mile of cornfields, block upon block of crumbling factories. (Willa Cather: "The only thing very noticeable about Nebraska was that it was still, all day long, Nebraska."[4])

But even used and battered landscapes have their particularity: Detroit's blight isn't Cleveland's blight, any more than Manchester's is Birmingham's. Nor are any two cornfields truly exactly alike, despite Monsanto's best efforts. The British cultural imagination has been formed by writers such as Thomas Hardy and D.H. Lawrence who are perfectly capable of distinguishing among bleaknesses; there's no reason the American imagination should not pay the Midwest the same tribute. Especially in a period when some of the more interesting art and music consists of similar procedures repeated on a massive canvas, when cultured people are trained to find meaning in the tiny variations of a Philip Glass symphony or an early John Adams tape piece, you'd think we could learn to truly see Midwestern flatness as something richer than mindless repetition. (Willa Cather again: "No one who had not grown up in a little prairie town could know anything about it. It was a kind of freemasonry.")[5]

Even if we insist, wrongly, on seeing the Midwest's physical geography as featureless, there's no reason to extend the mistake, as many even within the region do, to its cultural landscape. In a 2015 essay for *Slate*, "The Rust-Belt Theory of Low-Cost High Culture," reporter Alec McGillis marveled at the cheapness—and, it seems, the mere presence—of good orchestra and museum tickets in interior cities:

> The Cleveland Orchestra, one of the best in the world, offers a "young professional package," with regular concerts and special events, for a mere $15 per month—$20 for a couple. When I visited the St. Louis Art Museum, a monumental building deep within verdant Forest Park, I was stunned by its wealth of German expressionists (it has the world's largest collection of Max Beckmanns)—all for the entrance fee of $0. In Milwaukee, I spent hours with my laptop at the cafe in the art museum's Calatrava-designed wing.... In Detroit, friends and I got a prime table at Baker's Keyboard Lounge, its oldest jazz club, for a $10 cover.[6]

I appreciate McGillis's enthusiasm, but why on earth was he so surprised? This is a part of the country where, the novelist Neal Stephenson observes, you can find small colleges "scattered about ... at intervals of approximately one tank of gas." Indeed, the grid-based zoning so often invoked to symbolize dullness actually attests to a love of education, he argues:

> People who often fly between the East and West Coasts of the United States will be familiar with the region, stretching roughly from the Ohio to the Platte, that, except in anomalous non-flat areas, is spanned by a Cartesian grid of roads. They may not be aware that the spacing between roads is exactly one mile. Unless they have a serious interest in nineteenth-century Midwestern cartography, they can't possibly be expected to know that when those grids were laid out, a schoolhouse was platted at every other road intersection. In this way it was assured that no child in the Midwest would ever live more than $\sqrt{2}$ miles [i.e., about 1.4 miles] from a place where he or she could be educated.[7]

Minnesota Danish farmers were into Kierkegaard long before the rest of the country.[8] They were descended, perhaps, from the pioneers Meridel LeSueur describes in her social history *North Star Country*:

> Simultaneously with building the sod shanties, breaking the prairie, schools were started, Athenaeums and debating and singing societies founded, poetry written and recited on winter evenings. The latest theories of the rights of man were discussed along with the making of a better breaking plow. Fourier, Marx, Rousseau, Darwin were discussed in covered wagons.[9]

If you've read Marilynne Robinson's Gilead trilogy, you know that many of these schools were founded as centers of abolitionist resistance, or even as stops on the Underground Railroad.

When, looking in your own mind for a sense of your own experiences in a region, you find only clichés and evasions—well, that is a clue worth following. So I began, here and there, collecting tidbits, hoarding anecdotes, savoring every chance piece of evidence that the Midwest was a distinctive region with its own history. In doing so I noticed yet another paradox: If the Midwest is a particular place that instead thinks of itself as an anyplace or no-place, it is likewise both present and not present in the national conversation. The Midwest is, in fact, fairly frequently written about, but almost always in a way that weirdly disclaims the possibility that it has ever been written or thought about before. The trope of featurelessness is matched by a trope of neglect (for what can one do with what is featureless but neglect it?). Katy Rossing, a poet and essayist, has described the formula:

> 1. Begin with a loquacious description of the Euclidean-flat homogeneity of the landscape. This place looks boring. It looks like there's nothing here worth thinking about. Example: "The sins of the Midwest: flatness, emptiness, a necessary acceptance of the familiar. Where is the romance in being buried alive? In growing old?" (Stewart O'Nan, *Songs for the Missing*)

> 2. In fact, it seems no one has really thought about it before, they all write. What IS the Midwest? The West, South, and East all have clear stories, stories that are told and retold in regionally interested textbooks, novels, movies. The Midwest? It's a humorously ingenuous, blank foil for another region. Example: *Fargo, Annie Hall.*

> 3. But wait a minute, the writers tell you, it turns out this place isn't empty at all! They spend the remainder of the article crouched in a defensive posture.[10]

Rossing misses one or two tricks—there must also be a resentful invocation of the term *flyover country* ("a stereotype," as one lexicographer points out, "about other people's stereotypes").[11] And one must end self-refutingly, by pointing out a number of example of Midwestern distinctiveness or high achievement, all of which—the frontier, Abraham Lincoln, populism, the Great Migration, Chicago, the growth and decline of manufacturing—are so thoroughly discussed as to bring the article's initial premise into question.[12] The density of these let's-stop-ignoring-the-Midwest takes only increased after the 2016 election[13], as national newspapers, ignoring the dozens of articles they had already published on the region, pledged themselves to the Rust Belt as though to a strict Lenten discipline.[14]

There is no dearth of commentary upon the Midwest, actually, once you begin to look for it. Historian and politico Jon Lauck points to the region's rich historiographic tradition in *The Lost Region*; journals devoted to the region's history and literature come and go (*MidAmerica; Midwestern Gothic*); the Society for the Study of Midwestern Literature sponsors superb, if frequently ignored, scholarship; regional independent presses win awards and capture attention (Coffee House, Greywolf, Dzanc, Belt, Two Dollar Radio); writers as major as Toni Morrison, Louise Erdrich, Marilynne Robinson, David Foster Wallace, and Richard Powers set book after book in the region. (Morrison in particular is so identified with the South—because, to be blunt, she's black—that people forget she's from Ohio. *The Bluest Eye, Sula*, and *Beloved* are set there, *Song of Solomon* in Michigan.) If you took English in high school, you read—or pretended you read—Cather, Scott Fitzgerald, Ernest Hemingway, Sherwood Anderson, Sandra Cisneros, and Theodore Dreiser, all of whom wrote of the region lovingly or ambivalently; if you took it in graduate school, you may also have read Wescott, William H. Gass, Saul Bellow, Jaimy Gordon, Dinaw Mengestu. The situation resembles nothing so much as the episode of the television show *Louie* in which the main character, stricken with guilt over his lapsed friendship with a less successful comedian, appears at the man's house and demands a reunion, a reckoning; whereupon the old friend, after a meaningful silence, remarks that Louie has delivered the same speech twice before: He'd forgotten each time. Our reckoning with the Midwest is perpetually arriving, perpetually deferred.

Andrew R.L. Cayton, one of the foremost historians of the region, gives a partial explanation for this neurotic repetition: Much of the discourse about the Midwest is mentally filed under the heading "local," not "regional."

> Historically, when people in the Midwest argue with each other over questions of identity, they fight over issues on universal, national, or local levels. They talk about what it means to be an American, a Lutheran, a farmer, a woman, a lesbian, a feminist, a black man; they almost never talk about what it means to be Midwestern, except in the most cursory fashion. In trying to locate a "heartland code," one ethicist found that residents of the St. Louis area invoked generalities, such as "respect for family," "respect for religion," "respect for education," "honesty," "selflessness," and "respect for the environment." They rarely got more specific than that.... In virtually all the recent work on the Midwest, it remains a setting, not a particular constellation of attitudes or behaviors.[15]

We Midwesterners talk about ourselves, and we are talked about by others, but in terms either universal or local: Abe Lincoln of the log cabin, or Abe Lincoln of world history, but not, despite the movie, Abe Lincoln of Illinois, who was formed in part by that "great interior region" he lauded in his 1862 Annual Message to Congress.[16] A Midwesterner may be a human, an American, a Detroiter, at most a Michigander, but a "Midwesterner" only when reminded of the fact. Cayton blames this lack of "regional consciousness" in part on geography: "Regional identity—the creation of an imagined community—requires a strong sense of isolation. And the Midwest is not, strictly speaking, isolated. It is in the middle." More important, however, is the intensity of local attachment: "But it is less regional *rootlessness* than local rootedness that makes the construction of a regional identity so difficult in the Midwest.... Localism, this pride in family, town, and state, leaves little room for interest in a coherent regional identity. In general, Midwesterners want to be left alone in worlds of their own making."[17]

Cayton's last remark, in particular, throws light on the way the Midwest is often depicted in American art, and the way Midwestern artists tend to function. Think of Grant Wood's farm couple, posted like sentries; of the intensely self-aware little Midwestern scenes that dot the landscape of American popular-music history like a series of private kingdoms: Motown in the '60s, Ann Arbor–Detroit in the late '60s and early '70s, Cleveland in the mid-'70s, Minneapolis in the early '80s. Think of Prince, who famously shot down Matt Damon's attempt at conversation—"I hear you live in Minnesota"—with that wonderful remark, at once quintessentially Prince and quintessentially Midwestern: "I live inside my own heart, Matt Damon."[18] From Prince in his private Paisley Park kingdom in the middle of Minnesota; to Robert Pollard in Dayton, with his one-person record industry; to Bob Dylan, cloistered in his private languages and allegories; from William H. Gass's novels and stories, walled and defended in purple prose and private grudges like old Michigan fort towns; to Marilynne Robinson's elaborately homemade worlds and worldview; to Gwendolyn Brooks's lifelong loyalty to Chicago, the Midwestern artist hunkers down on the landscape; she lives in her own heart. We remember her, then, as the artist of that patch of landscape, not as a "Midwestern artist."

If it is not the Midwest that is missing from American history or culture, or even from the national conversation, but simply a Midwestern "regional consciousness," as Cayton puts it, one naturally wonders whether such a category is important in the first place. Do

Midwesterners need another "grid" (to borrow a term from the social critic George W.S. Trow) on which to plot their own lives? We already have families, towns and cities, a country, a species. Perhaps we are simply Americans, with no need for further differentiation.

It's certainly tempting to think so—because this idea is actually the one that gives the Midwest its most persistent self-understanding, the frame in which we see ourselves and through which others see us. We think of ourselves as basic Americans, with no further qualification. "The West, South, and East all have clear stories," as Katy Rossing puts it. But in the Midwest, we don't. We're free. And that is our story.

The authors of this story are not terribly hard to name. One of them is Lincoln, who, in his 1862 address to Congress having already labeled the Midwest the "great interior region," went even further, commending it as "territorially speaking...the great body of the republic."[19] It's a part of the country, but also, give or take, the country. Another author was Frederick Jackson Turner, whose *The Frontier in American History* (1920) characterizes the Middle West (as the slightly more dignified phrase of his day had it) as follows:

> Both native settler and European immigrant saw in this free and competitive movement of the frontier the chance to break the bondage of social rank, and to rise to a higher plane of existence. The pioneer was passionately desirous to secure for himself and for his family a favorable place in the midst of these large and free but vanishing opportunities. It took a century for this society to fit itself into the conditions of the whole province.... Little by little, nature pressed into her mold the plastic pioneer life.... From this society, seated amidst a wealth of material advantages, and breeding individualism, energetic competition, inventiveness, and spaciousness of design, came the triumph of the strongest. The captains of industry arose and seized on nature's gifts. Struggling with one another, increasing the scope of their ambitions as the largeness of the resources and the extent of the fields of activity revealed themselves, they were forced to accept the natural conditions of a province vast in area but simple in structure. Competition grew into consolidation.[20]

Turner's Middle West is a sort of buffer zone between capitalism and the democracy of yeoman farmers, the straw mattress on which Hamilton lies down with Jefferson. "The task of the Middle West is that of adapting democracy to the vast economic organization of the present," he writes.[21] One might have thought this was everybody's job. By tasking the Midwest in particular with the work all citizens of a developed democracy must do, Turner cannot help suggesting that the region is defined solely by a sort of extra degree of Americanness, by being American to the nth power. (Wescott again: "What seems local is national, what seems national is universal, what seems Middle Western is in the commonest way human."[22]) As the geographer James Shortridge puts it, "The Middle West came to symbolize the nation...to be seen as the most American part of America."[23] Nor is average Americanness quite the same as average Russianness or average Scandinavianness, for the United States has always understood itself, however self-flatteringly, as an experiment on behalf of humanity. Thus, Midwestern averageness, whatever form it may take, has consequences for the entire world; what we make here sets the world's template. The historian Susan Gray has even detected echoes in Turner's language of Lamarckian evolution, a theory dominant among biologists a century ago, when Turner was writing. The new characteristics that the "old" races of the world acquired in their struggle to build a world among the prairies and forests would create an actual new, American race.[24]

Small wonder, then, that Midwestern cities, institutions, and people show up again and again in the twentieth-century effort to determine what, in America, is normal. George Gallup was born in Iowa, began his career in Des Moines at Drake University, and worked for a time at Northwestern; Alfred Kinsey scandalized the country from—of all places—Bloomington, Indiana. Robert and Helen Lynd, setting out in the 1920s to study the "interwoven trends that are the life of a small American city," did not even feel the need to defend the assumption that the chosen city "should, if possible, be in that common-denominator of America, the Middle West." They chose Muncie, Indiana, and called it Middletown.[25] We cannot be surprised that the filmgoers of Peoria became proverbial, or that newscasters are still coached to sound like they're from Kansas.[26] Nor that a recent defender of the region's distinctiveness feels he must concede, in the same breath, that it "was always less distinctive than other regions",[27] or that a historian can call "ordinariness" the Midwest's "historic burden."[28] If it is to serve as the epitome of America for Americans, and of humanity for the world, the place had better not be too distinctly anything. It has no features worth naming. It's anywhere, and also nowhere.

What does it do to people to see themselves as normal? On the one hand, one might adopt a posture of vigilant defense, both internal and external, against anything that might detract from such a fully, finally achieved humanness. On the other hand, a person might feel intense alienation and disgust, which one might project inward—*What is wrong with me?*—or outward, in a kind of bomb-the-suburbs reflex. A third possibility—a simple, contented *being normal*—arises often in our culture's fictions about the Midwest, both the stupid versions (the contented families of old sitcoms) and the more sophisticated ones (*Fargo's* Marge Gunderson, that living argument for the value of banal goodness). I have yet to meet any real people who manage it. A species is a bounded set of variations on a template, not an achieved state of being.

I took the first option. As a child, I accepted without thinking that my small town, a city of 9,383 people, contained within it every possible human type; if I could not fit in here, I would not fit in anywhere. ("Fitting in" I defined as being occupied on Friday nights and, sooner or later, kissing a girl.) Every week that passed in which I did not meet these criteria—which was most of them—became a prophecy. Every perception, every idea, every opinion that I could not make immediately legible to my peers became proof of an almost metaphysical estrangement, an oceanic differentness that could not be changed and could not be borne. I would obsessively examine tiny failures of communication for days, always blaming myself. It never occurred to me that this problem might be accidental or temporary. I knew that cities existed, but they were all surely just Michigan farm towns joined together n number of times, depending on population. Owing to a basically phlegmatic temperament, and the fear of hurting my parents, I made it to college without committing suicide; there, the thing solved itself. But I worry what would have happened—what does often happen—to the kid like me, but with worse test scores, bad parents, an unlocked gun cabinet.

But I also worry about the people who *can* pass as Midwestern-normal. At its least toxic, this can lead to a kind of self-contempt: the nice, intelligent young women in my classes at the University of Michigan who describe themselves and their friends, with flat malice, as "basic bitches." In artists, it can lead to self-destructive behavior, to the pursuit of danger in the belief that one's actual experiences have furnished nothing in the way of material. It also leads us to one of the other great stereotypes of Midwesterners, one that I think has a little more truth to it than the nonsense about hard work and humility: We are repressed. Any emotion spiky or passionate enough to disrupt the smooth surface of normality must be shunted away. Garrison Keillor, and in some ways David Letterman, made careers from talking about this repression in a comic mode that both embodies it and transmutes it into art. The Minnesota writer Carol Bly finds it less amusing:

> [In the Midwest] there is a restraint against feeling in general. There is a restraint against enthusiasm ("real nice" is the adjective—not "marvelous"); there is restraint in grief ("real sober" instead of "heartbroken"); and always, always, restraint in showing your feelings, lest someone be drawn closer to you.... When someone has stolen all four wheels off your car you say, "Oh, when I saw that car, with the wheels stripped off like that, I just thought ohhhhhhhh."[29]

Critiques of emotional repression always risk imposing a single model for the Healthy Expression of the Emotions on a healthy range of variations. But anyone who has lived in the Midwest will recognize the mode Bly describes, and if you've lived there long enough, you'll have seen some of the consequences she describes:

> You repress your innate right to evaluate events and people, but...energy comes from making your own evaluations and then acting on them, so...therefore your natural energy must be replaced by indifferent violence.[30]

Donald Trump won the Midwestern states in part because he bothered to contest them at all, while his opponent did not. But we cannot forget the *way* he contested them: raucous rallies that promised, and in some views incited, random violence against a laundry list of enemies. Since his victory, the Three Percent Militia has become a recurring, and unwelcome, character in Michigan politics.

A regional identity built on its own denial, on the idea of an unqualified normality: This sounds, of course, like whiteness—a racial identity that consists only of the absence of certain kinds of oppression. (White people can, of course, be economically oppressed, though if the oppression goes on in one place long enough they tend to lose some of their whiteness, to be racialized as that Snopes branch of the human family, the white trash.) And here we hit upon the last major stereotype of the Midwest, its snowy-whiteness.

If the South depends on having black people to kick around, Midwestern whites often see people of color as ever new and out of place, decades after the Great Migration. The thinking goes like this: America is an experiment, carried out in its purest form here in the Midwest; people of color threaten the cohesion on which the whole experiment may depend. Thus, while Southern history yields story after story of the most savage, intimate racist violence—of men castrated and barbecued before smiling crowds, dressed as for a picnic—Midwestern history is a study in racial quarantine.[31] Midwestern cities often dominate in rankings of the country's most segregated. And though the region has seen its share of Klan activity and outright lynchings—I write this days after the acquittal of the St. Anthony, Minnesota, police officer who killed Philando Castile—the Midwest's racism most frequently appears in the history books in the form of riots: Detroit, 1943; Cleveland, 1966; Milwaukee, Cincinnati, and Detroit again, 1967; Chicago, Cincinnati again, and Kansas City, 1968; Detroit again, 1975; Cincinnati again, 2001; Ferguson, 2014; Milwaukee again, 2016. A riot is, among other things, a refusal to be quarantined. And the Midwest quarantines its nonwhite immigrants, too—the people from Mexico and further south, from the hills of Laos or the highlands of Somalia, and from the Middle East, who commute from their heavily segregated neighborhoods to harvest the grain, empty the bedpans, and drive the snowplows. This is not to mention the people whose forced removal or confinement gave rise to the notion of the Midwest as an empty canvas in the first place. The twentieth-century history of racism in the Midwest is, on the whole, both a terrible betrayal of the abolitionist impulse that led to the settlement of so much of the region and a fulfillment of the violence inherent in the idea of "settling" what was already occupied.

Our bland, featureless Midwest—on some level, it is a fantasy. The easiest, most tempting tack for a cultural critic to take with fantasies is to condemn them. Given what ideas of normalness, in particular, have done to this country, to its nonwhite, nonstraight, non–middle-class, nonmale—and also to those who are all of those things, and are driven slightly or fully crazy by the effort to live up to the norm that is their birthright—it is tempting simply to try to fumigate the myth away.

Tempting, but probably not possible. As the English moral philosopher Mary Midgley argues, myths are "organic parts of our lives, cognitive and emotional habits, structures that shape our thinking."[32] Since thinking cannot be structureless, a frontal attack on one myth usually leaves us in a state of uncritical, unnamed acceptance of a new one. Self-conscious attempts to create new myths, meanwhile, are like constructed languages;

they never quite lose their plastic smell. We should ask instead whether our story of the Midwest—this undifferentiated human place—contains any lovelier, more useful, or more radical possibilities. At the very least, we should try to name what there is in us for it to appeal to.

Marilynne Robinson's Gilead trilogy has been read so often as to be reduced to a gingham study in Americana, and Robinson, a complex and in some ways cranky thinker, to "an Iowa abbess delivering profundities in humble dress."[33] This is a strange way to think about the story of a man dying before his son's tenth birthday; of an emotionally distant drifter who fails at prostitution and eventually marries a pastor; of an Eisenhower Republican family that loses its chance at partial redemption because the kindly dad is a racist. If conflating Marilynne Robinson with Jan Karon gets more people to buy Robinson's books, I suppose I can't object too strenuously, but it may lead some readers to miss the strangeness of passages such as this one in *Home* (2008):

> In college all of them had studied the putative effects of deracination, which were angst and anomie, those dull horrors of the modern world. They had been examined on the subject, had rehearsed bleak and portentous philosophies in term papers, and they had done it with the earnest suspension of doubt that afflicts the highly educable. And then their return to the pays natal, where the same old willows swept the same ragged lawns, where the same old prairie arose and bloomed as negligence permitted. Home. What kinder place could there be on earth, and why did it seem to them all like exile? Oh, to be passing anonymously through an impersonal landscape! Oh, not to know every stump and stone, not to remember how the fields of Queen Anne's lace figured in the childish happiness they had offered to their father's hopes, God bless him.... Strangers in some vast, cold city might notice the grief in her eyes, even remember it for an hour or two as they would a painting or a photograph, but they would not violate her anonymity.[34]

This passage offers a stunning inversion of the trope of featurelessness. While acknowledging that the place (in this case Gilead, Iowa) has a history ("the childish happiness they had offered to their father's hopes"), Glory Boughton, the narrator, longs for the "anonymity" and "impersonal landscape" of a "vast, cold city" (Chicago, Minneapolis, Milwaukee).

She longs for "deracination," for the sense of being an anyone moving through an anyplace. Why should a person long for this? Anonymity is usually felt as a burden, and the sense that one is a mere "basic person" can imprison as much as it liberates.

Yet the passage resonates, because we humans need to feel that we are more than our communities, more than our histories, more even than ourselves. We need to feel this because it is true. The cultural conservative ideal, with its deeply rooted communities—an idea that finds a strange echo in the less nuanced kinds of identity politics—is a reduction as dangerous to human flourishing and self-understanding as is the reduction of the mind to the brain or the soul to the body. The "deeply rooted community" is, in reality, at least as often as not, a cesspit of nasty gossips, an echo chamber in which minor misunderstandings amplify until they prevent people from seeing each other accurately, or at all. As for the identities that drive so much of our politics, they are a necessary part of the naming and dismantling of specific kinds of oppression—but we've all met people for whom they become a cul-de-sac, people who ration their sympathy into smaller and smaller tranches of shared similarity until they begin to resemble crabbed white men. Moral imaginations, like economies, tend to shrink under an austerity regime.

Every human is a vast set of unexpressed possibilities. And I never feel this to be truer than when I drive through the Midwest, looking at all the towns that could, on paper, have been my town, all the lives that, on paper, could have been my life. The factories are shuttered, the climate is changing, the towns are dying. My freedom so to drive is afforded, in part, by my whiteness. I know all this, and when I drive, now, and look at those towns, those lives, I try to maintain a kind of double consciousness, or double vision—the Midwest as an America not yet achieved; the Midwest as an America soaked in the same old American sins. But I cannot convince myself that the promise the place still seems to hold, the promise of flatness, of the freedom of anonymity, of being anywhere and nowhere at once, is a lie all the way through. Instead, I find myself daydreaming—there is no sky so conducive to daydreaming—of a Midwest that makes, and keeps, these promises to everybody.

And then I arrive at the house that, out of all these little houses, by some inconceivable coincidence, happens to be mine. I park the car. I check the mail. I pet the cat. I ready myself for bed. I can't stay up too late. Between the Midwest that exists and the other Midwest, the utopic no-place that I dream of, is hard work enough for a life.

1. Glenway Wescott, *Good-Bye, Wisconsin* (New York, NY: Harper, 1928), 39. Quoted in Richard Nelson Current, Wisconsin: *A History* (Urbana, IL: University of Illinois Press, 2001), 161.

2. See C. K. Hyde, *Arsenal of Democracy: The American Automobile Industry in World War II* (Detroit, MI: Wayne State University Press, 2013).

3. Edward Watts, *An American Colony: Regionalism and the Roots of Midwestern Culture* (Athens, OH: Ohio University Press, 2001), xii. See also Watts's "The Midwest as a Colony: Transnational Regionalism," in *Regionalism and the Humanities*, ed. Timothy Mahoney and Wendy J. Katz (Omaha, NE: University of Nebraska Press, 2009) 166–89.

4. Willa Cather, *My Ántonia* (Boston, MA: Houghton Mifflin, 1954), 5. First published 1918.

5. Ibid, 1.

6. Alec McGillis, "The Rust-Belt Theory of Low-Cost Culture," *Slate*, January 1, 2015, http://www.slate.com/articles/arts/culturebox/2015/01/cheap_high_culture_in_baltimore_buffalo_detroit_and_other_midsize_cities.html.

7. Neal Stephenson, "*Everything and More* Foreword," in *Some Remarks* (New York, NY: HarperCollins, 2012), 273.

8. See Thomas Wetzel, "A Graveyard of the Midwest," *MidAmerica* 26 (1999): 10–24.

9. Meridel LeSueur, *Ripening: Selected Work*, 1927–1980 (Old Westbury, NY: Feminist Press, 1982), 36.

10. Katy Rossing, "Smothered: American Nostalgia and the Small Wisconsin Town," *Hypocrite Reader*, January 2012, http://hypocritereader.com/12/smothered-american-nostalgia.

11. This supposed pejorative appears to have been popularized by *Midwesterners* reacting defensively to the region's supposed unpopularity in the coastal mind. See Gabe Bullard, "The Surprising Origin of the Phrase 'Flyover Country,'" *National Geographic*, March 14, 2016, http://news.nationalgeographic.com/2016/03/160314-flyover-country-origin-language-midwest.

12. For two examples, see Matthew Wolfson, "The Midwest Is Not Flyover Country," *The New Republic*, March 22, 2014, https://newrepublic.com/article/117113/midwest-not-flyover-country-its-not-heartland-either, and Michael Dirda's review of Jon Lauck's *The Lost Region, Washington Post*, February 4, 2014, https://www.washingtonpost.com/entertainment/books/the-lost-region-toward-a-revival-of-midwestern-history-by-jon-k-lauck/2014/02/05/55e90e08-8a90-11e3-833c-33098f9e5267_story.html?utm_term=.62c430eef907. Alternatively, one might simply Google the phrase "Not just flyover country."

13. Eric Schulzke, "The One County That Tipped Michigan to Trump," *Deseret News*, November 16, 2016, http://www.deseretnews.com/article/865667328/The-one-county-that-tipped-Michigan-to-Trump-and-why-ignoring-it-is-not-an-option.html.

14. See Anne Trubek, "The Media Didn't Forget the Rust Belt—You Did," *Refinery29*, November 17, 2016, http://www.refinery29.com/2016/11/130147/rust-belt-trump-voters-election-media-issues.

15. Andrew R.L. Cayton, "The Anti-Region," in Cayton and Susan E. Gray, *The American Midwest: Essays on Regional History* (Bloomington, IN: Indiana University Press, 2001), 148.

16. Abraham Lincoln, "Second Annual Message to Congress," in *Lincoln: Political Writings and Speeches*, ed. Terence Ball (New York, NY: Cambridge University Press, 2013), 157. >

17. Ibid., 149, 150.

18. Kenzie Bryant, "Prince Had No Time for Matt Damon's Small Talk," *Vanity Fair*, July 18, 2016, http://www.vanityfair.com/style/2016/07/matt-damon-prince-small-talk.

19. Lincoln's delimitation of a "great interior region"— "bounded east by the Alleghenies, north by the British dominions, west by the Rocky Mountains, and south by the line along which the culture of corn and cotton meets"—doesn't exactly conform to the U.S. Census Bureau's definition of the Midwest, nor to any of a half-dozen other common definitions. (Source for additional quote is Lincoln, "Second Annual Message," 157.) Referring to the West, which at that time included Michigan, the nineteenth-century novelist Caroline Kirkland wrote, "How much does that expression mean to include? I never have been able to discover its limits." Me neither. (Kirkland is quoted in Edwin S. Fussell, *Frontier in American Literature* [Princeton, NJ: Princeton University Press, 1954], 3.)

20. Frederick Jackson Turner, *The Frontier in American History* (New York, NY: Holt, 1950), 154. First published 1920.

21. Ibid., 155.

22. Quoted in Ronald Weber, *The Midwestern Ascendancy in American Writing* (Bloomington, IN: Indiana University Press, 1992), 7.

23. James Shortridge, *The Middle West* (Lawrence, KS: University of Kansas Press, 1989), 33.

24. Susan E. Gray, "Stories Written in the Blood: Race and Midwestern History," in Cayton and Gray, *The American Midwest*, 127.

25. Robert S. Lynd and Helen Merrell Lynd, *Middletown: A Study in American Culture* (New York, NY: Harcourt, Brace, 1959), 7–8. First published 1929. The identification of Middletown and Muncie is attested in a number of places; see the chapter on *Middletown* in Sarah E. Igo, *The Averaged American: Surveys, Citizens, and the Making of a Mass Public* (Cambridge, MA: Harvard University Press, 2008).

26. See Edward McClelland's delightful *How to Speak Midwestern* (Cleveland, OH: Belt Publishing, 2016), 9–10.

27. Wolfson, "The Midwest Is Not Flyover Country."

28. Nicole Etcheson, "Barbecued Kentuckians and Six-Foot Texas Rangers: The Construction of Midwestern Identity," in Gray and Cayton, *The American Midwest*, 78.

29. Carol Bly, "From the Lost Swede Towns," in *Letters from the Country* (New York, NY: Harper and Row, 1981), 4.

30. Ibid., 5–6.

31. I mean this more or less literally. The book exists; see Thomas Sugrue, *The Origins of the Urban Crisis* (Princeton, NJ: Princeton University Press, 1997).

32. Mary Midgley, *Myths We Live By* (London, England: Routledge Classics, 214), 7.

33. Mark Athitakis, *The (New) Midwest* (Cleveland, OH: Belt Publishing, 2017), 9.

34. Marilynne Robinson, *Home* (New York, NY: Farrar, Straus and Giroux, 2008), 282.

CONTRIBUTORS

Dana Aritonovich is a lifelong left-winger (except for a brief lapse in judgment in sixth grade) who relishes every opportunity to prove right-wingers wrong. The death of her Trump-loving uncle weeks after the inauguration and the health scares of several other Republican relatives later that year revealed an unpleasant reality about her own judgmental stubbornness when it comes to politics. Dana wants to believe that everyone is multi-dimensional, but that's getting increasingly difficult as the years go by and people become more invested in their own backyards than in the community as a whole. She studied political science, holds degrees in communications and American history, and is currently pursuing her MFA in creative nonfiction. The blog *What I Like I Sounds* (https://whatilikeissounds.wordpress.com) is dedicated to exploring her entire music collection and how each piece has influenced her.

Sydney Boles is an investigative reporter covering immigration detention and the criminal justice system in the Midwest. She is pursuing an MSJ from Medill School of Journalism.

Bridget Callahan is a writer and comedian from Cleveland, Ohio. Her writing has been nominated for a 2017 Pushcart Prize, and the 2018 Best Small Fictions. Her daily coverage of the 2016 Republican National Convention street scene can be found at *The Tusk*, an online literary humor magazine where she serves as fiction editor. She is actively recruiting a secret dog army.

Phil Christman teaches first-year writing at the University of Michigan and is the editor of the *Michigan Review of Prisoner Creative Writing*. His work has appeared or is forthcoming in The *Hedgehog Review, Commonweal, The American Scholar, The Christian Century, Books & Culture*, and other publications.

John Counts has published fiction and essays in the *Chicago Tribune's* "Printers Row Journal," the *Chicago Reader, Joyland, Midwestern Gothic,* and Belt's *A Detroit Anthology*. He works as an investigative reporter for *The Ann Arbor News* and MLive Media Group. He is also an editor at the *Great Lakes Review* literary journal, where he conceived and edits the Narrative Map essay project.

Chris Drabick is a former rock music journalist whose fiction has appeared in *Midwestern Gothic, After the Pause* and *Great Lakes Review*, and non-fiction in *BULL* and *Stoneboat*. He was the recipient of a 2012 Juniper Summer Fellowship, as well as winner of the Marion Smith Short Story Prize. He teaches English at the University of Akron in Ohio, where he lives with his wife, their two sons and too many vinyl LPs.

Dan Gilman currently serves on the Pittsburgh City Council representing the 8th District, including the neighborhoods of Oakland, Point Breeze, Shadyside and Squirrel Hill. During his first term, Councilman Gilman has focused on creating a more accountable city government, embracing Pittsburgh's technological renaissance in order to improve City services, and making Pittsburgh a more family-friendly and progressive city. Gilman has received many awards and accolades for his hard work, including recognition by The New DEAL, a national network committed to highlighting pragmatic progressives with innovative ideas at the state and local level, and nomination as one of Pittsburgh's "40 Under 40" by *Pittsburgh Magazine* and Pittsburgh Urban Magnet Project, as well as one of Pittsburgh's "50 Finest" by *Whirl Magazine*. Councilman Gilman graduated from Pittsburgh's Shady Side Academy, and then with honors from Carnegie Mellon University with a degree in Ethics, History, and Public Policy.

Vince Guerrieri is a journalist and author in the Cleveland area. He attended college at Bowling Green State University, and was a newspaper editor in Northwest Ohio for eight years.

Justin Kern is a writer and a nonprofit marketing human who lives in Milwaukee with his wife and cats. A former daily news reporter, his fiction and nonfiction words have run in *Utne Reader, Great Lakes Review, Forth, Buffalo Spree, Milwaukee Record* and Belt's Buffalo anthology. He's a card-carrying member of four of Dunkirk's finer social clubs. His book, "Conniving for Nothing," will be out eventually.

Trent Kay Maverick is a professor of communications at John Carroll University and manages WJCU 88.7 FM, John Carroll's college radio station. Before entering academia, Trent tried really hard to become fluent in Hawaiian, dragged an iffy number of acquaintances to Rocky Horror, and spent a year in Japan teaching English and eating all the food.

Sarah Kendzior is a writer who lives in St. Louis. She covers U.S. and international politics for a number of publications, including the *Globe and Mail, De Correpondent*, NBC News and *Fast Company*. She has a PhD in anthropology from Washington University in St Louis, where she researched authoritarian states in Central Asia. Her best-selling essay collection, *The View From Flyover Country,* will be available in an updated print release in April 2018.

Amanda Lewan is an entrepreneur and writer living in Detroit. Her work has been been recognized and published in *NPR, The Nation, Journal of American*a and more. She is currently at work on her first novel. Visit her website at www.amandalewan.com for more.

Rowan Lynam is a journalist covering environmental racism and immigration detention in the Midwest. They are pursuing an MSJ from Medill School of Journalism.

Allison Lynn is the author of the novels *The Exiles* (Little A/Houghton Mifflin Harcourt) and *Now You See It* (Touchstone/Simon & Schuster), as well as articles, essays, and book reviews for publications that include *The New York Times Book Review, People* magazine, and *Post Road*. She lives in Indianapolis with her husband and son.

Annie Maroon is a writer from western Pennsylvania. She previously worked as a reporter for *MassLive*, and is now a freelance writer and photographer in the Boston area. Her work is online at anniemaroon.com.

Greggor Mattson, a native of small-town Washington, is Associate Professor of Sociology at Oberlin College, where he directs the Program in Gender, Sexuality, and Feminist Studies. He is the author of a book on prostitution regulation, other essays for Belt, and is working on a book about gay bars.

Edward McClelland is the author of *Folktales and Legends of the Middle West, How to Speak Midwestern, Nothin' But Blue Skies: The Heyday, Hard Times, and Hopes of America's Industrial Heartland, and The Third Coast: Sailors, Strippers, Fishermen, Folksingers, Long-Haired Ojibway Painters, and God-Save-the-Queen Monarchists of the Great Lakes.* His writing has also appeared in the *New York Times, Los Angeles Times, Columbia Journalism Review, Salon, Slate*, and the *Nation*.

Samantha Phillips is a city reporter for the Youngstown Vindicator, covering crime, administration and education, and writing up some feel-good features. She loves being a storyteller for a living. She graduated from Youngstown State University in May 2017 with a Bachelor of Arts in Communication. When Samantha is not writing, she is spending time with loved ones, playing with her pitbull, volunteering, reading, obsessing over *Black Mirror*, or enjoying the outdoors.

Angela Anagnost Repke lives with her family of four in Michigan. Her degrees in English and counseling suddenly mean more to her since becoming a stay-at-home-mom to help her mother in her triumphant battle against cancer. She turns to writing to help in both her daily blunders and rediscovering herself again outside of being a mother. Angela is a contributor at PopSugar and has been published in *Good Morning America, ABC News, Scary Mommy, MSN Lifestyle, Mothers Always Write,* and more. She is at work on *Mothers Lie*, a cross-generational memoir.

Mark V. Reynolds is a Chicago-based writer who reflects upon the intersection of history, race and culture for Popmatters.com and other publications. He received first-place honors from the Ohio Society of Professional Journalists in 2004 for media criticism, in the magazine Urban Dialect. He is a native of Cleveland, OH, and carries love for the Browns, Cavaliers, Indians and Stadium Mustard wherever he goes. In 2016-17, he served as Director of Marketing & Communications at Antioch College in Yellow Springs, his alma mater.

Tara Rose is an essayist, television critic, and daughter of the Rust Belt who now lives in Winston-Salem, NC.

Bill Savage teaches Chicago literature, history, and culture at Northwestern University and the Newberry Library of Chicago. He has published book reviews, op-ed essays, and various polemics, jeremiads, and diatribes in the *Chicago Tribune, Crain's Chicago Business,* the *Chicago Reader,* and other publications with "Chicago" in their masthead. He is currently at work on a book entitled "The City Logical," about reading Chicago's history through quirks in its grid of street names and addresses. He is a lifelong resident of Chicago's Rogers Park neighborhood.

Ed Simon is the author of *America and Other Fictions: On Radical Faith and Post-Religion* and *The Anthology of Babel*. A frequent contributor at several different sites, including *The Atlantic, The Paris Review Daily, The Washington Post, Newsweek*, and *Aeon* among others, he holds a PhD in Renaissance and early American literature from Lehigh University. He can be followed on Twitter @WithEdSimon, or on his Facebook author's page.

Tory Sparks graduated from Oberlin College in 2017 with Highest Honors in Gender, Sexuality, and Feminist Studies, specializing in studies of space, queer organizing, and generational politics. She served as the research assistant for the Who Needs Gay Bars? project by Professor Greggor Mattson in Summer of 2017, interviewing owners and patrons at rural, isolated gay bars across the American south and Midwest. She currently resides in Ann Arbor, Michigan with her cat, where she is the Washtenaw County Community Outreach Educator for Planned Parenthood. When she's not teaching sex ed or working with high school peer educators, she enjoys bar trivia, road trips, and feminist rants.

Lori Tucker-Sullivan is a freelance writer, whose poems, essays, stories, and reviews have appeared in various magazines and journals, including *Now & Then: The Magazine of Appalachia, Passages North, The Sun, About the Girl, The Cancer Poetry Project, Midwestern Gothic,* and others. Her essay, "Detroit, 2015" about her decision to return to Detroit after the death of her husband, was nominated for a Pushcart Prize and was listed as a Notable Essay of 2015 in *Best American Essays, 2016.* Her essay "Bused in and Bused Out: How Federal Mandates Changed Warrendale," was included in Belt Publishing's *Detroit Neighborhood Guidebook* in 2017. She is the author of the blog A Widow's Apprenticeship. She holds an MFA from Spalding University with a focus in Creative Nonfiction and is working on a memoir about how friendships with the widows of 1970s rock stars helped her grief journey. She lives in Detroit.

Christopher Vondracek appears as the poet Rattlesnake on South Dakota Public Broadcasting's "Rock Garden Tour." He is a journeyman English adjunct instructor and writes frequently on Lawrence Welk.

Wendy Welch directs the Graduate Medical Education Consortium of Southwest Virginia, working at the intersection of health and economic development. With her husband Jack Beck (presenter of "Celtic Clanjamphry" for NPR) she runs a shop that is the subject of her 2012 memoir *Little Bookstore of Big Stone Gap.* Editor of the volume *Public Health in*

Appalachia, her most recent book is Fall or Fly, telling the story of foster care in Coalfields Appalachia. And she is ringmaster of the all-volunteer cat rescue APPALACHIAN FELINE FRIENDS. She sleeps between these things. Find her online at wendywelchbigstonegap.wordpress.com.

AUTOBIOGRAPHY OF JOHN STUART MILL

by

JOHN STUART MILL

COMPASS CIRCLE

Autobiography of John Stuart Mill

Current edition published by Compass Circle in 2019.

Published by Compass Circle
A Division of Garcia & Kitzinger Pty Ltd
Cover copyright ©2019 by Compass Circle.

All rights reserved. No part of this publication may be reproduced, stored in a retrieval system, or transmitted, in any form or by any means, electronic, mechanical, photocopying, recording or otherwise without the prior permission of the publisher.

Note:
All efforts have been made to preserve original spellings and punctuation of the original edition which may include old-fashioned English spellings of words and archaic variants.

This book is a product of its time and does not reflect the same views on race, gender, sexuality, ethnicity, and interpersonal relations as it would if it were written today.

For information contact :
information@compass-circle.com

It is not because men's desires are strong that they act ill; it is because their consciences are weak.

JOHN STUART MILL

SECRET WISDOM OF THE AGES SERIES

Life presents itself, it advances in a fast way. Life indeed never stops. It never stops until the end. The most diverse questions peek and fade in our minds. Sometimes we seek for answers. Sometimes we just let time go by.

The book you have now in your hands has been waiting to be discovered by you. This book may reveal the answers to some of your questions.

Books are friends. Friends who are always by your side and who can give you great ideas, advice or just comfort your soul.

A great book can make you see things in your soul that you have not yet discovered, make you see things in your soul that you were not aware of.

Great books can change your life for the better. They can make you understand fascinating theories, give you new ideas, inspire you to undertake new challenges or to walk along new paths.

Life philosophies like the one of Henry Ford, John D. Rockefeller, Benjamin Franklin, Adam Smith, among others, are indeed a secret to many, but for those of us lucky enough to have discovered them, by one way or another, these books can enlighten us. They can open a wide range of possibilities to us. Because achieving greatness requires knowledge.

The series SECRET WISDOM OF THE AGES presented by Compass Circle try to bring you the great timeless masterpieces of personal development, positive thinking, and the law of attraction.

We welcome you to discover with us fascinating works by Henry Ford, John D. Rockefeller, Benjamin Franklin, Adam Smith, Wallace Wattles, Thomas Troward, James Allen, among others.

Contents

I

Childhood And Early Education

It seems proper that I should prefix to the following biographical sketch some mention of the reasons which have made me think it desirable that I should leave behind me such a memorial of so uneventful a life as mine. I do not for a moment imagine that any part of what I have to relate can be interesting to the public as a narrative or as being connected with myself. But I have thought that in an age in which education and its improvement are the subject of more, if not of profounder, study than at any former period of English history, it may be useful that there should be some record of an education which was unusual and remarkable, and which, whatever else it may have done, has proved how much more than is commonly supposed may be taught, and well taught, in those early years which, in the common modes of what is called instruction, are little better than wasted. It has also seemed to me that in an age of transition in opinions, there may be somewhat both of interest and of benefit in noting the successive phases of any mind which was always pressing forward, equally ready to learn and to unlearn either from its own thoughts or from those of others. But a motive which weighs more with me than either of these, is a desire to make acknowledgment of the debts which my intellectual and moral development owes to other persons; some of them of recognised eminence, others less known than they deserve to be, and the one to whom most of all is due, one whom the world had no opportunity of knowing. The reader whom these things do not interest, has only himself to blame if he reads farther, and I do

1

not desire any other indulgence from him than that of bearing in mind that for him these pages were not written.

I was born in London, on the 20th of May, 1806, and was the eldest son of James Mill, the author of the *History of British India*. My father, the son of a petty tradesman and (I believe) small farmer, at Northwater Bridge, in the county of Angus, was, when a boy, recommended by his abilities to the notice of Sir John Stuart, of Fettercairn, one of the Barons of the Exchequer in Scotland, and was, in consequence, sent to the University of Edinburgh, at the expense of a fund established by Lady Jane Stuart (the wife of Sir John Stuart) and some other ladies for educating young men for the Scottish Church. He there went through the usual course of study, and was licensed as a Preacher, but never followed the profession; having satisfied himself that he could not believe the doctrines of that or any other Church. For a few years he was a private tutor in various families in Scotland, among others that of the Marquis of Tweeddale, but ended by taking up his residence in London, and devoting himself to authorship. Nor had he any other means of support until 1819, when he obtained an appointment in the India House.

In this period of my father's life there are two things which it is impossible not to be struck with: one of them unfortunately a very common circumstance, the other a most uncommon one. The first is, that in his position, with no resource but the precarious one of writing in periodicals, he married and had a large family; conduct than which nothing could be more opposed, both as a matter of good sense and of duty, to the opinions which, at least at a later period of life, he strenuously upheld. The other circumstance, is the extraordinary energy which was required to lead the life he led, with the disadvantages under which he laboured from the first, and with those which he brought upon himself by his marriage. It would have been no small thing, had he done no more than to support himself and his family during so many years by writing, without ever being in debt, or in any pecuniary difficulty; holding, as he did, opinions, both in politics and in religion, which were more odious to all persons of influence, and to the common run of prosperous Englishmen, in that generation than either before or since; and being not only a man whom nothing would have induced to write against his convictions, but one who invariably threw into everything he wrote, as much of his convictions as he thought the circumstances would in any way permit: being, it must also be said, one who never did anything negligently; never undertook any task, literary or other, on which he did not conscientiously bestow all the labour necessary for performing it adequately. But he, with these burdens on him, planned, commenced, and completed, the *History of India*; and this in the course of about ten years, a shorter time than has been occupied (even by writers who had no other employment) in the production of almost any other historical work of equal bulk, and of anything approaching to the same amount of reading and research. And to this is to be added, that during the whole period, a considerable part of almost every day was employed in the instruction of his children: in the case of one of whom, myself, he exerted an amount of labour, care, and perseverance rarely, if ever, employed for a similar purpose, in endeavouring to give, according to his own conception, the highest order of intellectual education.

A man who, in his own practice, so vigorously acted up to the principle of losing no time, was likely to adhere to the same rule in the instruction of his pupil. I have no remembrance of the time when I began to learn Greek; I have been told that it was when I was three years old. My earliest recollection on the subject, is that of committing to memory what my father termed vocables, being lists of common Greek words, with their signification in English, which he wrote out for me on cards. Of grammar, until some years later, I learnt no more than the inflections of the nouns and verbs, but, after a course of vocables, proceeded at once to translation; and I faintly remember going through Aesop's *Fables*, the first Greek book which I read. The *Anabasis*, which I remember better, was the second. I learnt no Latin until my eighth year. At that time I had read, under my father's tuition, a number of Greek prose authors, among whom I remember the whole of Herodotus, and of Xenophon's *Cyropaedia* and *Memorials of Socrates*; some of the lives of the philosophers by Diogenes Laertius; part of Lucian, and Isocrates ad Demonicum and Ad Nicoclem. I also read, in 1813, the first six dialogues (in the common arrangement) of Plato, from the Euthyphron to the Theoctetus inclusive: which last dialogue, I venture to think, would have been better omitted, as it was totally impossible I should understand it. But my father, in all his teaching, demanded of me not only the utmost that I could do, but much that I could by no possibility have done. What he was himself willing to undergo for the sake of my instruction, may be judged from the fact, that I went through the whole process of preparing my Greek lessons in the same room and at the same table at which he was writing: and as in those days Greek and English lexicons were not, and I could make no more use of a Greek and Latin lexicon than could be made without having yet begun to learn Latin, I was forced to have recourse to him for the meaning of every word which I did not know. This incessant interruption, he, one of the most impatient of men, submitted to, and wrote under that interruption several volumes of his History and all else that he had to write during those years.

The only thing besides Greek, that I learnt as a lesson in this part of my childhood, was arithmetic: this also my father taught me: it was the task of the evenings, and I well remember its disagreeableness. But the lessons were only a part of the daily instruction I received. Much of it consisted in the books I read by myself, and my father's discourses to me, chiefly during our walks. From 1810 to the end of 1813 we were living in Newington Green, then an almost rustic neighbourhood. My father's health required considerable and constant exercise, and he walked habitually before breakfast, generally in the green lanes towards Hornsey. In these walks I always accompanied him, and with my earliest recollections of green fields and wild flowers, is mingled that of the account I gave him daily of what I had read the day before. To the best of my remembrance, this was a voluntary rather than a prescribed exercise. I made notes on slips of paper while reading, and from these in the morning walks, I told the story to him; for the books were chiefly histories, of which I read in this manner a great number: Robertson's histories, Hume, Gibbon; but my greatest delight, then and for long afterwards, was Watson's *Philip the Second and Third*. The heroic defence of the Knights of Malta against the Turks, and of the revolted Provinces of the Netherlands against Spain, excited in me an intense and lasting interest. Next to Watson, my favourite historical reading was Hooke's *History of Rome*. Of Greece I had seen at that time no regular history, except school abridgments and the last two or three volumes of a translation of Rollin's *Ancient History*, beginning with Philip of Macedon. But I read with great delight Langhorne's translation of Plutarch. In English history, beyond the time at which Hume leaves off, I remember reading Burnet's *History of his Own Time*, though I cared little for anything in it except the wars and battles; and the historical part of the *Annual Register*, from the beginning to about 1788, where the volumes my father borrowed for me from Mr. Bentham left off. I felt a lively interest in Frederic of Prussia during his difficulties, and in Paoli, the Corsican patriot; but when I came to the American War, I took my part, like a child as I was (until set right by my father) on the wrong side, because it was called the English side. In these frequent talks about the books I read, he used, as opportunity offered, to give me explanations and ideas respecting civilization, government, morality, mental cultivation, which he required me afterwards to restate to him in my own words. He also made me read, and give him a verbal account of, many books which would not have interested me sufficiently to induce me to read them of myself: among other's Millar's *Historical View of the English Government*, a book of great merit for its time, and which he highly valued; Mosheim's *Ecclesiastical History*, McCrie's *Life of John Knox*, and even Sewell and Rutty's Histories of the Quakers. He was fond of putting into my hands books which exhibited men of energy and resource in unusual circumstances, struggling against difficulties and overcoming them: of such works I remember Beaver's *African Memoranda*, and Collins's *Account of the First Settlement of New South Wales*. Two books which I never wearied of reading were Anson's Voyages, so delightful to most young persons, and a collection (Hawkesworth's, I believe) of *Voyages round the World*, in four volumes, beginning with Drake and ending with Cook and Bougainville. Of children's books, any more than of playthings, I had scarcely any, except an occasional gift from a relation or acquaintance: among those I had, *Robinson Crusoe* was pre-eminent, and continued to delight me through all my boyhood. It was no part, however, of my father's system to exclude books of amusement, though he allowed them very sparingly. Of such books he possessed at that time next to none, but he borrowed several for me; those which I remember are the *Arabian Nights*, Cazotte's *Arabian Tales*, *Don Quixote*, Miss Edgeworth's *Popular Tales*, and a book of some reputation in its day, Brooke's *Fool of Quality*.

In my eighth year I commenced learning Latin, in conjunction with a younger sister, to whom I taught it as I went on, and who afterwards repeated the lessons to my father; from this time, other sisters and brothers being successively added as pupils, a considerable part of my day's work consisted of this preparatory teaching. It was a part which I greatly disliked; the more so, as I was held responsible for the lessons of my pupils, in almost as full a sense as for my own: I, however, derived from this discipline the great advantage, of learning more thoroughly and retaining more lastingly the things which I was set to teach: perhaps, too, the practice it afforded in explaining difficulties to others, may even at that age have been useful. In other respects, the experience of my boyhood is not favourable to the plan of teaching children by means of one another. The teaching, I am sure, is very inefficient as teaching, and I well know that the relation between teacher and taught is not a good moral discipline to either. I went in this manner through the Latin grammar, and a considerable part of Cornelius Nepos and Caesar's Commentaries, but afterwards added to the superintendence of these lessons, much longer ones of my own.

In the same year in which I began Latin, I made my first commencement in the Greek poets with the Iliad. After I had made some progress in this, my father put Pope's translation into my hands. It was the first English verse I had cared to read, and it became one of the books in which for many years I most delighted: I think I must have read it from twenty to thirty times through. I should not have thought it worth while to mention a taste apparently so natural to boyhood, if I had not, as I think, observed that the keen enjoyment of this brilliant specimen of narrative and versification is not so universal with boys, as I should have expected both *a priori* and from my individual experience. Soon after this time I commenced Euclid, and somewhat later, Algebra, still under my father's tuition.

From my eighth to my twelfth year, the Latin books which I remember reading were, the *Bucolics* of Virgil, and the first six books of the Aeneid; all Horace, except the Epodes; the Fables of Phaedrus; the first five books of Livy (to which from my love of the subject I voluntarily added, in my hours of leisure, the remainder of the first decade); all Sallust; a considerable part of Ovid's *Metamorphoses*; some plays of Terence; two or three books of Lucretius; several of the Orations of Cicero, and of his writings on oratory; also his letters to Atticus, my father taking the trouble to translate to me from the French the historical explanations in Mingault's notes. In Greek I read the *Iliad* and *Odyssey* through; one or two plays of Sophocles, Euripides, and Aristophanes, though by these I profited little; all Thucydides; the *Hellenics* of Xenophon; a great part of Demosthenes, Aeschines, and Lysias; Theocritus; Anacreon; part of the *Anthology*; a little of Dionysius; several books of Polybius; and lastly Aristotle's *Rhetoric*, which, as the first expressly scientific treatise on any moral or psychological subject which I had read, and containing many of the best observations of the ancients on human nature and life, my father made me study with peculiar care, and throw the matter of it into synoptic tables. During the same years I learnt elementary geometry and algebra thoroughly, the differential calculus, and other portions of the higher mathematics far from thoroughly: for my father, not having kept up

7

this part of his early acquired knowledge, could not spare time to qualify himself for removing my difficulties, and left me to deal with them, with little other aid than that of books: while I was continually incurring his displeasure by my inability to solve difficult problems for which he did not see that I had not the necessary previous knowledge.

As to my private reading, I can only speak of what I remember. History continued to be my strongest predilection, and most of all ancient history. Mitford's Greece I read continually; my father had put me on my guard against the Tory prejudices of this writer, and his perversions of facts for the whitewashing of despots, and blackening of popular institutions. These points he discoursed on, exemplifying them from the Greek orators and historians, with such effect that in reading Mitford my sympathies were always on the contrary side to those of the author, and I could, to some extent, have argued the point against him: yet this did not diminish the ever new pleasure with which I read the book. Roman history, both in my old favourite, Hooke, and in Ferguson, continued to delight me. A book which, in spite of what is called the dryness of its style, I took great pleasure in, was the *Ancient Universal History*, through the incessant reading of which, I had my head full of historical details concerning the obscurest ancient people, while about modern history, except detached passages, such as the Dutch War of Independence, I knew and cared comparatively little. A voluntary exercise, to which throughout my boyhood I was much addicted, was what I called writing histories. I successively composed a Roman History, picked out of Hooke; and an Abridgment of the *Ancient Universal History*; a History of Holland, from my favourite Watson and from an anonymous compilation; and in my eleventh and twelfth year I occupied myself with writing what I flattered myself was something serious. This was no less than a History of the Roman Government, compiled (with the assistance of Hooke) from Livy and Dionysius: of which I wrote as much as would have made an octavo volume, extending to the epoch of the Licinian Laws. It was, in fact, an account of the struggles between the patricians and plebeians, which now engrossed all the interest in my mind which I had previously felt in the mere wars and conquests of the Romans. I discussed all the constitutional points as they arose: though quite ignorant of Niebuhr's researches, I, by such lights as my father had given me, vindicated the Agrarian Laws on the evidence of Livy, and upheld, to the best of my ability, the Roman Democratic party. A few years later, in my contempt of my childish efforts, I destroyed all these papers, not then anticipating that I could ever feel any curiosity about my first attempts at writing and reasoning. My father encouraged me in this useful amusement, though, as I think judiciously, he never asked to see what I wrote; so that I did not feel that in writing it I was accountable to any one, nor had the chilling sensation of being under a critical eye.

But though these exercises in history were never a compulsory lesson, there was another kind of composition which was so, namely, writing verses, and it was one of the most disagreeable of my tasks. Greek and Latin verses I did not write, nor learnt the prosody of those languages. My father, thinking this not worth the time it required, contented himself with making me read aloud to him, and correcting false quantities. I never composed at all in Greek, even in prose, and but little in Latin. Not that my father could be indifferent to the value of this practice, in giving a thorough knowledge of these languages, but because there really was not time for it. The verses I was required to write were English. When I first read Pope's Homer, I ambitiously attempted to compose something of the same kind, and achieved as much as one book of a continuation of the *Iliad*. There, probably, the spontaneous promptings of my poetical ambition would have stopped; but the exercise, begun from choice, was continued by command. Conformably to my father's usual practice of explaining to me, as far as possible, the reasons for what he required me to do, he gave me, for this, as I well remember, two reasons highly characteristic of him: one was, that some things could be expressed better and more forcibly in verse than in prose: this, he said, was a real advantage. The other was, that people in general attached more value to verse than it deserved, and the power of writing it, was, on this account, worth acquiring. He generally left me to choose my own subjects, which, as far as I remember, were mostly addresses to some mythological personage or allegorical abstraction; but he made me translate into English verse many of Horace's shorter poems: I also remember his giving me Thomson's *Winter* to read, and afterwards making me attempt (without book) to write something myself on the same subject. The verses I wrote were, of course, the merest rubbish, nor did I ever attain any facility of versification, but the practice may have been useful in making it easier for me, at a later period, to acquire readiness of expression.[1] I had read, up to this time, very little English poetry. Shakspeare my father had put into my hands, chiefly for the sake of the historical plays, from which, however, I went on to the others. My father never was a great admirer of Shakspeare, the English idolatry of whom he used to attack with some severity. He cared little for any English poetry except Milton (for whom he had the highest admiration), Goldsmith, Burns, and Gray's *Bard*, which he preferred to his Elegy: perhaps I may add Cowper and Beattie. He had some value for Spenser, and I remember his reading to me (unlike his usual practice of making me read to him) the first book of the *Fairie Queene*; but I took little pleasure in it. The poetry of the present century he saw scarcely any merit in, and I hardly became acquainted with any of it till I was grown up to manhood, except the metrical romances of Walter Scott, which I read at his recommendation and was intensely delighted with; as I always was with animated narrative. Dryden's Poems were among my father's books, and many of these he made me read, but I never cared for any of them except *Alexander's Feast*, which, as well as many of the songs in Walter Scott, I used to sing internally, to a music of my own: to some of the latter, indeed, I went so far as to compose airs, which I still remember. Cowper's short poems I read with some pleasure, but never got far into the longer ones; and nothing in the two volumes interested me like the prose account of his three hares. In my thirteenth year I met with

Campbell's poems, among which *Lochiel, Hohenlinden, The Exile of Erin*, and some others, gave me sensations I had never before experienced from poetry. Here, too, I made nothing of the longer poems, except the striking opening of *Gertrude of Wyoming*, which long kept its place in my feelings as the perfection of pathos.

During this part of my childhood, one of my greatest amusements was experimental science; in the theoretical, however, not the practical sense of the word; not trying experiments—a kind of discipline which I have often regretted not having had—nor even seeing, but merely reading about them. I never remember being so wrapt up in any book, as I was in Joyce's *Scientific Dialogues*; and I was rather recalcitrant to my father's criticisms of the bad reasoning respecting the first principles of physics, which abounds in the early part of that work. I devoured treatises on Chemistry, especially that of my father's early friend and schoolfellow, Dr. Thomson, for years before I attended a lecture or saw an experiment.

From about the age of twelve, I entered into another and more advanced stage in my course of instruction; in which the main object was no longer the aids and appliances of thought, but the thoughts themselves. This commenced with Logic, in which I began at once with the *Organon*, and read it to the Analytics inclusive, but profited little by the Posterior Analytics, which belong to a branch of speculation I was not yet ripe for. Contemporaneously with the *Organon*, my father made me read the whole or parts of several of the Latin treatises on the scholastic logic; giving each day to him, in our walks, a minute account of what I had read, and answering his numerous and most searching questions. After this, I went in a similar manner through the *Computatio sive Logica* of Hobbes, a work of a much higher order of thought than the books of the school logicians, and which he estimated very highly; in my own opinion beyond its merits, great as these are. It was his invariable practice, whatever studies he exacted from me, to make me as far as possible understand and feel the utility of them: and this he deemed peculiarly fitting in the case of the syllogistic logic, the usefulness of which had been impugned by so many writers of authority. I well remember how, and in what particular walk, in the neighbourhood of Bagshot Heath (where we were on a visit to his old friend Mr. Wallace, then one of the Mathematical Professors at Sandhurst) he first attempted by questions to make me think on the subject, and frame some conception of what constituted the utility of the syllogistic logic, and when I had failed in this, to make me understand it by explanations. The explanations did not make the matter at all clear to me at the time; but they were not therefore useless; they remained as a nucleus for my observations and reflections to crystallize upon; the import of his general remarks being interpreted to me, by the particular instances which came under my notice afterwards. My own consciousness and experience ultimately led me to appreciate quite as highly as he did, the value of an early practical familiarity with the school logic. I know of nothing, in my education, to which I think myself more indebted for whatever capacity of thinking I have attained. The first intellectual operation in which I arrived at any proficiency, was dissecting a bad argument, and finding in what part the fallacy lay: and though whatever capacity of this sort I attained, was due to the fact that it was an intellectual exercise in which I was most perseveringly drilled by my father, yet it is also true that the school logic, and the mental habits acquired in studying it, were among the principal instruments of this drilling. I am persuaded that nothing, in modern education, tends so much, when properly used, to form exact thinkers, who attach a precise meaning to words and propositions, and are not imposed on by vague, loose, or ambiguous terms. The boasted influence of mathematical studies is nothing to it; for in mathematical processes, none of the real difficulties of correct ratiocination occur. It is also a study peculiarly adapted to an early stage in the education of philosophical students, since it does not presuppose the slow process of acquiring, by experience and reflection, valuable thoughts of their own. They may become capable of disentangling the intricacies of confused and self-contradictory thought, before their own thinking faculties are much advanced; a power which, for want of some such discipline, many otherwise able men altogether lack; and when they have to answer opponents, only endeavour, by such arguments as they can command, to support the opposite conclusion, scarcely even attempting to confute the reasonings of their antagonists; and, therefore, at the utmost, leaving the question, as far as it depends on argument, a balanced one.

During this time, the Latin and Greek books which I continued to read with my father were chiefly such as were worth studying, not for the language merely, but also for the thoughts. This included much of the orators, and especially Demosthenes, some of whose principal orations I read several times over, and wrote out, by way of exercise, a full analysis of them. My father's comments on these orations when I read them to him were very instructive to me. He not only drew my attention to the insight they afforded into Athenian institutions, and the principles of legislation and government which they often illustrated, but pointed out the skill and art of the orator—how everything important to his purpose was said at the exact moment when he had brought the minds of his audience into the state most fitted to receive it; how he made steal into their minds, gradually and by insinuation, thoughts which, if expressed in a more direct manner, would have roused their opposition. Most of these reflections were beyond my capacity of full comprehension at the time; but they left seed behind, which germinated in due season. At this time I also read the whole of Tacitus, Juvenal, and Quintilian. The latter, owing to his obscure style and to the scholastic details of which many parts of his treatise are made up, is little read, and seldom sufficiently appreciated. His book is a kind of encyclopaedia of the thoughts of the ancients on the whole field of education and culture; and I have retained through life many valuable ideas which I can distinctly trace to my reading of him, even at that early age. It was at this period that I read, for the first time, some of the most important dialogues of Plato, in particular the *Gorgias*, the *Protagoras*, and the *Republic*. There is no author to whom my father thought himself more indebted for his own mental culture, than Plato, or whom he more frequently recommended to young students. I can bear similar testimony in regard to myself. The Socratic method, of which the Platonic dialogues are the chief example, is unsurpassed as a discipline for correcting the errors, and clearing up the confusions incident to the *intellectus sibi permissus*, the understanding which has made up all its bundles of associations under the guidance of popular phraseology. The close, searching *elenchus* by which the man of vague generalities is constrained either to express his meaning to himself in definite terms, or to confess that he does not know what he is talking about; the perpetual testing of all general statements by particular instances; the siege in form which is laid to the meaning of large abstract terms, by fixing upon some still larger class-name which includes that and more, and dividing down to the thing sought—marking out its limits and definition by a series of accurately drawn distinctions between it and each of the cognate objects which are successively parted off from it —all this, as an education for precise thinking, is inestimable, and all this, even at that age, took such hold of me that it became part of my own mind. I have felt ever since that the title of Platonist belongs by far better right to those who have been nourished in and have endeavoured to practise Plato's mode of investigation, than to those who are distinguished only by the adoption of certain dogmatical conclusions, drawn mostly from the least intelligible of his works, and which the character of his mind and writings makes it uncertain whether he himself regarded as anything more than poetic fancies, or philosophic conjectures.

In going through Plato and Demosthenes, since I could now read these authors, as far as the language was concerned, with perfect ease, I was not required to construe them sentence by sentence, but to read them aloud to my father, answering questions when asked: but the particular attention which he paid to elocution (in which his own excellence was remarkable) made this reading aloud to him a most painful task. Of all things which he required me to do, there was none which I did so constantly ill, or in which he so perpetually lost his temper with me. He had thought much on the principles of the art of reading, especially the most neglected part of it, the inflections of the voice, or *modulation*, as writers on elocution call it (in contrast with *articulation* on the one side, and *expression* on the other), and had reduced it to rules, grounded on the logical analysis of a sentence. These rules he strongly impressed upon me, and took me severely to task for every violation of them: but I even then remarked (though I did not venture to make the remark to him) that though he reproached me when I read a sentence ill, and *told* me how I ought to have read it, he never by reading it himself, *showed* me how it ought to be read. A defect running through his otherwise admirable modes of instruction, as it did through all his modes of thought, was that of trusting too much to the intelligibleness of the abstract, when not embodied in the concrete. It was at a much later period of my youth, when practising elocution by myself, or with companions of my own age, that I for the first time understood the object of his rules, and saw the psychological grounds of them. At that time I and others followed out the subject into its ramifications, and could have composed a very useful treatise, grounded on my father's principles. He himself left those principles and rules unwritten. I regret that when my mind was full of the subject, from systematic practice, I did not put them, and our improvements of them, into a formal shape.

A book which contributed largely to my education, in the best sense of the term, was my father's *History of India*. It was published in the beginning of 1818. During the year previous, while it was passing through the press, I used to read the proof sheets to him; or rather, I read the manuscript to him while he corrected the proofs. The number of new ideas which I received from this re-markable book, and the impulse and stimulus as well as guidance given to my thoughts by its criticism and disquisitions on society and civilization in the Hindoo part, on institutions and the acts of governments in the English part, made my early familiarity with it eminently useful to my subsequent progress. And though I can perceive deficiencies in it now as compared with a perfect standard, I still think it, if not the most, one of the most instructive histories ever written, and one of the books from which most benefit may be derived by a mind in the course of making up its opinions.

The Preface, among the most characteristic of my father's writings, as well as the richest in materials of thought, gives a picture which may be entirely depended on, of the sentiments and expectations with which he wrote the History. Saturated as the book is with the opinions and modes of judgment of a democratic radicalism then regarded as extreme; and treating with a severity, at that time most unusual, the English Constitution, the English law, and all parties and classes who possessed any considerable influence in the country; he may have expected reputation, but certainly not advancement in life, from its publication; nor could he have supposed that it would raise up anything but enemies for him in powerful quarters: least of all could he have expected favour from the East India Company, to whose commercial privileges he was unqualifiedly hostile, and on the acts of whose government he had made so many severe comments: though, in various parts of his book, he bore a testimony in their favour, which he felt to be their just due, namely, that no Government had on the whole given so much proof, to the extent of its lights, of good intention towards its subjects; and that if the acts of any other Government had the light of publicity as completely let in upon them, they would, in all probability, still less bear scrutiny.

On learning, however, in the spring of 1819, about a year after the publication of the History, that the East India Directors desired to strengthen the part of their home establishment which was employed in carrying on the correspondence with India, my father declared himself a candidate for that employment, and, to the credit of the Directors, successfully. He was appointed one of the Assistants of the Examiner of India Correspondence; officers whose duty it was to prepare drafts of despatches to India, for consideration by the Directors, in the principal departments of administration. In this office, and in that of Examiner, which he subsequently attained, the influence which his talents, his reputation, and his decision of character gave him, with superiors who really desired the good government of India, enabled him to a great extent to throw into his drafts of despatches, and to carry through the ordeal of the Court of Directors and Board of Control, without having their force much weakened, his real opinions on Indian subjects. In his History he had set forth, for the first time, many of the true principles of Indian administration: and his despatches, following his History, did more than had ever been done before to promote the improvement of India, and teach Indian officials to understand their business. If a selection of them were published, they would, I am convinced, place his character as a practical statesman fully on a level with his eminence as a speculative writer.

This new employment of his time caused no relaxation in his attention to my education. It was in this same year, 1819, that he took me through a complete course of political economy. His loved and intimate friend, Ricardo, had shortly before published the book which formed so great an epoch in political economy; a book which would never have been published or written, but for the entreaty and strong encouragement of my father; for Ricardo, the most modest of men, though firmly convinced of the truth of his doctrines, deemed himself so little capable of doing them justice in exposition and expression, that he shrank from the idea of publicity. The same friendly encouragement induced Ricardo, a year or two later, to become a member of the House of Commons; where, during the remaining years of his life, unhappily cut short in the full vigour of his intellect, he rendered so much service to his and my father's opinions both on political economy and on other subjects.

Though Ricardo's great work was already in print, no didactic treatise embodying its doctrines, in a manner fit for learners, had yet appeared. My father, therefore, commenced instructing me in the science by a sort of lectures, which he delivered to me in our walks. He expounded each day a portion of the subject, and I gave him next day a written account of it, which he made me rewrite over and over again until it was clear, precise, and tolerably complete. In this manner I went through the whole extent of the science; and the written outline of it which resulted from my daily *compte rendu*, served him afterwards as notes from which to write his *Elements of Political Economy*. After this I read Ricardo, giving an account daily of what I read, and discussing, in the best manner I could, the collateral points which offered themselves in our progress.

On Money, as the most intricate part of the subject, he made me read in the same manner Ricardo's admirable pamphlets, written during what was called the Bullion controversy; to these succeeded Adam Smith; and in this reading it was one of my father's main objects to make me apply to Smith's more superficial view of political economy, the superior lights of Ricardo, and detect what was fallacious in Smith's arguments, or erroneous in any of his conclusions. Such a mode of instruction was excellently calculated to form a thinker; but it required to be worked by a thinker, as close and vigorous as my father. The path was a thorny one, even to him, and I am sure it was so to me, notwithstanding the strong interest I took in the subject. He was often, and much beyond reason, provoked by my failures in cases where success could not have been expected; but in the main his method was right, and it succeeded. I do not believe that any scientific teaching ever was more thorough, or better fitted for training the faculties, than the mode in which logic and political economy were taught to me by my father. Striving, even in an exaggerated degree, to call forth the activity of my faculties, by making me find out everything for myself, he gave his explanations not before, but after, I had felt the full force of the difficulties; and not only gave me an accurate knowledge of these two great subjects, as far as they were then understood, but made me a thinker on both. I thought for myself almost from the first, and occasionally thought differently from him, though for a long time only on minor points, and making his opinion the ultimate standard. At a later period I even occasionally convinced him, and altered his opinion on some points of detail: which I state to his honour, not my own. It at once exemplifies his perfect candour, and the real worth of his method of teaching.

At this point concluded what can properly be called my lessons:

when I was about fourteen I left England for more than a year; and after my return, though my studies went on under my father's general direction, he was no longer my schoolmaster. I shall therefore pause here, and turn back to matters of a more general nature connected with the part of my life and education included in the preceding reminiscences.

In the course of instruction which I have partially retraced, the point most superficially apparent is the great effort to give, during the years of childhood, an amount of knowledge in what are considered the higher branches of education, which is seldom acquired (if acquired at all) until the age of manhood. The result of the experiment shows the ease with which this may be done, and places in a strong light the wretched waste of so many precious years as are spent in acquiring the modicum of Latin and Greek commonly taught to schoolboys; a waste which has led so many educational reformers to entertain the ill-judged proposal of discarding these languages altogether from general education. If I had been by nature extremely quick of apprehension, or had possessed a very accurate and retentive memory, or were of a remarkably active and energetic character, the trial would not be conclusive; but in all these natural gifts I am rather below than above par; what I could do, could assuredly be done by any boy or girl of average capacity and healthy physical constitution: and if I have accomplished anything, I owe it, among other fortunate circumstances, to the fact that through the early training bestowed on me by my father, I started, I may fairly say, with an advantage of a quarter of a century over my contemporaries.

There was one cardinal point in this training, of which I have already given some indication, and which, more than anything else, was the cause of whatever good it effected. Most boys or youths who have had much knowledge drilled into them, have their mental capacities not strengthened, but overlaid by it. They are crammed with mere facts, and with the opinions or phrases of other people, and these are accepted as a substitute for the power to form opinions of their own; and thus the sons of eminent fathers, who have spared no pains in their education, so often grow up mere parroters of what they have learnt, incapable of using their minds except in the furrows traced for them. Mine, however, was not an education of cram. My father never permitted anything which I learnt to degenerate into a mere exercise of memory. He strove to make the understanding not only go along with every step of the teaching, but, if possible, precede it. Anything which could be found out by thinking I never was told, until I had exhausted my efforts to find it out for myself. As far as I can trust my remembrance, I acquitted myself very lamely in this department; my recollection of such matters is almost wholly of failures, hardly ever of success. It is true the failures were often in things in which success, in so early a stage of my progress, was almost impossible. I remember at some time in my thirteenth year, on my happening to use the word idea, he asked me what an idea was; and expressed some displeasure at my ineffectual efforts to define the word: I recollect also his indignation at my using the common expression that something was true in theory but required correction in practice; and how, after making me vainly strive to define the word theory, he explained its meaning, and showed the fallacy of the vulgar form of speech which I had used; leaving me fully persuaded that in being unable to give a correct definition of Theory, and in speaking of it as something which might be at variance with practice, I had shown unparalleled ignorance. In this he seems, and perhaps was, very unreasonable; but I think, only in being angry at my failure. A pupil from whom nothing is ever demanded which he cannot do, never does all he can.

One of the evils most liable to attend on any sort of early proficiency, and which often fatally blights its promise, my father most anxiously guarded against. This was self-conceit. He kept me, with extreme vigilance, out of the way of hearing myself praised, or of being led to make self-flattering comparisons between myself and others. From his own intercourse with me I could derive none but a very humble opinion of myself; and the standard of comparison he always held up to me, was not what other people did, but what a man could and ought to do. He completely succeeded in preserving me from the sort of influences he so much dreaded. I was not at all aware that my attainments were anything unusual at my age. If I accidentally had my attention drawn to the fact that some other boy knew less than myself—which happened less often than might be imagined—I concluded, not that I knew much, but that he, for some reason or other, knew little, or that his knowledge was of a different kind from mine. My state of mind was not humility, but neither was it arrogance. I never thought of saying to myself, I am, or I can do, so and so. I neither estimated myself highly nor lowly: I did not estimate myself at all. If I thought anything about myself, it was that I was rather backward in my studies, since I always found myself so, in comparison with what my father expected from me. I assert this with confidence, though it was not the impression of various persons who saw me in my childhood. They, as I have since found, thought me greatly and disagreeably self-conceited; probably because I was disputatious, and did not scruple to give direct contradictions to things which I heard said. I suppose I acquired this bad habit from having been encouraged in an unusual degree to talk on matters beyond my age, and with grown persons, while I never had inculcated on me the usual respect for them. My father did not correct this ill-breeding and impertinence, probably from not being aware of it, for I was always too much in awe of him to be otherwise than extremely subdued and quiet in his presence. Yet with all this I had no notion of any superiority in myself; and well was it for me that I had not. I remember the very place in Hyde Park where, in my fourteenth year, on the eve of leaving my father's house for a long absence, he told me that I should find, as I got acquainted with new people, that I had been taught many things which youths of my age did not commonly know; and that many persons would be disposed to talk to me of this, and to compliment me upon it. What other things he said on this topic I remember very imperfectly; but he wound up by saying, that whatever I knew more than others, could not be ascribed to any merit in me, but to the very unusual advantage which had fallen to my lot, of having a father who was able to teach me, and willing to give the necessary trouble and time; that it was no matter of praise to me, if I knew more than those who had not had a similar advantage, but the deepest disgrace to me if I did not. I have a distinct remembrance, that the suggestion thus for the first time made to me, that I knew more than other youths who were considered well educated, was to me a piece of information, to which, as to all other things which my father told me, I gave implicit credence, but which did not at all impress me as a personal matter. I felt no disposition to glorify myself upon the circumstance that there were other persons who did not know what I knew; nor had I ever flattered myself that my acquirements, whatever they might be, were any merit of mine: but, now when my attention was called to the subject, I felt that what my father had said respecting my peculiar advantages was exactly the truth and common sense of the matter, and it fixed my opinion and feeling from that time forward.

II

Moral Influences In Early Youth. My Father's Character And Opinions

In my education, as in that of everyone, the moral influences, which are so much more important than all others, are also the most complicated, and the most difficult to specify with any approach to completeness. Without attempting the hopeless task of detailing the circumstances by which, in this respect, my early character may have been shaped, I shall confine myself to a few leading points, which form an indispensable part of any true account of my education.

I was brought up from the first without any religious belief, in the ordinary acceptation of the term. My father, educated in the creed of Scotch Presbyterianism, had by his own studies and reflections been early led to reject not only the belief in Revelation, but the foundations of what is commonly called Natural Religion. I have heard him say, that the turning point of his mind on the subject was reading Butler's *Analogy*. That work, of which he always continued to speak with respect, kept him, as he said, for some considerable time, a believer in the divine authority of Christianity; by proving to him that whatever are the difficulties in believing that the Old and New Testaments proceed from, or record the acts of, a perfectly wise and good being, the same and still greater difficul-

23

ties stand in the way of the belief, that a being of such a character can have been the Maker of the universe. He considered Butler's argument as conclusive against the only opponents for whom it was intended. Those who admit an omnipotent as well as perfectly just and benevolent maker and ruler of such a world as this, can say little against Christianity but what can, with at least equal force, be retorted against themselves. Finding, therefore, no halting place in Deism, he remained in a state of perplexity, until, doubtless after many struggles, he yielded to the conviction, that concerning the origin of things nothing whatever can be known. This is the only correct statement of his opinion; for dogmatic atheism he looked upon as absurd; as most of those, whom the world has considered Atheists, have always done. These particulars are important, because they show that my father's rejection of all that is called religious belief, was not, as many might suppose, primarily a matter of logic and evidence: the grounds of it were moral, still more than intellectual. He found it impossible to believe that a world so full of evil was the work of an Author combining infinite power with perfect goodness and righteousness. His intellect spurned the subtleties by which men attempt to blind themselves to this open contradiction. The Sabaean, or Manichaean theory of a Good and an Evil Principle, struggling against each other for the government of the universe, he would not have equally condemned; and I have heard him express surprise, that no one revived it in our time. He would have regarded it as a mere hypothesis; but he would have ascribed to it no depraving influence. As it was, his aversion to religion, in the sense usually attached to the term, was of the same kind with that of Lucretius: he regarded it with the feelings due not to a mere mental delusion, but to a great moral evil. He looked upon it as the greatest enemy of morality: first, by setting up fictitious excellences—belief in creeds, devotional feelings, and ceremonies, not connected with the good of human-kind—and causing these to be accepted as substitutes for genuine virtues: but above all, by radically vitiating the standard of morals; making it consist in doing the will of a being, on whom it lavishes indeed

24

all the phrases of adulation, but whom in sober truth it depicts as eminently hateful. I have a hundred times heard him say that all ages and nations have represented their gods as wicked, in a constantly increasing progression; that mankind have gone on adding trait after trait till they reached the most perfect conception of wickedness which the human mind can devise, and have called this God, and prostrated themselves before it. This *ne plus ultra* of wickedness he considered to be embodied in what is commonly presented to mankind as the creed of Christianity. Think (he used to say) of a being who would make a Hell—who would create the human race with the infallible foreknowledge, and therefore with the intention, that the great majority of them were to be consigned to horrible and everlasting torment. The time, I believe, is drawing near when this dreadful conception of an object of worship will be no longer identified with Christianity; and when all persons, with any sense of moral good and evil, will look upon it with the same indignation with which my father regarded it. My father was as well aware as anyone that Christians do not, in general, undergo the demoralizing consequences which seem inherent in such a creed, in the manner or to the extent which might have been expected from it. The same slovenliness of thought, and subjection of the reason to fears, wishes, and affections, which enable them to accept a theory involving a contradiction in terms, prevents them from perceiving the logical consequences of the theory. Such is the facility with which mankind believe at one and the same time things inconsistent with one another, and so few are those who draw from what they receive as truths, any consequences but those recommended to them by their feelings, that multitudes have held the undoubting belief in an Omnipotent Author of Hell, and have nevertheless identified that being with the best conception they were able to form of perfect goodness. Their worship was not paid to the demon which such a being as they imagined would really be, but to their own ideal of excellence. The evil is, that such a belief keeps the ideal wretchedly low; and opposes the most obstinate resistance to all thought which has a tendency to raise it higher.

Believers shrink from every train of ideas which would lead the mind to a clear conception and an elevated standard of excellence, because they feel (even when they do not distinctly see) that such a standard would conflict with many of the dispensations of nature, and with much of what they are accustomed to consider as the Christian creed. And thus morality continues a matter of blind tradition, with no consistent principle, nor even any consistent feeling, to guide it.

It would have been wholly inconsistent with my father's ideas of duty, to allow me to acquire impressions contrary to his convictions and feelings respecting religion: and he impressed upon me from the first, that the manner in which the world came into existence was a subject on which nothing was known: that the question, "Who made me?" cannot be answered, because we have no experience or authentic information from which to answer it; and that any answer only throws the difficulty a step further back, since the question immediately presents itself, "Who made God?" He, at the same time, took care that I should be acquainted with what had been thought by mankind on these impenetrable problems. I have mentioned at how early an age he made me a reader of ecclesiastical history; and he taught me to take the strongest interest in the Reformation, as the great and decisive contest against priestly tyranny for liberty of thought.

I am thus one of the very few examples, in this country, of one who has not thrown off religious belief, but never had it: I grew up in a negative state with regard to it. I looked upon the modern exactly as I did upon the ancient religion, as something which in no way concerned me. It did not seem to me more strange that English people should believe what I did not, than that the men I read of in Herodotus should have done so. History had made the variety of opinions among mankind a fact familiar to me, and this was but a prolongation of that fact. This point in my early education had, however, incidentally one bad consequence deserving notice. In giving me an opinion contrary to that of the world, my father thought it necessary to give it as one which could not prudently be avowed to the world. This lesson of keeping my thoughts to myself, at that early age, was attended with some moral disadvantages; though my limited intercourse with strangers, especially such as were likely to speak to me on religion, prevented me from being placed in the alternative of avowal or hypocrisy. I remember two occasions in my boyhood, on which I felt myself in this alternative, and in both cases I avowed my disbelief and defended it. My opponents were boys, considerably older than myself: one of them I certainly staggered at the time, but the subject was never renewed between us: the other who was surprised and somewhat shocked, did his best to convince me for some time, without effect.

The great advance in liberty of discussion, which is one of the most important differences between the present time and that of my childhood, has greatly altered the moralities of this question; and I think that few men of my father's intellect and public spirit, holding with such intensity of moral conviction as he did, unpopular opinions on religion, or on any other of the great subjects of thought, would now either practise or inculcate the withholding of them from the world, unless in the cases, becoming fewer every day, in which frankness on these subjects would either risk the loss of means of subsistence, or would amount to exclusion from some sphere of usefulness peculiarly suitable to the capacities of the individual. On religion in particular the time appears to me to have come when it is the duty of all who, being qualified in point of knowledge, have on mature consideration satisfied themselves that the current opinions are not only false but hurtful, to make their dissent known; at least, if they are among those whose station or reputation gives their opinion a chance of being attended to. Such an avowal would put an end, at once and for ever, to the vulgar prejudice, that what is called, very improperly, unbelief, is connected with any bad qualities either of mind or heart. The world would be astonished if it knew how great a proportion of its brightest ornaments—of those most distinguished even in popular estimation for wisdom and virtue—are complete sceptics in religion; many of them refraining from avowal, less from personal considerations than from a conscientious, though now in my opinion a most mistaken, apprehension, lest by speaking out what would tend to weaken existing beliefs, and by consequence (as they suppose) existing restraints, they should do harm instead of good.

Of unbelievers (so called) as well as of believers, there are many species, including almost every variety of moral type. But the best among them, as no one who has had opportunities of really knowing them will hesitate to affirm, are more genuinely religious, in the best sense of the word religion, than those who exclusively arrogate to themselves the title. The liberality of the age, or in other words the weakening of the obstinate prejudice which makes men unable to see what is before their eyes because it is contrary to their expectations, has caused it be very commonly admitted that a Deist may be truly religious: but if religion stands for any graces of character and not for mere dogma, the assertion may equally be made of many whose belief is far short of Deism. Though they may think the proof incomplete that the universe is a work of design, and though they assuredly disbelieve that it can have an Author and Governor who is *absolute* in power as well as perfect in goodness, they have that which constitutes the principal worth of all religions whatever, an ideal conception of a Perfect Being, to which they habitually refer as the guide of their conscience; and this ideal of Good is usually far nearer to perfection than the objective Deity of those who think themselves obliged to find absolute goodness in the author of a world so crowded with suffering and so deformed by injustice as ours.

My father's moral convictions, wholly dissevered from religion, were very much of the character of those of the Greek philosophers; and were delivered with the force and decision which characterized all that came from him. Even at the very early age at which I read with him the *Memorabilia* of Xenophon, I imbibed from that work and from his comments a deep respect for the character of Socrates; who stood in my mind as a model of ideal excellence: and I well remember how my father at that time impressed upon me the lesson of the "Choice of Hercules." At a somewhat later period the lofty moral standard exhibited in the writings of Plato operated upon me with great force. My father's moral inculcations were at all times mainly those of the "Socratici viri"; justice, temperance (to which he gave a very extended application), veracity, perseverance, readiness to encounter pain and especially labour; regard for the public good; estimation of persons according to their merits, and of things according to their intrinsic usefulness; a life of exertion in contradiction to one of self-indulgent ease and sloth. These and other moralities he conveyed in brief sentences, uttered as occasion arose, of grave exhortation, or stern reprobation and contempt.

But though direct moral teaching does much, indirect does more; and the effect my father produced on my character, did not depend solely on what he said or did with that direct object, but also, and still more, on what manner of man he was.

In his views of life he partook of the character of the Stoic, the Epicurean, and the Cynic, not in the modern but the ancient sense of the word. In his personal qualities the Stoic predominated. His standard of morals was Epicurean, inasmuch as it was utilitarian, taking as the exclusive test of right and wrong, the tendency of actions to produce pleasure or pain. But he had (and this was the Cynic element) scarcely any belief in pleasure; at least in his later years, of which alone, on this point, I can speak confidently. He was not insensible to pleasures; but he deemed very few of them worth the price which, at least in the present state of society, must be paid for them. The greater number of miscarriages in life he considered to be attributable to the overvaluing of pleasures. Accordingly, temperance, in the large sense intended by the Greek philosophers —stopping short at the point of moderation in all indulgences—was with him, as with them, almost the central point of educational precept. His inculcations of this virtue fill a large place in my childish remembrances. He thought human life a poor thing at best, after the freshness of youth and of unsatisfied curiosity had gone by. This was a topic on which he did not often speak, especially, it may be supposed, in the presence of young persons: but when he did, it was with an air of settled and profound conviction. He would sometimes say that if life were made what it might be, by good government and good education, it would be worth having: but he never spoke with anything like enthusiasm even of that possibility. He never varied in rating intellectual enjoyments above all others, even in value as pleasures, independently of their ulterior benefits. The pleasures of the benevolent affections he placed high in the scale; and used to say, that he had never known a happy old man, except those who were able to live over again in the pleasures of the young. For passionate emotions of all sorts, and for everything which bas been said or written in exaltation of them, he professed the greatest contempt. He regarded them as a form of madness. "The intense" was with him a bye-word of scornful disapprobation. He regarded as an aberration of the moral standard of modern times, compared with that of the ancients, the great stress laid upon feeling. Feelings, as such, he considered to be no proper subjects of praise or blame. Right and wrong, good and bad, he regarded as qualities solely of conduct—of acts and omissions; there being no feeling which may not lead, and does not frequently lead, either to good or to bad actions: conscience itself, the very desire to act right, often leading people to act wrong. Consistently carrying out the doctrine that the object of praise and blame should be the discouragement of wrong conduct and the encouragement of right, he refused to let his praise or blame be influenced by the motive of the agent. He blamed as severely what he thought a bad action, when the motive was a feeling of duty, as if the agents had been consciously evil doers. He would not have accepted as a plea in mitigation for inquisitors, that they sincerely believed burning heretics to be an obligation of conscience. But though he did not allow honesty of purpose to soften his disapprobation of actions, it had its full effect on his estimation of characters. No one prized conscientiousness and rectitude of intention more highly, or was more incapable of valuing any person in whom he did not feel assurance of it. But he disliked people quite as much for any other deficiency, provided he thought it equally likely to make them act ill. He disliked, for instance, a fanatic in any bad cause, as much as or more than one who adopted the same cause from self-interest, because he thought him even more likely to be practically mischievous. And thus, his aversion to many intellectual errors, or what he regarded as such, partook, in a certain sense, of the character of a moral feeling. All this is merely saying that he, in a degree once common, but now very unusual, threw his feelings into his opinions; which truly it is difficult to understand how anyone who possesses much of both, can fail to do. None but those who do not care about opinions will confound this with intolerance. Those who, having opinions which they hold to be immensely important, and their contraries to be prodigiously hurtful, have any deep regard for the general good, will necessarily dislike, as a class and in the abstract, those who think wrong what they think right, and right what they think wrong: though they need not therefore be, nor was my father, insensible to good qualities in an opponent, nor governed in their estimation of individuals by one general presumption, instead of by the whole of their character. I grant that an earnest person, being no more infallible than other men, is liable to dislike people on account of opinions which do not merit dislike; but if he neither himself does them any ill office, nor connives at its being done by others, he is not intolerant: and the forbearance which flows from a conscientious sense of the importance to mankind of the equal freedom of all opinions, is the only tolerance which is commendable, or, to the highest moral order of minds, possible.

It will be admitted, that a man of the opinions, and the character, above described, was likely to leave a strong moral impression on any mind principally formed by him, and that his moral teaching was not likely to err on the side of laxity or indulgence. The element which was chiefly deficient in his moral relation to his children was that of tenderness. I do not believe that this deficiency lay in his own nature. I believe him to have had much more feeling than he habitually showed, and much greater capacities of feeling than were ever developed. He resembled most Englishmen in being ashamed of the signs of feeling, and, by the absence of demonstration, starving the feelings themselves. If we consider further that he was in the trying position of sole teacher, and add to this that his temper was constitutionally irritable, it is impossible not to feel true pity for a father who did, and strove to do, so much for his children, who would have so valued their affection, yet who must have been constantly feeling that fear of him was drying it up at its source. This was no longer the case later in life, and with his younger children. They loved him tenderly: and if I cannot say so much of myself, I was always loyally devoted to him. As regards my own education, I hesitate to pronounce whether I was more a loser or gainer by his severity. It was not such as to prevent me from having a happy childhood. And I do not believe that boys can be induced to apply themselves with vigour, and—what is so much more difficult—perseverance, to dry and irksome studies, by the sole force of persuasion and soft words. Much must be done, and much must be learnt, by children, for which rigid discipline, and known liability to punishment, are indispensable as means. It is, no doubt, a very laudable effort, in modern teaching, to render as much as possible of what the young are required to learn, easy and interesting to them. But when this principle is pushed to the length of not requiring them to learn anything *but* what has been made easy and interesting, one of the chief objects of education is sacrificed. I rejoice in the decline of the old brutal and tyrannical system of teaching, which, however, did succeed in enforcing habits of application; but the new, as it seems to me, is training up a race of men who will be incapable of doing anything which is disagreeable to them. I do not, then, believe that fear, as an element in education, can be dispensed with; but I am sure that it ought not to be the main element; and when it predominates so much as to preclude love and confidence on the part of the child to those who should be the unreservedly trusted advisers of after years, and perhaps to seal up the fountains of frank and spontaneous communicativeness in the child's nature, it is an evil for which a large abatement must be made from the benefits, moral and intellectual, which may flow from any other part of the education.

During this first period of my life, the habitual frequenters of my father's house were limited to a very few persons, most of them little known to the world, but whom personal worth, and more or less of congeniality with at least his political opinions (not so frequently to be met with then as since), inclined him to cultivate; and his conversations with them I listened to with interest and instruction. My being an habitual inmate of my father's study made me acquainted with the dearest of his friends, David Ricardo, who by his benevolent countenance, and kindliness of manner, was very attractive to young persons, and who, after I became a student of political economy, invited me to his house and to walk with him in order to converse on the subject. I was a more frequent visitor (from about 1817 or 1818) to Mr. Hume, who, born in the same part of Scotland as my father, and having been, I rather think, a younger schoolfellow or college companion of his, had on returning from India renewed their youthful acquaintance, and who—coming, like many others, greatly under the influence of my father's intellect and energy of character—was induced partly by that influence to go into Parliament, and there adopt the line of conduct which has given him an honourable place in the history of his country. Of Mr. Bentham I saw much more, owing to the close intimacy which existed between him and my father. I do not know how soon after my father's first arrival in England they became acquainted. But my father was the earliest Englishman of any great mark, who thoroughly understood, and in the main adopted, Bentham's general views of ethics, government and law: and this was a natural foundation for sympathy between them, and made them familiar companions in a period of Bentham's life during which he admitted much fewer visitors than was the case subsequently. At this time Mr. Bentham passed some part of every year at Barrow Green House, in a beautiful part of the Surrey Hills, a few miles from Godstone, and there I each summer accompanied my father in a long visit. In 1813 Mr. Bentham, my father, and I made an excursion, which included Oxford, Bath and

Bristol, Exeter, Plymouth, and Portsmouth. In this journey I saw many things which were instructive to me, and acquired my first taste for natural scenery, in the elementary form of fondness for a "view." In the succeeding winter we moved into a house very near Mr. Bentham's, which my father rented from him, in Queen Square, Westminster. From 1814 to 1817 Mr. Bentham lived during half of each year at Ford Abbey, in Somersetshire (or rather in a part of Devonshire surrounded by Somersetshire), which intervals I had the advantage of passing at that place. This sojourn was, I think, an important circumstance in my education. Nothing contributes more to nourish elevation of sentiments in a people, than the large and free character of their habitations. The middle-age architecture, the baronial hall, and the spacious and lofty rooms, of this fine old place, so unlike the mean and cramped externals of English middle-class life, gave the sentiment of a larger and freer existence, and were to me a sort of poetic cultivation, aided also by the character of the grounds in which the Abbey stood; which were *riant* and secluded, umbrageous, and full of the sound of falling waters.

I owed another of the fortunate circumstances in my education, a year's residence in France, to Mr. Bentham's brother, General Sir Samuel Bentham. I had seen Sir Samuel Bentham and his family at their house near Gosport in the course of the tour already mentioned (he being then Superintendent of the Dockyard at Portsmouth), and during a stay of a few days which they made at Ford Abbey shortly after the Peace, before going to live on the Continent. In 1820 they invited me for a six months' visit to them in the South of France, which their kindness ultimately prolonged to nearly a twelvemonth. Sir Samuel Bentham, though of a character of mind different from that of his illustrious brother, was a man of very considerable attainments and general powers, with a decided genius for mechanical art. His wife, a daughter of the celebrated chemist, Dr. Fordyce, was a woman of strong will and decided character, much general knowledge, and great practical good sense of the Edgeworth kind: she was the ruling spirit of the household, as she deserved, and was well qualified, to be. Their family consisted of one son (the eminent botanist) and three daughters, the youngest about two years my senior. I am indebted to them for much and various instruction, and for an almost parental interest in my welfare. When I first joined them, in May, 1820, they occupied the Chbteau of Pompignan (still belonging to a descendant of Voltaire's enemy) on the heights overlooking the plain of the Garonne between Montauban and Toulouse. I accompanied them in an excursion to the Pyrenees, including a stay of some duration at Bagnhres de Bigorre, a journey to Pau, Bayonne, and Bagnhres de Luchon, and an ascent of the Pic du Midi de Bigorre.

This first introduction to the highest order of mountain scenery made the deepest impression on me, and gave a colour to my tastes through life. In October we proceeded by the beautiful mountain route of Castres and St. Pons, from Toulouse to Montpellier, in which last neighbourhood Sir Samuel had just bought the estate of Restinclihre, near the foot of the singular mountain of St. Loup. During this residence in France I acquired a familiar knowledge of the French language, and acquaintance with the ordinary French literature; I took lessons in various bodily exercises, in none of which, however, I made any proficiency; and at Montpellier I attended the excellent winter courses of lectures at the Faculti des Sciences, those of M. Anglada on chemistry, of M. Provengal on zoology, and of a very accomplished representative of the eighteenth century metaphysics, M. Gergonne, on logic, under the name of Philosophy of the Sciences. I also went through a course of the higher mathematics under the private tuition of M. Lenthiric, a professor at the Lycie of Montpellier. But the greatest, perhaps, of the many advantages which I owed to this episode in my education, was that of having breathed for a whole year, the free and genial atmosphere of Continental life. This advantage was not the less real though I could not then estimate, nor even consciously feel it. Having so little experience of English life, and the few people I knew being mostly such as had public objects, of a large and personally disinterested kind, at heart, I was ignorant of the low moral tone of what, in England, is called society; the habit of, not indeed professing, but taking for granted in every mode of implication, that conduct is of course always directed towards low and petty objects; the absence of high feelings which manifests itself by sneering depreciation of all demonstrations of them, and by general abstinence (except among a few of the stricter religionists) from professing any high principles of action at all, except in those preordained cases in which such profession is put on as part of the costume and formalities of the occasion. I could not then know or estimate the difference between this manner of existence, and that of a people like the French, whose faults, if equally real, are at all events different; among whom sentiments, which by comparison at least may be called elevated, are the current coin of human intercourse, both in books and in private life; and though often evaporating in profession, are yet kept alive in the nation at large by constant exercise, and stimulated by sympathy, so as to form a living and active part of the existence of great numbers of persons, and to be recognised and understood by all. Neither could I then appreciate the general culture of the understanding, which results from the habitual exercise of the feelings, and is thus carried down into the most uneducated classes of several countries on the Continent, in a degree not equalled in England among the so-called educated, except where an unusual tenderness of conscience leads to a habitual exercise of the intellect on questions of right and wrong. I did not know the way in which, among the ordinary English, the absence of interest in things of an unselfish kind, except occasionally in a special thing here and there, and the habit of not speaking to others, nor much even to themselves, about the things in which they do feel interest, causes both their feelings and their intellectual faculties to remain undeveloped, or to develop themselves only in some single and very limited direction; reducing them, considered as spiritual beings, to a kind of negative existence. All these things I did not perceive till long afterwards; but I even then felt, though without stating it clearly to myself, the contrast between the frank sociability and amiability of French personal intercourse, and the English mode of existence, in which everybody acts as if everybody else (with few, or no exceptions) was either an enemy or a bore. In France, it is true, the bad as well as the good points, both of individual and of national character, come more to the surface, and break out more fearlessly in ordinary intercourse, than in England: but the general habit of the people is to show, as well as to expect, friendly feeling in every one towards every other, wherever there is not some positive cause for the opposite. In England it is only of the best bred people, in the upper or upper middle ranks, that anything like this can be said.

In my way through Paris, both going and returning, I passed some time in the house of M. Say, the eminent political economist, who was a friend and correspondent of my father, having become acquainted with him on a visit to England a year or two after the Peace. He was a man of the later period of the French Revolution, a fine specimen of the best kind of French Republican, one of those who had never bent the knee to Bonaparte though courted by him to do so; a truly upright, brave, and enlightened man. He lived a quiet and studious life, made happy by warm affections, public and private. He was acquainted with many of the chiefs of the Liberal party, and I saw various noteworthy persons while staying at this house; among whom I have pleasure in the recollection of having once seen Saint-Simon, not yet the founder either of a philosophy or a religion, and considered only as a clever original. The chief fruit which I carried away from the society I saw, was a strong and permanent interest in Continental Liberalism, of which I ever afterwards kept myself *au courant*, as much as of English politics: a thing not at all usual in those days with Englishmen, and which had a very salutary influence on my development, keeping me free from the error always prevalent in England—and from which even my father, with all his superiority to prejudice, was not exempt—of judging universal questions by a merely English standard. After passing a few weeks at Caen with an old friend of my father's, I returned to England in July, 1821 and my education resumed its ordinary course.

III

Last Stage Of Education, And First Of Self-Education

For the first year or two after my visit to France, I continued my old studies, with the addition of some new ones. When I returned, my father was just finishing for the press his *Elements of Political Economy*, and he made me perform an exercise on the manuscript, which Mr. Bentham practised on all his own writings, making what he called "marginal contents"; a short abstract of every paragraph, to enable the writer more easily to judge of, and improve, the order of the ideas, and the general character of the exposition. Soon after, my father put into my hands Condillac's *Traiti des Sensations*, and the logical and metaphysical volumes of his *Cours d'Etudes*; the first (notwithstanding the superficial resemblance between Condillac's psychological system and my father's) quite as much for a warning as for an example. I am not sure whether it was in this winter or the next that I first read a history of the French Revolution. I learnt with astonishment that the principles of democracy, then apparently in so insignificant and hopeless a minority everywhere in Europe, had borne all before them in France thirty years earlier, and had been the creed of the nation. As may be supposed from this, I had previously a very vague idea of that great commotion. I knew only that the French had thrown off the absolute monarchy of Louis XIV. and XV., had put the King and Queen to death, guillotined many persons, one of whom was Lavoisier, and had ultimately fallen under the despotism of Bonaparte. From this time, as was natural,

39

the subject took an immense hold of my feelings. It allied itself with all my juvenile aspirations to the character of a democratic champion. What had happened so lately, seemed as if it might easily happen again: and the most transcendent glory I was capable of conceiving, was that of figuring, successful or unsuccessful, as a Girondist in an English Convention.

During the winter of 1821-2, Mr. John Austin, with whom at the time of my visit to France my father had but lately become acquainted, kindly allowed me to read Roman law with him. My father, notwithstanding his abhorrence of the chaos of barbarism called English Law, had turned his thoughts towards the bar as on the whole less ineligible for me than any other profession: and these readings with Mr. Austin, who had made Bentham's best ideas his own, and added much to them from other sources and from his own mind, were not only a valuable introduction to legal studies, but an important portion of general education. With Mr. Austin I read Heineccius on the Institutes, his *Roman Antiquities*, and part of his exposition of the Pandects; to which was added a considerable portion of Blackstone. It was at the commencement of these studies that my father, as a needful accompaniment to them, put into my hands Bentham's principal speculations, as interpreted to the Continent, and indeed to all the world, by Dumont, in the *Traiti de Ligislation*. The reading of this book was an epoch in my life; one of the turning points in my mental history.

My previous education had been, in a certain sense, already a course of Benthamism. The Benthamic standard of "the greatest happiness" was that which I had always been taught to apply; I was even familiar with an abstract discussion of it, forming an episode in an unpublished dialogue on Government, written by my father on the Platonic model. Yet in the first pages of Bentham it burst upon me with all the force of novelty. What thus impressed me was the chapter in which Bentham passed judgment on the common modes of reasoning in morals and legislation, deduced from phrases like "law of nature," "right reason," "the moral sense," "natural rectitude," and the like, and characterized them as dogmatism in disguise, imposing its sentiments upon others under cover of sounding expressions which convey no reason for the sentiment, but set up the sentiment as its own reason. It had not struck me before, that Bentham's principle put an end to all this. The feeling rushed upon me, that all previous moralists were superseded, and that here indeed was the commencement of a new era in thought. This impression was strengthened by the manner in which Bentham put into scientific form the application of the happiness principle to the morality of actions, by analysing the various classes and orders of their consequences. But what struck me at that time most of all, was the Classification of Offences, which is much more clear, compact, and imposing in Dumont's *ridaction* than in the original work of Bentham from which it was taken. Logic and the dialectics of Plato, which had formed so large a part of my previous training, had given me a strong relish for accurate classification. This taste had been strengthened and enlightened by the study of botany, on the principles of what is called the Natural Method, which I had taken up with great zeal, though only as an amusement, during my stay in France; and when I found scientific classification applied to the great and complex subject of Punishable Acts, under the guidance of the ethical principle of Pleasurable and Painful Consequences, followed out in the method of detail introduced into these subjects by Bentham, I felt taken up to an eminence from which I could survey a vast mental domain, and see stretching out into the distance intellectual results beyond all computation. As I proceeded further, there seemed to be added to this intellectual clearness, the most inspiring prospects of practical improvement in human affairs. To Bentham's general view of the construction of a body of law I was not altogether a stranger, having read with attention that admirable compendium, my father's article on Jurisprudence: but I had read it with little profit, and scarcely any interest, no doubt from its extremely general and abstract character, and also because it concerned the form more than the substance of the *corpus juris*, the logic rather than the ethics of law. But Bentham's subject was Legislation, of which

Jurisprudence is only the formal part: and at every page he seemed to open a clearer and broader conception of what human opinions and institutions ought to be, how they might be made what they ought to be, and how far removed from it they now are. When I laid down the last volume of the *Traiti*, I had become a different being. The "principle of utility," understood as Bentham understood it, and applied in the manner in which he applied it through these three volumes, fell exactly into its place as the keystone which held together the detached and fragmentary component parts of my knowledge and beliefs. It gave unity to my conceptions of things. I now had opinions; a creed, a doctrine, a philosophy; in one among the best senses of the word, a religion; the inculcation and diffusion of which could be made the principal outward purpose of a life. And I had a grand conception laid before me of changes to be effected in the condition of mankind through that doctrine. The *Traiti de Legislation* wound up with what was to me a most impressive picture of human life as it would be made by such opinions and such laws as were recommended in the treatise. The anticipations of practicable improvement were studiously moderate, deprecating and discountenancing as reveries of vague enthusiasm many things which will one day seem so natural to human beings, that injustice will probably be done to those who once thought them chimerical. But, in my state of mind, this appearance of superiority to illusion added to the effect which Bentham's doctrines produced on me, by heightening the impression of mental power, and the vista of improvement which he did open was sufficiently large and brilliant to light up my life, as well as to give a definite shape to my aspirations.

After this I read, from time to time, the most important of the other works of Bentham which had then seen the light, either as written by himself or as edited by Dumont. This was my private reading: while, under my father's direction, my studies were carried into the higher branches of analytic psychology. I now read Locke's *Essay*, and wrote out an account of it, consisting of a complete abstract of every chapter, with such remarks as occurred to me; which was read by, or (I think) to, my father, and discussed throughout. I performed the same process with *Helvetius de L'Esprit*, which I read of my own choice. This preparation of abstracts, subject to my father's censorship, was of great service to me, by compelling precision in conceiving and expressing psychological doctrines, whether accepted as truths or only regarded as the opinion of others. After Helvetius, my father made me study what he deemed the really master-production in the philosophy of mind, Hartley's *Observations on Man*. This book, though it did not, like the *Traiti de Ligislation*, give a new colour to my existence, made a very similar impression on me in regard to its immediate subject. Hartley's explanation, incomplete as in many points it is, of the more complex mental phenomena by the law of association, commended itself to me at once as a real analysis, and made me feel by contrast the insufficiency of the merely verbal generalizations of Condillac, and even of the instructive gropings and feelings about for psychological explanations, of Locke. It was at this very time that my father commenced writing his *Analysis* of the Mind, which carried Hartley's mode of explaining the mental phenomena to so much greater length and depth. He could only command the concentration of thought necessary for this work, during the complete leisure of his holiday for a month or six weeks annually: and he commenced it in the summer of 1822, in the first holiday he passed at Dorking; in which neighbourhood, from that time to the end of his life, with the exception of two years, he lived, as far as his official duties permitted, for six months of every year. He worked at the *Analysis* during several successive vacations, up to the year 1829, when it was published, and allowed me to read the manuscript, portion by portion, as it advanced. The other principal English writers on mental philosophy I read as I felt inclined, particularly Berkeley, Hume's *Essays*, Reid, Dugald Stewart and Brown on Cause and Effect. Brown's *Lectures* I did not read until two or three years later, nor at that time had my father himself read them.

Among the works read in the course of this year, which contributed materially to my development, I owe it to mention a book (written on the foundation of some of Bentham's manuscripts and published under the pseudonyme of Philip Beauchamp) entitled *Analysis of the Influence of Natural Religion on the Temporal Happiness of Mankind.* This was an examination not of the truth, but of the usefulness of religious belief, in the most general sense, apart from the peculiarities of any special revelation; which, of all the parts of the discussion concerning religion, is the most important in this age, in which real belief in any religious doctrine is feeble and precarious, but the opinion of its necessity for moral and social purposes almost universal; and when those who reject revelation, very generally take refuge in an optimistic Deism, a worship of the order of Nature, and the supposed course of Providence, at least as full of contradictions, and perverting to the moral sentiments, as any of the forms of Christianity, if only it is as completely realized. Yet very little, with any claim to a philosophical character, has been written by sceptics against the usefulness of this form of belief. The volume bearing the name of Philip Beauchamp had this for its special object. Having been shown to my father in manuscript, it was put into my hands by him, and I made a marginal analysis of it as I had done of the *Elements of Political Economy.* Next to the *Traiti de Ligislation,* it was one of the books which by the searching character of its analysis produced the greatest effect upon me. On reading it lately after an interval of many years, I find it to have some of the defects as well as the merits of the Benthamic modes of thought, and to contain, as I now think, many weak arguments, but with a great overbalance of sound ones, and much good material for a more completely philosophic and conclusive treatment of the subject.

I have now, I believe, mentioned all the books which had any considerable effect on my early mental development. From this point I began to carry on my intellectual cultivation by writing still more than by reading. In the summer of 1822 I wrote my first argumentative essay. I remember very little about it, except that it was an attack on what I regarded as the aristocratic prejudice, that the rich were, or were likely to be, superior in moral qualities to the poor. My performance was entirely argumentative, without any of the declamation which the subject would admit of, and might be expected to suggest to a young writer. In that department, however, I was, and remained, very inapt. Dry argument was the only thing I could, manage, or willingly attempted; though passively I was very susceptible to the effect of all composition, whether in the form of poetry or oratory, which appealed to the feelings on any basis of reason. My father, who knew nothing of this essay until it was finished, was well satisfied, and, as I learnt from others, even pleased with it; but, perhaps from a desire to promote the exercise of other mental faculties than the purely logical, he advised me to make my next exercise in composition one of the oratorical kind; on which suggestion, availing myself of my familiarity with Greek history and ideas, and with the Athenian orators, I wrote two speeches, one an accusation, the other a defence of Pericles, on a supposed impeachment for not marching out to fight the Lacedemonians on their invasion of Attica. After this I continued to write papers on subjects often very much beyond my capacity, but with great benefit both from the exercise itself, and from the discussions which it led to with my father.

I had now also begun to converse, on general subjects, with the instructed men with whom I came in contact: and the opportunities of such contact naturally became more numerous. The two friends of my father from whom I derived most, and with whom I most associated, were Mr. Grote and Mr. John Austin. The acquaintance of both with my father was recent, but had ripened rapidly into intimacy. Mr. Grote was introduced to my father by Mr. Ricardo, I think in 1819 (being then about twenty-five years old), and sought assiduously his society and conversation. Already a highly instructed man, he was yet, by the side of my father, a tyro in the great subjects of human opinion; but he rapidly seized on my father's best ideas; and in the department of political opinion he made himself known as early as 1820, by a pamphlet in defence of Radical Reform, in reply to a celebrated article by Sir

James Mackintosh, then lately published in he *Edinburgh Review.* Mr. Grote's father, the banker, was, I believe, a thorough Tory, and his mother intensely Evangelical; so that for his liberal opinions he was in no way indebted to home influences. But, unlike most persons who have the prospect of being rich by inheritance, he had, though actively engaged in the business of banking, devoted a great portion of time to philosophic studies; and his intimacy with my father did much to decide the character of the next stage in his mental progress. Him I often visited, and my conversations with him on political, moral, and philosophical subjects gave me, in addition to much valuable instruction, all the pleasure and benefit of sympathetic communion with a man of the high intellectual and moral eminence which his life and writings have since manifested to the world.

Mr. Austin, who was four or five years older than Mr. Grote, was the eldest son of a retired miller in Suffolk, who had made money by contracts during the war, and who must have been a man of remarkable qualities, as I infer from the fact that all his sons were of more than common ability and all eminently gentlemen. The one with whom we are now concerned, and whose writings on jurisprudence have made him celebrated, was for some time in the army, and served in Sicily under Lord William Bentinck. After the Peace he sold his commission and studied for the bar, to which he had been called for some time before my father knew him. He was not, like Mr. Grote, to any extent, a pupil of my father, but he had attained, by reading and thought, a considerable number of the same opinions, modified by his own very decided individuality of character. He was a man of great intellectual powers, which in conversation appeared at their very best; from the vigour and richness of expression with which, under the excitement of discussion, he was accustomed to maintain some view or other of most general subjects; and from an appearance of not only strong, but deliberate and collected will; mixed with a certain bitterness, partly derived from temperament, and partly from the general cast of his feelings and reflections. The dissatisfaction with life and the world, felt more or less in the present state of society and intellect by every discerning and highly conscientious mind, gave in his case a rather melancholy tinge to the character, very natural to those whose passive moral susceptibilities are more than proportioned to their active energies. For it must be said, that the strength of will of which his manner seemed to give such strong assurance, expended itself principally in manner. With great zeal for human improvement, a strong sense of duty, and capacities and acquirements the extent of which is proved by the writings he has left, he hardly ever completed any intellectual task of magnitude. He had so high a standard of what ought to be done, so exaggerated a sense of deficiencies in his own performances, and was so unable to content himself with the amount of elaboration sufficient for the occasion and the purpose, that he not only spoilt much of his work for ordinary use by overlabouring it, but spent so much time and exertion in superfluous study and thought, that when his task ought to have been completed, he had generally worked himself into an illness, without having half finished what he undertook. From this mental infirmity (of which he is not the sole example among the accomplished and able men whom I have known), combined with liability to frequent attacks of disabling though not dangerous ill-health, he accomplished, through life, little in comparison with what he seemed capable of; but what he did produce is held in the very highest estimation by the most competent judges; and, like Coleridge, he might plead as a set-off that he had been to many persons, through his conversation, a source not only of much instruction but of great elevation of character. On me his influence was most salutary. It was moral in the best sense. He took a sincere and kind interest in me, far beyond what could have been expected towards a mere youth from a man of his age, standing, and what seemed austerity of character. There was in his conversation and demeanour a tone of high-mindedness which did not show itself so much, if the quality existed as much, in any of the other persons with whom at that time I associated. My intercourse with him was the more beneficial, owing to his being of a different mental type from all other intellectual men whom I frequented, and he from the first set himself decidedly against the prejudices and narrownesses which are almost sure to be found in a young man formed by a particular mode of thought or a particular social circle.

His younger brother, Charles Austin, of whom at this time and for the next year or two I saw much, had also a great effect on me, though of a very different description. He was but a few years older than myself, and had then just left the University, where he had shone with great *iclat* as a man of intellect and a brilliant orator and converser. The effect he produced on his Cambridge contemporaries deserves to be accounted an historical event; for to it may in part be traced the tendency towards Liberalism in general, and the Benthamic and politico-economic form of it in particular, which showed itself in a portion of the more active-minded young men of the higher classes from this time to 1830. The Union Debating Society, at that time at the height of its reputation, was an arena where what were then thought extreme opinions, in politics and philosophy, were weekly asserted, face to face with their opposites, before audiences consisting of the *ilite* of the Cambridge youth: and though many persons afterwards of more or less note (of whom Lord Macaulay is the most celebrated) gained their first oratorical laurels in those debates, the really influential mind among these intellectual gladiators was Charles Austin. He continued, after leaving the University, to be, by his conversation and personal ascendency, a leader among the same class of young men who had been his associates there; and he attached me among others to his car. Through him I became acquainted with Macaulay, Hyde and Charles Villiers, Strutt (now Lord Belper), Romilly (now Lord Romilly and Master of the Rolls), and various others who subsequently figured in literature or politics, and among whom I heard discussions on many topics, as yet to a certain degree new to me. The influence of Charles Austin over me differed from that of the persons I have hitherto mentioned, in being not the influence of a man over a boy, but that of an elder contemporary. It was through him that I first felt myself, not a pupil under teachers, but a man among men. He was the first person of intellect whom I met on a ground of equality, though as yet much his inferior on that common ground. He was a man who never failed to impress greatly those with whom he came in contact, even when their opinions were the very reverse of his. The impression he gave was that of boundless strength, together with talents which, combined with such apparent force of will and character, seemed capable of dominating the world. Those who knew him, whether friendly to him or not, always anticipated that he would play a conspicuous part in public life. It is seldom that men produce so great an immediate effect by speech, unless they, in some degree, lay themselves out for it; and he did this in no ordinary degree. He loved to strike, and even to startle. He knew that decision is the greatest element of effect, and he uttered his opinions with all the decision he could throw into them, never so well pleased as when he astonished anyone by their audacity. Very unlike his brother, who made war against the narrower interpretations and applications of the principles they both professed, he, on the contrary, presented the Benthamic doctrines in the most startling form of which they were susceptible, exaggerating everything in them which tended to consequences offensive to anyone's preconceived feelings. All which, he defended with such verve and vivacity, and carried off by a manner so agreeable as well as forcible, that he always either came off victor, or divided the honours of the field. It is my belief that much of the notion popularly entertained of the tenets and sentiments of what are called Benthamites or Utilitarians had its origin in paradoxes thrown out by Charles Austin. It must be said, however, that his example was followed, *haud passibus aequis*, by younger proselytes, and that to *outrer* whatever was by anybody considered offensive in the doctrines and maxims of Benthamism, became at one time the badge of a small coterie of youths. All of these who had anything in them, myself among others, quickly outgrew this boyish vanity; and those who had not, became tired of differing from other people, and gave up both the good and the bad part of the heterodox opinions they had for some time professed.

It was in the winter of 1822-3 that I formed the plan of a little society, to be composed of young men agreeing in fundamental principles—acknowledging Utility as their standard in ethics and politics, and a certain number of the principal corollaries drawn from it in the philosophy I had accepted—and meeting once a fortnight to read essays and discuss questions conformably to the premises thus agreed on. The fact would hardly be worth mentioning, but for the circumstance, that the name I gave to the society I had planned was the Utilitarian Society. It was the first time that anyone had taken the title of Utilitarian; and the term made its way into the language, from this humble source. I did not invent the word, but found it in one of Galt's novels, the *Annals of the Parish*, in which the Scotch clergyman, of whom the book is a supposed autobiography, is represented as warning his parishioners not to leave the Gospel and become utilitarians. With a boy's fondness for a name and a banner I seized on the word, and for some years called myself and others by it as a sectarian appellation; and it came to be occasionally used by some others holding the opinions which it was intended to designate. As those opinions attracted more notice, the term was repeated by strangers and opponents, and got into rather common use just about the time when those who had originally assumed it, laid down that along with other sectarian characteristics. The Society so called consisted at first of no more than three members, one of whom, being Mr. Bentham's amanuensis, obtained for us permission to hold our meetings in his house. The number never, I think, reached ten, and the Society was broken up in 1826. It had thus an existence of about three years and a half. The chief effect of it as regards myself, over and above the benefit of practice in oral discussion, was that of bringing me in contact with several young men at that time less advanced than myself, among whom, as they professed the same opinions, I was for some time a sort of leader, and had considerable influence on their mental progress. Any young man of education who fell in my way, and whose opinions were not incompatible with those of the

Society, I endeavoured to press into its service; and some others I probably should never have known, had they not joined it. Those of the members who became my intimate companions—no one of whom was in any sense of the word a disciple, but all of them independent thinkers on their own basis—were William Eyton Tooke, son of the eminent political economist, a young man of singular worth both moral and intellectual, lost to the world by an early death; his friend William Ellis, an original thinker in the field of political economy, now honourably known by his apostolic exertions for the improvement of education; George Graham, afterwards official assignee of the Bankruptcy Court, a thinker of originality and power on almost all abstract subjects; and (from the time when he came first to England to study for the bar in 1824 or 1825) a man who has made considerably more noise in the world than any of these, John Arthur Roebuck.

In May, 1823, my professional occupation and status for the next thirty-five years of my life, were decided by my father's obtaining for me an appointment from the East India Company, in the office of the Examiner of India Correspondence, immediately under himself. I was appointed in the usual manner, at the bottom of the list of clerks, to rise, at least in the first instance, by seniority; but with the understanding that I should be employed from the beginning in preparing drafts of despatches, and be thus trained up as a successor to those who then filled the higher departments of the office. My drafts of course required, for some time, much revision from my immediate superiors, but I soon became well acquainted with the business, and by my father's instructions and the general growth of my own powers, I was in a few years qualified to be, and practically was, the chief conductor of the correspondence with India in one of the leading departments, that of the Native States. This continued to be my official duty until I was appointed Examiner, only two years before the time when the abolition of the East India Company as a political body determined my retirement. I do not know any one of the occupations by which a subsistence can now be gained, more suitable than such as this to anyone who, not being in independent circumstances, desires to devote a part of the twenty-four hours to private intellectual pursuits. Writing for the press cannot be recommended as a permanent resource to anyone qualified to accomplish anything in the higher departments of literature or thought: not only on account of the uncertainty of this means of livelihood, especially if the writer has a conscience, and will not consent to serve any opinions except his own; but also because the writings by which one can live are not the writings which themselves live, and are never those in which the writer does his best. Books destined to form future thinkers take too much time to write, and when written come, in general, too slowly into notice and repute, to be relied on for subsistence. Those who have to support themselves by their pen must depend on literary drudgery, or at best on writings addressed to the multitude; and can employ in the pursuits of their own choice, only such time as they can spare from those of necessity; which is generally less than the leisure allowed by office occupations, while the effect on the mind is far more enervating and fatiguing. For my own part I have, through life, found office duties an actual rest from the other mental occupations which I have carried on simultaneously with them. They were sufficiently intellectual not to be a distasteful drudgery, without being such as to cause any strain upon the mental powers of a person used to abstract thought, or to the labour of careful literary composition. The drawbacks, for every mode of life has its drawbacks, were not, however, unfelt by me. I cared little for the loss of the chances of riches and honours held out by some of the professions, particularly the bar, which had been, as I have already said, the profession thought of for me. But I was not indifferent to exclusion from Parliament, and public life: and I felt very sensibly the more immediate unpleasantness of confinement to London; the holiday allowed by India House practice not exceeding a month in the year, while my taste was strong for a country life, and my sojourn in France had left behind it an ardent desire of travelling. But though these tastes could not be freely indulged, they were at no time entirely sacrificed. I passed most Sundays, throughout the year, in the country, taking long rural walks on that day even when residing in London. The month's holiday was, for a few years, passed at my father's house in the country; afterwards a part or the whole was spent in tours, chiefly pedestrian, with some one or more of the young men who were my chosen companions; and, at a later period, in longer journeys or excursions, alone or with other friends. France, Belgium, and Rhenish Germany were within easy reach of the annual holiday: and two longer absences, one of three, the other of six months, under medical advice, added Switzerland, the Tyrol, and Italy to my list. Fortunately, also, both these journeys occurred rather early, so as to give the benefit and charm of the remembrance to a large portion of life.

I am disposed to agree with what has been surmised by others, that the opportunity which my official position gave me of learning by personal observation the necessary conditions of the practical conduct of public affairs, has been of considerable value to me as a theoretical reformer of the opinions and institutions of my time. Not, indeed, that public business transacted on paper, to take effect on the other side of the globe, was of itself calculated to give much practical knowledge of life. But the occupation accustomed me to see and hear the difficulties of every course, and the means of obviating them, stated and discussed deliberately with a view to execution: it gave me opportunities of perceiving when public measures, and other political facts, did not produce the effects which had been expected of them, and from what causes; above all, it was valuable to me by making me, in this portion of my activity, merely one wheel in a machine, the whole of which had to work together. As a speculative writer, I should have had no one to consult but myself, and should have encountered in my speculations none of the obstacles which would have started up whenever they came to be applied to practice. But as a Secretary conducting political correspondence, I could not issue an order, or express an opinion, without satisfying various persons very unlike myself, that the thing was fit to be done. I was thus in a good position for finding out by practice the mode of putting a thought which gives it easiest admittance into minds not prepared for it by habit; while I became practically conversant with the difficulties of moving bodies of men, the necessities of compromise, the art of sacrificing the non-essential to preserve the essential. I learnt how to obtain the best I could, when I could not obtain everything; instead of being indignant or dispirited because I could not have entirely my own way, to be pleased and encouraged when I could have the smallest part of it; and when even that could not be, to bear with complete equanimity the being overruled altogether. I have found, through life, these acquisitions to be of the greatest possible importance for personal happiness, and they are also a very necessary condition for enabling anyone, either as theorist or as practical man, to effect the greatest amount of good compatible with his opportunities.

IV

Youthful Propagandism. The "Westminster Review"

The occupation of so much of my time by office work did not relax my attention to my own pursuits, which were never carried on more vigorously. It was about this time that I began to write in newspapers. The first writings of mine which got into print were two letters published towards the end of 1822, in the *Traveller* evening newspaper. The *Traveller* (which afterwards grew into the *Globe and Traveller*, by the purchase and incorporation of the *Globe*) was then the property of the well-known political economist, Colonel Torrens, and under the editorship of an able man, Mr. Walter Coulson (who, after being an amanuensis of Mr. Bentham, became a reporter, then an editor, next a barrister and conveyancer, and died Counsel to the Home Office), it had become one of the most important newspaper organs of Liberal politics. Colonel Torrens himself wrote much of the political economy of his paper; and had at this time made an attack upon some opinion of Ricardo and my father, to which, at my father's instigation, I attempted an answer, and Coulson, out of consideration for my father and goodwill to me, inserted it. There was a reply by Torrens, to which I again rejoined. I soon after attempted something considerably more ambitious. The prosecutions of Richard Carlile and his wife and sister for publications hostile to Christianity were then exciting much attention, and nowhere more than among the people I frequented. Freedom of discussion even in politics, much more in religion, was at that time far from being, even in theory, the conceded point which it at least seems to be now; and the holders of obnoxious opinions had to be always ready to argue and re-argue for the liberty of expressing them. I wrote a series of five letters, under the signature of Wickliffe, going over the whole length and breadth of the question of free publication of all opinions on religion, and offered them to the *Morning Chronicle*. Three of them were published in January and February, 1823; the other two, containing things too outspoken for that journal, never appeared at all. But a paper which I wrote soon after on the same subject, '*propos* of a debate in the House of Commons, was inserted as a leading article; and during the whole of this year, 1823, a considerable number of my contributions were printed in the *Chronicle* and *Traveller*: sometimes notices of books, but oftener letters, commenting on some nonsense talked in Parliament, or some defect of the law, or misdoings of the magistracy or the courts of justice. In this last department the *Chronicle* was now rendering signal service. After the death of Mr. Perry, the editorship and management of the paper had devolved on Mr. John Black, long a reporter on its establishment; a man of most extensive reading and information, great honesty and simplicity of mind; a particular friend of my father, imbued with many of his and Bentham's ideas, which he reproduced in his articles, among other valuable thoughts, with great facility and skill. From this time the *Chronicle* ceased to be the merely Whig organ it was before, and during the next ten years became to a considerable extent a vehicle of the opinions of the Utilitarian Radicals. This was mainly by what Black himself wrote, with some assistance from Fonblanque, who first showed his eminent qualities as a writer by articles and *jeux d'esprit* in the *Chronicle*. The defects of the law, and of the administration of justice, were the subject on which that paper rendered most service to improvement. Up to that time hardly a word had been said, except by Bentham and my father, against that most peccant part of English institutions and of their administration. It was the almost universal creed of Englishmen, that the law of England, the judicature of England, the unpaid magistracy of England, were models of excellence. I do not go beyond the mark in saying, that after Bentham, who supplied the principal materials, the greatest share of the merit of breaking down this wretched superstition belongs to Black, as editor of the *Morning Chronicle*. He kept up an incessant fire against it, exposing the absurdities and vices of the law and the courts of justice, paid and unpaid, until he forced some sense of them into people's minds. On many other questions he became the organ of opinions much in advance of any which had ever before found regular advocacy in the newspaper press. Black was a frequent visitor of my father, and Mr. Grote used to say that he always knew by the Monday morning's article whether Black had been with my father on the Sunday. Black was one of the most influential of the many channels through which my father's conversation and personal influence made his opinions tell on the world; cooperating with the effect of his writings in making him a power in the country such as it has rarely been the lot of an individual in a private station to be, through the mere force of intellect and character: and a power which was often acting the most efficiently where it was least seen and suspected. I have already noticed how much of what was done by Ricardo, Hume, and Grote was the result, in part, of his prompting and persuasion. He was the good genius by the side of Brougham in most of what he did for the public, either on education, law reform, or any other subject. And his influence flowed in minor streams too numerous to be specified. This influence was now about to receive a great extension by the foundation of the *Westminster Review*.

Contrary to what may have been supposed, my father was in no degree a party to setting up the *Westminster Review*. The need of a Radical organ to make head against the *Edinburgh* and *Quarterly* (then in the period of their greatest reputation and influence) had been a topic of conversation between him and Mr. Bentham many years earlier, and it had been a part of their *Chbteau en Espagne* that my father should be the editor; but the idea had never assumed any practical shape. In 1823, however, Mr. Bentham determined to establish the *Review* at his own cost, and offered the editorship to my father, who declined it as incompatible with his India House appointment. It was then entrusted to Mr. (now Sir John) Bowring, at that time a merchant in the City. Mr. Bowring had been for two or three years previous an assiduous frequenter of Mr. Bentham, to whom he was recommended by many personal good qualities, by an ardent admiration for Bentham, a zealous adoption of many, though not all of his opinions, and, not least, by an extensive acquaintanceship and correspondence with Liberals of all countries, which seemed to qualify him for being a powerful agent in spreading Bentham's fame and doctrines through all quarters of the world. My father had seen little of Bowring, but knew enough of him to have formed a strong opinion, that he was a man of an entirely different type from what my father considered suitable for conducting a political and philosophical Review: and he augured so ill of the enterprise that he regretted it altogether, feeling persuaded not only that Mr. Bentham would lose his money, but that discredit would probably be brought upon Radical principles. He could not, however, desert Mr. Bentham, and he consented to write an article for the first number. As it had been a favourite portion of the scheme formerly talked of, that part of the work should be devoted to reviewing the other Reviews, this article of my father's was to be a general criticism of the *Edinburgh Review* from its commencement. Before writing it he made me read through all the volumes of the *Review*, or as much of each as seemed of any importance (which was not so arduous a task in 1823 as it would be now), and make notes for him of the articles which I thought he would wish to examine, either on account of their good or their bad qualities. This paper of my father's was the chief cause of the sensation which the *Westminster Review* produced at its first appearance, and is, both in conception and in execution, one of the most striking of all his writings. He began by an analysis of the tendencies of periodical literature in general; pointing out, that it cannot, like books, wait for success, but must succeed immediately or not at all, and is hence almost certain to profess and inculcate the opinions already held by the public to which it addresses itself, instead of attempting to rectify or improve those opinions. He next, to characterize the position of the *Edinburgh Review* as a political organ, entered into a complete analysis, from the Radical point of view, of the British Constitution. He held up to notice its thoroughly aristocratic character: the nomination of a majority of the House of Commons by a few hundred families; the entire identification of the more independent portion, the county members, with the great landholders; the different classes whom this narrow oligarchy was induced, for convenience, to admit to a share of power; and finally, what he called its two props, the Church, and the legal profession. He pointed out the natural tendency of an aristocratic body of this composition, to group itself into two parties, one of them in possession of the executive, the other endeavouring to supplant the former and become the predominant section by the aid of public opinion, without any essential sacrifice of the aristocratical predominance. He described the course likely to be pursued, and the political ground occupied, by an aristocratic party in opposition, coquetting with popular principles for the sake of popular support. He showed how this idea was realized in the conduct of the Whig party, and of the *Edinburgh Review* as its chief literary organ. He described, as their main characteristic, what he termed "seesaw"; writing alternately on both sides of the question which touched the power or interest of the governing classes; sometimes in different articles, sometimes in different parts of the same article: and illustrated his position by copious specimens. So formidable an attack on the Whig party and policy had never before been made; nor had so great a blow ever been struck, in this country, for Radicalism; nor was there, I believe, any living person capable of writing that article except my father.[2]

In the meantime the nascent *Review* had formed a junction with another project, of a purely literary periodical, to be edited by Mr. Henry Southern, afterwards a diplomatist, then a literary man by profession. The two editors agreed to unite their corps, and divide the editorship, Bowring taking the political, Southern the literary department. Southern's Review was to have been published by

Longman, and that firm, though part proprietors of the *Edinburgh*, were willing to be the publishers of the new journal. But when all the arrangements had been made, and the prospectuses sent out, the Longmans saw my father's attack on the *Edinburgh*, and drew back. My father was now appealed to for his interest with his own publisher, Baldwin, which was exerted with a successful result. And so in April, 1824, amidst anything but hope on my father's part, and that of most of those who afterwards aided in carrying on the *Review*, the first number made its appearance.

That number was an agreeable surprise to most of us. The average of the articles was of much better quality than had been expected. The literary and artistic department had rested chiefly on Mr. Bingham, a barrister (subsequently a police magistrate), who had been for some years a frequenter of Bentham, was a friend of both the Austins, and had adopted with great ardour Mr. Bentham's philosophical opinions. Partly from accident, there were in the first number as many as five articles by Bingham; and we were extremely pleased with them. I well remember the mixed feeling I myself had about the *Review*; the joy of finding, what we did not at all expect, that it was sufficiently good to be capable of being made a creditable organ of those who held the opinions it professed; and extreme vexation, since it was so good on the whole, at what we thought the blemishes of it. When, however, in addition to our generally favourable opinion of it, we learned that it had an extraordinary large sale for a first number, and found that the appearance of a Radical Review, with pretensions equal to those of the established organs of parties, had excited much attention, there could be no room for hesitation, and we all became eager in doing everything we could to strengthen and improve it.

My father continued to write occasional articles. The *Quarterly Review* received its exposure, as a sequel to that of the *Edinburgh*. Of his other contributions, the most important were an attack on Southey's *Book of the Church*, in the fifth number, and a political article in the twelfth. Mr. Austin only contributed one paper, but one of great merit, an argument against primogeniture, in reply to an article then lately published in the *Edinburgh Review* by McCulloch. Grote also was a contributor only once; all the time he could spare being already taken up with his *History of Greece.* The article he wrote was on his own subject, and was a very complete exposure and castigation of Mitford. Bingham and Charles Austin continued to write for some time; Fonblanque was a frequent contributor from the third number. Of my particular associates, Ellis was a regular writer up to the ninth number; and about the time when he left off, others of the set began; Eyton Tooke, Graham, and Roebuck. I was myself the most frequent writer of all, having contributed, from the second number to the eighteenth, thirteen articles; reviews of books on history and political economy, or discussions on special political topics, as corn laws, game laws, law of libel. Occasional articles of merit came in from other acquaintances of my father's, and, in time, of mine; and some of Mr. Bowring's writers turned out well. On the whole, however, the conduct of the Review was never satisfactory to any of the persons strongly interested in its principles, with whom I came in contact. Hardly ever did a number come out without containing several things extremely offensive to us, either in point of opinion, of taste, or by mere want of ability. The unfavourable judgments passed by my father, Grote, the two Austins, and others, were re-echoed with exaggeration by us younger people; and as our youthful zeal rendered us by no means backward in making complaints, we led the two editors a sad life. From my knowledge of what I then was, I have no doubt that we were at least as often wrong as right; and I am very certain that if the *Review* had been carried on according to our notions (I mean those of the juniors), it would have been no better, perhaps not even so good as it was. But it is worth noting as a fact in the history of Benthamism, that the periodical organ, by which it was best known, was from the first extremely unsatisfactory to those whose opinions on all subjects it was supposed specially to represent.

Meanwhile, however, the *Review* made considerable noise in the world, and gave a recognised *status*, in the arena of opinion and discussion, to the Benthamic type of Radicalism, out of all proportion to the number of its adherents, and to the personal merits and abilities, at that time, of most of those who could be reckoned among them. It was a time, as is known, of rapidly rising Liberalism. When the fears and animosities accompanying the war with France had been brought to an end, and people had once more a place in their thoughts for home politics, the tide began to set towards reform. The renewed oppression of the Continent by the old reigning families, the countenance apparently given by the English Government to the conspiracy against liberty called the Holy Alliance, and the enormous weight of the national debt and taxation occasioned by so long and costly a war, rendered the government and parliament very unpopular. Radicalism, under the leadership of the Burdetts and Cobbetts, had assumed a character and importance which seriously alarmed the Administration: and their alarm had scarcely been temporarily assuaged by the celebrated Six Acts, when the trial of Queen Caroline roused a still wider and deeper feeling of hatred. Though the outward signs of this hatred passed away with its exciting cause, there arose on all sides a spirit which had never shown itself before, of opposition to abuses in detail. Mr. Hume's persevering scrutiny of the public expenditure, forcing the House of Commons to a division on every objectionable item in the estimates, had begun to tell with great force on public opinion, and had extorted many minor retrenchments from an unwilling administration. Political economy had asserted itself with great vigour in public affairs, by the petition of the merchants of London for free trade, drawn up in 1820 by Mr. Tooke and presented by Mr. Alexander Baring; and by the noble exertions of Ricardo during the few years of his parliamentary life. His writings, following up the impulse given by the Bullion controversy, and followed up in their turn by the expositions and comments of my father and McCulloch (whose writings in the *Edinburgh Review* during those years were most valuable), had drawn general attention to the subject, making at least partial converts in the Cabinet itself; and Huskisson, supported by Canning, had commenced that gradual demolition of the protective system, which one of their colleagues virtually completed in 1846, though the last vestiges were only swept away by Mr. Gladstone in 1860. Mr. Peel, then Home Secretary, was entering cautiously into the untrodden and peculiarly Benthamic path of Law Reform. At this period, when Liberalism seemed to be becoming the tone of the time, when improvement of institutions was preached from the highest places, and a complete change of the constitution of Parliament was loudly demanded in the lowest, it is not strange that attention should have been roused by the regular appearance in controversy of what seemed a new school of writers, claiming to be the legislators and theorists of this new tendency. The air of strong conviction with which they wrote, when scarcely anyone else seemed to have an equally strong faith in as definite a creed; the boldness with which they tilted against the very front of both the existing political parties; their uncompromising profession of opposition to many of the generally received opinions, and the suspicion they lay under of holding others still more heterodox than they professed; the talent and verve of at least my father's articles, and the appearance of a corps behind him sufficient to carry on a Review; and finally, the fact that the *Review* was bought and read, made the so-called Bentham school in philosophy and politics fill a greater place in the public mind than it had held before, or has ever again held since other equally earnest schools of thought have arisen in England. As I was in the headquarters of it, knew of what it was composed, and as one of the most active of its very small number, might say without undue assumption, *quorum pars magna fui*, it belongs to me more than to most others, to give some account of it.

This supposed school, then, had no other existence than what was constituted by the fact, that my father's writings and conversation drew round him a certain number of young men who had already imbibed, or who imbibed from him, a greater or smaller portion of his very decided political and philosophical opinions. The notion that Bentham was surrounded by a band of disciples who received their opinions from his lips, is a fable to which my father did justice in his "Fragment on Mackintosh," and which, to all who knew Mr. Bentham's habits of life and manner of conversation, is simply ridiculous. The influence which Bentham exercised was by his writings. Through them he has produced, and is producing, effects on the condition of mankind, wider and deeper, no doubt, than any which can be attributed to my father. He is a much greater name in history. But my father exercised a far greater personal ascendency. He *was* sought for the vigour and instructiveness of his conversation, and did use it largely as an instrument for the diffusion of his opinions. I have never known any man who could do such ample justice to his best thoughts in colloquial discussion. His perfect command over his great mental resources, the terseness and expressiveness of his language and the moral earnestness as well as intellectual force of his delivery, made him one of the most striking of all argumentative conversers: and he was full of anecdote, a hearty laugher, and, when with people whom he liked, a most lively and amusing companion. It was not solely, or even chiefly, in diffusing his merely intellectual convictions that his power showed itself: it was still more through the influence of a quality, of which I have only since learnt to appreciate the extreme rarity: that exalted public spirit, and regard above all things to the good of the whole, which warmed into life and activity every germ of similar virtue that existed in the minds he came in contact with: the desire he made them feel for his approbation, the shame at his disapproval; the moral support which his conversation and his very existence gave to those who were aiming at the same objects, and the encouragement he afforded to the fainthearted or desponding among them, by the firm confidence which (though the reverse of sanguine as to the results to be expected in any one particular case) he always felt in the power of reason, the general progress of improvement, and the good which individuals could do by judicious effort.

If was my father's opinions which gave the distinguishing character to the Benthamic or utilitarian propagandism of that time. They fell singly, scattered from him, in many directions, but they flowed from him in a continued stream principally in three channels. One was through me, the only mind directly formed by his instructions, and through whom considerable influence was exercised over various young men, who became, in their turn, propagandists. A second was through some of the Cambridge contemporaries of Charles Austin, who, either initiated by him or under the general mental impulse which he gave, had adopted many opinions allied to those of my father, and some of the more considerable of whom afterwards sought my father's acquaintance and frequented his house. Among these may be mentioned Strutt, afterwards Lord Belper, and the present Lord Romilly, with whose eminent father, Sir Samuel, my father had of old been on terms of friendship. The third channel was that of a younger generation of Cambridge undergraduates, contemporary, not with Austin, but with Eyton Tooke, who were drawn to that estimable person by affinity of opinions, and introduced by him to my father: the most notable of these was Charles Buller. Various other persons individually received and transmitted a considerable amount of my father's influence: for example, Black (as before mentioned) and Fonblanque: most of these, however, we accounted only partial allies; Fonblanque, for instance, was always divergent from us on many important points. But indeed there was by no means complete unanimity among any portion of us, nor had any of us adopted implicitly all my father's opinions. For example, although his *Essay on Government* was regarded probably by all of us as a masterpiece of political wisdom, our adhesion by no means extended to the paragraph of it in which he maintains that women may, consistently with good government, be excluded from the suffrage, because their interest is the same with that of men. From this doctrine, I, and all those who formed my chosen associates, most positively dissented. It is due to my father to say that he denied having intended to affirm that women *should* be excluded, any more than men under the age of forty, concerning whom he maintained in the very next paragraph an exactly similar thesis. He was, as he truly said, not discussing whether the suffrage had better be restricted, but only (assuming that it is to be restricted) what is the utmost limit of restriction which does not necessarily involve a sacrifice of the securities for good government. But I thought then, as I have always thought since that the opinion which he acknowledged, no less than that which he disclaimed, is as great an error as any of those against which the *Essay* was directed; that the interest of women is included in that of men exactly as much as the interest of subjects is included in that of kings, and no more; and that every reason which exists for giving the suffrage to anybody, demands that it should not be withheld from women. This was also the general opinion of the younger proselytes; and it is pleasant to be able to say that Mr. Bentham, on this important point, was wholly on our side.

But though none of us, probably, agreed in every respect with my father, his opinions, as I said before, were the principal element which gave its colour and character to the little group of young men who were the first propagators of what was afterwards called "Philosophic Radicalism." Their mode of thinking was not characterized by Benthamism in any sense which has relation to Bentham as a chief or guide, but rather by a combination of Bentham's point of view with that of the modern political economy, and with the Hartleian metaphysics. Malthus's population principle was quite as much a banner, and point of union among us, as any opinion specially belonging to Bentham. This great doctrine, originally brought forward as an argument against the indefinite improvability of human affairs, we took up with ardent zeal in the contrary sense, as indicating the sole means of realizing that improvability by securing full employment at high wages to the whole labouring population through a voluntary restriction of the increase of their numbers. The other leading characteristics of the creed, which we held in common with my father, may be stated as follows:

In politics, an almost unbounded confidence in the efficacy of two things: representative government, and complete freedom of discussion. So complete was my father's reliance on the influence of reason over the minds of mankind, whenever it is allowed to reach them, that he felt as if all would be gained if the whole population were taught to read, if all sorts of opinions were allowed to be addressed to them by word and in writing, and if by means of the suffrage they could nominate a legislature to give effect to the opinions they adopted. He thought that when the legislature no longer represented a class interest, it would aim at the general interest, honestly and with adequate wisdom; since the people would be sufficiently under the guidance of educated intelligence, to make in general a good choice of persons to represent them, and having done so, to leave to those whom they had chosen a liberal discretion. Accordingly aristocratic rule, the government of the Few in any of its shapes, being in his eyes the only thing which stood between mankind and an administration of their affairs by the best wisdom to be found among them, was the object of his sternest disapprobation, and a democratic suffrage the principal article of his political creed, not on the ground of liberty, Rights of Man, or any of the phrases, more or less significant, by which, up to that time, democracy had usually been defended, but as the most essential of "securities for good government." In this, too, he held fast only to what he deemed essentials; he was comparatively indifferent to monarchical or republican forms—far more so than Bentham, to whom a king, in the character of "corrupter-general," appeared necessarily very noxious. Next to aristocracy, an established church, or corporation of priests, as being by position the great depravers of religion, and interested in opposing the progress of the human mind, was the object of his greatest detestation; though he disliked no clergyman personally who did not deserve it, and was on terms of sincere friendship with several. In ethics his moral feelings were energetic and rigid on all points which he deemed important to human well being, while he was supremely indifferent in opinion (though his indifference did not show itself in personal conduct) to all those doctrines of the common morality, which he thought had no foundation but in asceticism and priestcraft. He looked forward, for example, to a considerable increase of freedom in the relations between the sexes, though without pretending to define exactly what would be, or ought to be, the precise conditions of that freedom. This opinion was connected in him with no sensuality either of a theoretical or of a practical kind. He anticipated, on the contrary, as one of the beneficial effects of increased freedom, that the imagination would no longer dwell upon the physical relation and its adjuncts, and swell this into one of the principal objects of life; a perversion of the imagination and feelings, which he regarded as one of the deepest seated and most pervading evils in the human mind. In psychology, his fundamental doctrine was the formation of all human character by circumstances, through the universal Principle of Association, and the consequent unlimited possibility of improving the moral and intellectual condition of mankind by education. Of all his doctrines none was more important than this, or needs more to be insisted on; unfortunately there is none which is more contradictory to the prevailing tendencies of speculation, both in his time and since.

These various opinions were seized on with youthful fanaticism by the little knot of young men of whom I was one: and we put into them a sectarian spirit, from which, in intention at least, my father was wholly free. What we (or rather a phantom substituted in the place of us) were sometimes, by a ridiculous exaggeration, called by others, namely a "school," some of us for a time really hoped and aspired to be. The French *philosophes* of the eighteenth century were the examples we sought to imitate, and we hoped to accomplish no less results. No one of the set went to so great excesses in his boyish ambition as I did; which might be shown by many particulars, were it not an useless waste of space and time.

All this, however, is properly only the outside of our existence; or, at least, the intellectual part alone, and no more than one side of that. In attempting to penetrate inward, and give any indication of what we were as human beings, I must be understood as speaking only of myself, of whom alone I can speak from sufficient knowledge; and I do not believe that the picture would suit any of my companions without many and great modifications.

I conceive that the description so often given of a Benthamite, as a mere reasoning machine, though extremely inapplicable to most of those who have been designated by that title, was during two or three years of my life not altogether untrue of me. It was perhaps as applicable to me as it can well be to anyone just entering into life, to whom the common objects of desire must in general have at least the attraction of novelty. There is nothing very extraordinary in this fact: no youth of the age I then was, can be expected to be more than one thing, and this was the thing I happened to be. Ambition and desire of distinction I had in abundance; and zeal for what I thought the good of mankind was my strongest sentiment, mixing with and colouring all others. But my zeal was as yet little else, at that period of my life, than zeal for speculative opinions. It had not its root in genuine benevolence, or sympathy with mankind; though these qualities held their due place in my ethical standard. Nor was it connected with any high enthusiasm for ideal nobleness. Yet of this feeling I was imaginatively very susceptible; but there was at that time an intermission of its natural aliment, poetical culture, while there was a superabundance of the discipline antagonistic to it, that of mere logic and analysis. Add to this that, as already mentioned, my father's teachings tended to the undervaluing of feeling. It was not that he was himself cold-hearted or insensible; I believe it was rather from the contrary quality; he thought that feeling could take care of itself; that there was sure to be enough of it if actions were properly cared about. Offended by the frequency with which, in ethical and philosophical controversy, feeling is made the ultimate reason and justification of conduct, instead of being itself called on for a justification, while, in practice, actions the effect of which on human happiness is mischievous, are defended as being required by feeling, and the character of a person of feeling obtains a credit for desert, which he thought only due to actions, he had a real impatience of attributing praise to feeling, or of any but the most sparing reference to it, either in the estimation of persons or in the discussion of things. In addition to the influence which this characteristic in him had on me and others, we found all the opinions to which we attached most importance, constantly attacked on the ground of feeling. Utility was denounced as cold calculation; political economy as hard-hearted; anti-population doctrines as repulsive to the natural feelings of mankind. We retorted by the word "sentimentality," which, along with "declamation" and "vague generalities," served us as common terms of opprobrium. Although we were generally in the right, as against those who were opposed to us, the effect was that the cultivation of feeling (except the feelings of public and private duty) was not in much esteem among us, and had very little place in the thoughts of most of us, myself in particular. What we principally thought of, was to alter people's opinions; to make them believe according to evidence, and know what was their real interest, which when they once knew, they would, we thought, by the instrument of opinion, enforce a regard to it upon one another. While fully recognising the superior excellence of unselfish benevolence and love of justice, we did not expect the regeneration of mankind from any direct action on those sentiments, but from the effect of educated intellect, enlightening the selfish feelings. Although this last is prodigiously important as a means of improvement in the hands of those who are themselves impelled by nobler principles of action, I do not believe that any one of the survivors of the Benthamites or Utilitarians of that day now relies mainly upon it for the general amendment of human conduct.

From this neglect both in theory and in practice of the cultivation of feeling, naturally resulted, among other things, an undervaluing of poetry, and of Imagination generally, as an element of human nature. It is, or was, part of the popular notion of Benthamites, that they are enemies of poetry: this was partly true of Bentham himself; he used to say that "all poetry is misrepresentation": but in the sense in which he said it, the same might have been said of all impressive speech; of all representation or inculcation more oratorical in its character than a sum in arithmetic. An article of Bingham's in the first number of the *Westminster Review*, in which he offered as an explanation of something which he disliked in Moore, that "Mr. Moore *is* a poet, and therefore is *not* a reasoner," did a good deal to attach the notion of hating poetry to the writers in the *Review*. But the truth was that many of us were great readers of poetry; Bingham himself had been a writer of it, while as regards me (and the same thing might be said of my father), the correct statement would be, not that I disliked poetry, but that I was theoretically indifferent to it. I disliked any sentiments in poetry which I should have disliked in prose; and that included a great deal. And I was wholly blind to its place in human culture, as a means of educating the feelings. But I was always personally very susceptible to some kinds of it. In the most sectarian period of my Benthamism, I happened to look into Pope's *Essay on Man*, and, though every opinion in it was contrary to mine, I well remember how powerfully it acted on my imagination. Perhaps at that time poetical composition of any higher type than eloquent discussion in verse, might not have produced a similar effect upon me: at all events I seldom gave it an opportunity. This, however, was a mere passive state. Long before I had enlarged in any considerable degree the basis of my intellectual creed, I had obtained, in the natural course of my mental progress, poetic culture of the most valuable kind, by means of reverential admiration for the lives and characters of heroic persons; especially the heroes of philosophy. The same inspiring effect which so many of the benefactors of mankind have left on record that they had experienced from Plutarch's *Lives*, was produced on me by Plato's pictures of Socrates, and by some modern biographies, above all by Condorcet's *Life of Turgot*; a book well calculated to rouse the best sort of enthusiasm, since it contains one of the wisest and noblest of lives, delineated by one of the wisest and noblest of men. The heroic virtue of these glorious representatives of the opinions with which I sympathized, deeply affected me, and I perpetually recurred to them as others do to a favourite poet, when needing to be carried up into the more elevated regions of feeling and thought. I may observe by the way that this book cured me of my sectarian follies. The two or three pages beginning "Il regardait toute secte comme nuisible," and explaining why Turgot always kept himself perfectly distinct from the Encyclopedists, sank deeply into my mind. I left off designating myself and others as Utilitarians, and by the pronoun "we," or any other collective designation, I ceased to *afficher* sectarianism. My real inward sectarianism I did not get rid of till later, and much more gradually.

About the end of 1824, or beginning of 1825, Mr. Bentham, having lately got back his papers on Evidence from M. Dumont (whose *Traiti des Preuves Judiciaires*, grounded on them, was then first completed and published), resolved to have them printed in the original, and bethought himself of me as capable of preparing them for the press; in the same manner as his *Book of Fallacies* had been recently edited by Bingham. I gladly undertook this task, and it occupied nearly all my leisure for about a year, exclusive of the time afterwards spent in seeing the five large volumes through the press. Mr. Bentham had begun this treatise three time's, at considerable intervals, each time in a different manner, and each time without reference to the preceding: two of the three times he had gone over nearly the whole subject. These three masses of manuscript it was my business to condense into a single treatise, adopting the one last written as the groundwork, and incorporating with it as much of the two others as it had not completely superseded. I had also to unroll such of Bentham's involved and parenthetical sentences as seemed to overpass by their complexity the measure of what readers were likely to take the pains to understand. It was further Mr. Bentham's particular desire that I should, from myself, endeavour to supply any *lacunae* which he had left; and at his instance I read, for this purpose, the most authoritative treatises on the English Law of Evidence, and commented on a few of the objectionable points of the English rules, which had escaped Bentham's notice. I also replied to the objections which had been made to some of his doctrines by reviewers of Dumont's book, and added a few supplementary remarks on some of the more abstract parts of the subject, such as the theory of improbability and impossibility. The controversial part of these editorial additions was written in a more assuming tone than became one so young and inexperienced as I was: but indeed I had never contemplated coming forward in my own person; and as an anonymous editor of Bentham I fell into the tone of my author, not thinking it unsuitable to him or to the subject, however it might be so to me. My name as editor was put to the book after it was printed, at Mr. Bentham's positive desire, which I in vain attempted to persuade him to forego.

The time occupied in this editorial work was extremely well employed in respect to my own improvement. The *Rationale of Judicial Evidence* is one of the richest in matter of all Bentham's productions. The theory of evidence being in itself one of the most important of his subjects, and ramifying into most of the others, the book contains, very fully developed, a great proportion of all his best thoughts: while, among more special things, it comprises the most elaborate exposure of the vices and defects of English law, as it then was, which is to be found in his works; not confined to the law of evidence, but including, by way of illustrative episode, the entire procedure or practice of Westminster Hall. The direct knowledge, therefore, which I obtained from the book, and which was imprinted upon me much more thoroughly than it could have been by mere reading, was itself no small acquisition. But this occupation did for me what might seem less to be expected; it gave a great start to my powers of composition. Everything which I wrote subsequently to this editorial employment, was markedly superior to anything that I had written before it. Bentham's later style, as the world knows, was heavy and cumbersome, from the excess of a good quality, the love of precision, which made him introduce clause within clause into the heart of every sentence, that the reader might receive into his mind all the modifications and qualifications simultaneously with the main proposition: and the habit grew on him until his sentences became, to those not accustomed to them, most laborious reading. But his earlier style, that of the *Fragment on Government, Plan of a Judicial Establishment*, etc., is a model of liveliness and ease combined with fulness of matter, scarcely ever surpassed: and of this earlier style there were many striking specimens in the manuscripts on Evidence, all of which I endeavoured to preserve. So long a course of this admirable writing had a considerable effect upon my own; and I added to it by the assiduous reading of other writers, both French and English, who combined, in a remarkable degree, ease with force, such as Goldsmith, Fielding, Pascal, Voltaire, and Courier. Through these influences my writing lost the jejuneness of my early compositions; the bones and cartilages began to clothe themselves with flesh, and the style became, at times, lively and almost light.

This improvement was first exhibited in a new field. Mr. Marshall, of Leeds, father of the present generation of Marshalls, the same who was brought into Parliament for Yorkshire, when the representation forfeited by Grampound was transferred to it, an earnest Parliamentary reformer, and a man of large fortune, of which he made a liberal use, had been much struck with Bentham's *Book of Fallacies*; and the thought had occurred to him that it would be useful to publish annually the Parliamentary Debates, not in the chronological order of Hansard, but classified according to subjects, and accompanied by a commentary pointing out the fallacies of the speakers. With this intention, he very naturally addressed himself to the editor of the *Book of Fallacies*; and Bingham, with the assistance of Charles Austin, undertook the editorship. The work was called *Parliamentary History and Review*. Its sale was not sufficient to keep it in existence, and it only lasted three years. It excited, however, some attention among parliamentary and political people. The best strength of the party was put forth in it; and its execution did them much more credit than that of the *Westminster Review* had ever done. Bingham and Charles Austin wrote much in it; as did Strutt, Romilly, and several other Liberal lawyers. My father wrote one article in his best style; the elder Austin another. Coulson wrote one of great merit. It fell to my lot to lead off the first number by an article on the principal topic of the session (that of 1825), the Catholic Association and the Catholic Disabilities. In the second number I wrote an elaborate Essay on the Commercial Crisis of 1825 and the Currency Debates. In the third I had two articles, one on a minor subject, the other on the Reciprocity

principle in commerce, '*propos* of a celebrated diplomatic correspondence between Canning and Gallatin. These writings were
no longer mere reproductions and applications of the doctrines I
had been taught; they were original thinking, as far as that name
can be applied to old ideas in new forms and connexions: and I
do not exceed the truth in saying that there was a maturity, and a
well-digested, character about them, which there had not been in
any of my previous performances. In execution, therefore, they
were not at all juvenile; but their subjects have either gone by, or
have been so much better treated since, that they are entirely superseded, and should remain buried in the same oblivion with my
contributions to the first dynasty of the *Westminster Review.*

While thus engaged in writing for the public, I did not neglect
other modes of self-cultivation. It was at this time that I learnt German; beginning it on the Hamiltonian method, for which purpose
I and several of my companions formed a class. For several years
from this period, our social studies assumed a shape which contributed very much to my mental progress. The idea occurred to us
of carrying on, by reading and conversation, a joint study of several
of the branches of science which we wished to be masters of. We assembled to the number of a dozen or more. Mr. Grote lent a room
of his house in Threadneedle Street for the purpose, and his partner, Prescott, one of the three original members of the Utilitarian
Society, made one among us. We met two mornings in every week,
from half-past eight till ten, at which hour most of us were called off
to our daily occupations. Our first subject was Political Economy.
We chose some systematic treatise as our text-book; my father's
Elements being our first choice. One of us read aloud a chapter, or
some smaller portion of the book. The discussion was then opened,
and anyone who had an objection, or other remark to make, made
it. Our rule was to discuss thoroughly every point raised, whether
great or small, prolonging the discussion until all who took part
were satisfied with the conclusion they had individually arrived
at; and to follow up every topic of collateral speculation which the
chapter or the conversation suggested, never leaving it until we

had untied every knot which we found. We repeatedly kept up the discussion of some one point for several weeks, thinking intently on it during the intervals of our meetings, and contriving solutions of the new difficulties which had risen up in the last morning's discussion. When we had finished in this way my father's *Elements*, we went in the same manner through Ricardo's *Principles of Political Economy*, and Bailey's *Dissertation on Value*. These close and vigorous discussions were not only improving in a high degree to those who took part in them, but brought out new views of some topics of abstract Political Economy. The theory of International Values which I afterwards published, emanated from these conversations, as did also the modified form of Ricardo's *Theory of Profits*, laid down in my *Essay on Profits and Interest*. Those among us with whom new speculations chiefly originated, were Ellis, Graham, and I; though others gave valuable aid to the discussions, especially Prescott and Roebuck, the one by his knowledge, the other by his dialectical acuteness. The theories of International Values and of Profits were excogitated and worked out in about equal proportions by myself and Graham: and if our original project had been executed, my *Essays on Some Unsettled Questions of Political Economy* would have been brought out along with some papers of his, under our joint names. But when my exposition came to be written, I found that I had so much over-estimated my agreement with him, and he dissented so much from the most original of the two Essays, that on International Values, that I was obliged to consider the theory as now exclusively mine, and it came out as such when published many years later. I may mention that among the alterations which my father made in revising his *Elements* for the third edition, several were founded on criticisms elicited by these conversations; and in particular he modified his opinions (though not to the extent of our new speculations) on both the points to which I have adverted.

When we had enough of political economy, we took up the syllogistic logic in the same manner, Grote now joining us. Our first text-book was Aldrich, but being disgusted with its superficiality, we reprinted one of the most finished among the many manuals of the school logic, which my father, a great collector of such books, possessed, the *Manuductio ad Logicam* of the Jesuit Du Trieu. After finishing this, we took up Whately's *Logic*, then first republished from the *Encyclopedia Metropolitana*, and finally the *Computatio sive Logica* of Hobbes. These books, dealt with in our manner, afforded a high range for original metaphysical speculation: and most of what has been done in the First Book of my *System of Logic*, to rationalize and correct the principles and distinctions of the school logicians, and to improve the theory of the Import of Propositions, had its origin in these discussions; Graham and I originating most of the novelties, while Grote and others furnished an excellent tribunal or test. From this time I formed the project of writing a book on Logic, though on a much humbler scale than the one I ultimately executed.

Having done with Logic, we launched into Analytic Psychology, and having chosen Hartley for our text-book, we raised Priestley's edition to an extravagant price by searching through London to furnish each of us with a copy. When we had finished Hartley, we suspended our meetings; but my father's *Analysis of the Mind* being published soon after, we reassembled for the purpose of reading it. With this our exercises ended. I have always dated from these conversations my own real inauguration as an original and independent thinker. It was also through them that I acquired, or very much strengthened, a mental habit to which I attribute all that I have ever done, or ever shall do, in speculation: that of never accepting half-solutions of difficulties as complete; never abandoning a puzzle, but again and again returning to it until it was cleared up; never allowing obscure corners of a subject to remain unexplored, because they did not appear important; never thinking that I perfectly understood any part of a subject until I understood the whole.

Our doings from 1825 to 1830 in the way of public speaking, filled a considerable place in my life during those years, and as they had important effects on my development, something ought to be said of them.

There was for some time in existence a society of Owenites, called the Co-operative Society, which met for weekly public discussions in Chancery Lane. In the early part of 1825, accident brought Roebuck in contact with several of its members, and led to his attending one or two of the meetings and taking part in the debate in opposition to Owenism. Some one of us started the notion of going there in a body and having a general battle: and Charles Austin and some of his friends who did not usually take part in our joint exercises, entered into the project. It was carried out by concert with the principal members of the Society, themselves nothing loth, as they naturally preferred a controversy with opponents to a tame discussion among their own body. The question of population was proposed as the subject of debate: Charles Austin led the case on our side with a brilliant speech, and the fight was kept up by adjournment through five or six weekly meetings before crowded auditories, including along with the members of the Society and their friends, many hearers and some speakers from the Inns of Court. When this debate was ended, another was commenced on the general merits of Owen's system: and the contest altogether lasted about three months. It was a *lutte corps ' corps* between Owenites and political economists, whom the Owenites regarded as their most inveterate opponents: but it was a perfectly friendly dispute. We who represented political economy, had the same objects in view as they had, and took pains to show it; and the principal champion on their side was a very estimable man, with whom I was well acquainted, Mr. William Thompson, of Cork, author of a book on the Distribution of Wealth, and of an " Appeal" in behalf of women against the passage relating to them in my father's *Essay on Government*. Ellis, Roebuck, and I took an active part in the debate, and among those from the Inns of Court who joined in it, I remember Charles Villiers. The other side obtained also, on the population question, very efficient support from without. The well-known Gale Jones, then an elderly man, made one of his florid speeches; but the speaker with whom I was most struck, though I dissented from nearly every word he said, was Thirlwall, the historian, since Bishop of St. David's, then a Chancery barrister, unknown except by a high reputation for eloquence acquired at the Cambridge Union before the era of Austin and Macaulay. His speech was in answer to one of mine. Before he had uttered ten sentences, I set him down as the best speaker I had ever heard, and I have never since heard anyone whom I placed above him.

The great interest of these debates predisposed some of those who took part in them, to catch at a suggestion thrown out by McCulloch, the political economist, that a Society was wanted in London similar to the Speculative Society at Edinburgh, in which Brougham, Horner, and others first cultivated public speaking. Our experience at the Co-operative Society seemed to give cause for being sanguine as to the sort of men who might be brought together in London for such a purpose. McCulloch mentioned the matter to several young men of influence, to whom he was then giving private lessons in political economy. Some of these entered warmly into the project, particularly George Villiers, after Earl of Clarendon. He and his brothers, Hyde and Charles, Romilly, Charles Austin and I, with some others, met and agreed on a plan. We determined to meet once a fortnight from November to June, at the Freemasons' Tavern, and we had soon a fine list of members, containing, along with several members of Parliament, nearly all the most noted speakers of the Cambridge Union and of the Oxford United Debating Society. It is curiously illustrative of the tendencies of the time, that our principal difficulty in recruiting for the Society was to find a sufficient number of Tory speakers. Almost all whom we could press into the service were Liberals, of different orders and degrees. Besides those already named, we had Macaulay, Thirlwall, Praed, Lord Howick, Samuel Wilberforce (afterwards Bishop of Oxford), Charles Poulett Thomson (afterwards Lord Sydenham), Edward and Henry Lytton Bulwer, Fonblanque, and many others whom I cannot now recollect, but who made themselves afterwards more or less conspicuous in public or literary life. Nothing could seem more promising. But when the time for action drew near, and it was necessary to fix on a President, and find somebody to open the first debate, none of our celebrities would consent to perform either office. Of the many who were pressed on the subject, the only one who could be prevailed on was a man of whom I knew very little, but who had taken high honours at Oxford and was said to have acquired a great oratorical reputation there; who some time afterwards became a Tory member of Parliament. He accordingly was fixed on, both for filling the President's chair and for making the first speech. The important day arrived; the benches were crowded; all our great speakers were present, to judge of, but not to help our efforts. The Oxford orator's speech was a complete failure. This threw a damp on the whole concern: the speakers who followed were few, and none of them did their best: the affair was a complete *fiasco*; and the oratorical celebrities we had counted on went away never to return, giving to me at least a lesson in knowledge of the world. This unexpected breakdown altered my whole relation to the project. I had not anticipated taking a prominent part, or speaking much or often, particularly at first, but I now saw that the success of the scheme depended on the new men, and I put my shoulder to the wheel. I opened the second question, and from that time spoke in nearly every debate. It was very uphill work for some time. The three Villiers and Romilly stuck to us for some time longer, but the patience of all the founders of the Society was at last exhausted, except me and Roebuck. In the season following, 1826-7, things began to mend. We had acquired two excellent Tory speakers, Hayward and Shee (afterwards Sergeant Shee): the Radical side was reinforced by Charles Buller, Cockburn, and others of the second generation of Cambridge Benthamities; and with their and other occasional aid, and the two Tories as well as Roebuck and me for regular speakers, almost every debate was a *bataille rangie* between the "philosophic Radicals" and the Tory lawyers; until our conflicts were talked about, and several persons of note and consideration came to hear us. This happened still more in the subsequent seasons, 1828 and 1829, when the Coleridgians, in the persons of Maurice and Sterling, made their appearance in the Society as a second Liberal and even Radical party, on totally different grounds from Benthamism and vehemently opposed to it; bringing into these discussions the general doctrines and modes of thought of the European reaction against the philosophy of the eighteenth century; and adding a third and very important belligerent party to our contests, which were now no bad exponent of the movement of opinion among the most cultivated part of the new generation. Our debates were very different from those of common debating societies, for they habitually consisted of the strongest arguments and most philosophic principles which either side was able to produce, thrown often into close and *serri* confutations of one another. The practice was necessarily very useful to us, and eminently so to me. I never, indeed, acquired real fluency, and had always a bad and ungraceful delivery; but I could make myself listened to: and as I always wrote my speeches when, from the feelings involved, or the nature of the ideas to be developed, expression seemed important, I greatly increased my power of effective writing; acquiring not only an ear for smoothness and rhythm, but a practical sense for *telling* sentences, and an immediate criterion of their telling property, by their effect on a mixed audience.

The Society, and the preparation for it, together with the preparation for the morning conversations which were going on simultaneously, occupied the greater part of my leisure; and made me feel it a relief when, in the spring of 1828, I ceased to write for the *Westminster*. The *Review* had fallen into difficulties. Though the sale of the first number had been very encouraging, the permanent sale had never, I believe, been sufficient to pay the expenses, on the scale on which the *Review* was carried on. Those expenses had been considerably, but not sufficiently, reduced. One of the editors, Southern, had resigned; and several of the writers, including my father and me, who had been paid like other contributors for our earlier articles, had latterly written without payment. Nevertheless, the original funds were nearly or quite exhausted, and if the *Review* was to be continued some new arrangement of its affairs had become indispensable. My father and I had several conferences with Bowring on the subject. We were willing to do our utmost for maintaining the *Review* as an organ of our opinions, but not under Bowring's editorship: while the impossibility of its any longer supporting a paid editor, afforded a ground on which, without affront to him, we could propose to dispense with his services. We and some of our friends were prepared to carry on the *Review* as unpaid writers, either finding among ourselves an unpaid editor, or sharing the editorship among us. But while this negotiation was proceeding with Bowring's apparent acquiescence, he was carrying on another in a different quarter (with Colonel Perronet Thompson), of which we received the first intimation in a letter from Bowring as editor, informing us merely that an arrangement had been made, and proposing to us to write for the next number, with promise of payment. We did not dispute Bowring's right to bring about, if he could, an arrangement more favourable to himself than the one we had proposed; but we thought the concealment which he had practised towards us, while seemingly entering into our own project, an affront: and even had we not thought so, we were indisposed to expend any more of our time and trouble in attempting to write up the *Review* under his management. Accordingly my father excused himself from writing; though two or three years later, on great pressure, he did write one more political article. As for me, I positively refused. And thus ended my connexion with the original *Westminster*. The last article which I wrote in it had cost me more labour than any previous; but it was a labour of love, being a defence of the early French Revolutionists against the Tory misrepresentations of Sir Walter Scott, in the introduction to his *Life of Napoleon*. The number of books which I read for this purpose, making notes and extracts—even the number I had to buy (for in those days there was no public or subscription library from which books of reference could be taken home)—far exceeded the worth of the immediate object; but I had at that time a half-formed intention of writing a History of the French Revolution; and though I never executed it, my collections afterwards were very useful to Carlyle for a similar purpose.

V

Crisis In My Mental History. One Stage Onward

For some years after this time I wrote very little, and nothing regularly, for publication: and great were the advantages which I derived from the intermission. It was of no common importance to me, at this period, to be able to digest and mature my thoughts for my own mind only, without any immediate call for giving them out in print. Had I gone on writing, it would have much disturbed the important transformation in my opinions and character, which took place during those years. The origin of this transformation, or at least the process by which I was prepared for it, can only be explained by turning some distance back.

From the winter of 1821, when I first read Bentham, and especially from the commencement of the *Westminster Review*, I had what might truly be called an object in life; to be a reformer of the world. My conception of my own happiness was entirely identified with this object. The personal sympathies I wished for were those of fellow labourers in this enterprise. I endeavoured to pick up as many flowers as I could by the way; but as a serious and permanent personal satisfaction to rest upon, my whole reliance was placed on this; and I was accustomed to felicitate myself on the certainty of a happy life which I enjoyed, through placing my happiness in something durable and distant, in which some progress might be always making, while it could never be exhausted by complete attainment. This did very well for several years, during which the general improvement going on in the world and the idea of myself as engaged with others in struggling to promote it, seemed enough to fill up an interesting and animated existence. But the time came when I awakened from this as from a dream. It was in the autumn of 1826. I was in a dull state of nerves, such as everybody is occasionally liable to; unsusceptible to enjoyment or pleasurable excitement; one of those moods when what is pleasure at other times, becomes insipid or indifferent; the state, I should think, in which converts to Methodism usually are, when smitten by their first "conviction of sin." In this frame of mind it occurred to me to put the question directly to myself: "Suppose that all your objects in life were realized; that all the changes in institutions and opinions which you are looking forward to, could be completely effected at this very instant: would this be a great joy and happiness to you?" And an irrepressible self-consciousness distinctly answered, "No!" At this my heart sank within me: the whole foundation on which my life was constructed fell down. All my happiness was to have been found in the continual pursuit of this end. The end had ceased to charm, and how could there ever again be any interest in the means? I seemed to have nothing left to live for.

At first I hoped that the cloud would pass away of itself; but it did not. A night's sleep, the sovereign remedy for the smaller vexations of life, had no effect on it. I awoke to a renewed consciousness of the woful fact. I carried it with me into all companies, into all occupations. Hardly anything had power to cause me even a few minutes' oblivion of it. For some months the cloud seemed to grow thicker and thicker. The lines in Coleridge's *Dejection*—I was not then acquainted with them—exactly describe my case:

"A grief without a pang, void, dark and drear,
A drowsy, stifled, unimpassioned grief,
Which finds no natural outlet or relief
In word, or sigh, or tear."

In vain I sought relief from my favourite books; those memorials of past nobleness and greatness from which I had always hitherto drawn strength and animation. I read them now without feeling, or with the accustomed feeling minus all its charm; and I became persuaded, that my love of mankind, and of excellence for its own sake, had worn itself out. I sought no comfort by speaking to others of what I felt. If I had loved anyone sufficiently to make confiding my griefs a necessity, I should not have been in the condition I was. I felt, too, that mine was not an interesting, or in any way respectable distress. There was nothing in it to attract sympathy. Advice, if I had known where to seek it, would have been most precious. The words of Macbeth to the physician often occurred to my thoughts. But there was no one on whom I could build the faintest hope of such assistance. My father, to whom it would have been natural to me to have recourse in any practical difficulties, was the last person to whom, in such a case as this, I looked for help. Everything convinced me that he had no knowledge of any such mental state as I was suffering from, and that even if he could be made to understand it, he was not the physician who could heal it. My education, which was wholly his work, had been conducted without any regard to the possibility of its ending in this result; and I saw no use in giving him the pain of thinking that his plans had failed, when the failure was probably irremediable, and, at all events, beyond the power of *his* remedies. Of other friends, I had at that time none to whom I had any hope of making my condition intelligible. It was, however, abundantly intelligible to myself; and the more I dwelt upon it, the more hopeless it appeared.

My course of study had led me to believe, that all mental and moral feelings and qualities, whether of a good or of a bad kind, were the results of association; that we love one thing, and hate another, take pleasure in one sort of action or contemplation, and pain in another sort, through the clinging of pleasurable or painful ideas to those things, from the effect of education or of experience. As a corollary from this, I had always heard it maintained by my father, and was myself convinced, that the object of education should be to form the strongest possible associations of the salutary class; associations of pleasure with all things beneficial to the great whole, and of pain with all things hurtful to it. This doctrine appeared inexpugnable; but it now seemed to me, on retrospect, that my teachers had occupied themselves but superficially with the means of forming and keeping up these salutary associations. They seemed to have trusted altogether to the old familiar instruments, praise and blame, reward and punishment. Now, I did not doubt that by these means, begun early, and applied unremittingly, intense associations of pain and pleasure, especially of pain, might be created, and might produce desires and aversions capable of lasting undiminished to the end of life. But there must always be something artificial and casual in associations thus produced. The pains and pleasures thus forcibly associated with things, are not connected with them by any natural tie; and it is therefore, I thought, essential to the durability of these associations, that they should have become so intense and inveterate as to be practically indissoluble, before the habitual exercise of the power of analysis had commenced. For I now saw, or thought I saw, what I had always before received with incredulity —that the habit of analysis has a tendency to wear away the feelings: as indeed it has, when no other mental habit is cultivated, and the analysing spirit remains without its natural complements and correctives. The very excellence of analysis (I argued) is that it tends to weaken and undermine whatever is the result of prejudice; that it enables us mentally to separate ideas which have only casually clung together: and no associations whatever could ultimately resist this dissolving force, were it not that we owe to analysis our clearest knowledge of the permanent sequences in nature; the real connexions between Things, not dependent on our will and feelings; natural laws, by virtue of which, in many cases, one thing is inseparable from another in fact; which laws, in proportion as they are clearly perceived and imaginatively realized, cause our ideas of things which are always joined together in Nature, to cohere more and more closely in our thoughts. Analytic habits may thus even strengthen the associations between causes and effects, means and ends, but tend altogether to weaken those which are, to speak familiarly, a *mere* matter of feeling. They are therefore (I thought) favourable to prudence and clear- sightedness, but a perpetual worm at the root both of the passions and of the virtues; and, above all, fearfully undermine all desires, and all pleasures, which are the effects of association, that is, according to the theory I held, all except the purely physical and organic; of the entire insufficiency of which to make life desirable, no one had a stronger conviction than I had. These were the laws of human nature, by which, as it seemed to me, I had been brought to my present state. All those to whom I looked up, were of opinion that the pleasure of sympathy with human beings, and the feelings which made the good of others, and especially of mankind on a large scale, the object of existence, were the greatest and surest sources of happiness. Of the truth of this I was convinced, but to know that a feeling would make me happy if I had it, did not give me the feeling. My education, I thought, had failed to create these feelings in sufficient strength to resist the dissolving influence of analysis, while the whole course of my intellectual cultivation had made precocious and premature analysis the inveterate habit of my mind. I was thus, as I said to myself, left stranded at the commencement of my voyage, with a well-equipped ship and a rudder, but no sail; without any real desire for the ends which I had been so carefully fitted out to work for: no delight in virtue, or the general good, but also just as little in anything else. The fountains of vanity and ambition seemed to have dried up within me, as completely as those of benevolence. I had had (as I reflected) some gratification of vanity at too early an age: I had obtained some distinction and felt myself of some importance, before the desire of distinction and of importance had grown into a passion: and little as it was which I had attained, yet having been attained too early, like all pleasures enjoyed too soon, it had made me *blasi* and indifferent to the pursuit. Thus neither selfish nor unselfish pleasures were pleasures to me. And there seemed no power in nature sufficient to begin the formation of my character anew, and create, in a mind now irretrievably analytic, fresh associations of pleasure with any of the objects of human desire.

These were the thoughts which mingled with the dry, heavy dejection of the melancholy winter of 1826-7. During this time I was not incapable of my usual occupations. I went on with them mechanically, by the mere force of habit. I had been so drilled in a certain sort of mental exercise, that I could still carry it on when all the spirit had gone out of it. I even composed and spoke several speeches at the debating society, how, or with what degree of success, I know not. Of four years' continual speaking at that society, this is the only year of which I remember next to nothing. Two lines of Coleridge, in whom alone of all writers I have found a true description of what I felt, were often in my thoughts, not at this time (for I had never read them), but in a later period of the same mental malady:

"Work without hope draws nectar in a sieve,
And hope without an object cannot live."

In all probability my case was by no means so peculiar as I fancied it, and I doubt not that many others have passed through a similar state; but the idiosyncrasies of my education had given to the general phenomenon a special character, which made it seem the natural effect of causes that it was hardly possible for time to remove. I frequently asked myself, if I could, or if I was bound to go on living, when life must be passed in this manner. I generally answered to myself that I did not think I could possibly bear it beyond a year. When, however, not more than half that duration of time had elapsed, a small ray of light broke in upon my gloom. I was reading, accidentally, Marmontel's *Mimoires*, and came to the passage which relates his father's death, the distressed position of the family, and the sudden inspiration by which he, then a mere boy, felt and made them feel that he would be everything to them— would supply the place of all that they had lost. A vivid conception of the scene and its feelings came over me, and I was moved to tears. From this moment my burden grew lighter. The oppression of the thought that all feeling was dead within me was gone. I was no longer hopeless: I was not a stock or a stone. I had still, it seemed, some of the material out of which all worth of character, and all capacity for happiness, are made. Relieved from my ever-present sense of irremediable wretchedness, I gradually found that the ordinary incidents of life could again give me some pleasure; that I could again find enjoyment, not intense, but sufficient for cheerfulness, in sunshine and sky, in books, in conversation, in public affairs; and that there was, once more, excitement, though of a moderate, kind, in exerting myself for my opinions, and for the public good. Thus the cloud gradually drew off, and I again enjoyed life; and though I had several relapses, some of which lasted many months, I never again was as miserable as I had been.

The experiences of this period had two very marked effects on my opinions and character. In the first place, they led me to adopt a theory of life, very unlike that on which I had before I acted, and having much in common with what at that time I certainly had never heard of, the anti-self- consciousness theory of Carlyle. I never, indeed, wavered in the conviction that happiness is the test of all rules of conduct, and the end of life. But I now thought that this end was only to be attained by not making it the direct end. Those only are happy (I thought) who have their minds fixed on some object other than their own happiness; on the happiness of others, on the improvement of mankind, even on some art or pursuit, followed not as a means, but as itself an ideal end. Aiming thus at something else, they find happiness by the way. The enjoyments of life (such was now my theory) are sufficient to make it a pleasant thing, when they are taken *en passant*, without being made a principal object. Once make them so, and they are immediately felt to be insufficient. They will not bear a scrutinizing examination. Ask yourself whether you are happy, and you cease to be so. The only chance is to treat, not happiness, but some end external to it, as the purpose of life. Let your self-consciousness, your scrutiny, your self-interrogation, exhaust themselves on that; and if otherwise fortunately circumstanced you will inhale happiness with the air you breathe, without dwelling on it or thinking about it, without either forestalling it in imagination, or putting it to flight by fatal questioning. This theory now became the basis of my philosophy of life. And I still hold to it as the best theory for all those who have but a moderate degree of sensibility and of capacity I for enjoyment; that is, for the great majority of mankind.

The other important change which my opinions at this time underwent, was that I, for the first time, gave its proper place, among the prime necessities of human well-being, to the internal culture of the individual. I ceased to attach almost exclusive importance to the ordering of outward circumstances, and the training of the human being for speculation and for action.

I had now learnt by experience that the passing susceptibilities needed to be cultivated as well as the active capacities, and required to be nourished and enriched as well as guided. I did not, for an instant, lose sight of, or undervalue, that part of the truth which I had seen before; I never turned recreant to intellectual culture, or ceased to consider the power and practice of analysis as an essential condition both of individual and of social improvement But l thought that it had consequences which required to be corrected, by joining other kinds of cultivation with it. The maintenance of a due balance among the faculties now seemed to be of primary importance. The cultivation of the feelings became one of the cardinal points in my ethical and philosophical creed. And my thoughts and inclinations turned in an increasing degree towards whatever seemed capable of being instrumental to that object.

I now began to find meaning in the things, which I had read or heard about the importance of poetry and art as instruments of human culture. But it was some time longer before I began to know this by personal experience. The only one of the imaginative arts in which I had from childhood taken great pleasure, was music; the best effect of which (and in this it surpasses perhaps every other art) consists in exciting enthusiasm; in winding up to a high pitch those feelings of an elevated kind which are already in the character, but to which this excitement gives a glow and a fervour, which, though transitory at its utmost height, is precious for sustaining them at other times. This effect of music I had often experienced; but, like all my pleasurable susceptibilities, it was suspended during the gloomy period. I had sought relief again and again from this quarter, but found none. After the tide had turned, and I was in process of recovery, I had been helped forward by music, but in a much less elevated manner. I at this time first became acquainted with Weber's *Oberon*, and the extreme pleasure which I drew from its delicious melodies did me good by showing me a source of pleasure to which I was as susceptible as ever. The good, however, was much impaired by the thought that the pleasure of music (as is quite true of such pleasure as this was, that of mere tune) fades with familiarity, and requires either to be revived by intermittence, or fed by continual novelty. And it is very characteristic both of my then state, and of the general tone of my mind at this period of my life, that I was seriously tormented by the thought of the exhaustibility of musical combinations. The octave consists only of five tones and two semi-tones, which can be put together in only a limited number of ways, of which but a small proportion are beautiful: most of these, it seemed to me, must have been already discovered, and there could not be room for a long succession of Mozarts and Webers, to strike out, as these had done, entirely new and surpassingly rich veins of musical beauty. This source of anxiety may, perhaps, be thought to resemble that of the philosophers of Laputa, who feared lest the sun should be burnt out. It was, however, connected with the best feature in my character, and the only good point to be found in my very unromantic and in no way honourable distress. For though my dejection, honestly looked at, could not be called other than egotistical, produced by the ruin, as I thought, of my fabric of happiness, yet the destiny of mankind in general was ever in my thoughts, and could not be separated from my own. I felt that the flaw in my life, must be a flaw in life itself; that the question was, whether, if the reformers of society and government could succeed in their objects, and every person in the community were free and in a state of physical comfort, the pleasures of life, being no longer kept up by struggle and privation, would cease to be pleasures. And I felt that unless I could see my way to some better hope than this for human happiness in general, my dejection must continue; but that if I could see such an outlet, I should then look on the world with pleasure; content, as far as I was myself concerned, with any fair share of the general lot.

This state of my thoughts and feelings made the fact of my reading Wordsworth for the first time (in the autumn of 1828), an important event of my life. I took up the collection of his poems from curiosity, with no expectation of mental relief from it, though I had before resorted to poetry with that hope. In the worst period of my depression, I had read through the whole of Byron (then new to me), to try whether a poet, whose peculiar department was supposed to be that of the intenser feelings, could rouse any feeling in me. As might be expected, I got no good from this reading, but the reverse. The poet's state of mind was too like my own. His was the lament of a man who had worn out all pleasures, and who seemed to think that life, to all who possess the good things of it, must necessarily be the vapid, uninteresting thing which I found it. His Harold and Manfred had the same burden on them which I had; and I was not in a frame of mind to desire any comfort from the vehement sensual passion of his Giaours, or the sullenness of his Laras. But while Byron was exactly what did not suit my condition, Wordsworth was exactly what did. I had looked into the *Excursion* two or three years before, and found little in it; and I should probably have found as little, had I read it at this time. But the miscellaneous poems, in the two-volume edition of 1815 (to which little of value was added in the latter part of the author's life), proved to be the precise thing for my mental wants at that particular juncture.

In the first place, these poems addressed themselves powerfully to one of the strongest of my pleasurable susceptibilities, the love of rural objects and natural scenery; to which I had been indebted not only for much of the pleasure of my life, but quite recently for relief from one of my longest relapses into depression. In this power of rural beauty over me, there was a foundation laid for taking pleasure in Wordsworth's poetry; the more so, as his scenery lies mostly among mountains, which, owing to my early Pyrenean excursion, were my ideal of natural beauty. But Wordsworth would never have had any great effect on me, if he had merely placed before me beautiful pictures of natural scenery. Scott does this still better than Wordsworth, and a very second-rate landscape does it more effectually than any poet. What made Wordsworth's poems a medicine for my state of mind, was that they expressed, not mere outward beauty, but states of feeling, and of thought coloured by feeling, under the excitement of beauty. They seemed to be the very culture of the feelings, which I was in quest of. In them I seemed to draw from a source of inward joy, of sympathetic and imaginative pleasure, which could be shared in by all human beings; which had no connection with struggle or imperfection, but would be made richer by every improvement in the physical or social condition of mankind. From them I seemed to learn what would be the perennial sources of happiness, when all the greater evils of life shall have been removed. And I felt myself at once better and happier as I came under their influence. There have certainly been, even in our own age, greater poets than Wordsworth; but poetry of deeper and loftier feeling could not have done for me at that time what his did. I needed to be made to feel that there was real, permanent happiness in tranquil contemplation. Wordsworth taught me this, not only without turning away from, but with a greatly increased interest in, the common feelings and common destiny of human beings. And the delight which these poems gave me, proved that with culture of this sort, there was nothing to dread from the most confirmed habit of analysis. At the conclusion of the Poems came the famous Ode, falsely called Platonic, "Intimations of Immortality": in which, along with more than his usual sweetness of melody and rhythm, and along with the two passages of grand imagery but bad philosophy so often quoted, I found that he too had had similar experience to mine; that he also had felt that the first freshness of youthful enjoyment of life was not lasting; but that he had sought for compensation, and found it, in the way in which he was now teaching me to find it. The result was that I gradually, but completely, emerged from my habitual depression, and was never again subject to it. I long continued to value Wordsworth less according to his intrinsic merits, than by the measure of what he had done for me. Compared with the greatest poets, he may be said to be the poet of unpoetical natures, possessed of quiet and contemplative tastes. But unpoetical natures are precisely those which require poetic cultivation. This cultivation Wordsworth is much more fitted to give, than poets who are intrinsically far more poets than he.

It so fell out that the merits of Wordsworth were the occasion of my first public declaration of my new way of thinking, and separation from those of my habitual companions who had not undergone a similar change. The person with whom at that time I was most in the habit of comparing notes on such subjects was Roebuck, and I induced him to read Wordsworth, in whom he also at first seemed to find much to admire: but I, like most Wordsworthians, threw myself into strong antagonism to Byron, both as a poet and as to his influence on the character. Roebuck, all whose instincts were those of action and struggle, had, on the contrary, a strong relish and great admiration of Byron, whose writings he regarded as the poetry of human life, while Wordsworth's, according to him, was that of flowers and butterflies. We agreed to have the fight out at our Debating Society, where we accordingly discussed for two evenings the comparative merits of Byron and Wordsworth, propounding and illustrating by long recitations our respective theories of poetry: Sterling also, in a brilliant speech, putting forward his particular theory. This was the first debate on any weighty subject in which Roebuck and I had been on opposite sides. The schism between us widened from this time more and more, though we continued for some years longer to be companions. In the beginning, our chief divergence related to the cultivation of the feelings. Roebuck was in many respects very different from the vulgar notion of a Benthamite or Utilitarian. He was a lover of poetry and of most of the fine arts. He took great pleasure in music, in dramatic performances, especially in painting, and himself drew and designed landscapes with great facility and beauty. But he never could be

made to see that these things have any value as aids in the formation of character. Personally, instead of being, as Benthamites are
supposed to be, void of feeling, he had very quick and strong sensi-
bilities. But, like most Englishmen who have feelings, he found his
feelings stand very much in his way. He was much more susceptible to the painful sympathies than to the pleasurable, and, looking
for his happiness elsewhere, he wished that his feelings should be
deadened rather than quickened. And, in truth, the English character, and English social circumstances, make it so seldom possible
to derive happiness from the exercise of the sympathies, that it is
not wonderful if they count for little in an Englishman's scheme
of life. In most other countries the paramount importance of the
sympathies as a constituent of individual happiness is an axiom,
taken for granted rather than needing any formal statement; but
most English thinkers always seem to regard them as necessary
evils, required for keeping men's actions benevolent and compas-
sionate. Roebuck was, or appeared to be, this kind of Englishman.
He saw little good in any cultivation of the feelings, and none at
all in cultivating them through the imagination, which he thought
was only cultivating illusions. It was in vain I urged on him that
the imaginative emotion which an idea, when vividly conceived,
excites in us, is not an illusion but a fact, as real as any of the other
qualities of objects; and, far from implying anything erroneous and
delusive in our mental apprehension of the object, is quite consistent with the most accurate knowledge and most perfect practical
recognition of all its physical and intellectual laws and relations.
The intensest feeling of the beauty of a cloud lighted by the setting
sun, is no hindrance to my knowing that the cloud is vapour of
water, subject to all the laws of vapours in a state of suspension;
and I am just as likely to allow for, and act on, these physical laws
whenever there is occasion to do so, as if I had been incapable of
perceiving any distinction between beauty and ugliness.

While my intimacy with Roebuck diminished, I fell more and
more into friendly intercourse with our Coleridgian adversaries
in the Society, Frederick Maurice and John Sterling, both sub-

sequently so well known, the former by his writings, the latter through the biographies by Hare and Carlyle. Of these two friends, Maurice was the thinker, Sterling the orator, and impassioned expositor of thoughts which, at this period, were almost entirely formed for him by Maurice.

With Maurice I had for some time been acquainted through Eyton Tooke, who had known him at Cambridge, and although my discussions with him were almost always disputes, I had carried away from them much that helped to build up my new fabric of thought, in the same way as I was deriving much from Coleridge, and from the writings of Goethe and other German authors which I read during these years. I have so deep a respect for Maurice's character and purposes, as well as for his great mental gifts, that it is with some unwillingness I say anything which may seem to place him on a less high eminence than I would gladly be able to accord to him. But I have always thought that there was more intellectual power wasted in Maurice than in any other of my contemporaries. Few of them certainly have had so much to waste. Great powers of generalization, rare ingenuity and subtlety, and a wide perception of important and unobvious truths, served him not for putting something better into the place of the worthless heap of received opinions on the great subjects of thought, but for proving to his own mind that the Church of England had known everything from the first, and that all the truths on the ground of which the Church and orthodoxy have been attacked (many of which he saw as clearly as anyone) are not only consistent with the Thirty-nine Articles, but are better understood and expressed in those Articles than by anyone who rejects them. I have never been able to find any other explanation of this, than by attributing it to that timidity of conscience, combined with original sensitiveness of temperament, which has so often driven highly gifted men into Romanism, from the need of a firmer support than they can find in the independent conclusions of their own judgment. Any more vulgar kind of timidity no one who knew Maurice would ever think of imputing to him, even if he had not given public proof of his freedom from it, by his ultimate collision with some of the opinions commonly regarded as orthodox, and by his noble origination of the Christian Socialist movement. The nearest parallel to him, in a moral point of view, is Coleridge, to whom, in merely intellectual power, apart from poetical genius, I think him decidedly superior. At this time, however, he might be described as a disciple of Coleridge, and Sterling as a disciple of Coleridge and of him. The modifications which were taking place in my old opinions gave me some points of contact with them; and both Maurice and Sterling were of considerable use to my development. With Sterling I soon became very intimate, and was more attached to him than I have ever been to any other man. He was indeed one of the most lovable of men. His frank, cordial, affectionate, and expansive character; a love of truth alike conspicuous in the highest things and the humblest; a generous and ardent nature, which threw itself with impetuosity into the opinions it adopted, but was as eager to do justice to the doctrines and the men it was opposed to, as to make war on what it thought their errors; and an equal devotion to the two cardinal points of Liberty and Duty, formed a combination of qualities as attractive to me as to all others who knew him as well as I did. With his open mind and heart, he found no difficulty in joining hands with me across the gulf which as yet divided our opinions. He told me how he and others had looked upon me (from hearsay information), as a "made" or manufactured man, having had a certain impress of opinion stamped on me which I could only reproduce; and what a change took place in his feelings when he found, in the discussion on Wordsworth and Byron, that Wordsworth, and all which that name implies, "belonged" to me as much as to him and his friends. The failure of his health soon scattered all his plans of life, and compelled him to live at a distance from London, so that after the first year or two of our acquaintance, we only saw each other at distant intervals. But (as he said himself in one of his letters to Carlyle) when we did meet it was like brothers. Though he was never, in the full sense of the word, a profound thinker, his openness of mind, and the moral courage in which he greatly surpassed Maurice, made him outgrow the dominion which Maurice and Coleridge had once exercised over his intellect; though he retained to the last a great but discriminating admiration of both, and towards Maurice a warm affection. Except in that short and transitory phasis of his life, during which he made the mistake of becoming a clergyman, his mind was ever progressive: and the advance he always seemed to have made when I saw him after an interval, made me apply to him what Goethe said of Schiller, "er hatte eine furchtliche Fortschreitung." He and I started from intellectual points almost as wide apart as the poles, but the distance between us was always diminishing: if I made steps towards some of his opinions, he, during his short life, was constantly approximating more and more to several of mine: and if he had lived, and had health and vigour to prosecute his ever assiduous self-culture, there is no knowing how much further this spontaneous assimilation might have proceeded.

After 1829 I withdrew from attendance on the Debating Society. I had had enough of speech-making, and was glad to carry on my private studies and meditations without any immediate call for outward assertion of their results. I found the fabric of my old and taught opinions giving way in many fresh places, and I never allowed it to fall to pieces, but was incessantly occupied in weaving it anew. I never, in the course of my transition, was content to remain, for ever so short a time, confused and unsettled. When I had taken in any new idea, I could not rest till I had adjusted its relation to my old opinions, and ascertained exactly how far its effect ought to extend in modifying or superseding them.

The conflicts which I had so often had to sustain in defending the theory of government laid down in Bentham's and my father's writings, and the acquaintance I had obtained with other schools of political thinking, made me aware of many things which that doctrine, professing to be a theory of government in general, ought to have made room for, and did not. But these things, as yet, remained with me rather as corrections to be made in applying the theory to practice, than as defects in the theory. I felt that politics could not be a science of specific experience; and that the accusations against the Benthamic theory of *being* a theory, of proceeding *a priori* by way of general reasoning, instead of Baconian experiment, showed complete ignorance of Bacon's principles, and of the necessary conditions of experimental investigation. At this juncture appeared in the *Edinburgh Review*, Macaulay's famous attack on my father's *Essay on Government*. This gave me much to think about. I saw that Macaulay's conception of the logic of politics was erroneous; that he stood up for the empirical mode of treating political phenomena, against the philosophical; that even in physical science his notions of philosophizing might have recognised Kepler, but would have excluded Newton and Laplace. But I could not help feeling, that though the tone was unbecoming (an error for which the writer, at a later period, made the most ample and honourable amends), there was truth in several of his strictures on my father's treatment of the subject; that my father's premises were really too narrow, and included but a small number of the general truths on which, in politics, the important consequences depend. Identity of interest between the governing body and the community at large is not, in any practical sense which can be attached to it, the only thing on which good government depends; neither can this identity of interest be secured by the mere conditions of election. I was not at all satisfied with the mode in which my father met the criticisms of Macaulay. He did not, as I thought he ought to have done, justify himself by saying, "I was not writing a scientific treatise on politics, I was writing an argument for parliamentary reform." He treated Macaulay's argument as simply irrational; an attack upon the reasoning faculty; an example of the saying of Hobbes, that When reason is against a man, a man will be against reason. This made me think that there was really something more fundamentally erroneous in my father's conception of philosophical method, as applicable to politics, than I had hitherto supposed there was. But I did not at first see clearly what the error might be. At last it flashed upon me all at once in the course of other studies. In the early part of 1830 I had begun to put on paper the ideas on

Logic (chiefly on the distinctions among Terms, and the import of Propositions) which had been suggested and in part worked out in the morning conversations already spoken of. Having secured these thoughts from being lost, I pushed on into the other parts of the subject, to try whether I could do anything further towards clearing up the theory of logic generally. I grappled at once with the problem of Induction, postponing that of Reasoning, on the ground that it is necessary to obtain premises before we can reason from them. Now, Induction is mainly a process for finding the causes of effects: and in attempting to fathom the mode of tracing causes and effects in physical science, I soon saw that in the more perfect of the sciences, we ascend, by generalization from particulars, to the tendencies of causes considered singly, and then reason downward from those separate tendencies, to the effect of the same causes when combined. I then asked myself, what is the ultimate analysis of this deductive process; the common theory of the syllogism evidently throwing no light upon it. My practice (learnt from Hobbes and my father) being to study abstract principles by means of the best concrete instances I could find, the Composition of Forces, in dynamics, occurred to me as the most complete example of the logical process I was investigating. On examining, accordingly, what the mind does when it applies the principle of the Composition of Forces, I found that it performs a simple act of addition. It adds the separate effect of the one force to the separate effect of the other, and puts down the sum of these separate effects as the joint effect. But is this a legitimate process? In dynamics, and in all the mathematical branches of physics, it is; but in some other cases, as in chemistry, it is not; and I then recollected that something not unlike this was pointed out as one of the distinctions between chemical and mechanical phenomena, in the introduction to that favourite of my boyhood, Thompson's *System of Chemistry*. This distinction at once made my mind clear as to what was perplexing me in respect to the philosophy of politics. I now saw, that a science is either deductive or experimental, according as, in the province it deals with, the effects of causes when conjoined, are or are not the sums of the effects which the same causes produce when separate. It followed that politics must be a deductive science. It thus appeared, that both Macaulay and my father were wrong; the one in assimilating the method of philosophizing in politics to the purely experimental method of chemistry; while the other, though right in adopting a deductive method, had made a wrong selection of one, having taken as the type of deduction, not the appropriate process, that of the deductive branches of natural philosophy, but the inappropriate one of pure geometry, which, not being a science of causation at all, does not require or admit of any summing-up of effects. A foundation was thus laid in my thoughts for the principal chapters of what I afterwards published on the Logic of the Moral Sciences; and my new position in respect to my old political creed, now became perfectly definite.

If I am asked, what system of political philosophy I substituted for that which, as a philosophy, I had abandoned, I answer, No system: only a conviction that the true system was something much more complex and many-sided than I had previously had any idea of, and that its office was to supply, not a set of model institutions, but principles from which the institutions suitable to any given circumstances might be deduced. The influences of European, that is to say, Continental, thought, and especially those of the reaction of the nineteenth century against the eighteenth, were now streaming in upon me. They came from various quarters: from the writings of Coleridge, which I had begun to read with interest even before the change in my opinions; from the Coleridgians with whom I was in personal intercourse; from what I had read of Goethe; from Carlyle's early articles in the *Edinburgh* and Foreign Reviews, though for a long time I saw nothing in these (as my father saw nothing in them to the last) but insane rhapsody. From these sources, and from the acquaintance I kept up with the French literature of the time, I derived, among other ideas which the general turning upside down of the opinions of European thinkers had brought uppermost, these in particular: That the human mind has a certain order of possible progress, in which some things must precede others, an order which governments and public instructors can modify to some, but not to an unlimited extent: that all questions of political institutions are relative, not absolute, and that different stages of human progress not only *will* have, but *ought* to have, different institutions: that government is always either in the hands, or passing into the hands, of whatever is the strongest power in society, and that what this power is, does not depend on institutions, but institutions on it: that any general theory or philosophy of politics supposes a previous theory of human progress, and that this is the same thing with a philosophy of history. These opinions, true in the main, were held in an exaggerated and violent manner by the thinkers with whom I was now most accustomed to compare notes, and who, as usual with a reaction, ignored that half of the truth which the thinkers of the eighteenth century saw. But though, at one period of my progress, I for some time undervalued that great century, I never joined in the reaction against it, but kept as firm hold of one side of the truth as I took of the other. The fight between the nineteenth century and the eighteenth always reminded me of the battle about the shield, one side of which was white and the other black. I marvelled at the blind rage with which the combatants rushed against one another. I applied to them, and to Coleridge himself, many of Coleridge's sayings about half truths; and Goethe's device, "many-sidedness," was one which I would most willingly, at this period, have taken for mine.

The writers by whom, more than by any others, a new mode of political thinking was brought home to me, were those of the St. Simonian school in France. In 1829 and 1830 I became acquainted with some of their writings. They were then only in the earlier stages of their speculations. They had not yet dressed out their philosophy as a religion, nor had they organized their scheme of Socialism. They were just beginning to question the principle of hereditary property. I was by no means prepared to go with them even this length; but I was greatly struck with the connected view which they for the first time presented to me, of the natural order of human progress; and especially with their division of all history into organic periods and critical periods. During the organic periods (they said) mankind accept with firm conviction some positive creed, claiming jurisdiction over all their actions, and containing more or less of truth and adaptation to the needs of humanity. Under its influence they make all the progress compatible with the creed, and finally outgrow it; when a period follows of criticism and negation, in which mankind lose their old convictions without acquiring any new ones, of a general or authoritative character, except the conviction that the old are false. The period of Greek and Roman polytheism, so long as really believed in by instructed Greeks and Romans, was an organic period, succeeded by the critical or sceptical period of the Greek philosophers. Another organic period came in with Christianity. The corresponding critical period began with the Reformation, has lasted ever since, still lasts, and cannot altogether cease until a new organic period has been inaugurated by the triumph of a yet more advanced creed. These ideas, I knew, were not peculiar to the St. Simonians; on the contrary, they were the general property of Europe, or at least of Germany and France, but they had never, to my knowledge, been so completely systematized as by these writers, nor the distinguishing characteristics of a critical period so powerfully set forth; for I was not then acquainted with Fichte's *Lectures on the Characteristics of the Present Age*. In Carlyle, indeed, I found bitter denunciations of an "age of unbelief," and of the present age as such, which I, like most people at that time, supposed to be passionate protests in favour of the old modes of belief. But all that was true in these denunciations, I thought that I found more calmly and philosophically stated by the St. Simonians. Among their publications, too, there was one which seemed to me far superior to the rest; in which the general idea was matured into something much more definite and instructive. This was an early work of Auguste Comte, who then called himself, and even announced himself in the title-page as, a pupil of Saint Simon. In this tract M. Comte first put forth the doctrine, which he afterwards so copiously illustrated, of the natural succession of three stages in every department of human knowledge:

first, the theological, next the metaphysical, and lastly, the positive stage; and contended, that social science must be subject to the same law; that the feudal and Catholic system was the concluding phasis of the theological state of the social science, Protestantism the commencement, and the doctrines of the French Revolution the consummation, of the metaphysical; and that its positive state was yet to come. This doctrine harmonized well with my existing notions, to which it seemed to give a scientific shape. I already regarded the methods of physical science as the proper models for political. But the chief benefit which I derived at this time from the trains of thought suggested by the St. Simonians and by Comte, was, that I obtained a clearer conception than ever before of the peculiarities of an era of transition in opinion, and ceased to mistake the moral and intellectual characteristics of such an era, for the normal attributes of humanity. I looked forward, through the present age of loud disputes but generally weak convictions, to a future which shall unite the best qualities of the critical with the best qualities of the organic periods; unchecked liberty of thought, unbounded freedom of individual action in all modes not hurtful to others; but also, convictions as to what is right and wrong, useful and pernicious, deeply engraven on the feelings by early education and general unanimity of sentiment, and so firmly grounded in reason and in the true exigencies of life, that they shall not, like all former and present creeds, religious, ethical, and political, require to be periodically thrown off and replaced by others.

M. Comte soon left the St. Simonians, and I lost sight of him and his writings for a number of years. But the St. Simonians I continued to cultivate. I was kept *au courant* of their progress by one of their most enthusiastic disciples, M. Gustave d'Eichthal, who about that time passed a considerable interval in England. I was introduced to their chiefs, Bazard and Enfantin, in 1830; and as long as their public teachings and proselytism continued, I read nearly everything they wrote. Their criticisms on the common doctrines of Liberalism seemed to me full of important truth; and it was partly by their writings that my eyes were opened to the very limited and temporary value of the old political economy, which assumes private property and inheritance as indefeasible facts, and freedom of production and exchange as the *dernier mot* of social improvement. The scheme gradually unfolded by the St. Simonians, under which the labour and capital of society would be managed for the general account of the community, every individual being required to take a share of labour, either as thinker, teacher, artist, or producer, all being classed according to their capacity, and remunerated according to their work, appeared to me a far superior description of Socialism to Owen's. Their aim seemed to me desirable and rational, however their means might be inefficacious; and though I neither believed in the practicability, nor in the beneficial operation of their social machinery, I felt that the proclamation of such an ideal of human society could not but tend to give a beneficial direction to the efforts of others to bring society, as at present constituted, nearer to some ideal standard. I honoured them most of all for what they have been most cried down for—the boldness and freedom from prejudice with which they treated the subject of the family, the most important of any, and needing more fundamental alterations than remain to be made in any other great social institution, but on which scarcely any reformer has the courage to touch. In proclaiming the perfect equality of men and women, and an entirely new order of things in regard to their relations with one another, the St. Simonians, in common with Owen and Fourier, have entitled themselves to the grateful remembrance of future generations.

In giving an account of this period of my life, I have only specified such of my new impressions as appeared to me, both at the time and since, to be a kind of turning points, marking a definite progress in my mode of thought. But these few selected points give a very insufficient idea of the quantity of thinking which I carried on respecting a host of subjects during these years of transition. Much of this, it is true, consisted in rediscovering things known to all the world, which I had previously disbelieved or disregarded. But the rediscovery was to me a discovery, giving me plenary possession of the truths, not as traditional platitudes, but fresh from their source; and it seldom failed to place them in some new light, by which they were reconciled with, and seemed to confirm while they modified, the truths less generally known which lay in my early opinions, and in no essential part of which I at any time wavered. All my new thinking only laid the foundation of these more deeply and strongly, while it often removed misapprehension and confusion of ideas which had perverted their effect. For example, during the later returns of my dejection, the doctrine of what is called Philosophical Necessity weighed on my existence like an incubus. I felt as if I was scientifically proved to be the helpless slave of antecedent circumstances; as if my character and that of all others had been formed for us by agencies beyond our control, and was wholly out of our own power. I often said to myself, what a relief it would be if I could disbelieve the doctrine of the formation of character by circumstances; and remembering the wish of Fox respecting the doctrine of resistance to governments, that it might never be forgotten by kings, nor remembered by subjects, I said that it would be a blessing if the doctrine of necessity could be believed by all *quoad* the characters of others, and disbelieved in regard to their own. I pondered painfully on the subject till gradually I saw light through it. I perceived, that the word Necessity, as a name for the doctrine of Cause and Effect applied to human action, carried with it a misleading association; and that this association was the operative force in the depressing and paralysing influence which I had experienced: I saw that though our character is formed by circumstances, our own desires can do much to shape those circumstances; and that what is really inspiriting and ennobling in the doctrine of freewill is the conviction that we have real power over the formation of our own character; that our will, by influencing some of our circumstances, can modify our future habits or capabilities of willing. All this was entirely consistent with the doctrine of circumstances, or rather, was that doctrine itself, properly understood. From that time I drew, in my own mind, a clear distinction between the doctrine of circumstances and Fatalism; discarding altogether the misleading word Necessity. The theory, which I now for the first time rightly apprehended, ceased altogether to be discouraging; and, besides the relief to my spirits, I no longer suffered under the burden—so heavy to one who aims at being a reformer in opinions—of thinking one doctrine true and the contrary doctrine morally beneficial. The train of thought which had extricated me from this dilemma seemed to me, in after years, fitted to render a similar service to others; and it now forms the chapter on Liberty and Necessity in the concluding Book of my *System of Logic.*

Again, in politics, though I no longer accepted the doctrine of the *Essay on Government* as a scientific theory; though I ceased to consider representative democracy as an absolute principle, and regarded it as a question of time, place, and circumstance; though I now looked upon the choice of political institutions as a moral and educational question more than one of material interests, thinking that it ought to be decided mainly by the consideration, what great improvement in life and culture stands next in order for the people concerned, as the condition of their further progress, and what institutions are most likely to promote that; nevertheless, this change in the premises of my political philosophy did not alter my practical political creed as to the requirements of my own time and country. I was as much as ever a Radical and Democrat for Europe, and especially for England. I thought the predominance of the aristocratic classes, the noble and the rich, in the English constitution, an evil worth any struggle to get rid of; not on account of taxes, or any such comparatively small inconvenience, but as the great demoralizing agency in the country. Demoralizing, first, because it made the conduct of the Government an example of gross public immorality, through the predominance of private over public interests in the State, and the abuse of the powers of legislation for the advantage of classes. Secondly, and in a still greater degree, because the respect of the multitude always attaching itself principally to that which, in the existing state of society, is the chief passport to power; and under English institutions, riches, hereditary or acquired, being the almost exclusive source of political importance; riches, and the signs of riches, were almost the only things really respected, and the life of the people was mainly devoted to the pursuit of them. I thought, that while the higher and richer classes held the power of government, the instruction and improvement of the mass of the people were contrary to the self-interest of those classes, because tending to render the people more powerful for throwing off the yoke: but if the democracy obtained a large, and perhaps the principal share, in the governing power, it would become the interest of the opulent classes to promote their education, in order to ward off really mischievous errors, and especially those which would lead to unjust violations of property. On these grounds I was not only as ardent as ever for democratic institutions, but earnestly hoped that Owenite, St. Simonian, and all other anti-property doctrines might spread widely among the poorer classes; not that I thought those doctrines true, or desired that they should be acted on, but in order that the higher classes might be made to see that they had more to fear from the poor when uneducated than when educated.

In this frame of mind the French Revolution of July found me: It roused my utmost enthusiasm, and gave me, as it were, a new existence. I went at once to Paris, was introduced to Lafayette, and laid the groundwork of the intercourse I afterwards kept up with several of the active chiefs of the extreme popular party. After my return I entered warmly, as a writer, into the political discussions of the time; which soon became still more exciting, by the coming in of Lord Grey's Ministry, and the proposing of the Reform Bill. For the next few years I wrote copiously in newspapers. It was about this time that Fonblanque, who had for some time written the political articles in the *Examiner*, became the proprietor and editor of the paper. It is not forgotten with what verve and talent, as well as fine wit, he carried it on, during the whole period of Lord Grey's Ministry, and what importance it assumed as the principal representative, in the newspaper press, of Radical opinions. The distinguishing character of the paper was given to it entirely by his own articles, which formed at least three-fourths of all the original writing contained in it: but of the remaining fourth I contributed during those years a much larger share than anyone else. I wrote nearly all the articles on French subjects, including a weekly summary of French politics, often extending to considerable length; together with many leading articles on general politics, commercial and financial legislation, and any miscellaneous subjects in which I felt interested, and which were suitable to the paper, including occasional reviews of books. Mere newspaper articles on the occurrences or questions of the moment, gave no opportunity for the development of any general mode of thought; but I attempted, in the beginning of 1831, to embody in a series of articles, headed "The Spirit of the Age," some of my new opinions, and especially to point out in the character of the present age, the anomalies and evils characteristic of the transition from a system of opinions which had worn out, to another only in process of being formed. These articles, were, I fancy, lumbering in style, and not lively or striking enough to be, at any time, acceptable to newspaper readers; but had they been far more attractive, still, at that particular moment, when great political changes were impending, and engrossing all minds, these discussions were ill-timed, and missed fire altogether. The only effect which I know to have been produced by them, was that Carlyle, then living in a secluded part of Scotland, read them in his solitude, and, saying to himself (as he afterwards told me) "Here is a new Mystic," inquired on coming to London that autumn respecting their authorship; an inquiry which was the immediate cause of our becoming personally acquainted.

I have already mentioned Carlyle's earlier writings as one of the channels through which I received the influences which enlarged my early narrow creed; but I do not think that those writings, by themselves, would ever have had any effect on my opinions. What truths they contained, though of the very kind which I was already receiving from other quarters, were presented in a form and vesture less suited than any other to give them access to a mind trained as mine had been. They seemed a haze of poetry and German metaphysics, in which almost the only clear thing was a strong animosity to most of the opinions which were the basis of my mode of thought; religious scepticism, utilitarianism, the doctrine of circumstances, and the attaching any importance to democracy, logic, or political economy. Instead of my having been taught anything, in the first instance, by Carlyle, it was only in proportion as I came to see the same truths through media more suited to my mental constitution, that I recognised them in his writings. Then, indeed, the wonderful power with which he put them forth made a deep impression upon me, and I was during a long period one of his most fervent admirers; but the good his writings did me, was not as philosophy to instruct, but as poetry to animate. Even at the time when our acquaintance commenced, I was not sufficiently advanced in my new modes of thought to appreciate him fully; a proof of which is, that on his showing me the manuscript of *Sartor Resartus*, his best and greatest work, which he just then finished, I made little of it; though when it came out about two years afterwards in *Fraser's Magazine* I read it with enthusiastic admiration and the keenest delight. I did not seek and cultivate Carlyle less on account of the fundamental differences in our philosophy. He soon found out that I was not "another mystic," and when for the sake of my own integrity I wrote to him a distinct profession of all those of my opinions which I knew he most disliked, he replied that the chief difference between us was that I "was as yet consciously nothing of a mystic." I do not know at what period he gave up the expectation that I was destined to become one; but though both his and my opinions underwent in subsequent years considerable changes, we never approached much nearer to each other's modes of thought than we were in the first years of our acquaintance. I did not, however, deem myself a competent judge of Carlyle. I felt that he was a poet, and that I was not; that he was a man of intuition, which I was not; and that as such, he not only saw many things long before me, which I could only, when they were pointed out to me, hobble after and prove, but that it was highly probable he could see many things which were not visible to me even after they were pointed out. I knew that I could not see round him, and could never be certain that I saw over him; and I never presumed to judge him with any definiteness, until he was interpreted to me by one greatly the superior of us both—who was more a poet than he, and more a thinker than I—whose own mind and nature included his, and infinitely more.

Among the persons of intellect whom I had known of old, the one with whom I had now most points of agreement was the elder Austin. I have mentioned that he always set himself in opposition to our early sectarianism; and latterly he had, like myself, come under new influences. Having been appointed Professor of Jurisprudence in the London University (now University College), he had lived for some time at Bonn to study for his Lectures; and the influences of German literature and of the German character and state of society had made a very perceptible change in his views of life. His personal disposition was much softened; he was less militant and polemic; his tastes had begun to turn themselves towards the poetic and contemplative. He attached much less importance than formerly to outward changes; unless accompanied by a better cultivation of the inward nature. He had a strong distaste for the general meanness of English life, the absence of enlarged thoughts and unselfish desires, the low objects on which the faculties of all classes of the English are intent. Even the kind of public interests which Englishmen care for, he held in very little esteem. He thought that there was more practical good government, and (which is true enough) infinitely more care for the education and mental improvement of all ranks of the people, under the Prussian monarchy, than under the English representative government: and he held, with the French *Economistes*, that the real security for good government is un *peuple iclairi*, which is not always the fruit of popular institutions, and which, if it could be had without them, would do their work better than they. Though he approved of the Reform Bill, he predicted, what in fact occurred, that it would not produce the great immediate improvements in government which many expected from it. The men, he said, who could do these great things did not exist in the country. There were many points of sympathy between him and me, both in the new opinions he had adopted and in the old ones which he retained. Like me, he never ceased to be a utilitarian, and, with all his love for the Germans and enjoyment of their literature, never became in the smallest degree reconciled to the innate-principle metaphysics. He cultivated more and more a kind of German religion, a religion of poetry and feeling with little, if anything, of positive dogma; while in politics (and here it was that I most differed with him) he acquired an indifference, bordering on contempt, for the progress of popular institutions: though he rejoiced in that of Socialism, as the most effectual means of compelling the powerful classes to educate the people, and to impress on them the only real means of permanently improving their material condition, a limitation of their numbers. Neither was he, at this time, fundamentally opposed to Socialism in itself as an ultimate result of improvement. He professed great disrespect for what he called "the universal principles of human nature of the political economists," and insisted on the evidence which history and daily experience afford of the "extraordinary pliability of human nature" (a phrase which I have somewhere borrowed from him); nor did he think it possible to set any positive bounds to the moral capabilities which might unfold themselves in mankind, under an enlightened direction of social and educational influences. Whether he retained all these opinions to the end of life I know not. Certainly the modes of thinking of his later years, and especially of his last publication, were much more Tory in their general character than those which he held at this time.

My father's tone of thought and feeling, I now felt myself at a great distance from: greater, indeed, than a full and calm explanation and reconsideration on both sides, might have shown to exist in reality. But my father was not one with whom calm and full explanations on fundamental points of doctrine could be expected, at least with one whom he might consider as, in some sort, a deserter from his standard. Fortunately we were almost always in strong agreement on the political questions of the day, which engrossed a large part of his interest and of his conversation. On those matters of opinion on which we differed, we talked little. He knew that the habit of thinking for myself, which his mode of education had fostered, sometimes led me to opinions different from his, and he perceived from time to time that I did not always tell him *how* different. I expected no good, but only pain to both of us, from discussing our differences: and I never expressed them but when he gave utterance to some opinion or feeling repugnant to mine, in a manner which would have made it disingenuousness on my part to remain silent.

It remains to speak of what I wrote during these years, which, independently of my contributions to newspapers, was considerable. In 1830 and 1831 I wrote the five Essays since published under the title of *Essays on some Unsettled Questions of political Economy*, almost as they now stand, except that in 1833 I partially rewrote the fifth Essay. They were written with no immediate purpose of publication; and when, some years later, I offered them to a publisher, he declined them. They were only printed in 1844, after the success of the *System of Logic*. I also resumed my speculations on this last subject, and puzzled myself, like others before me, with the great paradox of the discovery of new truths by general reasoning. As to the fact, there could be no doubt. As little could it be doubted, that all reasoning is resolvable into syllogisms, and that in every syllogism the conclusion is actually contained and implied in the premises. How, being so contained and implied, it could be new truth, and how the theorems of geometry, so different in appearance from the definitions and axioms, could be all contained in these, was a difficulty which no, one, I thought, had sufficiently felt, and which, at all events, no one had succeeded in clearing up. The explanations offered by Whately and others, though they might give a temporary satisfaction, always, in my mind, left a mist still hanging over the subject. At last, when reading a second or third time the chapters on Reasoning in the second volume of Dugald Stewart, interrogating myself on every point, and following out, as far as I knew how, every topic of thought which the book suggested, I came upon an idea of his respecting the use of axioms in ratiocination, which I did not remember to have before noticed, but which now, in meditating on it, seemed to me not only true of axioms, but of all general propositions whatever, and to be the key of the whole perplexity. From this germ grew the theory of the Syllogism propounded in the Second Book of the *Logic*; which I immediately fixed by writing it out. And now, with greatly increased hope of being able to produce a work on Logic, of some originality and value, I proceeded to write the First Book, from the rough and imperfect draft I had already made. What I now wrote became the basis of that part of the subsequent Treatise; except that it did not contain the Theory of Kinds, which was a later addition, suggested by otherwise inextricable difficulties which met me in my first attempt to work out the subject of some of the concluding chapters of the Third Book. At the point which I had now reached I made a halt, which lasted five years. I had come to the end of my tether; I could make nothing satisfactory of Induction, at this time. I continued to read any book which seemed to promise light on the subject, and appropriated, as well as I could, the results; but for a long time I found nothing which seemed to open to me any very important vein of meditation.

In 1832 I wrote several papers for the first series of *Tait's Magazine*, and one for a quarterly periodical called the *Jurist*, which had been founded, and for a short time carried on, by a set of friends, all lawyers and law reformers, with several of whom I was acquainted. The paper in question is the one on the rights and duties of the State respecting Corporation and Church Property, now standing first among the collected *Dissertations and Discussions*; where one of my articles in *Tait*, "The Currency Juggle," also appears. In the whole mass of what I wrote previous to these, there is nothing of sufficient permanent value to justify reprinting. The paper in the *Jurist*, which I still think a very complete discussion of the rights of the State over Foundations, showed both sides of my opinions, asserting as firmly as I should have done at any time, the doctrine that all endowments are national property, which the government may and ought to control; but not, as I should once have done, condemning endowments in themselves, and proposing that they should be taken to pay off the national debt. On the contrary, I urged strenuously the importance of a provision for education, not dependent on the mere demand of the market, that is, on the knowledge and discernment of average parents, but calculated to establish and keep up a higher standard of instruction than is likely to be spontaneously demanded by the buyers of the article. All these opinions have been confirmed and strengthened by the whole of my subsequent reflections.

VI

Commencement Of The Most Valuable Friendship Of My Life. My Father's Death. Writings And Other Proceedings Up To 1840.

It was the period of my mental progress which I have now reached that I formed the friendship which has been the honour and chief blessing of my existence, as well as the source of a great part of all that I have attempted to do, or hope to effect hereafter, for human improvement. My first introduction to the lady who, after a friendship of twenty years, consented to become my wife, was in 1830, when I was in my twenty-fifth and she in her twenty-third year. With her husband's family it was the renewal of an old acquaintanceship. His grandfather lived in the next house to my father's in Newington Green, and I had sometimes when a boy been invited to play in the old gentleman's garden. He was a fine specimen of the old Scotch puritan; stern, severe, and powerful, but very kind to children, on whom such men make a lasting impression. Although it was years after my introduction to Mrs. Taylor before my acquaintance with her became at all intimate or confidential, I very soon felt her to be the most admirable person I had ever known. It is not to be supposed that she was, or that any one, at the age at which I first saw her, could be, all that she afterwards became. Least of all could this be true of her, with whom self-improvement, progress in the highest and in all senses, was a law of her nature; a necessity equally from the ardour with which she sought it, and from the spontaneous tendency of faculties which could not receive an impression or an experience without making it the source or the occasion of an accession of wisdom. Up to the time when I first saw her, her rich and powerful nature had chiefly unfolded itself according to the received type of feminine genius. To her outer circle she was a beauty and a wit, with an air of natural distinction, felt by all who approached her: to the inner, a woman of deep and strong feeling, of penetrating and intuitive intelligence, and of an eminently meditative and poetic nature. Married at an early age to a most upright, brave, and honourable man, of liberal opinions and good education, but without the intellectual or artistic tastes which would have made him a companion for her, though a steady and affectionate friend, for whom she had true esteem and the strongest affection through life, and whom she most deeply lamented when dead; shut out by the social disabilities of women from any adequate exercise of her highest faculties in action on the world without; her life was one of inward meditation, varied by familiar intercourse with a small circle of friends, of whom one only (long since deceased) was a person of genius, or of capacities of feeling or intellect kindred with her own, but all had more or less of alliance with her in sentiments and opinions. Into this circle I had the good fortune to be admitted, and I soon perceived that she possessed in combination, the qualities which in all other persons whom I had known I had been only too happy to find singly. In her, complete emancipation from every kind of superstition (including that which attributes a pretended perfection to the order of nature and the universe), and an earnest protest against many things which are still part of the established constitution of society, resulted not from the hard intellect, but from strength of noble and elevated feeling, and co-existed with a highly reverential nature. In general spiritual characteristics, as well as in temperament and organisation, I have often compared her, as she was at this time, to

Shelley: but in thought and intellect, Shelley, so far as his powers were developed in his short life, was but a child compared with what she ultimately became. Alike in the highest regions of speculation and in the smaller practical concerns of daily life, her mind was the same perfect instrument, piercing to the very heart and marrow of the matter; always seizing the essential idea or principle. The same exactness and rapidity of operation, pervading as it did her sensitive as well as her mental faculties, would, with her gifts of feeling and imagination, have fitted her to be a consummate artist, as her fiery and tender soul and her vigorous eloquence would certainly have made her a great orator, and her profound knowledge of human nature and discernment and sagacity in practical life, would, in the times when such a *carrihre* was open to women, have made her eminent among the rulers of mankind. Her intellectual gifts did but minister to a moral character at once the noblest and the best balanced which I have ever met with in life. Her unselfishness was not that of a taught system of duties, but of a heart which thoroughly identified itself with the feelings of others, and often went to excess in consideration for them by imaginatively investing their feelings with the intensity of its own. The passion of justice might have been thought to be her strongest feeling, but for her boundless generosity, and a lovingness ever ready to pour itself forth upon any or all human beings who were capable of giving the smallest feeling in return. The rest of her moral characteristics were such as naturally accompany these qualities of mind and heart: the most genuine modesty combined with the loftiest pride; a simplicity and sincerity which were absolute, towards all who were fit to receive them; the utmost scorn of whatever was mean and cowardly, and a burning indignation at everything brutal or tyrannical, faithless or dishonourable in conduct and character, while making the broadest distinction between *mala in se* and mere *mala prohibita*—between acts giving evidence of intrinsic badness in feeling and character, and those which are only violations of conventions either good or bad, violations which, whether in themselves right or wrong, are capable of being committed by persons in every other respect lovable or admirable.

To be admitted into any degree of mental intercourse with a being of these qualities, could not but have a most beneficial influence on my development; though the effect was only gradual, and many years elapsed before her mental progress and mine went forward in the complete companionship they at last attained. The benefit I received was far greater than any which I could hope to give; though to her, who had at first reached her opinions by the moral intuition of a character of strong feeling, there was doubtless help as well as encouragement to be derived from one who had arrived at many of the same results by study and reasoning: and in the rapidity of her intellectual growth, her mental activity, which converted everything into knowledge, doubtless drew from me, as it did from other sources, many of its materials. What I owe, even intellectually, to her, is in its detail, almost infinite; of its general character a few words will give some, though a very imperfect, idea.

With those who, like all the best and wisest of mankind, are dissatisfied with human life as it is, and whose feelings are wholly identified with its radical amendment, there are two main regions of thought. One is the region of ultimate aims; the constituent elements of the highest realizable ideal of human life. The other is that of the immediately useful and practically attainable. In both these departments, I have acquired more from her teaching, than from all other sources taken together. And, to say truth, it is in these two extremes principally, that real certainty lies. My own strength lay wholly in the uncertain and slippery intermediate region, that of theory, or moral and political science: respecting the conclusions of which, in any of the forms in which I have received or originated them, whether as political economy, analytic psychology, logic, philosophy of history, or anything else, it is not the least of my intellectual obligations to her that I have derived from her a wise scepticism, which, while it has not hindered me from following out the honest exercise of my thinking faculties to whatever conclusions might result from it, has put me on my guard against holding or announcing these conclusions with a degree of confidence which the nature of such speculations does not warrant, and has kept my mind not only open to admit, but prompt to welcome and eager to seek, even on the questions on which I have most meditated, any prospect of clearer perceptions and better evidence. I have often received praise, which in my own right I only partially deserve, for the greater practicality which is supposed to be found in my writings, compared with those of most thinkers who have been equally addicted to large generalizations. The writings in which this quality has been observed, were not the work of one mind, but of the fusion of two, one of them as pre-eminently practical in its judgments and perceptions of things present, as it was high and bold in its anticipations for a remote futurity. At the present period, however, this influence was only one among many which were helping to shape the character of my future development: and even after it became, I may truly say, the presiding principle of my mental progress, it did not alter the path, but only made me move forward more boldly, and, at the same time, more cautiously, in the same course. The only actual revolution which has ever taken place in my modes of thinking, was already complete. My new tendencies had to be confirmed in some respects, moderated in others: but the only substantial changes of opinion that were yet to come, related to politics, and consisted, on one hand, in a greater approximation, so far as regards the ultimate prospects of humanity, to a qualified Socialism, and on the other, a shifting of my political ideal from pure democracy, as commonly understood by its partisans, to the modified form of it, which is set forth in my *Considerations on Representative Government*.

This last change, which took place very gradually, dates its commencement from my reading, or rather study, of M. de Tocqueville's *Democracy in America*, which fell into my hands immediately after its first appearance. In that remarkable work, the excellences of democracy were pointed out in a more conclusive, because a more specific manner than I had ever known them to be, even by the most enthusiastic democrats; while the specific dangers which beset democracy, considered as the government of the numerical majority, were brought into equally strong light, and subjected to a masterly analysis, not as reasons for resisting what the author considered as an inevitable result of human progress, but as indications of the weak points of popular government, the defences by which it needs to be guarded, and the correctives which must be added to it in order that while full play is given to its beneficial tendencies, those which are of a different nature may be neutralized or mitigated. I was now well prepared for speculations of this character, and from this time onward my own thoughts moved more and more in the same channel, though the consequent modifications in my practical political creed were spread over many years, as would be shown by comparing my first review of *Democracy in America*, written and published in 1835, with the one in 1840 (reprinted in the *Dissertations*), and this last, with the *Considerations on Representative Government*.

A collateral subject on which also I derived great benefit from the study of Tocqueville, was the fundamental question of centralization. The powerful philosophic analysis which he applied to American and to French experience, led him to attach the utmost importance to the performance of as much of the collective business of society, as can safely be so performed, by the people themselves, without any intervention of the executive government, either to supersede their agency, or to dictate the manner of its exercise. He viewed this practical political activity of the individual citizen, not only as one of the most effectual means of training the social feelings and practical intelligence of the people, so important in themselves and so indispensable to good government, but also as the specific counteractive to some of the characteristic infirmities of democracy, and a necessary protection against its degenerating into the only despotism of which, in the modern world, there is real danger—the absolute rule of the head of the executive over a congregation of isolated individuals, all equals but all slaves. There was, indeed, no immediate peril from this source on the British side of the channel, where nine-tenths of the internal business which elsewhere devolves on the government, was transacted by agencies independent of it; where centralization was, and is, the subject not only of rational disapprobation, but of unreasoning prejudice; where jealousy of Government interference was a blind feeling preventing or resisting even the most beneficial exertion of legislative authority to correct the abuses of what pretends to be local self-government, but is, too often, selfish mismanagement of local interests, by a jobbing and *borni* local oligarchy. But the more certain the public were to go wrong on the side opposed to centralization, the greater danger was there lest philosophic reformers should fall into the contrary error, and overlook the mischiefs of which they had been spared the painful experience. I was myself, at this very time, actively engaged in defending important measures, such as the great Poor Law Reform of 1834, against an irrational clamour grounded on the anti-centralization prejudice: and had it not been for the lessons of Tocqueville, I do not know that I might not, like many reformers before me, have been hurried into the excess opposite to that, which, being the one prevalent in my own country, it was generally my business to combat. As it is, I have steered carefully between the two errors, and whether I have or have not drawn the line between them exactly in the right place, I have at least insisted with equal emphasis upon the evils on both sides, and have made the means of reconciling the advantages of both, a subject of serious study.

In the meanwhile had taken place the election of the first Reformed Parliament, which included several of the most notable of my Radical friends and acquaintances—Grote, Roebuck, Buller, Sir William Molesworth, John and Edward Romilly, and several more; besides Warburton, Strutt, and others, who were in parliament already. Those who thought themselves, and were called by their friends, the philosophic Radicals, had now, it seemed, a fair opportunity, in a more advantageous position than they had ever before occupied, for showing what was in them; and I, as well as my father, founded great hopes on them. These hopes were destined to be disappointed. The men were honest, and faithful to their opinions, as far as votes were concerned; often in spite of much discouragement. When measures were proposed, flagrantly at variance with their principles, such as the Irish Coercion Bill, or the Canada Coercion in 1837, they came forward manfully, and braved any amount of hostility and prejudice rather than desert the right. But on the whole they did very little to promote any opinions; they had little enterprise, little activity: they left the lead of the Radical portion of the House to the old hands, to Hume and O'Connell. A partial exception must be made in favour of one or two of the younger men; and in the case of Roebuck, it is his title to permanent remembrance, that in the very first year during which he sat in Parliament, he originated (or re-originated after the unsuccessful attempt of Mr. Brougham) the parliamentary movement for National Education; and that he was the first to commence, and for years carried on almost alone, the contest for the self-government of the Colonies. Nothing, on the whole equal to these two things, was done by any other individual, even of those from whom most was expected. And now, on a calm retrospect, I can perceive that the men were less in fault than we supposed, and that we had expected too much from them. They were in unfavourable circumstances. Their lot was cast in the ten years of inevitable reaction, when, the Reform excitement being over, and the few legislative improvements which the public really called for having been rapidly effected, power gravitated back in its natural direction, to those who were for keeping things as they were; when the public mind desired rest, and was less disposed than at any other period since the Peace, to let itself be moved by attempts to work up the Reform feeling into fresh activity in favour of new things. It would have required a great political leader, which no one is to be blamed for not being, to have effected really great things by parliamentary discussion when the nation was in this mood. My father and I had hoped that some competent leader might arise; some man of philosophic attainments and popular talents, who could have put heart into the many younger or less distinguished men that would have been ready to join him—could have made them available, to the extent of their talents, in bringing advanced ideas before the public—could have used the House of Commons as a rostra or a teacher's chair for instructing and impelling the public mind; and would either have forced the Whigs to receive their measures from him, or have taken the lead of the Reform party out of their hands. Such a leader there would have been, if my father had been in Parliament. For want of such a man, the instructed Radicals sank into a mere *Ctti Gauche* of the Whig party. With a keen, and as I now think, an exaggerated sense of the possibilities which were open to the Radicals if they made even ordinary exertion for their opinions, I laboured from this time till 1839, both by personal influence with some of them, and by writings, to put ideas into their heads, and purpose into their hearts. I did some good with Charles Buller, and some with Sir William Molesworth; both of whom did valuable service, but were unhappily cut off almost in the beginning of their usefulness. On the whole, however, my attempt was vain. To have had a chance of succeeding in it, required a different position from mine. It was a task only for one who, being himself in Parliament, could have mixed with the Radical members in daily consultation, could himself have taken the initiative, and instead of urging others to lead, could have summoned them to follow.

What I could do by writing, I did. During the year 1833 I continued working in the *Examiner* with Fonblanque who at that time was zealous in keeping up the fight for Radicalism against the Whig ministry. During the session of 1834 I wrote comments on passing events, of the nature of newspaper articles (under the title "Notes on the Newspapers"), in the *Monthly Repository*, a magazine conducted by Mr. Fox, well known as a preacher and political orator, and subsequently as member of parliament for Oldham; with whom I had lately become acquainted, and for whose sake chiefly I wrote in his magazine. I contributed several other articles to this periodical, the most considerable of which (on the theory of Poetry), is reprinted in the "Dissertations." Altogether, the writings (independently of those in newspapers) which I published from 1832 to 1834, amount to a large volume. This, however, includes abstracts of several of Plato's Dialogues, with introductory remarks, which, though not published until 1834, had been written several years earlier; and which I afterwards, on various occasions, found to have been read, and their authorship known, by more people than were aware of anything else which I had written, up to that time. To complete the tale of my writings at this period, I may add that in 1833, at the request of Bulwer, who was just then completing his *England and the English* (a work, at that time, greatly in advance of the public mind), I wrote for him a critical account of Bentham's philosophy, a small part of which he incorporated in his text, and printed the rest (with an honourable acknowledgment), as an appendix. In this, along with the favourable, a part also of the unfavourable side of my estimation of Bentham's doctrines, considered as a complete philosophy, was for the first time put into print.

But an opportunity soon offered, by which, as it seemed, I might have it in my power to give more effectual aid, and at the same time, stimulus, to the "philosophic Radical" party, than I had done hitherto. One of the projects occasionally talked of between my father and me, and some of the parliamentary and other Radicals who frequented his house, was the foundation of a periodical organ of philosophic radicalism, to take the place which the *Westminster Review* had been intended to fill: and the scheme had gone so far as to bring under discussion the pecuniary contributions which could be looked for, and the choice of an editor. Nothing, however, came of it for some time: but in the summer of 1834 Sir William Molesworth, himself a laborious student, and a precise and metaphysical thinker, capable of aiding the cause by his pen as well as by his purse, spontaneously proposed to establish a Review, provided I would consent to be the real, if I could not be the ostensible, editor. Such a proposal was not to be refused; and the Review was founded, at first under the title of the *London Review*, and afterwards under that of the *London and Westminster*, Molesworth having bought the *Westminster* from its proprietor, General Thompson, and merged the two into one. In the years between 1834 and 1840 the conduct of this Review occupied the greater part of my spare time. In the beginning, it did not, as a whole, by any means represent my opinions. I was under the necessity of conceding much to my inevitable associates. The *Review* was established to be the representative of the "philosophic Radicals," with most of whom I was now at issue on many essential points, and among whom I could not even claim to be the most important individual. My father's co-operation as a writer we all deemed indispensable, and he wrote largely in it until prevented by his last illness. The subjects of his articles, and the strength and decision with which his opinions were expressed in them, made the *Review* at first derive its tone and colouring from him much more than from any of the other writers. I could not exercise editorial control over his articles, and I was sometimes obliged to sacrifice to him portions of my own. The old *Westminster Review* doctrines, but little modified, thus formed the staple of the *Review*; but I hoped by the side of these, to introduce other ideas and another tone, and to obtain for my own shade of opinion a fair representation, along with those of other members of the party. With this end chiefly in view, I made it one of the peculiarities of the work that every article should bear an initial, or some other signature, and be held to express the opinions solely of the individual writer; the editor being only responsible for its being worth publishing and not in conflict with the objects for which the *Review* was set on foot. I had an opportunity of putting in practice my scheme of conciliation between the old and the new "philosophic radicalism," by the choice of a subject for my own first contribution. Professor Sedgwick, a man of eminence in a particular walk of natural science, but who should not have trespassed into philosophy, had lately published his *Discourse on the Studies of Cambridge*, which had as its most prominent feature an intemperate assault on analytic psychology and utilitarian ethics, in the form of an attack on Locke and Paley. This had excited great indignation in my father and others, which I thought it fully deserved. And here, I imagined, was an opportunity of at the same time repelling an unjust attack, and inserting into my defence of Hartleianism and

Utilitarianism a number of the opinions which constituted my view of those subjects, as distinguished from that of my old associates. In this I partially succeeded, though my relation to my father would have made it painful to me in any case, and impossible in a Review for which he wrote, to speak out my whole mind on the subject at this time.

I am, however, inclined to think that my father was not so much opposed as he seemed, to the modes of thought in which I believed myself to differ from him; that he did injustice to his own opinions by the unconscious exaggerations of an intellect emphatically polemical; and that when thinking without an adversary in view, he was willing to make room for a great portion of the truths he seemed to deny. I have frequently observed that he made large allowance in practice for considerations which seemed to have no place in his theory. His *Fragment on Mackintosh*, which he wrote and published about this time, although I greatly admired some parts of it, I read as a whole with more pain than pleasure; yet on reading it again, long after, I found little in the opinions it contains, but what I think in the main just; and I can even sympathize in his disgust at the *verbiage* of Mackintosh, though his asperity towards it went not only beyond what was judicious, but beyond what was even fair. One thing, which I thought, at the time, of good augury, was the very favourable reception he gave to Tocqueville's *Democracy in America*. It is true, he said and thought much more about what Tocqueville said in favour of democracy, than about what he said of its disadvantages. Still, his high appreciation of a book which was at any rate an example of a mode of treating the question of government almost the reverse of his—wholly inductive and analytical, instead of purely ratiocinative—gave me great encouragement. He also approved of an article which I published in the first number following the junction of the two reviews, the essay reprinted in the *Dissertations*, under the title "Civilization"; into which I threw many of my new opinions, and criticised rather emphatically the mental and moral tendencies of the time, on grounds and in a manner which I certainly had not learnt from him.

All speculation, however, on the possible future developments of my father's opinions, and on the probabilities of permanent co-operation between him and me in the promulgation of our thoughts, was doomed to be cut short. During the whole of 1835 his health had been declining: his symptoms became unequivocally those of pulmonary consumption, and after lingering to the last stage of debility, he died on the 23rd of June, 1836. Until the last few days of his life there was no apparent abatement of intellectual vigour; his interest in all things and persons that had interested him through life was undiminished, nor did the approach of death cause the smallest wavering (as in so strong and firm a mind it was impossible that it should) in his convictions on the subject of religion. His principal satisfaction, after he knew that his end was near, seemed to be the thought of what he had done to make the world better than he found it; and his chief regret in not living longer, that he had not had time to do more.

His place is an eminent one in the literary, and even in the political history of his country; and it is far from honourable to the generation which has benefited by his worth, that he is so seldom mentioned, and, compared with men far his inferiors, so little remembered. This is probably to be ascribed mainly to two causes. In the first place, the thought of him merges too much in the deservedly superior fame of Bentham. Yet he was anything but Bentham's mere follower or disciple. Precisely because he was himself one of the most original thinkers of his time, he was one of the earliest to appreciate and adopt the most important mass of original thought which had been produced by the generation preceding him. His mind and Bentham's were essentially of different construction. He had not all Bentham's high qualities, but neither had Bentham all his. It would, indeed, be ridiculous to claim for him the praise of having accomplished for mankind such splendid services as Bentham's. He did not revolutionize, or rather create, one of the great departments of human thought. But, leaving out of the reckoning all that portion of his labours in which he benefited by what Bentham had done, and counting only what he achieved in a province in which Bentham had done nothing, that of analytic psychology, he will be known to posterity as one of the greatest names in that most important branch of speculation, on which all the moral and political sciences ultimately rest, and will mark one of the essential stages in its progress. The other reason which has made his fame less than he deserved, is that notwithstanding the great number of his opinions which, partly through his own efforts, have now been generally adopted, there was, on the whole, a marked opposition between his spirit and that of the present time. As Brutus was called the last of the Romans, so was he the last of the eighteenth century: he continued its tone of thought and sentiment into the nineteenth (though not unmodified nor unimproved), partaking neither in the good nor in the bad influences of the reaction against the eighteenth century, which was the great characteristic of the first half of the nineteenth. The eighteenth century was a great age, an age of strong and brave men, and he was a fit companion for its strongest and bravest. By his writings and his personal influence he was a great centre of light to his generation. During his later years he was quite as much the head and leader of the intellectual radicals in England, as Voltaire was of the *philosophes* of France. It is only one of his minor merits, that he was the originator of all sound statesmanship in regard to the subject of his largest work, India. He wrote on no subject which he did not enrich with valuable thought, and excepting the *Elements of Political Economy*, a very useful book when first written, but which has now for some time finished its work, it will be long before any of his books will be wholly superseded, or will cease to be instructive reading to students of their subjects. In the power of influencing by mere force of mind and character, the convictions and purposes of others, and in the strenuous exertion of that power to promote freedom and progress, he left, as far as my knowledge extends, no equal among men and but one among women.

Though acutely sensible of my own inferiority in the qualities by which he acquired his personal ascendancy, I had now to try what it might be possible for me to accomplish without him: and the *Review* was the instrument on which I built my chief hopes of establishing a useful influence over the liberal and democratic section of the public mind. Deprived of my father's aid, I was also exempted from the restraints and reticences by which that aid had been purchased. I did not feel that there was any other radical writer or politician to whom I was bound to defer, further than consisted with my own opinions: and having the complete confidence of Molesworth, I resolved henceforth to give full scope to my own opinions and modes of thought, and to open the *Review* widely to all writers who were in sympathy with Progress as I understood it, even though I should lose by it the support of my former associates. Carlyle, consequently became from this time a frequent writer in the *Review*; Sterling, soon after, an occasional one; and though each individual article continued to be the expression of the private sentiments of its writer, the general tone conformed in some tolerable degree to my opinions. For the conduct of the *Review*, under, and in conjunction with me, I associated with myself a young Scotchman of the name of Robertson, who had some ability and information, much industry, and an active scheming head, full of devices for making the *Review* more saleable, and on whose capacities in that direction I founded a good deal of hope: insomuch, that when Molesworth, in the beginning of 1837, became tired of carrying on the *Review* at a loss, and desirous of getting rid of it (he had done his part honourably, and at no small pecuniary cost,) I, very imprudently for my own pecuniary interest, and very much from reliance on Robertson's devices, determined to continue it at my own risk, until his plans should have had a fair trial. The devices were good, and I never had any reason to change my opinion of them. But I do not believe that any devices would have made a radical and democratic review defray its expenses, including a paid editor or sub-editor, and a liberal payment to writers. I myself and several frequent contributors gave our labour gratuitously, as we had done for Molesworth; but the paid contributors continued to be remunerated on the usual scale of the *Edinburgh* and *Quarterly Reviews*; and this could not be done from the proceeds of the sale.

In the same year, 1837, and in the midst of these occupations, I resumed the *Logic*. I had not touched my pen on the subject for five years, having been stopped and brought to a halt on the threshold of Induction. I had gradually discovered that what was mainly wanting, to overcome the difficulties of that branch of the subject, was a comprehensive, and, at the same time, accurate view of the whole circle of physical science, which I feared it would take me a long course of study to acquire; since I knew not of any book, or other guide, that would spread out before me the generalities and processes of the sciences, and I apprehended that I should have no choice but to extract them for myself, as I best could, from the details. Happily for me, Dr. Whewell, early in this year, published his *History of the Inductive Sciences*. I read it with eagerness, and found in it a considerable approximation to what I wanted. Much, if not most, of the philosophy of the work appeared open to objection; but the materials were there, for my own thoughts to work upon: and the author had given to those materials that first degree of elaboration, which so greatly facilitates and abridges the subsequent labour. I had now obtained what I had been waiting for. Under the impulse given me by the thoughts excited by Dr. Whewell, I read again Sir J. Herschel's *Discourse on the Study of Natural Philosophy*: and I was able to measure the progress my mind had made, by the great help I now found in this work— though I had read and even reviewed it several years before with little profit. I now set myself vigorously to work out the subject in thought and in writing. The time I bestowed on this had to be stolen from occupations more urgent. I had just two months to spare, at this period, in the intervals of writing for the *Review*. In these two months I completed the first draft of about a third, the most difficult third, of the book. What I had before written, I estimate at another third, so that one-third remained. What I wrote at this time consisted of the remainder of the doctrine of Reasoning (the theory of Trains of Reasoning, and Demonstrative Science), and the greater part of the Book on Induction. When this was done, I had, as it seemed to me, untied all the really hard knots, and the completion of the book had become only a question of time. Having got thus far, I had to leave off in order to write two articles for the next number of the *Review*. When these were written, I returned to the subject, and now for the first time fell in with Comte's *Cours de Philosophie Positive*, or rather with the two volumes of it which were all that had at that time been published. My theory of Induction was substantially completed before I knew of Comte's book; and it is perhaps well that I came to it by a different road from his, since the consequence has been that my treatise contains, what his certainly does not, a reduction of the inductive process to strict rules and to a scientific test, such as the syllogism is for ratiocination. Comte is always precise and profound on the method of investigation, but he does not even attempt any exact definition of the conditions of proof: and his writings show that he never attained a just conception of them. This, however, was specifically the problem, which, in treating of Induction, I had proposed to myself. Nevertheless, I gained much from Comte, with which to enrich my chapters in the subsequent rewriting: and his book was of essential service to me in some of the parts which still remained to be thought out. As his subsequent volumes successively made their appearance, I read them with avidity, but, when he reached the subject of Social Science, with varying feelings. The fourth volume disappointed me: it contained those of his opinions on social subjects with which I most disagree. But the fifth, containing the connected view of history, rekindled all my enthusiasm; which the sixth (or concluding) volume did not materially abate. In a merely logical point of view, the only leading conception for which I am indebted to him is that of the Inverse Deductive Method, as the one chiefly applicable to the complicated subjects of History and Statistics: a process differing from the more common form of the deductive method in this—that instead of arriving at its conclusions by general reasoning, and verifying them by specific experience (as is the natural order in the deductive branches of physical science), it obtains its generalizations by a collation of specific experience, and verifies them by ascertaining whether they are such as would follow from known general principles. This was an idea entirely new to me when I found it in Comte: and but for him I might not soon (if ever) have arrived at it.

I had been long an ardent admirer of Comte's writings before I had any communication with himself; nor did I ever, to the last, see him in the body. But for some years we were frequent correspondents, until our correspondence became controversial, and our zeal cooled. I was the first to slacken correspondence; he was the first to drop it. I found, and he probably found likewise, that I could do no good to his mind, and that all the good he could do to mine, he did by his books. This would never have led to discontinuance of intercourse, if the differences between us had been on matters of simple doctrine. But they were chiefly on those points of opinion which blended in both of us with our strongest feelings, and determined the entire direction of our aspirations. I had fully agreed with him when he maintained that the mass of mankind, including even their rulers in all the practical departments of life, must, from the necessity of the case, accept most of their opinions on political and social matters, as they do on physical, from the authority of those who have bestowed more study on those subjects than they generally have it in their power to do. This lesson had been strongly impressed on me by the early work of Comte, to which I have adverted. And there was nothing in his great Treatise which I admired more than his remarkable exposition of the benefits which the nations of modern Europe have historically derived from the separation, during the Middle Ages, of temporal and spiritual power, and the distinct organization of the latter. I agreed with him that the moral and intellectual ascendancy, once exercised by priests, must in time pass into the hands of philosophers, and will naturally do so when they become sufficiently unanimous, and in other respects worthy to possess it. But when he exaggerated this line of thought into a practical system, in which philosophers were to be organized into a kind of corporate hierarchy, invested with almost the same spiritual supremacy (though without any secular power) once possessed by the Catholic Church; when I found him relying on this spiritual authority as the only security for good government, the sole bulwark against practical oppression, and expecting that by it a system of despotism in the state and despotism in the family would be rendered innocuous and beneficial; it is not surprising, that while as logicians we were nearly at one, as sociologists we could travel together no further. M. Comte lived to carry out these doctrines to their extremest consequences, by planning, in his last work, the *Systhme de Politique Positive*, the completest system of spiritual and temporal despotism which ever yet emanated from a human brain, unless possibly that of Ignatius Loyola: a system by which the yoke of general opinion, wielded by an organized body of spiritual teachers and rulers, would be made supreme over every action, and as far as is in human possibility, every thought, of every member of the community, as well in the things which regard only himself, as in those which concern the interests of others. It is but just to say that this work is a considerable improvement, in many points of feeling, over Comte's previous writings on the same subjects: but as an accession to social philosophy, the only value it seems to me to possess, consists in putting an end to the notion that no effectual moral authority can be maintained over society without the aid of religious belief; for Comte's work recognises no religion except that of Humanity, yet it leaves an irresistible conviction that any moral beliefs concurred in by the community generally may be brought to bear upon the whole conduct and lives of its individual members, with an energy and potency truly alarming to think of. The book stands a monumental warning to thinkers on society and politics, of what happens when once men lose sight, in their speculations, of the value of Liberty and of Individuality.

To return to myself. The *Review* engrossed, for some time longer, nearly all the time I could devote to authorship, or to thinking with authorship in view. The articles from the *London and Westminster Review* which are reprinted in the *Dissertations*, are scarcely a fourth part of those I wrote. In the conduct of the *Review* I had two principal objects. One was to free philosophic radicalism from the reproach of sectarian Benthamism. I desired, while retaining the precision of expression, the definiteness of meaning, the contempt of declamatory phrases and vague generalities, which were so honourably characteristic both of Bentham and of my father, to give a wider basis and a more free and genial character to Radical speculations; to show that there was a Radical philosophy, better and more complete than Bentham's, while recognizing and incorporating all of Bentham's which is permanently valuable. In this first object I, to a certain extent, succeeded. The other thing I attempted, was to stir up the educated Radicals, in and out of Parliament, to exertion, and induce them to make themselves, what I thought by using the proper means they might become —a powerful party capable of taking the government of the country, or at least of dictating the terms on which they should share it with the Whigs. This attempt was from the first chimerical: partly because the time was unpropitious, the Reform fervour being in its period of ebb, and the Tory influences powerfully rallying; but still more, because, as Austin so truly said, "the country did not contain the men." Among the Radicals in Parliament there were several qualified to be useful members of an enlightened Radical party, but none capable of forming and leading such a party. The exhortations I addressed to them found no response. One occasion did present itself when there seemed to be room for a bold and successful stroke for Radicalism. Lord Durham had left the ministry, by reason, as was thought, of their not being sufficiently Liberal; he afterwards accepted from them the task of ascertaining and removing the causes of the Canadian rebellion; he had shown a disposition to surround himself at the outset with Radical advisers; one of his earliest measures, a good measure both in intention and in effect, having been disapproved and reversed by the Government at home, he had resigned his post, and placed himself openly in a position of quarrel with the Ministers. Here was a possible chief for a Radical party in the person of a man of importance, who was hated by the Tories and had just been injured by the Whigs. Any one who had the most elementary notions of party tactics, must have attempted to make something of such an opportunity. Lord Durham was bitterly attacked from all sides, inveighed against by enemies, given up by timid friends; while those who would willingly have defended him did not know what to say. He appeared to be returning a defeated and discredited man. I had followed the Canadian events from the beginning; I had been one of the prompters of his prompters; his policy was almost exactly what mine would have been, and I was in a position to defend it. I wrote and published a manifesto in the *Review*, in which I took the very highest ground in his behalf, claiming for him not mere acquittal, but praise and honour. Instantly a number of other writers took up the tone: I believe there was a portion of truth in what Lord Durham, soon after, with polite exaggeration, said to me—that to this article might be ascribed the almost triumphal reception which he met with on his arrival in England. I believe it to have been the word in season, which, at a critical moment, does much to decide the result; the touch which determines whether a stone, set in motion at the top of an eminence, shall roll down on one side or on the other. All hopes connected with Lord Durham as a politician soon vanished; but with regard to Canadian, and generally to colonial policy, the cause was gained: Lord Durham's report, written by Charles Buller, partly under the inspiration of Wakefield, began a new era; its recommendations, extending to complete internal self-government, were in full operation in Canada within two or three years, and have been since extended to nearly all the other colonies, of European race, which have any claim to the character of important communities. And I may say that in successfully upholding the reputation of Lord Durham and his advisers at the most important moment, I contributed materially to this result.

One other case occurred during my conduct of the *Review*, which similarly illustrated the effect of taking a prompt initiative. I believe that the early success and reputation of Carlyle's *French Revolution*, were considerably accelerated by what I wrote about it in the *Review*. Immediately on its publication, and before the commonplace critics, all whose rules and modes of judgment it set at defiance, had time to pre-occupy the public with their disapproval of it, I wrote and published a review of the book, hailing it as one of those productions of genius which are above all rules, and are a law to themselves. Neither in this case nor in that of Lord Durham do I ascribe the impression, which I think was produced by what I wrote, to any particular merit of execution: indeed, in at least one of the cases (the article on Carlyle) I do not think the execution was good. And in both instances, I am persuaded that anybody, in a position to be read, who had expressed the same opinion at the same precise time, and had made any tolerable statement of the just grounds for it, would have produced the same effect. But, after the complete failure of my hopes of putting a new life into Radical politics by means of the *Review*, I am glad to look back on these two instances of success in an honest attempt to do mediate service to things and persons that deserved it. After the last hope of the formation of a Radical party had disappeared, it was time for me to stop the heavy expenditure of time and money which the *Review* cost me. It had to some extent answered my personal purpose as a vehicle for my opinions. It had enabled me to express in print much of my altered mode of thought, and to separate myself in a marked manner from the narrower Benthamism of my early writings. This was done by the general tone of all I wrote, including various purely literary articles, but especially by the two papers (reprinted in the *Dissertations*) which attempted a philosophical estimate of Bentham and of Coleridge. In the first of these, while doing full justice to the merits of Bentham, I pointed out what I thought the errors and deficiencies of his philosophy. The substance of this criticism *I* still think perfectly just; but I have sometimes doubted whether it was right to publish it at that time. I have often felt that Bentham's philosophy, as an instrument of progress, has been to some extent discredited before it had done its work, and that to lend a hand towards lowering its reputation was doing more harm than service to improvement. Now, however, when a counter-reaction appears to be setting in towards what is good in Benthamism, I can look with more satisfaction on this criticism of its defects, especially as I have myself balanced it by vindications of the fundamental principles of Bentham's philosophy, which are reprinted along with it in the same collection. In the essay on Coleridge I attempted to characterize the European reaction against the negative philosophy of the eighteenth century: and here, if the effect only of this one paper were to be considered, I might be thought to have erred by giving undue prominence to the favourable side, as I had done in the case of Bentham to the unfavourable. In both cases, the impetus with which I had detached myself from what was untenable in the doctrines of Bentham and of the eighteenth century, may have carried me, though in appearance rather than in reality, too far on the contrary side. But as far as relates to the article on Coleridge, my defence is, that I was writing for Radicals and Liberals, and it was my business to dwell most on that, in writers of a different school, from the knowledge of which they might derive most improvement.

The number of the *Review* which contained the paper on Coleridge, was the last which was published during my proprietorship. In the spring of 1840 I made over the *Review* to Mr. Hickson, who had been a frequent and very useful unpaid contributor under my management: only stipulating that the change should be marked by a resumption of the old name, that of *Westminster Review.* Under that name Mr. Hickson conducted it for ten years, on the plan of dividing among contributors only the net proceeds of the *Review* giving his own labour as writer and editor gratuitously. Under the difficulty in obtaining writers, which arose from this low scale of payment, it is highly creditable to him that he was able to maintain, in some tolerable degree, the character of the *Review* as an organ of radicalism and progress. I did not cease altogether to write for the *Review*, but continued to send it occasional contributions, not, however, exclusively; for the greater circulation of the *Edinburgh Review* induced me from this time to offer articles to it also when I had anything to say for which it appeared to be a suitable vehicle. And the concluding volumes of *Democracy in America*, having just then come out, I inaugurated myself as a contributor to the *Edin-*

burgh, by the article on that work, which heads the second volume of the *Dissertations*.

General View Of The Remainder Of My Life.

From this time, what is worth relating of my life will come into a very small compass; for I have no further mental changes to tell of, but only, as I hope, a continued mental progress; which does not admit of a consecutive history, and the results of which, if real, will be best found in my writings. I shall, therefore, greatly abridge the chronicle of my subsequent years.

The first use I made of the leisure which I gained by disconnecting myself from the *Review*, was to finish the *Logic*. In July and August, 1838, I had found an interval in which to execute what was still undone of the original draft of the Third Book. In working out the logical theory of those laws of nature which are not laws of Causation, nor corollaries from such laws, I was led to recognize kinds as realities in nature, and not mere distinctions for convenience; a light which I had not obtained when the First Book was written, and which made it necessary for me to modify and enlarge several chapters of that Book. The Book on Language and Classification, and the chapter on the Classification of Fallacies, were drafted in the autumn of the same year; the remainder of the work, in the summer and autumn of 1840. From April following to the end of 1841, my spare time was devoted to a complete rewriting of the book from its commencement. It is in this way that all my books have been composed. They were always written at least twice over; a first draft of the entire work was completed to the very end of the subject, then the whole begun again *de novo*; but incorporating, in the second writing, all sentences and parts of sentences of the old draft, which appeared as suitable to my purpose as anything which I could write in lieu of them. I have found great advantages in this system of double redaction. It combines, better than any other mode of composition, the freshness and vigour of the first conception, with the superior precision and completeness resulting from prolonged thought. In my own case, moreover, I have found that the patience necessary for a careful elaboration of the details of composition and expression, costs much less effort after the entire subject has been once gone through, and the substance of all that I find to say has in some manner, however imperfect, been got upon paper. The only thing which I am careful, in the first draft, to make as perfect as I am able, is the arrangement. If that is bad, the whole thread on which the ideas string themselves becomes twisted; thoughts placed in a wrong connection are not expounded in a manner that suits the right, and a first draft with this original vice is next to useless as a foundation for the final treatment.

During the re-writing of the *Logic*, Dr. Whewell's *Philosophy of the Inductive Sciences* made its appearance; a circumstance fortunate for me, as it gave me what I greatly desired, a full treatment of the subject by an antagonist, and enabled me to present my ideas with greater clearness and emphasis as well as fuller and more varied development, in defending them against definite objections, or confronting them distinctly with an opposite theory. The controversies with Dr. Whewell, as well as much matter derived from Comte, were first introduced into the book in the course of the re-writing.

At the end of 1841, the book being ready for the press, I offered it to Murray, who kept it until too late for publication that season, and then refused it, for reasons which could just as well have been given at first. But I have had no cause to regret a rejection which led to my offering it to Mr. Parker, by whom it was published in the spring of 1843. My original expectations of success were extremely limited. Archbishop Whately had, indeed, rehabilitated the name of Logic, and the study of the forms, rules, and fallacies of Ratiocination; and Dr. Whewell's writings had begun to excite an interest in the other part of my subject, the theory of Induction. A treatise, however, on a matter so abstract, could not be expected to be popular; it could only be a book for students, and students on such subjects were not only (at least in England) few, but addicted chiefly to the opposite school of metaphysics, the ontological and "innate principles" school. I therefore did not expect that the book

would have many readers, or approvers; and looked for little practical effect from it, save that of keeping the tradition unbroken of
what I thought a better philosophy. What hopes I had of exciting
any immediate attention, were mainly grounded on the polemical
propensities of Dr Whewell; who, I thought, from observation of
his conduct in other cases, would probably do something to bring
the book into notice, by replying, and that promptly, to the attack
on his opinions. He did reply but not till 1850, just in time for me
to answer him in the third edition. How the book came to have,
for a work of the kind, so much success, and what sort of persons
compose the bulk of those who have bought, I will not venture
to say read, it, I have never thoroughly understood. But taken in
conjunction with the many proofs which have since been given of a
revival of speculation, speculation too of a free kind, in many quarters, and above all (where at one time I should have least expected
it) in the Universities, the fact becomes partially intelligible. I have
never indulged the illusion that the book had made any considerable impression on philosophical opinion. The German, or *a priori*
view of human knowledge, and of the knowing faculties, is likely
for some time longer (though it may be hoped in a diminishing
degree) to predominate among those who occupy themselves with
such inquiries, both here and on the Continent. But the "System of
Logic" supplies what was much wanted, a text-book of the opposite
doctrine—that which derives all knowledge from experience, and
all moral and intellectual qualities principally from the direction
given to the associations. I make as humble an estimate as anybody of what either an analysis of logical processes, or any possible
canons of evidence, can do by themselves towards guiding or recti-
fying the operations of the understanding. Combined with other
requisites, I certainly do think them of great use; but whatever
may be the practical value of a true philosophy of these matters, it
is hardly possible to exaggerate the mischiefs of a false one. The
notion that truths external to the mind may be known by intuition
or consciousness, independently of observation and experience,
is, I am persuaded, in these times, the great intellectual support of

false doctrines and bad institutions. By the aid of this theory, every inveterate belief and every intense feeling, of which the origin is not remembered, is enabled to dispense with the obligation of justifying itself by reason, and is erected into its own all-sufficient voucher and justification. There never was such an instrument devised for consecrating all deep-seated prejudices. And the chief strength of this false philosophy in morals, politics, and religion, lies in the appeal which it is accustomed to make to the evidence of mathematics and of the cognate branches of physical science. To expel it from these, is to drive it from its stronghold: and because this had never been effectually done, the intuitive school, even after what my father had written in his *Analysis of the Mind*, had in appearance, and as far as published writings were concerned, on the whole the best of the argument. In attempting to clear up the real nature of the evidence of mathematical and physical truths, the *System of Logic* met the intuitive philosophers on ground on which they had previously been deemed unassailable; and gave its own explanation, from experience and association, of that peculiar character of what are called necessary truths, which is adduced as proof that their evidence must come from a deeper source than experience. Whether this has been done effectually, is still *sub judice*; and even then, to deprive a mode of thought so strongly rooted in human prejudices and partialities, of its mere speculative support, goes but a very little way towards overcoming it; but though only a step, it is a quite indispensable one; for since, after all, prejudice can only be successfully combated by philosophy, no way can really be made against it permanently until it has been shown not to have philosophy on its side.

Being now released from any active concern in temporary politics, and from any literary occupation involving personal communication with contributors and others, I was enabled to indulge the inclination, natural to thinking persons when the age of boyish vanity is once past, for limiting my own society to a very few persons. General society, as now carried on in England, is so insipid an affair, even to the persons who make it what it is, that it is kept up for any reason rather than the pleasure it affords. All serious discussion on matters on which opinions differ, being considered ill-bred, and the national deficiency in liveliness and sociability having prevented the cultivation of the art of talking agreeably on trifles, in which the French of the last century so much excelled, the sole attraction of what is called society to those who are not at the top of the tree, is the hope of being aided to climb a little higher in it; while to those who are already at the top, it is chiefly a compliance with custom, and with the supposed requirements of their station. To a person of any but a very common order in thought or feeling, such society, unless he has personal objects to serve by it, must be supremely unattractive: and most people, in the present day, of any really high class of intellect, make their contact with it so slight, and at such long intervals, as to be almost considered as retiring from it altogether. Those persons of any mental superiority who do otherwise, are, almost without exception, greatly deteriorated by it. Not to mention loss of time, the tone of their feelings is lowered: they become less in earnest about those of their opinions respecting which they must remain silent in the society they frequent: they come to look upon their most elevated objects as unpractical, or, at least, too remote from realization to be more than a vision, or a theory, and if, more fortunate than most, they retain their higher principles unimpaired, yet with respect to the persons and affairs of their own day they insensibly adopt the modes of feeling and judgment in which they can hope for sympathy from the company they keep. A person of high intellect should never go into unintellectual society unless he can enter it as an apostle; yet he is the only person with high objects who can safely enter it at all. Persons even of intellectual aspirations had much better, if they can, make their habitual associates of at least their equals, and, as far as possible, their superiors, in knowledge, intellect, and elevation of sentiment. Moreover, if the character is formed, and the mind made up, on the few cardinal points of human opinion, agreement of conviction and feeling on these, has been felt in all times to be an essential requisite of anything worthy the name of friendship, in a really earnest mind. All these circumstances united, made the number very small of those whose society, and still more whose intimacy, I now voluntarily sought.

Among these, by far the principal was the incomparable friend of whom I have already spoken. At this period she lived mostly with one young daughter, in a quiet part of the country, and only occasionally in town, with her first husband, Mr. Taylor. I visited her equally in both places; and was greatly indebted to the strength of character which enabled her to disregard the false interpretations liable to be put on the frequency of my visits to her while living generally apart from Mr. Taylor, and on our occasionally travelling together, though in all other respects our conduct during those years gave not the slightest ground for any other supposition than the true one, that our relation to each other at that time was one of strong affection and confidential intimacy only. For though we did not consider the ordinances of society binding on a subject so entirely personal, we did feel bound that our conduct should be such as in no degree to bring discredit on her husband, nor therefore on herself.

In this third period (as it may be termed) of my mental progress, which now went hand in hand with hers, my opinions gained equally in breadth and depth, I understood more things, and those which I had understood before I now understood more thoroughly. I had now completely turned back from what there had been of excess in my reaction against Benthamism. I had, at the height of that reaction, certainly become much more indulgent to the common opinions of society and the world, and more willing to be content with seconding the superficial improvement which had begun to take place in those common opinions, than became one whose convictions on so many points, differed fundamentally from them. I was much more inclined, than I can now approve, to put in abeyance the more decidedly heretical part of my opinions, which I now look upon as almost the only ones, the assertion of which tends in any way to regenerate society. But in addition to this, our opinions were far *more* heretical than mine had been in the days of my most extreme Benthamism. In those days I had seen little further than the old school of political economists into the possibilities of fundamental improvement in social arrangements. Private property, as now understood, and inheritance, appeared to me, as to them, the *dernier mot* of legislation: and I looked no further than to mitigating the inequalities consequent on these institutions, by getting rid of primogeniture and entails. The notion that it was possible to go further than this in removing the injustice—for injustice it is, whether admitting of a complete remedy or not—involved in the fact that some are born to riches and the vast majority to poverty, I then reckoned chimerical, and only hoped that by universal education, leading to voluntary restraint on population, the portion of the poor might be made more tolerable. In short, I was a democrat, but not the least of a Socialist. We were now much less democrats than I had been, because so long as education continues to be so wretchedly imperfect, we dreaded the ignorance and especially the selfishness and brutality of the mass: but our ideal of ultimate improvement went far beyond Democracy, and would class us decidedly under the general designation of Socialists. While we repudiated with the greatest energy that tyranny of society over the individual which most Socialistic systems are supposed to involve, we yet looked forward to a time when society will no longer be divided into the idle and the industrious; when the rule that they who do not work shall not eat, will be applied not to paupers only, but impartially to all; when the division of the produce of labour, instead of depending, as in so great a degree it now does, on the accident of birth, will be made by concert on an acknowledged principle of justice; and when it will no longer either be, or be thought to be, impossible for human beings to exert themselves strenuously in procuring benefits which are not to be exclusively their own, but to be shared with the society they belong to. The social problem of the future we considered to be, how to unite the greatest individual liberty of action, with a common ownership in the raw material of the globe, and an equal participation of all in the benefits of combined labour. We had not the presumption to suppose that we could already foresee, by what precise form of institutions these objects could most effectually be attained, or at how near or how distant a period they would become practicable. We saw clearly that to render any such social transformation either possible or desirable, an equivalent change of character must take place both in the uncultivated herd who now compose the labouring masses, and in the immense majority of their employers. Both these classes must learn by practice to labour and combine for generous, or at all events for public and social purposes, and not, as hitherto, solely for narrowly interested ones. But the capacity to do this has always existed in mankind, and is not, nor is ever likely to be, extinct. Education, habit, and the cultivation of the sentiments, will make a common man dig or weave for his country, as readily as fight for his country. True enough, it is only by slow degrees, and a system of culture prolonged through successive generations, that men in general can be brought up to this point. But the hindrance is not in the essential constitution of human nature. Interest in the common good is at present so weak a motive in the generality not because it can never be otherwise, but because the mind is not accustomed to dwell on it as it dwells from morning till night on things which tend only to personal advantage. When called into activity, as only self-interest now is, by the daily course of life, and spurred from behind by the love of distinction and the fear of shame, it is capable of producing, even in common men, the most strenuous exertions as well as the most heroic sacrifices. The deep-rooted selfishness which forms the general character of the existing state of society, is *so* deeply rooted, only because the whole course of existing institutions tends to foster it; and modern institutions in some respects more than ancient, since the occasions on which the individual is called on to do anything for the public without receiving its pay, are far less frequent in modern life, than the smaller commonwealths of antiquity. These considerations did not make us overlook the folly of premature attempts to dispense with the inducements of private interest in social affairs, while no substitute for them has been or

can be provided: but we regarded all existing institutions and social arrangements as being (in a phrase I once heard from Austin)
"merely provisional," and we welcomed with the greatest pleasure
and interest all socialistic experiments by select individuals (such
as the Co-operative Societies), which, whether they succeeded or
failed, could not but operate as a most useful education of those
who took part in them, by cultivating their capacity of acting upon
motives pointing directly to the general good, or making them
aware of the defects which render them and others incapable of
doing so.

In the *Principles of Political Economy*, these opinions were pro-
mulgated, less clearly and fully in the first edition, rather more so
in the second, and quite unequivocally in the third. The difference
arose partly from the change of times, the first edition having been
written and sent to press before the French Revolution of 1848,
after which the public mind became more open to the reception
of novelties in opinion, and doctrines appeared moderate which
would have been thought very startling a short time before. In the
first edition the difficulties of Socialism were stated so strongly, that
the tone was on the whole that of opposition to it. In the year or
two which followed, much time was given to the study of the best
Socialistic writers on the Continent, and to meditation and discussion on the whole range of topics involved in the controversy: and
the result was that most of what had been written on the subject
in the first edition was cancelled, and replaced by arguments and
reflections which represent a more advanced opinion.

The *Political Economy* was far more rapidly executed than the
Logic, or indeed than anything of importance which I had previously written. It was commenced in the autumn of 1845, and was
ready for the press before the end of 1847. In this period of little
more than two years there was an interval of six months during
which the work was laid aside, while I was writing articles in the
Morning Chronicle (which unexpectedly entered warmly into my
purpose) urging the formation of peasant properties on the waste
lands of Ireland. This was during the period of the Famine, the

winter of 1846-47, when the stern necessities of the time seemed to afford a chance of gaining attention for what appeared to me the only mode of combining relief to immediate destitution with permanent improvement of the social and economical condition of the Irish people. But the idea was new and strange; there was no English precedent for such a proceeding: and the profound ignorance of English politicians and the English public concerning all social phenomena not generally met with in England (however common elsewhere), made my endeavours an entire failure. Instead of a great operation on the waste lands, and the conversion of cottiers into proprietors, Parliament passed a Poor Law for maintaining them as paupers: and if the nation has not since found itself in inextricable difficulties from the joint operation of the old evils and the quack remedy it is indebted for its deliverance to that most unexpected and surprising fact, the depopulation of ireland, commenced by famine, and continued by emigration.

The rapid success of the *Political Economy* showed that the public wanted, and were prepared for such a book. Published early in 1848, an edition of a thousand copies was sold in less than a year. Another similar edition was published in the spring of 1849; and a third, of 1250 copies, early in 1852. It was, from the first, continually cited and referred to as an authority, because it was not a book merely of abstract science, but also of application, and treated Political Economy not as a thing by itself, but as a fragment of a greater whole; a branch of Social Philosophy, so interlinked with all the other branches, that its conclusions, even in its own peculiar province, are only true conditionally, subject to interference and counteraction from causes not directly within its scope: while to the character of a practical guide it has no pretension, apart from other classes of considerations. Political Economy, in truth, has never pretended to give advice to mankind with no lights but its own; though people who knew nothing but political economy (and therefore knew that ill) have taken upon themselves to advise, and could only do so by such lights as they had. But the numerous sentimental enemies of political economy, and its still more numerous

interested enemies in sentimental guise, have been very successful in gaining belief for this among other unmerited imputations
against it, and the *Principles* having, in spite of the freedom of many
of its opinions, become for the present the most popular treatise
on the subject, has helped to disarm the enemies of so important
a study. The amount of its worth as an exposition of the science,
and the value of the different applications which it suggests, others
of course must judge.

For a considerable time after this, I published no work of magnitude; though I still occasionally wrote in periodicals, and my
correspondence (much of it with persons quite unknown to me),
on subjects of public interest, swelled to a considerable bulk. During these years I wrote or commenced various Essays, for eventual
publication, on some of the fundamental questions of human and
social life, with regard to several of which I have already much exceeded the severity of the Horatian precept. I continued to watch
with keen interest the progress of public events. But it was not, on
the whole, very encouraging to me. The European reaction after
1848, and the success of an unprincipled usurper in December, 1851,
put an end, as it seemed, to all present hope for freedom or social
improvement in France and the Continent. In England, I had seen
and continued to see many of the opinions of my youth obtain
general recognition, and many of the reforms in institutions, for
which I had through life contended, either effected or in course
of being so. But these changes had been attended with much less
benefit to human well-being than I should formerly have anticipated, because they had produced very little improvement in that
which all real amelioration in the lot of mankind depends on, their
intellectual and moral state: and it might even be questioned if
the various causes of deterioration which had been at work in the
meanwhile, had not more than counterbalanced the tendencies
to improvement. I had learnt from experience that many false
opinions may be exchanged for true ones, without in the least altering the habits of mind of which false opinions are the result. The
English public, for example, are quite as raw and undiscerning on

subjects of political economy since the nation has been converted to free-trade, as they were before; and are still further from having acquired better habits of thought and feeling, or being in any way better fortified against error, on subjects of a more elevated character. For, though they have thrown off certain errors, the general discipline of their minds, intellectually and morally, is not altered. I am now convinced, that no great improvements in the lot of mankind are possible, until a great change takes place in the fundamental constitution of their modes of thought. The old opinions in religion, morals, and politics, are so much discredited in the more intellectual minds as to have lost the greater part of their efficacy for good, while they have still life enough in them to be a powerful obstacle to the growing up of any better opinions on those subjects. When the philosophic minds of the world can no longer believe its religion, or can only believe it with modifications amounting to an essential change of its character, a transitional period commences, of weak convictions, paralysed intellects, and growing laxity of principle, which cannot terminate until a renovation has been effected in the basis of their belief leading to the evolution of some faith, whether religious or merely human, which they can really believe: and when things are in this state, all thinking or writing which does not tend to promote such a renovation, is of very little value beyond the moment. Since there was little in the apparent condition of the public mind, indicative of any tendency in this direction, my view of the immediate prospects of human improvement was not sanguine. More recently a spirit of free speculation has sprung up, giving a more encouraging prospect of the gradual mental emancipation of England; and concurring with the renewal under better auspices, of the movement for political freedom in the rest of Europe, has given to the present condition of human affairs a more hopeful aspect.[3]

Between the time of which I have now spoken, and the present, took place the most important events of my private life. The first of these was my marriage, in April, 1851, to the lady whose incomparable worth had made her friendship the greatest source to me both of happiness and of improvement, during many years in which we never expected to be in any closer relation to one another. Ardently as I should have aspired to this complete union of our lives at any time in the course of my existence at which it had been practicable, I, as much as my wife, would far rather have foregone that privilege for ever, than have owed it to the premature death of one for whom I had the sincerest respect, and she the strongest affection. That event, however, having taken place in July, 1849, it was granted to me to derive from that evil my own greatest good, by adding to the partnership of thought, feeling, and writing which had long existed, a partnership of our entire existence. For seven and a-half years that blessing was mine; for seven and a-half only! I can say nothing which could describe, even in the faintest manner, what that loss was and is. But because I know that she would have wished it, I endeavour to make the best of what life I have left, and to work on for her purposes with such diminished strength as can be derived from thoughts of her, and communion with her memory.

When two persons have their thoughts and speculations completely in common; when all subjects of intellectual or moral interest are discussed between them in daily life, and probed to much greater depths than are usually or conveniently sounded in writings intended for general readers; when they set out from the same principles, and arrive at their conclusions by processes pursued jointly, it is of little consequence in respect to the question of originality, which of them holds the pen; the one who contributes least to the composition may contribute more to the thought; the writings which result are the joint product of both, and it must often be impossible to disentangle their respective parts, and affirm that this belongs to one and that to the other. In this wide sense, not only during the years of our married life, but during many of the years of confidential friendship which preceded, all my published writings were as much here work as mine; her share in them constantly increasing as years advanced. But in certain cases, what belongs to her can be distinguished, and specially identified. Over and above the general influence which her mind had over mine, the most valuable ideas and features in these joint productions—those which have been most fruitful of important results, and have contributed most to the success and reputation of the works themselves—originated with her, were emanations from her mind, my part in them being no greater than in any of the thoughts which I found in previous writers, and made my own only by incorporating them with my own system of thought! During the greater part of my literary life I have performed the office in relation to her, which from a rather early period I had considered as the most useful part that I was qualified to take in the domain of thought, that of an interpreter of original thinkers, and mediator between them and the public; for I had always a humble opinion of my own powers as an original thinker, except in abstract science (logic, metaphysics, and the theoretic principles of political economy and politics), but thought myself much superior to most of my contemporaries in willingness and ability to learn from everybody; as I found hardly anyone who made such a point of examining what was said in defence of all opinions, however new or however old, in the conviction that even if they were errors there might be a substratum of truth underneath them, and that in any case the discovery of what it was that made them plausible, would be a benefit to truth. I had, in consequence, marked this out as a sphere of usefulness in which I was under a special obligation to make myself active; the more so, as the acquaintance I had formed with the ideas of the Coleridgians, of the German thinkers, and of Carlyle, all of them fiercely opposed to the mode of thought in which I had been brought up, had convinced me that along with much error they possessed much truth, which was veiled from minds otherwise capable of receiving it by the transcendental and mystical phraseology in which they were accustomed to shut it up, and from which they neither cared, nor knew how, to disengage it; and I did not despair of separating the truth from the error, and exposing it in terms which would be intelligible and not repulsive to those on my own side in philosophy. Thus prepared, it will easily be believed that when I came into close intellectual communion with a person of the most eminent faculties, whose genius, as it grew and unfolded itself in thought, continually struck out truths far in advance of me, but in which I could not, as I had done in those others, detect any mixture of error, the greatest part of my mental growth consisted in the assimilation of those truths, and the most valuable part of my intellectual work was in building the bridges and clearing the paths which connected them with my general system of thought.[4]

The first of my books in which her share was conspicious was the *Principles of Political Economy*. The *System of Logic* owed little to her except in the minuter matters of composition, in which respect my writings, both great and small, have largely benefited by her accurate and clear-sighted criticism.[5] The chapter of the *Political Econonomy* which has had a greater influence on opinion than all the rest, that on 'the Probable Future of the Labouring Classes,' is entirely due to her; in the first draft of the book, that chapter did not exist. She pointed out the need of such a chapter, and the extreme imperfection of the book without it; she was the cause of my writing it; and the more general part of the chapter, the statement and discussion of the two opposite theories respecting the proper condition of the labouring classes, was wholly an exposition of her thoughts, often in words taken from her own lips. The purely scientific part of the *Political Economy* I did not learn from her; but it was chiefly her influence that gave to the book that general tone by which it is distinguished from all previous expositions of Political Economy that had any pretension to being scientific, and which has made it so useful in conciliating minds which those previous expositions had repelled. This tone consisted chiefly in making the proper distinction between the laws of the Production of Wealth—which are laws of nature, dependent on the properties of objects—and the modes of its Distribution, which, subject to certain conditions, depend on human will. The commom run of political economists confuse these together, under the designation of economic laws, which they deem incapable of being defeated or modified by human effort; ascribing the same necessity to things dependent on the unchangeable conditions of our earthly existence, and to those which, being but the necessary consequences of particular social arrangements, are merely co-extensive with these; given certain institutions and customs, wages, profits, and rent will be determined by certain causes; but this class of political economists drop the indispensable presupposition, and argue that these causes must, by an inherent necessity, against which no human means can avail, determine the shares which fall, in the division of the produce, to labourers, capitalists, and landlords. The *Principles of Political Economy* yielded to none of its predecessors in aiming at the scientific appreciation of the action of these causes, under the conditions which they presuppose; but it set the example of not treating those conditions as final. The economic generalizations which depend not on necessaties of nature but on those combined with the existing arrangements of society, it deals with only as provisional, and as liable to be much altered by the progress of social improvement. I had indeed partially learnt this view of things from the thoughts awakened in me by the speculations of the St. Simonians; but it was made a living principle pervading and animating the book by my wife's promptings. This example illustrates well the general character of what she contributed to my writings. What was abstract and purely scientific was generally mine; the properly human element came from her: in all that concerned the application of philosophy to the exigencies of human society and progress, I was her pupil, alike in boldness of speculation and cautiousness of practical judgment. For, on the one hand, she was much more courageous and far-sighted than without her I should have been, in anticipation of an order of things to come, in which many of the limited generalizations now so often confounded with universal principles will cease to be applicable. Those parts of my writings, and especially of the *Political Economy*, which contemplate possibilities in the future such as, when affirmed by Socialists, have in general been fiercely denied by political economists, would, but for her, either have been absent, or the suggestions would have been made much more timidly and in a more qualified form. But while she thus rendered me bolder in speculation on human affairs, her practical turn of mind, and her almost unerring estimate of practical obstacles, repressed in me all tendencies that were really visionary. Her mind invested all ideas in a concrete shape, and formed to itself a conception of how they would actually work: and her knowledge of the existing feelings and conduct of mankind was so seldom at fault, that the weak point in any unworkable suggestion seldom escapes her.[6]

During the two years which immediately preceded the cessation of my official life, my wife and I were working together at the "Liberty." I had first planned and written it as a short essay in 1854. It was in mounting the steps of the Capitol, in January, 1855, that the thought first arose of converting it into a volume. None of my writings have been either so carefully composed, or so sedulously corrected as this. After it had been written as usual twice over, we kept it by us, bringing it out from time to time, and going through it *de novo*, reading, weighing, and criticizing every sentence. Its final revision was to have been a work of the winter of 1858-9, the first after my retirement, which we had arranged to pass in the south of Europe. That hope and every other were frustrated by the most unexpected and bitter calamity of her death—at Avignon, on our way to Montpellier, from a sudden attack of pulmonary congestion.

Since then I have sought for such alleviation as my state admitted of, by the mode of life which most enabled me to feel her still near me. I bought a cottage as close as possible to the place where she is buried, and there her daughter (my fellow-sufferer and now my chief comfort) and I, live constantly during a great portion of the year. My objects in life are solely those which were hers; my pursuits and occupations those in which she shared, or sympathized, and which are indissolubly associated with her. Her memory is to me a religion, and her approbation the standard by which, summing up as it does all worthiness, I endeavour to regulate my life.

After my irreparable loss, one of my earliest cares was to print and publish the treatise, so much of which was the work of her whom I had lost, and consecrate it to her memory. I have made no alteration or addition to it, nor shall I ever. Though it wants the last touch of her hand, no substitute for that touch shall ever be attempted by mine.

The *Liberty* was more directly and literally our joint production than anything else which bears my name, for there was not a sentence of it that was not several times gone through by us together, turned over in many ways, and carefully weeded of any faults, either in thought or expression, that we detected in it. It is in consequence of this that, although it never underwent her final revision, it far surpasses, as a mere specimen of composition, anything which has proceeded from me either before or since. With regard to the thoughts, it is difficult to identify any particular part or element as being more hers than all the rest. The whole mode of thinking of which the book was the expression, was emphatically hers. But I also was so thoroughly imbued with it, that the same thoughts naturally occurred to us both. That I was thus penetrated with it, however, I owe in a great degree to her. There was a moment in my mental progress when I might easily have fallen into a tendency towards over-government, both social and political; as there was also a moment when, by reaction from a contrary excess, I might have become a less thorough radical and democrat than I am. In both these points, as in many others, she benefited me as much by keeping me right where I was right, as by leading me to new truths, and ridding me of errors. My great readiness and eagerness to learn from everybody, and to make room in my opinions for every new acquisition by adjusting the old and the new to one another, might, but for her steadying influence, have seduced me into modifying my early opinions too much. She was in nothing more valuable to my mental development than by her just measure of the relative importance of different considerations, which often protected me from allowing to truths I had only recently learnt to see, a more important place in my thoughts than was properly their due.

The *Liberty* is likely to survive longer than anything else that I have written (with the possible exception of the *Logic*), because the conjunction of her mind with mine has rendered it a kind of philosophic text-book of a single truth, which the changes progressively taking place in modern society tend to bring out into ever stronger relief: the importance, to man and society of a large variety in types of character, and of giving full freedom to human nature to expand itself in innumerable and conflicting directions. Nothing can better show how deep are the foundations of this truth, than the great impression made by the exposition of it at a time which, to superficial observation, did not seem to stand much in need of such a lesson. The fears we expressed, lest the inevitable growth of social equality and of the government of public opinion, should impose on mankind an oppressive yoke of uniformity in opinion and practice, might easily have appeared chimerical to those who looked more at present facts than at tendencies; for the gradual revolution that is taking place in society and institutions has, thus far, been decidedly favourable to the development of new opinions, and has procured for them a much more unprejudiced hearing than they previously met with. But this is a feature belonging to periods of transition, when old notions and feelings have been unsettled, and no new doctrines have yet succeeded to their ascendancy. At such times people of any mental activity, having given up their old beliefs, and not feeling quite sure that those they still retain can stand unmodified, listen eagerly to new opinions. But this state of things is necessarily transitory: some particular body of doctrine in time rallies the majority round it, organizes social institutions and modes of action conformably to itself, education impresses this new creed upon the new generations without the mental processes that have led to it, and by degrees it acquires the very same power of compression, so long exercised by the creeds of which it had taken the place. Whether this noxious power will be exercised, depends on whether mankind have by that time become aware that it cannot be exercised without stunting and dwarfing human nature. It is then that the teachings of the *Liberty* will have their greatest value. And it is to be feared that they will retain that value a long time.

As regards originality, it has of course no other than that which every thoughtful mind gives to its own mode of conceiving and expressing truths which are common property. The leading thought of the book is one which though in many ages confined to insulated thinkers, mankind have probably at no time since the beginning of civilization been entirely without. To speak only of the last few generations, it is distinctly contained in the vein of important thought respecting education and culture, spread through the European mind by the labours and genius of Pestalozzi. The unqualified championship of it by Wilhelm von Humboldt is referred to in the book; but he by no means stood alone in his own country. During the early part of the present century the doctrine of the rights of individuality, and the claim of the moral nature to develop itself in its own way, was pushed by a whole school of German authors even to exaggeration; and the writings of Goethe, the most celebrated of all German authors, though not belonging to that or to any other school, are penetrated throughout by views of morals and of conduct in life, often in my opinion not defensible, but which are incessantly seeking whatever defence they admit of in the theory of the right and duty of self-development. In our own country before the book *On Liberty* was written, the doctrine of Individuality had been enthusiastically asserted, in a style of vigorous declamation sometimes reminding one of Fichte, by Mr. William Maccall, in a series of writings of which the most elaborate is entitled *Elements of Individualism*: and a remarkable American, Mr. Warren, had framed a System of Society, on the foundation of *the Sovereignty of the individual*, had obtained a number of followers, and had actually commenced the formation of a Village Community (whether it now exists I know not), which, though bearing a superficial resemblance to some of the projects of Socialists, is diametrically opposite to them in principle, since it recognizes no authority whatever in Society over the individual, except to enforce equal freedom of development for all individualities. As the book which bears my name claimed no originality for any of its doctrines, and was not intended to write their history, the only author who had preceded me in their assertion, of whom I thought it appropriate to say anything, was Humboldt, who furnished the motto to the work; although in one passage I borrowed from the Warrenites their phrase, the sovereignty of the individual. It is hardly necessary here to remark that there are abundant differences in detail, between the conception of the doctrine by any of the predecessors I have mentioned, and that set forth in the book.

The political circumstances of the time induced me, shortly after, to complete and publish a pamphlet (*Thoughts on Parliamentary Reform*), part of which had been written some years previously on the occasion of one of the abortive Reform Bills, and had at the time been approved and revised by her. Its principal features were, hostility to the Ballot (a change of opinion in both of us, in which she rather preceded me), and a claim of representation for minorities; not, however, at that time going beyond the cumulative vote proposed by Mr. Garth Marshall. In finishing the pamphlet for publication, with a view to the discussions on the Reform Bill of Lord Derby's and Mr. Disraeli's Government in 1859, I added a third feature, a plurality of votes, to be given, not to property, but to proved superiority of education. This recommended itself to me as a means of reconciling the irresistible claim of every man or woman to be consulted, and to be allowed a voice, in the regulation of affairs which vitally concern them, with the superiority of weight justly due to opinions grounded on superiority of knowledge. The suggestion, however, was one which I had never discussed with my almost infallible counsellor, and I have no evidence that she would have concurred in it. As far as I have been able to observe, it has found favour with nobody; all who desire any sort of inequality in the electoral vote, desiring it in favour of property and not of intelligence or knowledge. If it ever overcomes the strong feeling which exists against it, this will only be after the establishment of a systematic National Education by which the various grades of politically valuable acquirement may be accurately defined and authenticated. Without this it will always remain liable to strong, possibly conclusive, objections; and with this, it would perhaps not be needed.

It was soon after the publication of *Thoughts on Parliamentary Reform*, that I became acquainted with Mr. Hare's admirable system of Personal Representation, which, in its present shape, was then for the first time published. I saw in this great practical and philosophical idea, the greatest improvement of which the system of representative government is susceptible; an improvement which, in the most felicitous manner, exactly meets and cures the grand, and what before seemed the inherent, defect of the representative system; that of giving to a numerical majority all power, instead of only a power proportional to its numbers, and enabling the strongest party to exclude all weaker parties from making their opinions heard in the assembly of the nation, except through such opportunity as may be given to them by the accidentally unequal distribution of opinions in different localities. To these great evils nothing more than very imperfect palliations had seemed possible; but Mr. Hare's system affords a radical cure. This great discovery, for it is no less, in the political art, inspired me, as I believe it has inspired all thoughtful persons who have adopted it, with new and more sanguine hopes respecting the prospects of human society; by freeing the form of political institutions towards which the whole civilized world is manifestly and irresistibly tending, from the chief part of what seemed to qualify, or render doubtful, its ultimate benefits. Minorities, so long as they remain minorities, are, and ought to be, outvoted; but under arrangements which enable any assemblage of voters, amounting to a certain number, to place in the legislature a representative of its own choice, minorities cannot be suppressed. Independent opinions will force their way into the council of the nation and make themselves heard there, a thing which often cannot happen in the existing forms of representative democracy; and the legislature, instead of being weeded of individual peculiarities and entirely made up of men who simply represent the creed of great political or religious parties, will comprise a large proportion of the most eminent individual minds in the country, placed there, without reference to party, by voters who appreciate their individual eminence. I can understand that persons, otherwise intelligent, should, for want of sufficient examination, be repelled from Mr. Hare's plan by what they think the complex nature of its machinery. But any one who does not feel the want which the scheme is intended to supply; any one who throws it over as a mere theoretical subtlety or crotchet, tending to no valuable purpose, and unworthy of the attention of practical men, may be pronounced an incompetent statesman, unequal to the politics of the future. I mean, unless he is a minister or aspires to become one: for we are quite accustomed to a minister continuing to profess unqualified hostility to an improvement almost to the very day when his conscience or his interest induces him to take it up as a public measure, and carry it.

Had I met with Mr. Hare's system before the publication of my pamphlet, I should have given an account of it there. Not having done so, I wrote an article in *Fraser's Magazine* (reprinted in my miscellaneous writings) principally for that purpose, though I included in it, along with Mr. Hare's book, a review of two other productions on the question of the day; one of them a pamphlet by my early friend, Mr. John Austin, who had in his old age become an enemy to all further Parliamentary reform; the other an able and vigourous, though partially erroneous, work by Mr. Lorimer.

In the course of the same summer I fulfilled a duty particularly incumbent upon me, that of helping (by an article in the *Edinburgh Review*) to make known Mr. Bain's profound treatise on the Mind, just then completed by the publication of its second volume. And I carried through the press a selection of my minor writings, forming the first two volumes of *Dissertations and Discussions*. The selection had been made during my wife's lifetime, but the revision, in concert with her, with a view to republication, had been barely commenced; and when I had no longer the guidance of her judgment I despaired of pursuing it further, and republished the papers as they were, with the exception of striking out such passages as were no longer in accordance with my opinions. My literary work of the year was terminated with an essay in *Fraser's Magazine* (afterwards republished in the third volume of *Dissertations and Discussions*), entitled "A Few Words on Non-Intervention." I was prompted to write this paper by a desire, while vindicating England from the imputations commonly brought against her on the Continent, of a peculiar selfishness in matters of foreign policy to warn Englishmen of the colour given to this imputation by the low tone in which English statesmen are accustomed to speak of English policy as concerned only with English interests, and by the conduct of Lord Palmerston at that particular time in opposing the Suez Canal; and I took the opportunity of expressing ideas which had long been in my mind (some of them generated by my Indian experience, and others by the international questions which then greatly occupied the European public), respecting the true principles of international morality, and the legitimate modifications made in it by difference of times and circumstances; a subject I had already, to some extent, discussed in the vindication of the French Provisional Government of 1848 against the attacks of Lord Brougham and others, which I published at the time in the *Westminster Review*, and which is reprinted in the *Dissertations*.

I had now settled, as I believed, for the remainder of my existence into a purely literary life; if that can be called literary which continued to be occupied in a pre-eminent degree with politics, and not merely with theoretical, but practical politics, although a great part of the year was spent at a distance of many hundred miles from the chief seat of the politics of my own country, to which, and primarily for which, I wrote. But, in truth, the modern facilities of communication have not only removed all the disadvantages, to a political writer in tolerably easy circumstances, of distance from the scene of political action, but have converted them into advantages. The immediate and regular receipt of newspapers and periodicals keeps him *au courant* of even the most temporary politics, and gives him a much more correct view of the state and progress of opinion than he could acquire by personal contact with

individuals: for every one's social intercourse is more or less limited to particular sets or classes, whose impressions and no others
reach him through that channel; and experience has taught me that
those who give their time to the absorbing claims of what is called
society, not having leisure to keep up a large acquaintance with
the organs of opinion, remain much more ignorant of the general
state either of the public mind, or of the active and instructed part
of it, than a recluse who reads the newspapers need be. There
are, no doubt, disadvantages in too long a separation from one's
country—in not occasionally renewing one's impressions of the
light in which men and things appear when seen from a position
in the midst of them; but the deliberate judgment formed at a distance, and undisturbed by inequalities of perspective, is the most
to be depended on, even for application to practice. Alternating
between the two positions, I combined the advantages of both. And,
though the inspirer of my best thoughts was no longer with me,
I was not alone: she had left a daughter, my stepdaughter, [Miss
Helen Taylor, the inheritor of much of her wisdom, and of all her
nobleness of character,] whose ever growing and ripening talents
from that day to this have been devoted to the same great purposes
[and have already made her name better and more widely known
than was that of her mother, though far less so than I predict, that
if she lives it is destined to become. Of the value of her direct co-
operation with me, something will be said hereafter, of what I owe
in the way of instruction to her great powers of original thought
and soundness of practical judgment, it would be a vain attempt to
give an adequate idea]. Surely no one ever before was so fortunate,
as, after such a loss as mine, to draw another prize in the lottery of
life [—another companion, stimulator, adviser, and instructor of
the rarest quality]. Whoever, either now or hereafter, may think
of me and of the work I have done, must never forget that it is the
product not of one intellect and conscience, but of three[, the least
considerable of whom, and above all the least original, is the one
whose name is attached to it].

The work of the years 1860 and 1861 consisted chiefly of two treatises, only one of which was intended for immediate publication. This was the *Considerations on Representative Government*; a connected exposition of what, by the thoughts of many years, I had come to regard as the best form of a popular constitution. Along with as much of the general theory of government as is necessary to support this particular portion of its practice, the volume contains many matured views of the principal questions which occupy the present age, within the province of purely organic institutions, and raises, by anticipation, some other questions to which growing necessities will sooner or later compel the attention both of theoretical and of practical politicians. The chief of these last, is the distinction between the function of making laws, for which a numerous popular assembly is radically unfit, and that of getting good laws made, which is its proper duty and cannot be satisfactorily fulfilled by any other authority: and the consequent need of a Legislative Commission, as a permanent part of the constitution of a free country; consisting of a small number of highly trained political minds, on whom, when Parliament has determined that a law shall be made, the task of making it should be devolved: Parliament retaining the power of passing or rejecting the bill when drawn up, but not of altering it otherwise than by sending proposed amendments to be dealt with by the Commission. The question here raised respecting the most important of all public functions, that of legislation, is a particular case of the great problem of modern political organization, stated, I believe, for the first time in its full extent by Bentham, though in my opinion not always satisfactorily resolved by him; the combination of complete popular control over public affairs, with the greatest attainable perfection of skilled agency.

The other treatise written at this time is the one which was published some years[7] later under the title of *The Subjection of Women*. It was written [at my daughter's suggestion] that there might, in any event, be in existence a written exposition of my opinions on that great question, as full and conclusive as I could make it. The intention was to keep this among other unpublished papers, improving it from time to time if I was able, and to publish it at the time when it should seem likely to be most useful. As ultimately published [it was enriched with some important ideas of my daughter's, and passages of her writing. But] in what was of my own composition, all that is most striking and profound belongs to my wife; coming from the fund of thought which had been made common to us both, by our innumerable conversations and discussions on a topic which filled so large a place in our minds.

Soon after this time I took from their repository a portion of the unpublished papers which I had written during the last years of our married life, and shaped them, with some additional matter, into the little work entitled *Utilitarianism*; which was first published, in three parts, in successive numbers of *Fraser's Magazine*, and afterwards reprinted in a volume.

Before this, however, the state of public affairs had become extremely critical, by the commencement of the American civil war. My strongest feelings were engaged in this struggle, which, I felt from the beginning, was destined to be a turning point, for good or evil, of the course of human affairs for an indefinite duration. Having been a deeply interested observer of the slavery quarrel in America, during the many years that preceded the open breach, I knew that it was in all its stages an aggressive enterprise of the slave-owners to extend the territory of slavery; under the combined influences of pecuniary interest, domineering temper, and the fanaticism of a class for its class privileges, influences so fully and powerfully depicted in the admirable work of my friend Professor Cairnes, *The Slave Power*. Their success, if they succeeded, would be a victory of the powers of evil which would give courage to the enemies of progress and damp the spirits of its friends all over the civilized world, while it would create a formidable military power, grounded on the worst and most anti-social form of the tyranny of men over men, and, by destroying for a long time the prestige of the great democratic republic, would give to all the privileged classes of Europe a false confidence, probably only to be extinguished in blood. On the other hand, if the spirit of the North was sufficiently roused to carry the war to a successful termination, and if that termination did not come too soon and too easily, I foresaw, from the laws of human nature, and the experience of revolutions, that when it did come it would in all probability be thorough: that the bulk of the Northern population, whose conscience had as yet been awakened only to the point of resisting the further extension of slavery, but whose fidelity to the Constitution of the United States made them disapprove of any attempt by the Federal Government to interfere with slavery in the States where it already existed, would acquire feelings of another kind when the Constitution had been shaken off by armed rebellion, would determine to have done for ever with the accursed thing, and would join their banner with that of the noble body of Abolitionists, of whom Garrison was the courageous and single-minded apostle, Wendell Phillips the eloquent orator, and John Brown the voluntary martyr.[8] Then, too, the whole mind of the United States would be let loose from its bonds, no longer corrupted by the supposed necessity of apologizing to foreigners for the most flagrant of all possible violations of the free principles of their Constitution; while the tendency of a fixed state of society to stereotype a set of national opinions would be at least temporarily checked, and the national mind would become more open to the recognition of whatever was bad in either the institutions or the customs of the people. These hopes, so far as related to slavery, have been completely, and in other respects are in course of being progressively realized. Foreseeing from the first this double set of consequences from the success or failure of the rebellion, it may be imagined with what feelings I contemplated the rush of nearly the whole upper and middle classes of my own country even those who passed for Liberals, into a furious pro-Southern partisanship: the working classes, and some of the literary and scientific men, being almost the sole exceptions to the general frenzy. I never before felt so keenly how little permanent improvement had reached the minds of our influential classes, and of what small value were the liberal opinions they had got into the habit of professing. None of the

Continental Liberals committed the same frightful mistake. But the generation which had extorted negro emancipation from our West India planters had passed away; another had succeeded which had not learnt by many years of discussion and exposure to feel strongly the enormities of slavery; and the inattention habitual with Englishmen to whatever is going on in the world outside their own island, made them profoundly ignorant of all the antecedents of the struggle, insomuch that it was not generally believed in England, for the first year or two of the war, that the quarrel was one of slavery. There were men of high principle and unquestionable liberality of opinion, who thought it a dispute about tariffs, or assimilated it to the cases in which they were accustomed to sympathize, of a people struggling for independence.

It was my obvious duty to be one of the small minority who protested against this perverted state of public opinion. I was not the first to protest. It ought to be remembered to the honour of Mr. Hughes and of Mr. Ludlow, that they, by writings published at the very beginning of the struggle, began the protestation. Mr. Bright followed in one of the most powerful of his speeches, followed by others not less striking. I was on the point of adding my words to theirs, when there occurred, towards the end of 1861, the seizure of the Southern envoys on board a British vessel, by an officer of the United States. Even English forgetfulness has not yet had time to lose all remembrance of the explosion of feeling in England which then burst forth, the expectation, prevailing for some weeks, of war with the United States, and the warlike preparations actually commenced on this side. While this state of things lasted, there was no chance of a hearing for anything favourable to the American cause; and, moreover, I agreed with those who thought the act unjustifiable, and such as to require that England should demand its disavowal. When the disavowal came, and the alarm of war was over, I wrote, in January, 1862, the paper, in *Fraser's Magazine*, entitled "The Contest in America," [and I shall always feel grateful to my daughter that her urgency prevailed on me to write it when I did, for we were then on the point of setting out for a journey

167

of some months in Greece and Turkey, and but for her, I should have deferred writing till our return.] Written and published when it was, this paper helped to encourage those Liberals who had felt overborne by the tide of illiberal opinion, and to form in favour of the good cause a nucleus of opinion which increased gradually, and, after the success of the North began to seem probable, rapidly. When we returned from our journey I wrote a second article, a review of Professor Cairnes' book, published in the *Westminster Review*. England is paying the penalty, in many uncomfortable ways, of the durable resentment which her ruling classes stirred up in the United States by their ostentatious wishes for the ruin of America as a nation; they have reason to be thankful that a few, if only a few, known writers and speakers, standing firmly by the Americans in the time of their greatest difficulty, effected a partial diversion of these bitter feelings, and made Great Britain not altogether odious to the Americans.

This duty having been performed, my principal occupation for the next two years was on subjects not political. The publication of Mr. Austin's *Lectures on Jurisprudence* after his decease, gave me an opportunity of paying a deserved tribute to his memory, and at the same time expressing some thoughts on a subject on which, in my old days of Benthamism, I had bestowed much study. But the chief product of those years was the *Examination of Sir William Hamilton's Philosophy*. His *Lectures*, published in 1860 and 1861, I had read towards the end of the latter year, with a half-formed intention of giving an account of them in a Review, but I soon found that this would be idle, and that justice could not be done to the subject in less than a volume. I had then to consider whether it would be advisable that I myself should attempt such a performance. On consideration, there seemed to be strong reasons for doing so. I was greatly disappointed with the *Lectures*. I read them, certainly, with no prejudice against Sir William Hamilton. I had up to that time deferred the study of his *Notes to Reid* on account of their unfinished state, but I had not neglected his *Discussions in Philosophy*; and though I knew that his general mode of treating the facts of mental philosophy differed from that of which I most approved, yet his vigorous polemic against the later Transcendentalists, and his strenuous assertion of some important principles, especially the Relativity of human knowledge, gave me many points of sympathy with his opinions, and made me think that genuine psychology had considerably more to gain than to lose by his authority and reputation. His *Lectures* and the *Dissertations on Reid* dispelled this illusion: and even the *Discussions*, read by the light which these throw on them, lost much of their value. I found that the points of apparent agreement between his opinions and mine were more verbal than real; that the important philosophical principles which I had thought he recognised, were so explained away by him as to mean little or nothing, or were continually lost sight of, and doctrines entirely inconsistent with them were taught in nearly every part of his philosophical writings. My estimation of him was therefore so far altered, that instead of regarding him as occupying a kind of intermediate position between the two rival philosophies, holding some of the principles of both, and supplying to both powerful weapons of attack and defence, I now looked upon him as one of the pillars, and in this country from his high philosophical reputation the chief pillar, of that one of the two which seemed to me to be erroneous.

Now, the difference between these two schools of philosophy, that of Intuition, and that of Experience and Association, is not a mere matter of abstract speculation; it is full of practical consequences, and lies at the foundation of all the greatest differences of practical opinion in an age of progress. The practical reformer has continually to demand that changes be made in things which are supported by powerful and widely-spread feelings, or to question the apparent necessity and indefeasibleness of established facts; and it is often an indispensable part of his argument to show, how those powerful feelings had their origin, and how those facts came to seem necessary and indefeasible. There is therefore a natural hostility between him and a philosophy which discourages the explanation of feelings and moral facts by circumstances and association, and prefers to treat them as ultimate elements of human nature; a philosophy which is addicted to holding up favourite doctrines as intuitive truths, and deems intuition to be the voice of Nature and of God, speaking with an authority higher than that of our reason. In particular, I have long felt that the prevailing tendency to regard all the marked distinctions of human character as innate, and in the main indelible, and to ignore the irresistible proofs that by far the greater part of those differences, whether between individuals, races, or sexes, are such as not only might but naturally would be produced by differences in circumstances, is one of the chief hindrances to the rational treatment of great social questions, and one of the greatest stumbling blocks to human improvement. This tendency has its source in the intuitional metaphysics which characterized the reaction of the nineteenth century against the eighteenth, and it is a tendency so agreeable to human indolence, as well as to conservative interests generally, that unless attacked at the very root, it is sure to be carried to even a greater length than is really justified by the more moderate forms of the intuitional philosophy. That philosophy not always in its moderate forms, had ruled the thought of Europe for the greater part of a century. My father's *Analysis of the Mind*, my own *Logic*, and Professor Bain's great treatise, had attempted to re-introduce a better mode of philosophizing, latterly with quite as much success as could be expected; but I had for some time felt that the mere contrast of the two philosophies was not enough, that there ought to be a hand-to-hand fight between them, that controversial as well as expository writings were needed, and that the time was come when such controversy would be useful. Considering, then, the writings and fame of Sir W. Hamilton as the great fortress of the intuitional philosophy in this country, a fortress the more formidable from the imposing character, and the in many respects great personal merits and mental endowments, of the man, I thought it might be a real service to philosophy to attempt a thorough examination of all his most important doctrines, and an estimate of his general claims to eminence as a philosopher; and I was confirmed in this resolution by observing that in the writings of at least one, and him one of the ablest, of Sir W. Hamilton's followers, his peculiar doctrines were made the justification of a view of religion which I hold to be profoundly immoral—that it is our duty to bow down in worship before a Being whose moral attributes are affirmed to be unknowable by us, and to be perhaps extremely different from those which, when we are speaking of our fellow-creatures, we call by the same names.

As I advanced in my task, the damage to Sir W. Hamilton's reputation became greater than I at first expected, through the almost incredible multitude of inconsistencies which showed themselves on comparing different passages with one another. It was my business, however, to show things exactly as they were, and I did not flinch from it. I endeavoured always to treat the philosopher whom I criticized with the most scrupulous fairness; and I knew that he had abundance of disciples and admirers to correct me if I ever unintentionally did him injustice. Many of them accordingly have answered me, more or less elaborately, and they have pointed out oversights and misunderstandings, though few in number, and mostly very unimportant in substance. Such of those as had (to my knowledge) been pointed out before the publication of the latest edition (at present the third) have been corrected there, and the remainder of the criticisms have been, as far as seemed necessary, replied to. On the whole, the book has done its work: it has shown the weak side of Sir William Hamilton, and has reduced his too great philosophical reputation within more moderate bounds; and by some of its discussions, as well as by two expository chapters, on the notions of Matter and of Mind, it has perhaps thrown additional light on some of the disputed questions in the domain of psychology and metaphysics.

After the completion of the book on Hamilton, I applied myself to a task which a variety of reasons seemed to render specially incumbent upon me; that of giving an account, and forming an estimate, of the doctrines of Auguste Comte. I had contributed more than any one else to make his speculations known in England,

and, in consequence chiefly of what I had said of him in my *Logic*, he had readers and admirers among thoughtful men on this side of the Channel at a time when his name had not yet in France emerged from obscurity. So unknown and unappreciated was he at the time when my *Logic* was written and published, that to criticize his weak points might well appear superfluous, while it was a duty to give as much publicity as one could to the important contributions he had made to philosophic thought. At the time, however, at which I have now arrived, this state of affairs had entirely changed. His name, at least, was known almost universally, and the general character of his doctrines very widely. He had taken his place in the estimation both of friends and opponents, as one of the conspicuous figures in the thought of the age. The better parts of his speculations had made great progress in working their way into those minds, which, by their previous culture and tendencies, were fitted to receive them: under cover of those better parts those of a worse character, greatly developed and added to in his later writings, had also made some way, having obtained active and enthusiastic adherents, some of them of no inconsiderable personal merit, in England, France, and other countries. These causes not only made it desirable that some one should undertake the task of sifting what is good from what is bad in M. Comte's speculations, but seemed to impose on myself in particular a special obligation to make the attempt. This I accordingly did in two essays, published in successive numbers of the *Westminster Review*, and reprinted in a small volume under the title *Auguste Comte and Positivism*.

The writings which I have now mentioned, together with a small number of papers in periodicals which I have not deemed worth preserving, were the whole of the products of my activity as a writer during the years from 1859 to 1865. In the early part of the last-mentioned year, in compliance with a wish frequently expressed to me by working men, I published cheap People's Editions of those of my writings which seemed the most likely to find readers among the working classes; viz, *Principles of Political Economy*, *Liberty*, and *Representative Government*. This was a considerable sacrifice of my pecuniary interest, especially as I resigned all idea of deriving profit from the cheap editions, and after ascertaining from my publishers the lowest price which they thought would remunerate them on the usual terms of an equal division of profits, I gave up my half share to enable the price to be fixed still lower. To the credit of Messrs. Longman they fixed, unasked, a certain number of years after which the copyright and stereotype plates were to revert to me, and a certain number of copies after the sale of which I should receive half of any further profit. This number of copies (which in the case of the *Political Economy* was 10,000) has for some time been exceeded, and the People's Editions have begun to yield me a small but unexpected pecuniary return, though very far from an equivalent for the diminution of profit from the Library Editions.

In this summary of my outward life I have now arrived at the period at which my tranquil and retired existence as a writer of books was to be exchanged for the less congenial occupation of a member of the House of Commons. The proposal made to me, early in 1865, by some electors of Westminster, did not present the idea to me for the first time. It was not even the first offer I had received, for, more than ten years previous, in consequence of my opinions on the Irish Land Question, Mr. Lucas and Mr. Duffy, in the name of the popular party in Ireland, offered to bring me into Parliament for an Irish county, which they could easily have done: but the incompatibility of a seat in Parliament with the office I then held in the India House, precluded even consideration of the proposal. After I had quitted the India House, several of my friends would gladly have seen me a member of Parliament; but there seemed no probability that the idea would ever take any practical shape. I was convinced that no numerous or influential portion of any electoral body, really wished to be represented by a person of my opinions; and that one who possessed no local connection or popularity, and who did not choose to stand as the mere organ of a party had small chance of being elected anywhere unless through the expenditure of money. Now it was, and is, my fixed conviction, that a candidate ought not to incur one farthing of expense for undertaking a public duty. Such of the lawful expenses of an election as have no special reference to any particular candidate, ought to be borne as a public charge, either by the State or by the locality. What has to be done by the supporters of each candidate in order to bring his claims properly before the constituency, should be done by unpaid agency or by voluntary subscription. If members of the electoral body, or others, are willing to subscribe money of their own for the purpose of bringing, by lawful means, into Parliament some one who they think would be useful there, no one is entitled to object: but that the expense, or any part of it, should fall on the candidate, is fundamentally wrong; because it amounts in reality to buying his seat. Even on the most favourable supposition as to the mode in which the money is expended, there is a legitimate suspicion that any one who gives money for leave to undertake a public trust, has other than public ends to promote by it; and (a consideration of the greatest importance) the cost of elections, when borne by the candidates, deprives the nation of the services, as members of Parliament, of all who cannot or will not afford to incur a heavy expense. I do not say that, so long as there is scarcely a chance for an independent candidate to come into Parliament without complying with this vicious practice, it must always be morally wrong in him to spend money, provided that no part of it is either directly or indirectly employed in corruption. But, to justify it, he ought to be very certain that he can be of more use to his country as a member of Parliament than in any other mode which is open to him; and this assurance, in my own case, I did not feel. It was by no means clear to me that I could do more to advance the public objects which had a claim on my exertions, from the benches of the House of Commons, than from the simple position of a writer. I felt, therefore, that I ought not to seek election to Parliament, much less to expend any money in procuring it.

But the conditions of the question were considerably altered when a body of electors sought me out, and spontaneously offered to bring me forward as their candidate. If it should appear, on explanation, that they persisted in this wish, knowing my opinions, and accepting the only conditions on which I could conscientiously serve, it was questionable whether this was not one of those calls upon a member of the community by his fellow-citizens, which he was scarcely justified in rejecting. I therefore put their disposition to the proof by one of the frankest explanations ever tendered, I should think, to an electoral body by a candidate. I wrote, in reply to the offer, a letter for publication, saying that I had no personal wish to be a member of Parliament, that I thought a candidate ought neither to canvass nor to incur any expense, and that I could not consent to do either. I said further, that if elected, I could not undertake to give any of my time and labour to their local interests. With respect to general politics, I told them without reserve, what I thought on a number of important subjects on which they had asked my opinion: and one of these being the suffrage, I made known to them, among other things, my conviction (as I was bound to do, since I intended, if elected, to act on it), that women were entitled to representation in Parliament on the same terms with men. It was the first time, doubtless, that such a doctrine had ever been mentioned to English electors; and the fact that I was elected after proposing it, gave the start to the movement which has since become so vigorous, in favour of women's suffrage. Nothing, at the time, appeared more unlikely than that a candidate (if candidate I could be called) whose professions and conduct set so completely at defiance all ordinary notions of electioneering, should nevertheless be elected. A well-known literary man[, who was also a man of society,] was heard to say that the Almighty himself would have no chance of being elected on such a programme. I strictly adhered to it, neither spending money nor canvassing, nor did I take any personal part in the election, until about a week preceding the day of nomination, when I attended a few public meetings to state my principles and give to any questions which the electors might exercise their just right of putting to me for their own guidance; answers as plain and unreserved as my address. On one subject only, my religious opinions, I announced from the beginning that

I would answer no questions; a determination which appeared to be completely approved by those who attended the meetings. My frankness on all other subjects on which I was interrogated, evidently did me far more good than my answers, whatever they might be, did harm. Among the proofs I received of this, one is too remarkable not to be recorded. In the pamphlet, *Thoughts on Parliamentary Reform*, I had said, rather bluntly, that the working classes, though differing from those of some other countries, in being ashamed of lying, are yet generally liars. This passage some opponent got printed in a placard, which was handed to me at a meeting, chiefly composed of the working classes, and I was asked whether I had written and published it. I at once answered "I did." Scarcely were these two words out of my mouth, when vehement applause resounded through the whole meeting. It was evident that the working people were so accustomed to expect equivocation and evasion from those who sought their suffrages, that when they found, instead of that, a direct avowal of what was likely to be disagreeable to them, instead of being affronted, they concluded at once that this was a person whom they could trust. A more striking instance never came under my notice of what, I believe, is the experience of those who best know the working classes, that the most essential of all recommendations to their favour is that of complete straightforwardness; its presence outweighs in their minds very strong objections, while no amount of other qualities will make amends for its apparent absence. The first working man who spoke after the incident I have mentioned (it was Mr. Odger) said, that the working classes had no desire not to be told of their faults; they wanted friends, not flatterers, and felt under obligation to any one who told them anything in themselves which he sincerely believed to require amendment. And to this the meeting heartily responded.

Had I been defeated in the election, I should still have had no reason to regret the contact it had brought me into with large bodies of my countrymen; which not only gave me much new experience, but enabled me to scatter my political opinions rather widely, and, by making me known in many quarters where I had never before been heard of, increased the number of my readers, and the presumable influence of my writings. These latter effects were of course produced in a still greater degree, when, as much to my surprise as to that of any one, I was returned to Parliament by a majority of some hundreds over my Conservative competitor.

I was a member of the House during the three sessions of the Parliament which passed the Reform Bill; during which time Parliament was necessarily my main occupation, except during the recess. I was a tolerably frequent speaker, sometimes of prepared speeches, sometimes extemporaneously. But my choice of occasions was not such as I should have made if my leading object had been Parliamentary influence. When I had gained the ear of the House, which I did by a successful speech on Mr. Gladstone's Reform Bill, the idea I proceeded on was that when anything was likely to be as well done, or sufficiently well done, by other people, there was no necessity for me to meddle with it. As I, therefore, in general reserved myself for work which no others were likely to do, a great proportion of my appearances were on points on which the bulk of the Liberal party, even the advanced portion of it, either were of a different opinion from mine, or were comparatively indifferent. Several of my speeches, especially one against the motion for the abolition of capital punishment, and another in favour of resuming the right of seizing enemies' goods in neutral vessels, were opposed to what then was, and probably still is, regarded as the advanced liberal opinion. My advocacy of women's suffrage and of Personal Representation, were at the time looked upon by many as whims of my own; but the great progress since made by those opinions, and especially the response made from almost all parts of the kingdom to the demand for women's suffrage, fully justified the timeliness of those movements, and have made what was undertaken as a moral and social duty, a personal success. Another duty which was particularly incumbent on me as one of the Metropolitan Members, was the attempt to obtain a Municipal Government for the Metropolis: but on that subject the indifference of the House of

Commons was such that I found hardly any help or support within its walls. On this subject, however, I was the organ of an active and intelligent body of persons outside, with whom, and not with me, the scheme originated, and who carried on all the agitation on the subject and drew up the Bills. My part was to bring in Bills already prepared, and to sustain the discussion of them during the short time they were allowed to remain before the House; after having taken an active part in the work of a Committee presided over by Mr. Ayrton, which sat through the greater part of the Session of 1866, to take evidence on the subject. The very different position in which the question now stands (1870) may justly be attributed to the preparation which went on during those years, and which produced but little visible effect at the time; but all questions on which there are strong private interests on one side, and only the public good on the other, have a similar period of incubation to go through.

The same idea, that the use of my being in Parliament was to do work which others were not able or not willing to do, made me think it my duty to come to the front in defence of advanced Liberalism on occasions when the obloquy to be encountered was such as most of the advanced Liberals in the House, preferred not to incur. My first vote in the House was in support of an amendment in favour of Ireland, moved by an Irish member, and for which only five English and Scotch votes were given, including my own: the other four were Mr. Bright, Mr. McLaren, Mr. T.B. Potter, and Mr. Hadfield. And the second speech I delivered[9] was on the bill to prolong the suspension of the Habeas Corpus in Ireland. In denouncing, on this occasion, the English mode of governing Ireland, I did no more than the general opinion of England now admits to have been just; but the anger against Fenianism was then in all its freshness; any attack on what Fenians attacked was looked upon as an apology for them; and I was so unfavourably received by the House, that more than one of my friends advised me (and my own judgment agreed with the advice) to wait, before speaking again, for the favourable opportunity that would be given by the first great debate on the Reform Bill. During this silence, many flattered themselves that I had turned out a failure, and that they should not be troubled with me any more. Perhaps their uncomplimentary comments may, by the force of reaction, have helped to make my speech on the Reform Bill the success it was. My position in the House was further improved by a speech in which I insisted on the duty of paying off the National Debt before our coal supplies are exhausted, and by an ironical reply to some of the Tory leaders who had quoted against me certain passages of my writings, and called me to account for others, especially for one in my *Considerations on Representative Government*, which said that the Conservative party was, by the law of its composition, the stupidest party. They gained nothing by drawing attention to the passage, which up to that time had not excited any notice, but the *sobriquet* of "the stupid party" stuck to them for a considerable time afterwards. Having now no longer any apprehension of not being listened to, I confined myself, as I have since thought too much, to occasions on which my services seemed specially needed, and abstained more than enough from speaking on the great party questions. With the exception of Irish questions, and those which concerned the working classes, a single speech on Mr. Disraeli's Reform Bill was nearly all that I contributed to the great decisive debates of the last two of my three sessions.

I have, however, much satisfaction in looking back to the part I took on the two classes of subjects just mentioned. With regard to the working classes, the chief topic of my speech on Mr. Gladstone's Reform Bill was the assertion of their claims to the suffrage. A little later, after the resignation of Lord Russell's Ministry and the succession of a Tory Government, came the attempt of the working classes to hold a meeting in Hyde Park, their exclusion by the police, and the breaking down of the park railing by the crowd. Though Mr. Beales and the leaders of the working men had retired under protest before this took place, a scuffle ensued in which many innocent persons were maltreated by the police, and the exasperation of the working men was extreme. They showed a determination to make another attempt at a meeting in the Park, to which many of them would probably have come armed; the Government made military preparations to resist the attempt, and something very serious seemed impending. At this crisis I really believe that I was the means of preventing much mischief. I had in my place in Parliament taken the side of the working men, and strongly censured the conduct of the Government. I was invited, with several other Radical members, to a conference with the leading members of the Council of the Reform League; and the task fell chiefly upon myself, of persuading them to give up the Hyde Park project, and hold their meeting elsewhere. It was not Mr. Beales and Colonel Dickson who needed persuading; on the contrary, it was evident that these gentlemen had already exerted their influence in the same direction, thus far without success. It was the working men who held out, and so bent were they on their original scheme, that I was obliged to have recourse to *les grands moyens*. I told them that a proceeding which would certainly produce a collision with the military, could only be justifiable on two conditions: if the position of affairs had become such that a revolution was desirable, and if they thought themselves able to accomplish one. To this argument, after considerable discussion, they at last yielded: and I was able to inform Mr. Walpole that their intention was given up. I shall never forget the depth of his relief or the warmth of his expressions of gratitude. After the working men had conceded so much to me, I felt bound to comply with their request that I would attend and speak at their meeting at the Agricultural Hall; the only meeting called by the Reform League which I ever attended. I had always declined being a member of the League, on the avowed ground that I did not agree in its programme of manhood suffrage and the ballot: from the ballot I dissented entirely; and I could not consent to hoist the flag of manhood suffrage, even on the assurance that the exclusion of women was not intended to be implied; since if one goes beyond what can be immediately carried, and professes to take one's stand on a principle, one should go the whole length of the principle. I have entered thus particularly into this matter because my conduct on this occasion gave great displeasure to the Tory and Tory-Liberal press, who have charged me ever since with having shown myself, in the trials of public life, intemperate and passionate. I do not know what they expected from me; but they had reason to be thankful to me if they knew from what I had, in all probability preserved them. And I do not believe it could have been done, at that particular juncture, by any one else. No other person, I believe, had at that moment the necessary influence for restraining the working classes, except Mr. Gladstone and Mr. Bright, neither of whom was available: Mr. Gladstone, for obvious reasons; Mr. Bright because he was out of town.

When, some time later, the Tory Government brought in a bill to prevent public meetings in the Parks, I not only spoke strongly in opposition to it, but formed one of a number of advanced Liberals, who, aided by the very late period of the session, succeeded in defeating the Bill by what is called talking it out. It has not since been renewed.

On Irish affairs also I felt bound to take a decided part. I was one of the foremost in the deputation of Members of Parliament who prevailed on Lord Derby to spare the life of the condemned Fenian insurgent, General Burke. The Church question was so vigorously handled by the leaders of the party, in the session of 1868, as to require no more from me than an emphatic adhesion: but the land question was by no means in so advanced a position; the superstitions of landlordism had up to that time been little challenged, especially in Parliament, and the backward state of the question, so far as concerned the Parliamentary mind, was evidenced by the extremely mild measure brought in by Lord Russell's government in 1866, which nevertheless could not be carried. On that bill I delivered one of my most careful speeches, in which I attempted to lay down some of the principles of the subject, in a manner calculated less to stimulate friends, than to conciliate and convince opponents. The engrossing subject of Parliamentary Reform prevented either this bill, or one of a similar character brought in by Lord Derby's Government, from being carried through. They never got beyond the second reading. Meanwhile the signs of Irish disaffection had become much more decided; the demand for complete separation between the two countries had assumed a menacing aspect, and there were few who did not feel that if there was still any chance of reconciling Ireland to the British connection, it could only be by the adoption of much more thorough reforms in the territorial and social relations of the country, than had yet been contemplated. The time seemed to me to have come when it would be useful to speak out my whole mind; and the result was my pamphlet *England and Ireland*, which was written in the winter of 1867, and published shortly before the commencement of the session of 1868. The leading features of the pamphlet were, on the one hand, an argument to show the undesirableness, for Ireland as well as England, of separation between the countries, and on the other, a proposal for settling the land question by giving to the existing tenants a permanent tenure, at a fixed rent, to be assessed after due inquiry by the State.

The pamphlet was not popular, except in Ireland, as I did not expect it to be. But, if no measure short of that which I proposed would do full justice to Ireland, or afford a prospect of conciliating the mass of the Irish people, the duty of proposing it was imperative; while if, on the other hand, there was any intermediate course which had a claim to a trial, I well knew that to propose something which would be called extreme, was the true way not to impede but to facilitate a more moderate experiment. It is most improbable that a measure conceding so much to the tenantry as Mr. Gladstone's Irish Land Bill, would have been proposed by a Government, or could have been carried through Parliament, unless the British public had been led to perceive that a case might be made, and perhaps a party formed, for a measure considerably stronger. It is the character of the British people, or at least of the higher and middle classes who pass muster for the British people, that to induce them to approve of any change, it is necessary that they should look upon it as a middle course: they think every proposal extreme and violent unless they hear of some other proposal going still farther, upon which their antipathy to extreme views may discharge itself. So it proved in the present instance; my proposal was condemned, but any scheme for Irish Land reform short of mine, came to be thought moderate by comparison. I may observe that the attacks made on my plan usually gave a very incorrect idea of its nature. It was usually discussed as a proposal that the State should buy up the land and become the universal landlord; though in fact it only offered to each individual landlord this as an alternative, if he liked better to sell his estate than to retain it on the new conditions; and I fully anticipated that most landlords would continue to prefer the position of landowners to that of Government annuitants, and would retain their existing relation to their tenants, often on more indulgent terms than the full rents on which the compensation to be given them by Government would have been based. This and many other explanations I gave in a speech on Ireland, in the debate on Mr. Maguire's Resolution, early in the session of 1868. A corrected report of this speech, together with my speech on Mr. Fortescue's Bill, has been published (not by me, but with my permission) in Ireland.

Another public duty, of a most serious kind, it was my lot to have to perform, both in and out of Parliament, during these years. A disturbance in Jamaica, provoked in the first instance by injustice, and exaggerated by rage and panic into a premeditated rebellion, had been the motive or excuse for taking hundreds of innocent lives by military violence, or by sentence of what were called courts-martial, continuing for weeks after the brief disturbance had been put down; with many added atrocities of destruction of property logging women as well as men, and a general display of the brutal recklessness which usually prevails when fire and sword are let loose. The perpetrators of those deeds were defended and applauded in England by the same kind of people who had so long upheld negro slavery: and it seemed at first as if the British nation was about to incur the disgrace of letting pass without even a protest, excesses of authority as revolting as any of those for which, when perpetrated by the instruments of other governments, Englishmen can hardly find terms sufficient to express their abhorrence. After a short time, however, an indignant feeling was roused: a voluntary Association formed itself under the name of the Jamaica Committee, to take such deliberation and action as the case might admit of, and adhesions poured in from all parts of the country. I was abroad at the time, but I sent in my name to the Committee as soon as I heard of it, and took an active part in the proceedings from the time of my return. There was much more at stake than only justice to the negroes, imperative as was that consideration. The question was, whether the British dependencies, and eventually, perhaps, Great Britain itself, were to be under the government of law, or of military licence; whether the lives and persons of British subjects are at the mercy of any two or three officers however raw and inexperienced or reckless and brutal, whom a panic-stricken Governor, or other functionary, may assume the right to constitute into a so-called court-martial. This question could only be decided by an appeal to the tribunals; and such an appeal the Committee determined to make. Their determination led to a change in the chairmanship of the Committee, as the chairman, Mr. Charles Buxton, thought it not unjust indeed, but inexpedient, to prosecute Governor Eyre and his principal subordinates in a criminal court: but a numerously attended general meeting of the Association having decided this point against him, Mr. Buxton withdrew from the Committee, though continuing to work in the cause, and I was, quite unexpectedly on my own part, proposed and elected chairman. It became, in consequence, my duty to represent the Committee in the House of Commons, sometimes by putting questions to the Government, sometimes as the recipient of questions, more or less provocative, addressed by individual members to myself; but especially as speaker in the important debate originated in the session of 1866, by Mr. Buxton: and the speech I then delivered is that which I should probably select as the best of my speeches in Parliament.[10] For more than two years we carried on the combat, trying every avenue legally open to us, to the Courts of Criminal Justice. A bench of magistrates in one of the most Tory counties in England dismissed our case: we were more successful before the magistrates at Bow Street; which gave an opportunity to the Lord Chief Justice of the Queen's Bench, Sir Alexander Cockburn, for delivering his celebrated charge, which settled the law of the question in favour of liberty, as far as it is in the power of a judge's charge to settle it. There, however, our success ended, for the Old Bailey Grand jury by throwing out our bill prevented the case from coming to trial. It was clear that to bring English functionaries to the bar of a criminal court for abuses of power committed against negroes and mulattoes was not a popular proceeding with the English middle classes. We had, however, redeemed, so far as lay in us, the character of our country, by showing that there was at any rate a body of persons determined to use all the means which the law afforded to obtain justice for the injured. We had elicited from the highest criminal judge in the nation an authoritative declaration that the law was what we maintained it to be; and we had given an emphatic warning to those who might be tempted to similar guilt hereafter, that, though they might escape the actual sentence of a criminal tribunal, they were not safe against being put to some trouble and expense in order to avoid it. Colonial governors and other persons in authority, will have a considerable motive to stop short of such extremities in future.

As a matter of curiosity I kept some specimens of the abusive letters, almost all of them anonymous, which I received while these proceedings were going on. They are evidence of the sympathy felt with the brutalities in Jamaica by the brutal part of the population at home. They graduated from coarse jokes, verbal and pictorial, up to threats of assassination.

Among other matters of importance in which I took an active part, but which excited little interest in the public, two deserve particular mention. I joined with several other independent Liberals in defeating an Extradition Bill introduced at the very end of the session of 1866, and by which, though surrender avowedly for political offences was not authorized, political refugees, if charged by a foreign Government with acts which are necessarily incident to all attempts at insurrection, would have been surrendered to be dealt with by the criminal courts of the Government against which they had rebelled: thus making the British Government an accomplice in the vengeance of foreign despotisms. The defeat of this proposal led to the appointment of a Select Committee (in which I was included), to examine and report on the whole subject of Extradition Treaties; and the result was, that in the Extradition Act which passed through Parliament after I had ceased to be a member, opportunity is given to any one whose extradition is demanded, of being heard before an English court of justice to prove that the offence with which he is charged, is really political. The cause of European freedom has thus been saved from a serious misfortune, and our own country from a great iniquity. The other subject to be mentioned is the fight kept up by a body of advanced Liberals in the session of 1868, on the Bribery Bill of Mr. Disraeli's Government, in which I took a very active part. I had taken counsel with several of those who had applied their minds most carefully to the details of the subject—Mr. W.D. Christie, Serjeant Pulling, Mr. Chadwick—as well as bestowed much thought of my own, for the purpose of framing such amendments and additional clauses as might make the Bill really effective against the numerous modes of corruption, direct and indirect, which might otherwise, as there was much reason to fear, be increased instead of diminished by the Reform Act. We also aimed at engrafting on the Bill, measures for diminishing the mischievous burden of what are called the legitimate expenses of elections. Among our many amendments, was that of Mr. Fawcett for making the returning officer's expenses a charge on the rates, instead of on the candidates; another was the prohibition of paid canvassers, and the limitation of paid agents to one for each candidate; a third was the extension of the precautions and penalties against bribery to municipal elections, which are well known to be not only a preparatory school for bribery at parliamentary elections, but an habitual cover for it. The Conservative Government, however, when once they had carried the leading provision of their Bill (for which I voted and spoke), the transfer of the jurisdiction in elections from the House of Commons to the Judges, made a determined resistance to all other improvements; and after one of our most important proposals, that of Mr. Fawcett, had actually obtained a majority, they summoned the strength of their party and threw out the clause in a subsequent stage. The Liberal party in the House was greatly dishonoured by the conduct of many of its members in giving no help whatever to this attempt to secure the necessary conditions of an honest representation of the people. With their large majority in the House they could have carried all the amendments, or better ones if they had better to propose. But it was late in the session; members were eager to set about their preparations for the impending General Election: and while some (such as Sir Robert Anstruther) honourably remained at their post, though rival candidates were already canvassing their constituency, a much greater number placed their electioneering interests before their public duty. Many Liberals also looked with indifference on legislation against bribery, thinking that it merely diverted public interest from the Ballot, which they considered— very mistakenly as I expect it will turn out—to be a sufficient, and the only, remedy. From these causes our fight, though kept up with great vigour for several nights, was wholly unsuccessful, and the practices which we sought to render more difficult, prevailed more widely than ever in the first General Election held under the new electoral law.

In the general debates on Mr. Disraeli's Reform Bill, my participation was limited to the one speech already mentioned; but I made the Bill an occasion for bringing the two great improvements which remain to be made in Representative Government, formally before the House and the nation. One of them was Personal, or, as it is called with equal propriety, Proportional Representation. I brought this under the consideration of the House, by an expository and argumentative speech on Mr. Hare's plan; and subsequently I was active in support of the very imperfect substitute for that plan, which, in a small number of constituencies, Parliament was induced to adopt. This poor makeshift had scarcely any recommendation, except that it was a partial recognition of the evil which it did so little to remedy. As such, however, it was attacked by the same fallacies, and required to be defended on the same principles, as a really good measure; and its adoption in a few Parliamentary elections, as well as the subsequent introduction of what is called the Cumulative Vote in the elections for the London School Board, have had the good effect of converting the equal claim of all electors to a proportional share in the representation, from a subject of merely speculative discussion, into a question of practical politics, much sooner than would otherwise have been the case.

This assertion of my opinions on Personal Representation cannot be credited with any considerable or visible amount of practical result. It was otherwise with the other motion which I made in the form of an amendment to the Reform Bill, and which was by far the most important, perhaps the only really important, public service I performed in the capacity of a Member of Parliament: a motion to strike out the words which were understood to limit the electoral franchise to males, and thereby to admit to the suffrage all women who, as householders or otherwise, possessed the qualification required of male electors. For women not to make their claim to the suffrage, at the time when the elective franchise was being largely extended, would have been to abjure the claim altogether; and a movement on the subject was begun in 1866, when I presented a petition for the suffrage, signed by a considerable number of distinguished women. But it was as yet uncertain whether the proposal would obtain more than a few stray votes in the House: and when, after a debate in which the speaker's on the contrary side were conspicuous by their feebleness, the votes recorded in favour of the motion amounted to 73—made up by pairs and tellers to above 80—the surprise was general, and the encouragement great: the greater, too, because one of those who voted for the motion was Mr. Bright, a fact which could only be attributed to the impression made on him by the debate, as he had previously made no secret of his nonconcurrence in the proposal. [The time appeared to my daughter, Miss Helen Taylor, to have come for forming a Society for the extension of the suffrage to women. The existence of the Society is due to my daughter's initiative; its constitution was planned entirely by her, and she was the soul of the movement during its first years, though delicate health and superabundant occupation made her decline to be a member of the Executive Committee. Many distinguished members of parliament, professors, and others, and some of the most eminent women of whom the country can boast, became members of the Society, a large proportion either directly or indirectly through my daughter's influence, she having written the greater number, and all the best, of the letters by which adhesions was obtained, even when those letters bore my signature. In two remarkable instances, those of Miss Nightingale and Miss Mary Carpenter, the reluctance those ladies had at first felt to come forward, (for it was not on their past difference of opinion) was overcome by appeals written by my daughter though signed by me. Associations for the same object were formed in various local centres, Manchester, Edinburgh, Birmingham, Bristol, and Glasgow; and others which have done much valuable work for the cause. All the Societies take the title of branches of the National Society for Women's Suffrage; but each has its own governing body, and acts in complete independence of the others.]

I believe I have mentioned all that is worth remembering of my proceedings in the House. But their enumeration, even if complete, would give but an inadequate idea of my occupations during that period, and especially of the time taken up by correspondence. For many years before my election to Parliament, I had been continually receiving letters from strangers, mostly addressed to me as a writer on philosophy, and either propounding difficulties or communicating thoughts on subjects connected with logic or political economy. In common, I suppose, with all who are known as political economists, I was a recipient of all the shallow theories and absurd proposals by which people are perpetually endeavouring to show the way to universal wealth and happiness by some artful reorganization of the currency. When there were signs of sufficient intelligence in the writers to make it worth while attempting to put them right, I took the trouble to point out their errors, until the growth of my correspondence made it necessary to dismiss such persons with very brief answers. Many, however, of the communications I received were more worthy of attention than these, and in some, oversights of detail were pointed out in my writings, which I was thus enabled to correct. Correspondence of this sort naturally multiplied with the multiplication of the subjects on which I wrote, especially those of a metaphysical character. But when I became a member of Parliament. I began to receive letters on private grievances and on every imaginable subject that related to any kind of public affairs, however remote from my knowledge or pursuits. It was not my constituents in Westminster who laid this burthen on me: they kept with remarkable fidelity to the understanding on which I had consented to serve. I received, indeed, now and then an application from some ingenuous youth to procure for him a small government appointment; but these were few, and how simple and ignorant the writers were, was shown by the fact that the applications came in about equally whichever party was in power. My invariable answer was, that it was contrary to the principles on which I was elected to ask favours of any Government. But, on the whole, hardly any part of the country gave me less trouble than my own constituents. The general mass of correspondence, however, swelled into an oppressive burthen.

[At this time, and thenceforth, a great proportion of all my letters (including many which found their way into the newspapers) were not written by me but by my daughter; at first merely from her willingness to help in disposing of a mass of letters greater than I could get through without assistance, but afterwards because I thought the letters she wrote superior to mine, and more so in proportion to the difficulty and importance of the occasion. Even those which I wrote myself were generally much improved by her, as is also the case with all the more recent of my prepared speeches, of which, and of some of my published writings, not a few passages, and those the most successful, were hers.]

While I remained in Parliament my work as an author was unavoidably limited to the recess. During that time I wrote (besides the pamphlet on Ireland, already mentioned), the Essay on Plato, published in the *Edinburgh Review*, and reprinted in the third volume of *Dissertations and Discussions*; and the address which, conformably to custom, I delivered to the University of St. Andrew's, whose students had done me the honour of electing me to the office of Rector. In this Discourse I gave expression to many thoughts and opinions which had been accumulating in me through life, respecting the various studies which belong to a liberal education, their uses and influences, and the mode in which they should be pursued to render their influences most beneficial. The position taken up, vindicating the high educational value alike of the old classic and the new scientific studies, on even stronger grounds than are urged by most of their advocates, and insisting that it is only the stupid inefficiency of the usual teaching which makes those studies be regarded as competitors instead of allies, was, I think, calculated, not only to aid and stimulate the improvement which has happily commenced in the national institutions for higher education, but to diffuse juster ideas than we often find, even in highly educated men, on the conditions of the highest mental cultivation.

During this period also I commenced (and completed soon after I had left Parliament) the performance of a duty to philosophy and to the memory of my father, by preparing and publishing an edition of the *Analysis of the Phenomena of the Human Mind*, with notes bringing up the doctrines of that admirable book to the latest improvements in science and in speculation. This was a joint undertaking: the psychological notes being furnished in about equal proportions by Mr. Bain and myself, while Mr. Grote supplied some valuable contributions on points in the history of philosophy incidentally raised, and Dr. Andrew Findlater supplied the deficiencies in the book which had been occasioned by the imperfect philological knowledge of the time when it was written. Having been originally published at a time when the current of metaphysical speculation ran in a quite opposite direction to the psychology of Experience and Association, the *Analysis* had not obtained the amount of immediate success which it deserved, though it had made a deep impression on many individual minds, and had largely contributed, through those minds, to create that more favourable atmosphere for the Association Psychology of which we now have the benefit. Admirably adapted for a class book of the Experience Metaphysics, it only required to be enriched, and in some cases corrected, by the results of more recent labours in the same school of thought, to stand, as it now does, in company with Mr. Bain's treatises, at the head of the systematic works on Analytic psychology.

In the autumn of 1868 the Parliament which passed the Reform Act was dissolved, and at the new election for Westminster I was thrown out; not to my surprise, nor, I believe, to that of my principal supporters, though in the few days preceding the election they had become more sanguine than before. That I should not have been elected at all would not have required any explanation; what excites curiosity is that I should have been elected the first time, or, having been elected then, should have been defeated afterwards. But the efforts made to defeat me were far greater on the second occasion than on the first. For one thing, the Tory Government was now struggling for existence, and success in any contest was of more importance to them. Then, too, all persons of Tory feelings were far more embittered against me individually than on the previous occasion; many who had at first been either favourable or indifferent, were vehemently opposed to my re-election. As I had shown in my political writings that I was aware of the weak points in democratic opinions, some Conservatives, it seems, had not been without hopes of finding me an opponent of democracy: as I was able to see the Conservative side of the question, they presumed that, like them, I could not see any other side. Yet if they had really read my writings, they would have known that after giving full weight to all that appeared to me well grounded in the arguments against democracy, I unhesitatingly decided in its favour, while recommending that it should be accompanied by such institutions as were consistent with its principle and calculated to ward off its inconveniences: one of the chief of these remedies being Proportional Representation, on which scarcely any of the Conservatives gave me any support. Some Tory expectations appear to have been founded on the approbation I had expressed of plural voting, under certain conditions: and it has been surmised that the suggestion of this sort made in one of the resolutions which Mr. Disraeli introduced into the House preparatory to his Reform Bill (a suggestion which meeting with no favour, he did not press), may have been occasioned by what I had written on the point: but if so, it was forgotten that I had made it an express condition that the privilege of a plurality of votes should be annexed to education, not to property, and even so, had approved of it only on the supposition of universal suffrage. How utterly inadmissible such plural voting would be under the suffrage given by the present Reform Act, is proved, to any who could otherwise doubt it, by the very small weight which the working classes are found to possess in elections, even under the law which gives no more votes to any one elector than to any other.

While I thus was far more obnoxious to the Tory interest, and to many Conservative Liberals than I had formerly been, the course I pursued in Parliament had by no means been such as to make Liberals generally at all enthusiastic in my support. It has already been mentioned, how large a proportion of my prominent appearances had been on questions on which I differed from most of the Liberal party, or about which they cared little, and how few occasions there had been on which the line I took was such as could lead them to attach any great value to me as an organ of their opinions. I had moreover done things which had excited, in many minds, a personal prejudice against me. Many were offended by what they called the persecution of Mr. Eyre: and still greater offence was taken at my sending a subscription to the election expenses of Mr. Bradlaugh. Having refused to be at any expense for my own election, and having had all its expenses defrayed by others, I felt under a peculiar obligation to subscribe in my turn where funds were deficient for candidates whose election was desirable. I accordingly sent subscriptions to nearly all the working class candidates, and among others to Mr. Bradlaugh. He had the support of the working classes; having heard him speak, I knew him to be a man of ability and he had proved that he was the reverse of a demagogue, by placing himself in strong opposition to the prevailing opinion of the democratic party on two such important subjects as Malthusianism and Personal Representation. Men of this sort, who, while sharing the democratic feelings of the working classes, judged political questions for themselves, and had courage to assert their individual convictions against popular opposition, were needed, as it seemed to me, in Parliament, and I did not think that Mr. Bradlaugh's anti-religious opinions (even though he had been intemperate in the expression of them) ought to exclude him. In subscribing, however, to his election, I did what would have been highly imprudent if I had been at liberty to consider only the interests of my own re-election; and, as might be expected, the utmost possible use, both fair and unfair, was made of this act of mine to stir up the electors of Westminster against me. To these various causes, combined with an unscrupulous use of the usual pecuniary and other influences on the side of my Tory competitor, while none were used on my side, it is to be ascribed that I failed at my second election after having succeeded at the first. No sooner was the result of the election known than I received three or four invitations to become a candidate for other constituencies, chiefly counties; but even if success could have been expected, and this without expense, I was not disposed to deny myself the relief of returning to private life. I had no cause to feel humiliated at my rejection by the electors; and if I had, the feeling would have been far outweighed by the numerous expressions of regret which I received from all sorts of persons and places, and in a most marked degree from those members of the liberal party in Parliament, with whom I had been accustomed to act.

Since that time little has occurred which there is need to commemorate in this place. I returned to my old pursuits and to the enjoyment of a country life in the south of Europe, alternating twice a year with a residence of some weeks or months in the neighbourhood of London. I have written various articles in periodicals (chiefly in my friend Mr. Morley's *Fortnightly Review*), have made a small number of speeches on public occasions, especially at the meetings of the Women's Suffrage Society, have published the *Subjection of Women*, written some years before, with some additions [by my daughter and myself,] and have commenced the preparation of matter for future books, of which it will be time to speak more particularly if I live to finish them. Here, therefore, for the present, this memoir may close.

Notes

[1]In a subsequent stage of boyhood, when these exercises had ceased to be compulsory, like most youthful writers I wrote tragedies; under the inspiration not so much of Shakspeare as of Joanna Baillie, whose *Constantine Paleologus* in particular appeared to me one of the most glorious of human compositions. I still think it one of the best dramas of the last two centuries.

[2]The continuation of this article in the second number of the *Review* was written by me under my father's eye, and (except as practice in composition, in which respect it was, to me, more useful than anything else I ever wrote) was of little or no value.

[3]Written about 1861.

[4]The steps in my mental growth for which I was indebted to her were far from being those which a person wholly uninformed on the subject would probably suspect. It might be supposed, for instance, that my strong convictions on the complete equality in all legal, political, social, and domestic relations, which ought to exist between men and women, may have been adopted or learnt from her. This was so far from being the fact, that those convictions were among the earliest results of the application of my mind to political subjects, and the strength with which I held them was, as I believe, more than anything else, the originating cause of the interest she felt in me. What is true is that, until I knew her, the opinion was in my mind little more than an abstract principle. I saw no more reason why women should be held in legal subjection to other people, than why men should. I was certain that their interests required fully as much protection as those of men, and were quite as little likely to obtain it without an equal voice in making the laws by which they were bound. But that perception of the vast practical bearings of women's disabilities which found expression in the book on the *Subjection of Women* was acquired mainly through her teaching. But for her rare knowledge of human nature and comprehension of moral and social influences, though I should doubtless have held my present opinions, I should have had a very insufficient perception of the mode in which the consequences of the inferior position of women intertwine themselves with all the evils of existing society and with all the difficulties of human improvement. I am indeed painfully conscious of how much of her best thoughts on the subject I have failed to reproduce, and how greatly that little treatise falls short of what it would have been if she had put on paper her entire mind on this question, or had lived to revise and improve, as she certainly would have done, my imperfect statement of the case.

[5]The only person from whom I received any direct assistence in the preparation of the *System of Logic* was Mr. Bain, since so justly celebrated for his philosophical writings. He went carefully through the manuscript before it was sent to the press, and enriched it with a great number of additional examples and illustrations from science; many of which, as well as some detached remarks of his own in confirmation of my logical views, I inserted nearly in his own words.

[6]A few dedicatory lines acknowledging what the book owed to her, were prefixed

to some of the presentation copies of the *Political Economy* on iets first publication. Her dislike of publicity alone prevented their insertion in the other copies of the work. During the years which intervened between the commencement of my married life and the catastrophe which closed it, the principal occurrences of my outward existence (unless I count as such a first attack of the family disease, and a consequent journey of more than six months for the recovery of health, in Italy, Sicily, and Greece) had reference to my position in the India House. In 1856 I was promoted to the rank of chief of the office in which I had served for upwards of thirty-three years. The appointment, that of Examiner of India Correspondence, was the highest, +next to that of Secretary, in the East India Company's home service, involving the general superintendence of all the correspondence with the Indian Governments, except the military, naval, and financial. I held this office as long as it continued to exist, being a little more than two years; after which it pleased Parliament, in other words Lord Palmerston, to put an end to the East india Company as a branch of the government of India under the Crown, and convert the administration of that country into a thing to be scrambled for by the second and third class of English parliamentary politicians. I was the chief manager of the resistance which the Company made to their own political extinction, and to the letters and petitions I wrote for them, and the concluding chapter of my treatise on Representative Government, I must refer for my opinions on the folly and mischief of this ill-considered change. Personally I considered myself a gainer by it, as I had given enough of my life to india, and was not unwilling to retire on the liberal compensation granted. After the change was consummated, Lord Stanley, the first Secretary of State for India, made me the honourable offer of a seat in the Council, and the proposal was subsequently renewed by the Council itself, on the first occasion of its having to supply a vacancy in its own body. But the conditions of Indian government under the new system made me anticipate nothing but useless vexation and waste of effort from any participation in it: and nothing that has since happened has had any tendency to make me regret my refusal.

[7]In 1869.

[8]The saying of this true hero, after his capture, that he was worth more for hanging than any other purpose, reminds one, by its combination of wit, wisdom, and self-devotion, of Sir Thomas More.

[9]The first was in answer to Mr. Lowe's reply to Mr. Bright on the Cattle Plague Bill, and was thought at the time to have helped to get rid of a provision in the Government measure which would have given to landholders a second indemnity, after they had already been once indemnified for the loss of some of their cattle by the increased selling price of the remainder.

[10]Among the most active members of the Committee were Mr. P.A. Taylor, M.P., always faithful and energetic in every assertion of the principles of liberty; Mr. Goldwin Smith, Mr. Frederic Harrison, Mr. Slack, Mr. Chamerovzow, Mr. Shaen, and Mr. Chesson, the Honorary Secretary of the Association.

Made in the USA
Columbia, SC
11 January 2021

30635175R00121